Gender Power, Leadership, and Governance

Gender Power, Leadership, and Governance

Edited by
Georgia Duerst-Lahti and Rita Mae Kelly

Ann Arbor

THE UNIVERSITY OF MICHIGAN PRESS

Copyright © by the University of Michigan 1995
All rights reserved
Published in the United States of America by
The University of Michigan Press
Manufactured in the United States of America
Typeset in 10 on 12 pt. Times Roman by Publication Assistance Center,
College of Public Programs, Arizona State University
♾Printed on acid-free paper

2006   2005   2004   2003   7   6   5   4

A CIP catalogue record for this book is available from the British Library.

Library of Congress Cataloging-in-Publication Data

Gender power, leadership, and governance / Georgia Duerst-Lahti and
    Rita Mae Kelly, editors.
            p.   cm.
    Includes bibliographical references (p.   ) and index.
    ISBN 0-472-09610-9 (alk. paper). — ISBN 0-472-06610-2 (pbk. :
alk. paper)
        1. Women in politics.   2. Women in politics—United States.
    3. Sexism.   4. Sexism—United States.   5. Power (Social studies)
    6. Power (Social studies)—United States.   7. Political leadership.
    8. Political leadership—United States.   I. Duerst-Lahti, Georgia,
    1955–   II. Kelly, Rita Mae.
    HQ1236.G462 1995
        305.3—dc20   95-30132
                                                                CIP

Acknowledgments

We wish to thank the many individuals who shared ideas and gave encouragement throughout this project. A special thanks to the contributors and to the University of Michigan staff. LeAnn Fields, our acquisitions editor, and Ellen McCarthy, our copyediting coordinator, facilitated a speedy and relatively painless processing. Janet Soper, of the Publication Assistance Center at Arizona State University, College of Public Programs, typeset the manuscript in a timely, quality fashion and with good humor, making our lives much easier. Dawn Spangler worked expeditiously to track the various citations that needed completing. Many thanks!

Our home institutions have also provided assistance. We acknowledge the Faculty Development Fund at Beloit College for their financial support, and the Arizona State University, College of Public Programs's Publication Assistance Center for their time and efforts on our behalf.

Our families supported us and manifested much needed patience and good will throughout. Georgia especially wishes to express her appreciation to Tris Elena, and Alex for their understanding and for helping make quiet time available. Rita says, thanks once again, to her family: Vince, Patrick, and Kathleen.

Contents

Introduction

Some readers may be surprised to learn that men have gender just as much as women have gender. Because most of the writing on gender concentrates exclusively on women, such a misconception is understandable. This book considers men and masculinity as well as women and femininity. From our vantage point, masculinity is hard to ignore in studying leadership and governance.

Most students of gender know men have gender too. They also are likely have thought about both men and women as gendered beings. Nonetheless, some who use gender in their research have not carefully considered the important distinction between sex and gender, using the two interchangeably, especially in quantitative analysis. Perhaps most importantly, too few who have begun to use gender as a variable have played with the profound implications of the shift in thinking that accompanies a careful use of sex and gender. Because many social scientists use the terms interchangeably on surveys or in reporting findings, overlooking this distinction and what it implies is both easy and common. While theorists who explore these concepts have established fine nuances among related concepts, seldom do theorists and empirical researchers meld their work. This book tries such a merging. We hope to persuade you that you need to master (mistress?) a few more concepts—*transgendered* and *gender power,* for example—to move us beyond essentialist boxes and stalemated points between women and men. We also hope to persuade readers that the conceptual clarity gained by making careful conceptual distinctions, will improve our understanding, lead to better scholarship, and fundamentally shift the way we see the topics covered in this book. In the end, we ambitiously hope students of leadership and governance are forever changed by some insight gained from reading this volume.

Finally, many, probably most, have long believed that feminism has ideological dimensions, or that feminism is an ideology. Few have ever pondered the possibility that feminism has an ideological parallel in masculinism. Masculinism and all such an ideology implies remain largely unexplored. What if? What if both feminism and masculinism constitute metaideologies that subsume other ideologies? Most introductory-level textbooks on political ideology now deal with liberalism, conservatism, fascism, anarchy, socialism, or Marxism; some cover nationalism, and most deal with feminism.

Political science has been slower than most social sciences in incorporating feminism into its repertoire, so some might think that feminists should be pleased to be included at all. However, two fundamental intellectual inconsistencies cloud even this basic advance. First, despite the fact outsiders pay little heed, feminists have long argued internally among various camps. Marxist feminists disagree with liberal feminists, who in turn diverge from postmodernists, and so on. For example, debates occur around how to treat difference. Should we recognize gender differences, acknowledge their consequences, and in strategies for change seek special treatment that accounts for differences? Or should we concentrate on treating women and men exactly the same and advocate only equal pay for equal work, for example, arguing that to do anything else is to reimpose gender demarcations where none need exist? Or, alternatively, should we advocate comparable pay for comparable worth on the grounds that men and women differ, particularly in their working situations? As scholars and activists have struggled with these issues, dominance by one gender all too often has reemerged, to the detriment of women.

Second, in the larger scheme of political ideologies the question becomes, why should feminism contain multiple, often inconsistent ideologies? If we find multiple, familiar ideologies inside feminism, why is feminism conceptually treated as a category equivalent to liberalism, for example, when it contains liberalism and socialism and Marxism, and more? If feminism contains these other ideologies, might it more reasonably be considered as a metaideology? And if feminism is a metaideology, then why don't we also recognize masculinism as a metaideology? Somehow political thinkers have been missing, ignoring, or otherwise not seeing a metaideology of masculinism in operation. We invite you to come along with us as we work through these possibilities.

The Aims of This Book

Leadership and governance are crucial to the well-being of the common good and public life. The common good and public life also shape each of our private lives; therefore, leadership and governance are crucial to individual good as well. This book intends (1) to offer the concept of gender power as crucial to our understanding of leadership and governance; (2) to build upon prior empirical research in sex and sex roles in order to move beyond into a richer conceptual and explanatory realm; and (3) to illustrate concrete ways to deploy the concept of gender power in a spectrum of leadership and governance arenas.

This book is unusual because it both crosses areas of study in political science by mixing theory with empirical research and compounds the mix by including cases from legislative, executive, and electoral politics. Policy and bureaucracy, symbolic politics and institutional structures all come under scrutiny.

The purposes of this book are essentially fivefold:

1. to demonstrate the difference between analyzing sex or sex-role variations and analyzing gender and gender power;
2. to contribute to the articulation of gender power as a concept central to the analysis of government and governance;
3. to show how knowledge derived from the women's studies literature can be used to improve our understanding of politics, leadership, governance, political institutions, and behavior;
4. to show how institutional sexism leads to differential gender power and hence to differential political power; and
5. to link the consequences of gender power to political leadership and governance.

Students of any, or any combination, of the subjects included in the title—gender, power, leadership, or governance—should find this volume of interest. Written largely by political scientists who have a familiarity with feminist scholarship and an interest in political organizations and institutions, this work provides a unique perspective on leadership and governance.

The authors owe an intellectual debt to Jean Lipman-Blumen for introducing the concept of gender power in institutions (*Gender Roles and Power,* 1984), but as a sociologist she pursued a social focus. Here we pursue gender power in explicitly political institutions, settings, symbolism, and behaviors. We also consider its relevance for how we study topics surrounding leadership and governance. A major strength of the volume resides in its analysis of gender power at multiple levels—individual, institutional, and social symbolic—with attention to the way gender power intersects with and operates at multiple levels simultaneously. It offers the opportunity to consider leadership through various dimensions of governance, aspects that often cross subfields of political science. As importantly, it points to the ways in which most analyses of political leadership continue to ignore gender.

Within political science, this book serves as a complement and corrective to most works on leadership. To take as an archtypical example, *Leadership and Politics,* edited by Bryan D. Jones (1989), has thirteen chapters replete with references to various men and masculine-rooted assumptions but fails to consider gender explicitly despite intermittently referring to "she." This absence is particularly revealing given the claim to an integrative approach, especially one that claims to covers "the 'two worlds' of political analysis," leadership as part of a social world and "a political world that is more similar to biology."[1] This absence is further compounded by acknowledgment that "*any* social force or institutional structure can limit the actions of leaders"[2] and that "[l]eadership opportunities are highly contextual."[3] That gender can remain so completely invisible to such a study of political leadership demonstrates the need to uncover the power that makes it possible—gender power.

The exploration of gender power in leadership and governance is part of the larger effort to place gender—for men as well as women—into the realm of political-science analysis and discourse. A spate of fine work is emerging: Wendy Brown's *Manhood and Politics* (1988) and Christine DiStefano's *Configurations of Masculinity* (1991) explore political theory; Sue Tolleson-Rinehart and Jeanie R. Stanley's *Claytie and the Lady* (1994) illustrate gender power through an encompassing case study; *The Political Interests of Gender* (1988), edited by Kathleen B. Jones and Anna G. Jonasdottir, and *Equality Politics and Gender* (1991), edited by Elizabeth Meehan and Selma Sevenhuijsen, are examples of theme-directed volumes; and Camilla Stivers's *Gender Images in Public Administration* (1993) and *Women and Men of the States* (1992), edited by Mary E. Guy, examine gender power in public administration. Political-science scholarship currently flourishes around the topic of gender in many subfields.

Gender has not been treated much in the literature on leadership, however. Multidisciplinary works such as Barbara Kellerman's *Leadership: Multidisciplinary Perspectives* (1984), or *Contemporary Issues in Leadership* (1984; 2d ed. 1989), edited by William E. Rosenbach and Robert L. Taylor, include women and/or gender in various ways but do not take up the question of gender power in shaping leadership. Albeit unevenly, Rosenbach and Taylor show a dramatic increase in attempts to include women or gendered aspects of leadership in their second edition. Kathleen Hall Jamieson, in *Beyond the Double Bind,* touches upon crucial aspects of leadership to show how women overcome obstacles in their paths to leadership. Many treatments of women and leadership employ a biographical approach: for example, *Women Leaders in Contemporary U.S. Politics* (1987), edited by Frank P. Le Veness and Jane P. Sweeney; others look at the individual styles of women, as does *The Female Advantage* (1990) by Sally Helgesen. While useful, these works do not systematically pursue why so few women lead and govern; hence, they provide little guidance for changing gender power relations in future governing.

In this volume we establish the ways gender power operates in the realm of leadership and governance. We do so by bridging alternative levels and methods of analysis. Each of our approaches in the empirical chapters pursues themes and questions familiar to mainstream political science. We do so with the intent of broadening the stream, however. Gender power exists as a central construct of the political world of governance. We aim to examine it through explorations of leadership.

We proceed toward these ends through the following arguments, which are empirically explored:

1. Gender is different from sex, which is rooted exclusively in biology.[4] Gender consists of a broader social construction, ultimately prescribing, and generally leading to, an entire way of being.
2. Gender is not limited to femaleness and maleness, but includes men, masculinity, and manliness as well as women, femininity, and womanliness.
3. Gender extends to normative sets of beliefs, which can be considered as feminism and masculinism. Masculinism is more than a way of being; like feminism, it can be considered as an ideology.
4. All facets of human interaction are gendered, although social science has historically ignored this aspect of social being. Consequently, it has produced biased results and partial truths.
5. Masculinism is considered the norm of being and acting in the United States and elsewhere, with feminism and femaleness considered deviant from this norm. This gives men and masculinity a privileged position in interpersonal institutional relations and the important structures of society.
6. Gender power emanates from the behavior patterns and social reality that gender fosters. Gender power can be assessed in any human interaction.
7. Gender power permeates and follows from all facets of human interaction. It operates at interpersonal levels, as a social category, within institutions, and normatively. It shapes political actions.
8. While gender power varies by circumstance, since men have controlled social and political institutions and conventions and have constructed those institutions in such a way as to suit their founders, men generally are advantaged inside institutions they constructed. Masculinism operates whether or not participants are aware of its influence.
9. Leadership and governance, in particular, have been defined in terms of masculinism. As a result, women and feminism are particularly disadvantaged in this crucial domain.

Warming Up to Concepts

The ideas surrounding gender that we present here are not necessarily straight-forward. We devote plenty of paper and ink to them later, in ways even those knowledgeable should find interesting. Here we want only to indicate some key terms with the hope you find them provocative enough, especially in relation to leadership and governance, to read on.

Sex relates to the biological categories we know as males and females. Biology is not as "given" as most believe, however.

Sex roles extend from biological categories we create. Most sex roles are rooted in structural-functionalist thinking. If females give birth to children, then only they mother. If males have greater physical strength, then males become protectors. *Sex roles* is an often misused concept.

Gender is the social construction of biological sex, how we take biological differences and give them social meaning. In the process, we create a set of practices and norms for interpersonal behavior, roles for individuals to perform, ways of being, ways of knowing, standpoints and worldviews.

Gender power pervades all human interaction. It is the power that results from our gendered (e)valuations of things and behaviors, our ways of being, behaving, and structuring social relations. It is rooted in interpretations that give meaning to biological sex and extend from the fact we understand sex differences as very important to the way we establish the social order.

Sex-role crossover occurs when a man or woman acts in a manner "appropriate" for the "opposite" sex. This concept is embedded in assumptions about rigidly prescribed social roles based upon dualistically fixed biological sex.

Transgendered moments or behaviors occur when we no longer believe a trait or behavior to be appropriate only for women or for men, yet we recognize that gender still matters. For example, women and men both can leave work early to care for their children, or both can be seen as acting appropriately in an assertive manner. Nevertheless, (e)valuations of these acts are not synonymous.

The Structure of This Book

The sections of the book each concentrate on one particular kind of analysis. Part 1 deals with theory related to gender and power in public leadership. It also considers how we know what we know about these important subjects. Part 2 contrasts sex and gender as social-science variables, revealing the opening into gender power available from the latter. Part 3 moves to gender power dynamics at an institutional level. It shows that analyses of institutional sexism and the gendered nature of actions inside organizations and institutions reveal different insights. Part 4 highlights "doing" gender, or gender as a set of interpersonal practices with political consequences. Part 5 tackles gender power in its symbolic manifestations, challenging readers to reexamine some otherwise unexamined imagery that leads to beliefs limiting women as leaders in governance.

The chapters of the book together also cross subfields of political science. Chapter 1 is largely theoretical and merges women's studies thinking with that of political science. Chapter 2 is an epistemological and ontological exploration that introduces the empirical chapters. Chapter 3 goes to executives in state government to explain the paucity of women at the top. Chapter 4 and 5 look at congressional behavior to consider gender's role in policy representation of women. The former presents a parsimonious model of representation appropriate for any subject but revealing of gender power also. Chapter 5 demonstrates the operation of gender power through committee structures on policies of crucial importance to women—reproductive policies. Chapter 6 illuminates long-ignored factors in the gendered nature of types of agencies and, as important, how we think about policy typologies more generally. Chapter 7 draws upon committees in a state legislature to reveal the power of gender in the interpersonal dynamics that govern governing. Chapter 8 uses findings from state executives to show the curtailing effect sexual harassment has upon women's leadership behavior. Chapter 9 draws upon the media construction of the "year of the woman" to question accepted and gendered symbols of representations and changes the year brought. Chapter 10 examines health care reform and the gender overlays that are manifested in response to Hillary Rodham Clinton and the institutionalized way gender patterns are played out in health care itself.

In the final chapter, we highlight the scholarly and normative implications of this volume and summarize the empirical findings about gender power. We also explore options for increasing gender awareness and gender balance in governance and leadership, as well as in our studies of these important phenomena. Throughout, we consider the new grounding of politics developed through the addition of the concept of gender power.

Notes

1. Bryan D. Jones, ed. *Leadership and Politics: New Perspectives in Political Science* (Lawrence: University Press of Kansas, 1989), viii.
2. Ibid., 4.
3. Ibid., 5.
4. Even claims to fixed biological sex can be readily disputed because some humans have XXX, XXY, or XYY genetic sex makeup. In addition, sex change operations truly confound claims to biological sex, along with hormone treatments and the like. We acknowledge this but will not pursue it extensively.

Part 1: Gender, Power, and Leadership

In Part 1 the historical linkages among the concepts and reality of masculinity, power, and leadership are laid bare. Masculinism is contrasted to feminism, and gender power is defined and established as a means to see masculinism's pervasive influence on governance. Our review of the literature on power and leadership reveals how rarely the words *women* and *feminine* are associated with them and how heavily men and masculinity saturate our understanding of power and leadership. We also articulate the distinction between sex and gender, both as variables and as the origin of conceptual frameworks. We give considerable attention to dimensions of gender, both because the term has too often been inappropriately used and because its theoretical uses have become complex and sophisticated in a very short span of time. Our aim is to introduce students of leadership and governance to the centrality of gender analysis for these topics. In chapter 2 we provide an overview of methodological approaches to the study of gender and gender power, illustrating the necessity of multiple levels of analysis if we are to capture the pervasive and reinforcing nature of gender power disparities under masculinism. Chapter 2 also provides an overview of the works presented in this volume.

Chapter 1

On Governance, Leadership, and Gender

Georgia Duerst-Lahti and Rita Mae Kelly

Governance and leadership are both large and amorphous concepts. Each incorporates aspects of institutions and organizations, individuals, and social symbolism. Each also involves actions, practices, consequences, and the use of power. Both governance and leadership are relational. As concepts, governance and leadership have many distinctive elements and can readily be considered separately from the other. We can, for example, consider institutional or structural arrangements of governance, such as federalism, without considering leadership. Similarly, third graders on the playground may contend with leadership struggles that have nothing to do with governance. Nonetheless, the two often overlap. Governance involves leadership much of the time, and some leaders govern. Surely, transforming the unwieldy forces of political life into good government involves processes we know as governance and leadership. Political thinkers have been pondering the relationships between governance and leadership at least since Plato, precisely because they inevitably combine in the real world of politics. It is hard to study one without bumping into the other.

Like governance and leadership, gender too is amorphous and relational. With the burgeoning study of it and the multitude of ways it has been used thus far, gender is also an analytically vague concept. The purpose of this book is to entangle gender, power, and leadership with each other more explicitly and to disentangle governance and leadership from their respective gender blinders, restrictions, and "givens."

In this chapter we review the literature on governance, leadership, and gender, revealing how gender power is seldom mentioned and how women, power, and leadership have rarely combined in either the literature or in reality. We begin first by defining the terms *governance* and *leadership*. Then we examine in greater detail understandings of gender and gender relations, highlighting the fact that men as well as women have gender and that masculinity permeates politics and power. We consider how we might understand gender as gender power, introduce the argument that masculinism is every bit as much an ideology as feminism, and discuss the interaction of masculinism with leadership. We conclude with a discussion of how gender and gender power interact with leadership.

Definitions

Governance can be defined as the process of implementing modern state power, of putting the program of those who govern into place. In a democracy we presume that the program reflects the desires and needs of citizens even though it may also spill into power relations among those holding public positions. Governance involves relations between those who govern and the citizenry as well as among those who govern. Such includes electoral arrangements that shape the nature of that relationship. Governance also involves institutional relationships between legislatures and executives or among various agencies. We can find governance relations rooted in positions such as those between a committee chair and committee members, among members of a legislative body or various administrative agency officials, even between the president and the first spouse. Power relations, few would deny, pervade these relations of governance.

In the case of the United States, we assume that transforming political life into governance includes all branches of government, federalism, and the sundry relations contained in the political context. We are most concerned here with governance at state and national levels, particularly in legislative and administrative branches—in portions of modern political life that occupy a long-standing place in notions of governance.

Leadership is difficult to define precisely because it has been defined in so many ways already. Perhaps the most common element among definitions is the notion that leadership involves influence but that influence might be applied to followers, tasks, or culture. Leadership also has been considered in terms of individual traits, leader behavior, patterns of interacting, role relationships, relations with followers, and follower perceptions. In his useful review article, Gary Yukl identifies the major approaches to leadership as those exploring traits, situational factors, behavior, and power.[1] He also identifies three major controversies: the tension between leadership as a shared phenomenon and that of the single "great" person who possesses more influence than others, confusion between leaders and managers, and the use of coercion in leader-follower relations. In any case, leaders by definition need followers, or they would not be leaders. Someone must follow for leadership to occur, even if we conceive of leadership as a shared phenomenon. Like governance, leadership is inherently relational.

While literatures on both governance and leadership have become vast over the years, seldom have scholars been conscious of gender as they explored these two topics. In the history of ideas and in politics more generally, gender has remained largely invisible. Even now when gender is identified as central to assumptions and arguments of "great" political writers, gender is seldom conceived as a category of analysis, either as a social force or as a determining standpoint for the proffered ideas and ideologies.

Leadership clearly is an amorphous concept. Adding the adjective *political* does only a little to narrow its conceptual possibilities. Even a cursory review of contemporary writings on political leadership, as exemplified by the works of Kellerman and of Mughan and Patterson, shows the categories mentioned above as well as attention to political leaders' personality, selection, socialization, motivations, and impact.[2] And because politics is itself pervasive, political leadership is too. Bryan Jones locates political leaders in formal theories, culture, and economics, along with situations and institutions.[3] Nonetheless, despite the inherent imprecision of a broad understanding of leadership, the central place of any elected or top appointed official in activities of governance recommends against an artificially narrow definition. As we will explore more fully below, merely holding a position of public authority places one in a leadership role in governance by virtue of positional power alone. Political leadership occurs through formal aspects of government and in a multitude of ways surrounding formal governing.

Gender and Gender Relations

In its simplest version, gender is the socially constructed meaning given to biological sex, especially sex differences. Gender is how we come to understand, and often to magnify, the minor differences that exist between biological males and females.[4] As we began to understand gender in the 1970s, generally we equated gender with sex roles and sex-role stereotypes. Girls were "sugar and spice" who cared for the home, boys were "snails and pails" who made their way in the public world of work and politics. We learned our gender through socialization for our sex roles, and then we assumed women and men should fit stereotypes accordingly. Please notice that both males and female are characterized by gender.

Gender is *not* synonymous with females, feminine, feminist, women; males have gender too. Reading the gender literature might lead one to believe otherwise. Until quite recently, women have predominated gender research as both authors and subjects. For example, *Gender Roles and Power,* by Jean Lipman-Blumen, does not even index *men* or *masculinity* though it includes many entries under "women" and "femininity."[5] In this fine and pathbreaking book, women's gender roles remain the focus, with men serving as the power-holding comparison. The desire to study women to the neglect of men sprang from a need to remedy centuries of neglect toward women, bringing some balance and fitting the needs of the moment. Ironically, men came to constitute "the other" in terms of gender knowledge, with only token attention being given to them as gendered beings until quite recently. But despite the irony, men do not face the full brunt of otherness because they remain so central in the world of resource distribution and control, cultural practices, and social expectations that determine how we live our lives.[6] Men are not tokens in the larger realm of gender power, so assumptions derived from the considerable literature on women as "other" do not explain men's gendered otherness well. In political studies at least, we increasingly turn our sights toward men and masculinity as subjects of gender scrutiny.[7]

The need to study men as gendered beings has become increasingly clear for several reasons. First, if we are to understand the crucial relational power embedded within the gender system, we must understand gender dynamics related to men as gender dynamics rather than as universal norms. Without this, we understand neither masculinity nor universal norms accurately. Second, all scholars, men as well as women, need to become cognizant of gender as an analytic category for their studies to capture a range of insights and findings on a variety of topics accurately. Third, without seeing themselves as part of the sex/gender system, men will not recognize the full range of human potential, for themselves or for women.

One improvement in gender analysis within political science is the lens through which we see and interpret classic texts. Many feminists who incorporate gender into their analysis begin to see prior writings in new ways. Christine DiStefano's *Configuration of Masculinity* serves as a prominent example.[8] She carefully and persuasively illustrates masculine assumptions embedded in classic political philosophy and points to alternative conclusions that might be reached if we began from women's standpoint. With this new lens we can immediately point to works that explicitly focused on men with little pretense of studying humans more generally. One such example is William F. Whyte's *Man and Organization*.[9] While today the book is readily identified as an explicit analysis of masculinity, at the time of its publication scholars lacked a gender vocabulary. As a result, most readers interpreted the book as a text about alienation from work, particular ways of organizing work life, and the effects of modernization on individuals (whose central subject, androcentrically, was assumed to be male).[10] Almost no one initially read the book as a text on the ideological construction of (white, suburban, professional) men and manliness. Now, with our current gender lens, the masculinist standpoint in the book seems self-evident.

Gender as a Category

To have such blindness about our very own scholarship suggests that gender is much larger and more complex than sex roles and social stereotypes about males and females. Too often discussions of gender become synonymous with sex roles or stereotypes, masking other power relations in the process. Gender can indeed be understood as a scheme for categorizing individuals that "recognizes biological differentiation while also creating social differentiations" through sex roles and social expectations for each gender.[11] But to limit our study of gender to this physiologically based notion is a mistake. As Linda Nicholson cogently explicates, while most scholars of gender begin from the common idea of "biological foundationalism," that idea itself represents a continuum and the physical body needs also to be analyzed.[12] Defining gender as simply two equal social categories makes the mistake of simply paralleling the use of sex as an analytical category. Many scholars today, especially those employing quantitative analysis, label categories as gender when in fact all they know is the reported sex of the respondent. One suspects that many find gender a more polite word than sex, given the propensity of the mistake. However, misuse of the term confounds a sophisticated understanding of gender dynamics and is especially detrimental in understanding gender power dynamics. Such use of *gender* does not facilitate analyzing the way gender is entangled with social resources—such as control of major institutions, wealth, and knowledge and the way they have been maldistributed between the sexes. With such maldistribution, public power is also maldistributed, and one sex dominates the other. Thus, the categories of men and women are not socially equal; the relationships between categories determine which is derogated as one category conflicts with the other. To assume empirical equality between men and women by making them equal categories is to predetermine the outcome of analysis. A broader approach to the study of gender and its definition is needed.

Gender as an Attribute

Students of gender have realized that in order for such sex roles and stereotypes to exist, much more was needed to establish and maintain this structure of meaning about sexes. A capacity to shape cultural assumptions, practices, norms, and belief systems had to be involved. The biological differences at stake are relatively modest and far more mutable than social constructions of the idea of "opposite sexes" allows.[13] Females *become* women through cultural belief systems and can become *known* as women through comparison to men; males become men through the same *process of engenderment,* even if the specific substance differs. Men come to be understood as masculine or manly through comparisons to women. The becoming, the knowing, and the process of engenderment constitute *normative* understandings of gender. Up to this time in history, *masculine* only has had meaning if *feminine* existed as a counterpoint. Gender was and is social and relational.

These gendered social relations are comprised of interrelated and interdependent parts whose individual components have no meaning separate from other discrete parts. As a social process, gender "enters into and partially constitutes all other social relations and activities." As a result, we must study gender because it "helps us to make sense out of particular social worlds."[14] To understand any social relation, we must know the social meaning of *male* and *female* and the consequences of being assigned to one or the other gender in a given situation. In other words, gender is dynamic and fluid, always dependent upon the situation and context; yet all social relations are partly determined by gendered meanings.

Gender as Normative

Growing awareness about gender led to several crucial discoveries. Teresa de Lauretis helped all to "see" more clearly through the technologies of gender.[15] Wendy Brown applied feminist knowledge of gender and gender systems to words of "great men" of political thinking.[16] She showed convincingly the capacity of gender—in this case manhood—to operate as a normative system in its own right. Brown showed that politics, as we know it in the Western tradition, is infused with manliness; politics is highly gendered.

Judith Butler's *Gender Trouble* is among the most transformative works on gender.[17] Butler called the notion of social construction itself into question. In her mind, we cannot think of gender as socially constructed biological sex without first questioning the means through which someone's given sex becomes "given." Because culture mediates all knowledge, sex itself can only be known through culture. "In such a case, not biology, but culture, becomes destiny."[18] Like many now thinking about transexuality and transvestites, she challenges the extent to which gender must depend upon sex. If gender is "performed," as transvestites and cross-dressers and powerful female athletes make apparent,[19] then we can think of gender as "radically independent of sex, [and] gender itself becomes a free floating artifice, with the consequence that *man* and *masculine* might just as easily signify a female body as a male one, and *woman* and *feminine* a male body as easily as a female one."[20] Freeing our notions of gender from biological sex opens new avenues of thought about gender.

This perspective has two critically useful insights about gender. First, gender is not necessarily tied to a human body; rather it is rooted in a generally coherent set of beliefs about what constitutes masculine or feminine.[21] Margaret Thatcher then could be understood as being highly masculine, even more so than some men, despite the fact she occupies a female body.[22] Second, if we all perform our gender, then gender is essentially something we "do"; it is a set of practices. To define gender, at least in part, as something people do, is to understand it as a feature that emerges from social settings rather than as an identity people *have* or a property of individuals. Gender becomes an action occurring between people in a particular setting.[23] Gender, then, as Wendy Brown illustrated, can apply to a way of "doing" or conducting politics as well as to the people who do politics. That is, gender can be a prescribed way of behaving, a normative stance or a normative position about "properness" in a setting that operates independent of any particular body.

Clearly, gender and gender relations have many aspects. Gender can be defined as a category, as an attribute or property, as something we do, or as a normative position. Commonly gender is also often understood as an identity people have along with other identities. People are situated along a number of identities that shape their lives and others' interpretations of them. Clearly race, class, ethnicity, and sexual orientation help determine the particular configuration of gender for any individual. White women, for example, have fought notions of "ladylike" behaviors that require feigned weakness on their part; they fight to be seen as strong and capable. In contrast, women of color struggle under assumptions that often cast them as strong physical laborers; they instead fight to be seen as capable of being "a lady," of being perceived as worthy of the cultural status that accompanies "ladies."[24]

Figure 1 attempts to represent gendered modes that currently operate in the United States at a structural and normative (valuing) level. Societal structures and values work such that they largely determine the options available to individuals in their self-presentation and interpersonal interactions.

The figure depicts a boundary area of manliness and womanliness, the dualisms that bind current common understandings of gender. Subsumed within these bounds are the melding possibilities of androgynous and/or gynandrous modes. While these modes offer "gender blending," they still derive from the basic dualisms. The "not" opening that cuts across the figure, extending beyond the structures and values, represents the thinking of those who seek to disrupt the dualism that constrains our understanding and construction of sexuality and gender. Such thinking tries to open our imaginations to other ways of understanding gender; yet, bound by our current knowledge, the opening remains embedded in the dualist mode of gender.

One can gain a sense of the valuing inherent within these modes in two ways. The first can be found in the enormous difficulty of breaking out of modes set by two "given" sexes with their socially constructed genders. Societal

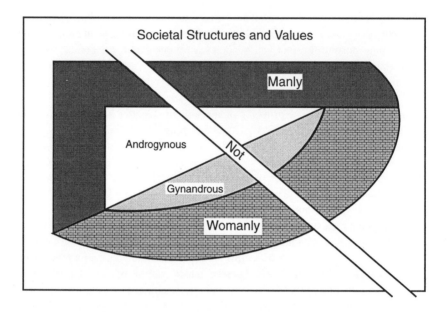

Fig. 1. Representation of gendered modes

structures and values relentlessly confine thinking to an understanding of "opposite" sexes by creating polar models for gender. Even the blending relies upon the opposites, with *gyn* and *andro* as the anchors. Second, the seldom used word *gynandrous,* or *gynandry,* alerts readers to the predominance of *andro,* or man, in the (e)valuation of these "opposites." While the notion of androgynous behavior has gained popular currency, many feminists quickly came to critique it as forcing women to become more like men without reciprocity.[25] The reason such primacy fell to the masculine aspects of this blending is rooted in power. It is "normal" to put men first, (e.g., "he and she") in self-serving circularity, because feminine aspects simply are not valued as much as the masculine in the workplace or society at large. The thought of granting the female or feminine primacy by putting the *gyn* first has gained little acceptance. The term is not even known or acknowledged outside narrow academic circles. Dualistic difference infuses societal structures and values as dualistic dominance.

Much like gender, these identities, categories, and modes of interaction carry normative strength for larger cultural values and belief systems and the societal rewards that accompany them. Disproportionately, class privilege or disadvantage turn on one's skin color, ethnic groups devise various expectations for women and men, heterosexual assumptions are legitimized by marital and property laws, and so on. Gender is but one aspect of societal power. It remains an important one for political analysis nonetheless, especially analysis of governance, where men emerge as leaders across salient U.S. categories. In fact, we contend that understandings of most aspects of leadership and governance are incomplete, often even erroneous, if they fail to consider gender.

We will argue and defend throughout this volume that concepts of leadership and governance are gendered, embedded inside assumptions, practices, norms, belief systems that make men normal. If masculinity permeates politics, as we will use Wendy Brown and others to show is in fact the case,[26] then males, who are much more aligned with masculinity than any female could be, have gender power as a permeating resource to maintain their predominance. In other words, precisely because gender is more than the socially constructed sex of individuals present in a situation, those who are masculine or who perform masculinity well have advantages in gaining and holding leadership positions in governance situations. Positions of leadership in the realm of governance carry with them an array of power resources that also accrue to men. Gender relations are also power relations.

Gender as Gender Power

Gender, and not sex (women or men as categories), needs to be the focal point in analyses of power relations. Because it is in the welter of *relations* between women and men and the consequences ensuing from them that we turn gender into gender power, gender must be the foundation for study. At a basic interpersonal level, relations between women and men occur constantly through intimacy, conversational exchange, contrasting self-presentation such as accepted clothing, the prescriptions for ladies and gentlemen, sex-specified jobs (e.g., doctors and nurses), marital roles, on so on. The crux of the problem rests in the way these relations and assumptions about gender mask and subsume power relations. As Flax has noted, "[G]ender relations so far as we have been able to understand them have been (more or less) relations of domination."[27] Gender relations then can be more accurately named gender power relations. Gender power occurs at the nexus of gender relations and power relations. From this vantage point gender relations can encompass relations between members of the same sex as well as members of different sexes.

In the American polity, all avenues of public power—and the authoritative organizations used in their implementation—have historically been controlled by males,[28] rooted at least as early as Hobbes, who disrupted patriarchy, or rule of fathers, only to replace it with rule of adult men. Jeff Hearn, writing of "men in the public eye," refers to such systems as *viriarchy,* or public patriarchies.[29] Public authority, whatever the particular arrangement, has rested with men.

Kathleen Jones argues this control of public authority has resulted in an authority—legitimized power—more common to men.[30]

One important but largely invisible by-product of men's domination of institutional power has been their ability to allocate society values and resources through a self-justifying ideology. Men's position atop social institutions has enabled them to structure institutions, create laws, legitimize particular knowledge, establish moral codes, and shape culture in ways that perpetuate their power over women.

While few would argue that elite men can fully inculcate all others with a singular ideology, masculine assumptions underpin the norms that become normal in social relations. So, when women enter and act within the realm of leadership and governance, they do so within ideological terms of masculine norms. Therein lies the transformation of gender relations into gender power relations.

Gender power may best be defined as power and power dynamics resulting from the practices of people performing gender within the normative constraints gender modes impose. These practices encompass (e)valuation of things, behaviors, and ways of being. The interpretation of these practices is implicitly and explicitly rooted in the social constructions that give meaning to biological-physiological sex (and the social interaction between the sexes more generally). Like gender, gender power is dynamic, fluid, and situationally derived; it can only be determined by the particular context, even though we find generally consistent patterns within contexts. So for example, the quarterback on the football team and the homecoming queen each derive a particular gender power from the normative (e)valuations of their gendered performance. A soldier who risks his life to save a wounded buddy and a mother who gently calms her infant each perform in gendered ways and derive power from their actions.

The gender power arrangements we find in the contemporary United States derive from masculinism, which, in turn, shapes the gender power. Consider, for example, the opportunity to accrue social resources from being a "gender star." More males have the opportunity to play football than females have to become honored athletes or cheerleaders, let alone homecoming queen. The rewards for being quarterback or any star player involve some quantity of fame, over several months or years, and the direct possibility of further resources such as a college scholarships or a professional contract. Cheerleaders attain little name recognition so derive little social capital. The homecoming queen is famous for a week and finds no systematic way to turn this honor into future resources. Similarly, mothers are simply expected to calm a fussy infant; in fact they are penalized in various ways if they do not meet the expectation of good mothers. In contrast, soldiers—still only men in frontline combat—are rewarded with medals, monuments, and parades for their valor. While both women and men have access to gender power, and while in the latter examples sex-role strictures have clearly begun to change, that access is highly differential. Masculinism sets the contours of that differentiation.

Gender, Gender Power, and Leadership Ideology: Masculinity as Masculinism

Ideology can be thought of as a systematic set of beliefs, especially "ideas about how power in society ought to be organized. These ideas are derived from a view of the problems and possibilities inherent in human nature in its individual and social aspects."[31] It is not the problems and possibilities themselves that count for ideologies but rather the *views* of them. According to Kenneth Hoover, images of power relationships provide the inspiration for any ideology's plan of action.

The main ideas of these images of power relations are made visible in two ways: (1) by questioning and evaluating the assumptions that lie behind them and (2) by establishing the distribution of power and privilege that follows from each image. Despite the fact that conflict in society often arises when people act upon contrasting ideological assumptions, these assumptions often are not clear to the user. The ideology becomes more potent precisely because its assumptions go unanalyzed.[32] Not only has masculinity gone unanalyzed even as its assumptions served as the foundation of norms in governance, masculinism remains almost entirely outside the ken of all who think about politics, even though governance as we understand it today is the explicit ideological manifestation of masculinity.[33] Such speaks to masculinism's potency as an ideology.

Ideology remains a crucial part of political life, serving as justification for obeying or defying some authority. "To understand an ideology is to see what its ideas about power involve and how these ideas are related to assumptions about individuals and community life."[34] If masculinity can in fact be considered an ideology, we should expect to find beliefs about human nature that focus on men and probably give greater credence to the potential men offer, to find power organized in society such that men predominate, and to find courses of action developed that are consistent with values associated with masculinity. So should we think of masculinity as an ideology—as masculinism—along with thinking of it as part of gender relations? An affirmative answer informs analyses of gender power in important ways. If masculinism operates, then, the organization of power, plans of action, and the resulting norms will serve as self-justifying systems to (re)inforce a masculine power.

Like its counterpart, feminism, masculinism is neither inherently good nor bad but does carry assumptions about the proper distribution of power and privilege and serves as the basis for a plan of action. Again, ideologies operate such that their underlying assumptions may not be clear to their users, and the invisibility of assumptions increases their potency. We all can participate in masculinist ideological arrangements without being aware of them, and the fact we are not aware gives strength to the masculinist actions that follow.

When Wendy Brown wrote of "manliness" in politics, she carefully scrutinized the writings of several "great" political thinkers—Aristotle, Machiavelli, and Weber—to reveal the influence of "the ideal of man and manhood" upon Western political thought.[35] Along with Christine DiStefano,[36] she was among the first to employ feminist gender analysis to study men and masculinity in politics, incisively opening new possibilities for seeing familiar ideas through her approach. She revealed that man's politics was inevitably intertwined with meanings of manhood as both developed throughout history. Her approach moved the discourse away from notions of patriarchy and rule by fathers to a far more subtle and complex understanding; the very meaning of politics could not be separated from the meaning of manhood. In ideological terms, Brown revealed the masculine assumptions that lay the foundation for Western politics.

Ideas about power in politics inevitably become debates about the distribution of privilege within manhood. Mark Kahn, for example, suggests respectfully that "fortune was a man" (most likely a bachelor) precisely because men had so much power they could afford to ignore women entirely during the founding of the United States.[37] In the Federalist Papers and elsewhere, the founding fathers debated which men were suited to govern and whose prosperity would be bolstered by emerging institutional arrangements of the great compromise. John Adams wrote his wife Abigail of the "masculine system" they were creating.[38] Jeff Hearn returns to the past to talk of the present because "'Public man' and 'public men' are still very much a reality, both as ideology and practice."[39]

Using the gender lens, it is highly noticeable that we have been studying men and masculinity for some time in the arena of governance, even though we rarely acknowledged it as such. For example, *Who Governs,* Dahl's[40] classic study of pluralism at New Haven was a study of men's opportunity to participate in leadership roles and women's systematic exclusion from them.[41] Still, neither Dahl nor feminist readers of political studies treat men and masculinity fully inside the realm of gender analysis.

Men on Masculinity

Male scholars have increasingly become interested in men, masculinity, and the study of gender for the past two decades, with a growing political force accompanying it. Kenneth Clatterbaugh has identified six contemporary perspectives on masculinity: conservative, profeminist, men's rights, spiritual, socialist, and group specific (e.g., black or gay).[42] While feminism may have given rise to some perspectives on masculinities, men could claim many of their own constructions and their own recognition of masculinist thought. This scholarship has a longer history than many students of gender or politics realize.

Joseph Pleck and Jack Sawyer published *Men and Masculinity* in 1974,[43] a work exploring many of the questions made evident by the rise of the women's movement, including chapters on "male liberation" and "unlearning." Other works in the 1970s considered male chauvinism,[44] the "hazards of being male" and a "new male,"[45] as well as presenting readings for "men against sexism," which could contrast with a belief in the "inevitability of patriarchy," and on the danger of men's "sexual suicide."[46] These works were as political as feminist writings of the time. They incorporate stances of profeminist men in support of women, radical men's rights advocates decrying the difficulties and discrimination men faced, or conservatives who saw extant gender arrangements as inevitable as well as preferable. Obviously, some of these writings occurred in reaction to feminism, but all of them implicitly or explicitly studied men as gendered beings.

The 1980s witnessed a maturing of the same strands of thought from both scholarly and men's activists' positions. Approaches include conservative George Gilder deploring changes in homes,[47] scrutiny of "myths of masculinity"[48] and the "male experience,"[49] and explorations of "why men are the way they are."[50] Research on men and masculinity flourished,[51] and various constructions of masculini*ties* have been recognized[52] and have been accompanied by the awareness that our understanding of males *as men* was socially constructed.[53] Men were looking to move "beyond patriarchy," and gay men were taking a place in the scholarship and activism.[54] Men have been very active over the past decades in studying masculinity and gender. If we study gender, we study both women and men. Clearly, men have gender too.

Despite all of the scholarship on masculinity by men, one fundamental political element remains unacknowledged: Seldom do these scholars acknowledge masculinism as ideological. Male scholars' inability to understand masculinity as having ideological dimensions (or their reticence or refusal to acknowledge masculinism) stands in sharp contrast to a general willingness to label feminism as ideological and to delimit its contributions to knowledge of politics accordingly. In other words, men have limited recognition that perspectives on masculinity taken as a whole contain ideas, beliefs, actions, and potentials parallel to feminism. Like feminism, masculinism represents ideological stances; it is a metaideology that incorporates multiple ideologies within it. That masculinity could for so long be denied as ideological is, as Wendy Brown states, a "kind of deafness [that] has a vitally political edge."[55] Clatterbaugh's "perspectives on masculinity," then, might better be named "variations on masculinist thought," in a fashion parallel to Rosemarie Tong's "feminist thought" or Alison Jaggar's "feminist politics."[56] The feminine or femininity is to feminism as the masculine or masculinity is to masculinism.

Masculinism and Leadership

Those who do gender analysis know well that, in the domain of leadership and governance, women clearly constitute the "other," or in Simone de Beauvoir's term, women are the "second sex."[57] Women have been mostly invisible in the public sphere. As the hoopla surrounding the 1992 elections made patently clear, women as a group still find themselves outside public leadership and positions of governance despite the few women who hold top spots. "More than any other kind of human activity, *politics* has historically borne an explicitly masculine identity. It has been more exclusively limited to men than any other realm of endeavor and has been more intensely, self-consciously masculine than most other social practices."[58]

This presents intractable problems for women who want to enter politics and govern effectively because they find entering manhood difficult, virtually by definition. And such masculine assumptions have been more potent for having gone unexamined—hence, the need to study gender power in relationship to governance. The invisible, gendered ideological roots of politics need to be made visible. While governance and leadership have been distinctively marked by men and masculinity, seldom have these concepts been acknowledged as gendered by scholars of the subjects.

Probably no notion illustrates this masculine marking better than the prevalence of the Great Man theory of leadership. In compiling an impressive sourcebook on political leadership—impressive because she has artfully drawn critical passages from writings throughout history—Barbara Kellerman shows us just how much masculinity permeates understandings of political leadership.[59] First, of the forty-three passages she selects, only two are written by women, so it is not surprising that men take a more central place if men are writing. Second, if she is to represent the writings on the subject accurately, she can scarcely avoid Great Men, heroes, philosopher kings, and princes. That is how we have come to know leaders. All of these images, of course, represent political leaders as masculine. None of the chapters explicitly includes women, and most implicitly exclude them. In Hoover's measure of ideology, these images indicate masculine power and masculinism at work.[60]

In another well-regarded recent book, *Leadership and Politics,* edited by Bryan D. Jones,[61] we find thirteen chapters replete with references to various men and masculine-rooted assumptions that fail to consider gender explicitly at all (except for intermittent references to "she"). This absence is particularly revealing given the claim to an integrative approach, especially one said to cover "the 'two worlds' of political analysis," leadership as part of a social world and "a political world that is more similar to biology."[62] This absence is further compounded by acknowledgment that "*any* social force or institutional structure can limit the actions of leaders" and that "[l]eadership opportunities are highly contextual."[63] That gender can remain so completely invisible to such a study of political leadership demonstrates the need to uncover the power that makes it possible—gender power.

In a third otherwise fine book, *Political Leadership in Democratic Societies,* edited by Anthony Mughan and Samuel C. Patterson,[64] we again find little awareness of gender and scant evidence that political leadership includes women. Here we find 23 chapters, with one by Pippa Norris on women, electoral systems, and parliamentary recruitment.[65] This section assumes that all who hold a public office are leaders and does not directly address broader questions of leadership. Another chapter on Margaret Thatcher by Anthony King makes no mention of gender, even though King declares Thatcher "an unusual prime minister" and "a minority inside her own party."[66] He remains oblivious to gender dynamics as he describe events surrounding the Falkland Islands War, which

> proved what some had doubted, that she was capable of performing effectively under the most extreme pressure. It vindicated her posture as a leader who could be counted on to take hard decisions and see them through to success. It made her for the time being a national hero ... her position of overall dominance was never again in doubt. (328)

As researchers at the Center for the Study of the American Woman and Politics have long known, women executives must prove that they are capable of being tough, especially in military matters, but this gender power differential goes unstated by King. Similarly, he ignores the way in which being a woman, an outsider, likely shaped her position as "unusual" or "a minority." As a woman she inevitably faced the prospect of being in an area that both assumes men as the norm and finds little female company. Interestingly, it was her actions as commander in chief, perhaps the most masculine of all leadership posts, that transformed her into a "hero" and made her dominant.[67]

Women's presence among governing leaders inevitably evokes comparisons to predecessors and incumbents (who consequentially happen mostly to be male). "What we took to be humanly inclusive problematics, concepts, theories, objective methodologies, and transcendental truths are in fact far less than that. Instead, these products of thought bear the mark of their collective and individual creators, and the creators in turn have been distinctively marked as to gender, class, races, and culture."[68] Leadership and governance are marked collectively by male ancestry and individually by great men. Until all of us, but especially men, acknowledge the existence of a gender power system, we will ignore tremendously important aspects of life, society, institutions, and power structures.

Gender and the Study of Leadership

Gender's invisibility in the realm of leadership and governance lies in masculine assumptions. As revealed in the above discussion, gender—especially in man, masculine, and manly variants—has always existed and persisted in discussions of governance and political leadership. The political world of men[69] that "has passed as a humanistically impartial vocabulary of power, reason, morality, interest, autonomy, justice, history, theory, progress, and enlightenment is actually imbued with gendered masculine meanings and values.[70] As a result of masculinism, males benefit from considerably more social power than females, and in the sexual division of labor men have been assigned most of the "power duties"[71] in society generally and in politics more specifically. Yet, most of us experience male political leadership as normal. How does that come to be? Under the feminist challenge, says Christine DiStefano, thoughts related to governance and leadership "can no longer claim ungendered innocence."[72]

But what can we claim for women in the realm of governance and leadership? Let us begin by looking more closely at what the literature shows us about gender and leadership. We will borrow Yukl's four major approaches to leadership studies to frame this exploration: trait and behavioral-style analysis, situational leadership, and the place of power. We begin with trait analysis because it is by far the most prevalent area, for reasons that should become readily apparent.

Traits and Styles: The Common Way of Studying Gender and Leadership

Any look at the topic of leadership and gender shows the centrality of trait analysis. Modern scholarship on leadership began with the study of leadership traits (e.g., the Ohio State and Michigan studies). That alone makes unremarkable the fact most explorations of gender and leadership began with the study of traits. Pamela Johnson can be credited with the most crucial foundation study in this area.[73] She revised earlier conclusions that no common trait could be found among leaders, instead finding that leaders share one trait: Leaders were almost uniformly male. Such a finding is crucial to knowledge about gender and leadership. Because of the particular trait and because it had been overlooked or assumed as a given for decades of study, Johnson's finding also suggests much about gender power and leadership.

We have tended to study gender and leadership by looking at traits or styles for another reason as well. We first came to "know" gender by looking at sex roles and sex-role stereotypes. Both of these ideas build upon sex-specified traits and styles. We invariably discuss gender in terms of associations of behaviors or traits with one sex or the other. Marilyn Loden's *Feminine Leadership* carefully detailed the traits of women's leadership style in contrast to men's style.[74] Similarly Sally Helgesen's "female advantage" flows from a remake of Mintzberg's study of men's leadership styles.[75] In both cases, we must first know what feminine or female means—how they are socially constructed as gendered—before we can understand women's leadership style. It should not go without notice that women's style is apparently demarcated from the normal style of men's leadership.

Kelly, Hale, and Burgess illustrated this latter point using a factor analysis on top-level administrators working for the state of Arizona.[76] They found that, although few differences existed between the male and female administrators on individual behavioral traits, substantial differences existed in terms of how the various traits were packaged. The traits of dominance, intimidation, attractiveness, and affection in particular were displayed very differently by men and women. Whereas dominance and intimidation could be used as positive forces for male managers, they were not typically used by women but rather were avoided. In addition, attractiveness and being affectionate were linked with being opportunistic for men but not for women. Being attractive seemed to be required for women to be viewed as good managers. Being affectionate was linked with a "gentle" behavioral style for women.

Duerst-Lahti and Johnson employed the trait approach to the study of gender and leadership styles by using gender stereotypes to test gendered valuations and styles.[77] In a two-step process, they first used gender stereotypes to see which traits and behaviors were valued in top-level administrators; then they compared self-reported assessments of leadership style according to gender stereotypes. They found that gender-neutral styles and traits were valued most in top-level administrators by both women and men, with feminine and masculine traits being valued equally after the neutral traits. Interestingly, however, in assessing their own styles and traits, female top-level administrators avoided feminine traits and styles, while men did not. Women "out-maled the men" or, more accurately, out-masculined the men. Nevertheless, women more than men also reported employing those traits and styles deemed most valuable to the organization. So while these female administrators seemed to avoid feminine traits, they did not wantonly accept masculine ones; rather, they adopted traits and behaviors seen as most consequential for the organization. Finally, these studies compared differences among the sexes as well as between them, finding greater differences among women and among men than between them. Top-level women and men shared far more traits and behavioral styles with each other than they shared with their middle-level sex-counterparts.

These studies lead to conclusions about the possibility of "gender neutral-ity," a phrase often used when quantitative comparisons of sex categories find "no difference." Much like Ann Morrison and her colleagues and Ragins and Sundstrom,[78] Kelly as well as Duerst-Lahti and Johnson conclude that gender perceptions and gender stereotypes so intrude upon assessments of traits and styles that none can be considered neutral.[79] Instead, it is much more productive to view traits and styles as *transgendered.*[80] By transgendered we mean that while it may be seen as appropriate for both women and men to display a particular trait or behavior, its meaning will not be understood the same. Think, for example, about the process of homemaking, comparing a housewife to a househusband. To illustrate the concept of transgendering in leadership behav-ioral style, consider assertiveness. Both women and men in leadership roles can be seen as gender appropriate when behaving assertively today. However, if we think about assertiveness as somewhere midway on a continuum of fully passive to fully aggressive, women are confined to a more limited range of appropriate assertive-aggressive behavior than men, and women's range falls closer to the passive end of the continuum than does men's range. Women are not seen as unusual if they are fully passive and reach the limit of acceptability with assertiveness. Anything beyond this limit passes the bounds of acceptability, and a woman is highly likely to face unflattering labels for being too aggressive. In contrast, men seem odd and perhaps weak if they are fully passive. For men, assertive behavior is often rewarded because gender expectations lead us to anticipate that men will behave in an aggressive manner. Therefore, when a man behaves assertively but not aggressively, we likely reward him for his consid-erate behavior. In this case, both women and men behave assertively, but the interpretations vary dramatically. This set of interpretations, the reader might note, is completely consistent with the propensity to reassert gender where none need exist, as in the case of the new ideas on "women's management styles" discussed above. Given the climate for gender today, *traits and behaviors cannot be neutral;* they can at best be understood as transgendered.

Situational Leadership and Gender

That mothers/women are accorded greater leadership potential in the realm of parenting comes as no surprise. One only need to consider the different images evoked in the phrase "to mother a child" and "to father a child" to understand their gendered meanings. Mothers' greater leadership potential with children is recognized by the common practice of awarding custody to them in cases of divorce. This is, of course, one of the prime situational differences that drives the men's rights movement. But such differences speak only vaguely to issues of leadership and governance.

Central to the situational leadership approach is the notion that individual leaders change their behavior according to the needs of followers and that in certain circumstances one style of leadership is more effective than another. One might think about the command-and-control leadership style prevalent in military settings; when an officer gives an order, the enlisted ranks are to follow without question, and the style is effective. Command and control is not effective when leaders and followers do not share a formalized hierarchical relationship, such as in a social movement in which leaders must cajole follows to follow, or when power is shared, as between, say, a Republican president and a Democratic Speaker of the House.

Several studies shed light on the way gender interacts situationally. First, women but not men face a proving period of about a year, according to a study of state administrative agencies. Further, women apparently need to reprove their competency with every new group they encounter.[81] Therefore, followers need additional reassurance from female leaders, forcing them continually to demonstrate and reassure followers of their competence. This is not the case with male leaders, who may even demonstrate incompetence without having their overall leadership called into question. The situational terrain, then, differs by gender interpretation.

Second, the organizational culture of agencies varies, and with these cultures come different gender ethoses. The ease with which women "fit" into agency cultures and the conduciveness of various agencies to female leadership tend to follow gender stereotypes quite closely.[82] The more consistent an agency's function with feminine stereotypes, the more likely women are to advance in leadership positions. The more consistent an agency's function with masculine stereotypes, the greater the predominance of men in leadership posts.

Third, inside "male bastion" agencies, those agencies in which men overwhelmingly fill the ranks in line positions, gender ethos alters situationally. In a study of women in foreign-policy agencies, Meredith Sarkees and Nancy McGlen find the command-and-control style of the Defense Department actually advantages women's leadership capacity over the more malleable and informal styles present in the State Department. Subordinates, apparently, will follow women when ordered to do so but are less likely to credit leadership potential in a situation that operates more by negotiation.[83]

Finally, as the work of Meredith Newman in this volume reveals, even the way we think about policy through policy typologies carries with it gendered dimensions. Women would be wise to enter distributive-type agencies, because more agency rewards accrue there. Such agencies also purport not to inspire controversy. Distributive agencies also are more likely to cover policy areas generally associated with men. Situations matter for gender; gender shifts meanings and power relations by situation.

Power and Leadership

This book is devoted to gender power and leadership. Power underpins leadership. The perception of power grants an individual an advantage in being accepted as a leader, and if one is a leader, one is more likely to be seen as powerful. Because men have more social power and hold more political leadership posts, they benefit more in the relationship between leadership and power. As Ragins and Sundstrom carefully delineate,[84] dynamics and resources at multiple levels interact to diminish women's power and enhance men's power (see chap. 2). We will explore the issue of leadership and power throughout this volume. Now we turn to a closer look at how it is possible to "do gender" and "do leadership" as a way to better understand gender power.[85]

Doing Leadership, Doing Gender, Seeing Gender Power

One way to see gender power operate is to think about doing gender and leadership simultaneously. Perhaps the easiest way to accomplish this is to consider political leadership in terms of sex-segregated occupations that, in turn, are embedded in the sexual division of labor. It is not unreasonable to think about political leadership as part of a career. Most who are considered political leaders hold public positions. For those who do not, Ross Perot for example, lifework or career builds in such way as to make an individual plausible as a political leader (and plays a large part in viability as a political candidate). In any case, by virtue of the resources, decision-making capacity, and influence, almost any top public job can be seen as enabling leadership of some kind. And although legislatures have institutional leadership structures and posts, almost any legislator can be seen as a leader by virtue of the capacity to respond or not, give direction to policy, or influence interests of a legislative district. So, doing the work of a public post can readily be understood as doing leadership. But how do we do gender in this context?

Following the model of Elaine Hall, we focus on the work role of political leaders rather than looking to the gender of the individual per se, because individuals cannot override the structural conditions of each social context.[86] A leader then does gender by doing a work role that is loaded with gender meaning. Remember above when Margaret Thatcher became a hero (not a heroine) through her ruthless military command during the Falkland Islands War. Because work roles are gendered, writes Hall, any job "involves managing both the gendered work activity and an individual gender category." The best way to maintain gender arrangements in political leadership (or any occupation) is to keep the leadership positions as a strictly sex-segregated occupation. If that fails, if we begin to have more than token numbers of female senators or congresswomen, then a process of reinterpretation occurs. Individuals do not apply gender meanings to supposedly abstract or ungendered behaviors; rather, the work behaviors themselves are loaded with gender. Gender is implicit in the mode of action as part of its interaction. Therefore, and this is important, a gendered mode of action is available to persons of both sexes. When men are nurses or women are admirals, they work in a mode of action that is itself gendered. So long as the sex of the individual is consistent with the gendered work activity, no dissonance occurs. However, when gender-atypical workers perform a task, the incongruity between the worker's gender and the gendered work role prompts a reinterpretation of the gendered meanings.

The process of reinterpreting the gender meanings of work usually includes a heightened importance of gender displays. Female marines are forced to take classes in grooming and makeup for example;[87] a male nurse seeks out specialty areas that provide greater authority and autonomy, higher pay, and closer collaboration with physicians; female political candidates find a "year of the woman" when the agenda shifts from foreign to domestic concerns. To maintain the gender meanings loaded on the work activities, often the work of any interloper is said to be performed differently. So, for example, we would expect to see the rise of books on feminine leadership styles as women successfully do leadership work. Such gender integration essentially splits the work role into two gendered forms, so that male nurses can find a masculine niche inside an occupation gendered femininely or, more to our point, women can do "masculine" leadership tasks.

Even if we set aside the problem women face being recognized as leaders at all, women can successfully enter masculine leadership roles but face two unhappy options, neither of which alters extant gender power relations. Either women must conform to artificially heightened gender differentiation as a leader and agree that feminine leaders' styles exist, thereby perpetuating gender differentiation in the process or women leaders can "do masculine leadership"; they can perform their leadership tasks in a way more masculine than men.

Neither option alters extant gender power. The former reinstates gender differentiation, which in turn perpetuates the probability of masculine domination. The latter leaves women reinforcing masculinist modes of leadership when women might prefer to operate by other modes. Both options reinforce masculine valuation and buttress masculinism's grip on "normal" leadership as masculine leadership. In Judith Lorber's words, we see "biology as ideology."[88]

Let us briefly return to the adjective *political* in our discussion of leaders. Above we said that leadership is sufficiently amorphous that narrowing its scope could artificially limit our potential to understand it. We also said that the power inherent in any position of public authority placed an office holder in a leadership position as they implement modern state power through governance. Several facets of such political leadership should be highlighted.

First, as we alluded, politics occurs within an organized context. Much of the work of governance is conducted by bureaucrats at various levels of government, and few students of leadership forget that public bureaucracies are organizations. However, those who study legislatures or the policy process seldom treat committees or the institution as organizations.

Organizational analysis of legislatures, studies that apply insights of organization theory to the behavior of legislatures or the people in them, are much harder to find than such analyses of the executive branch. Nonetheless, legislative settings and their policymaking activities operate every bit as much in an organized context as bureaucracies. So knowledge about gender power and leadership derived from other organizations applies to legislatures as well.

Second, like gender, the organized context of governance is constructed socially. However formalized over time, all governmental bodies are reifications: We think them up and make them real by acting accordingly. They are "politically negotiated orders" whose structures are "emergent entities" that result from the conscious political decisions of particular people.[89]

Recent reforms of congressional committee structures again serves as a case in point. Men and women create a particular order and structure the organized context in a particular way. However, because organizations emerge as people negotiate their environments and these environments themselves are constantly in flux, organizations are continuously subject to change. This creates uncertainty, and uncertainty leads those involved in an organization to engage in politics to control the context and construct the setting as they prefer.

Politics involves the use of concrete resources and symbolic forms of power. Because all organizations exist inside larger social arrangements, larger social arrangements shape organizational politics and the power dynamics accompanying them. These larger social arrangements include gender arrangements as a central component of power arrangements, whether or not those engaged in any particular act of politics or governance are aware of gender.

Third, all of this activity involves assumptions about the proper distribution of power, or in Hoover's terms, all of this constitutes ideologically rooted behavior. Again, if the assumptions remain below levels of awareness, the ideology operates with greater potency than if those involved readily acknowledge its existence.

Finally, gender is a complex concept and phenomenon. It generates from bodies that are biologically sexed but only gains meaning through its social construction. Because gender is socially constructed, it is composed of ideas, or more specifically normative beliefs about valuation, modes of behavior, and being. Gender is something one can do or perform as a result. And because males and females are not socially equal categories, ideas about gender inevitably are ideas about gender power. Underpinning all of these ideas we can find masculinism, the ideology that follows from ideas about gender, power arrangements in society, and the related plans of action.

Every social act inevitably is interpreted through a gender lens. Therefore, even if some particular behavior or position is deemed acceptable for both women and men and so might seem "gender neutral," we can only know it through gendered prescriptions; neutrality cannot exist. And gender relations are power relations. Gender categories are not equivalent. We can, as a result, more accurately think of phenomena such as leadership as transgendered rather than neutral. While women may enter governance and leadership today, they do so in a transgendered context still in the process of shifting from masculinity and masculinism.

Notes

1. Gary A. Yukl, *Leadership in Organizations,* 2d ed. (Englewood Cliffs, N.J.: Prentice-Hall, 1989), and "Managerial Leadership: A Review of Theory and Research," *Journal of Management* 15 (2) (1989): 251–59.
2. Barbara Kellerman, ed., *Political Leadership: A Source Book* (Pittsburgh: University of Pittsburgh Press, 1986). In fairness to Kellerman, her earlier edited volume *Leadership: Multidisciplinary Perspectives* (Englewood Cliffs, N.J.: Prentice-Hall, 1984), has twelve chapters with five written by women, including one on "feminist scholarship on political leadership" by Susan Carroll. The difference between these two works points out the masculine bias of leadership when sources for a sourcebook are so dominated by male writers. See also Anthony Mughan and Samuel C. Patterson, eds., *Political Leadership in Democratic Societies* (Chicago: Nelson-Hall Publishers, 1992).
3. Bryan Jones, ed., *Leadership and Politics: New Perspectives in Political Science* (Lawrence: University of Kansas Press, 1989).
4. Studies now confirm the ambiguity of biological sex with, for example, XXY gene combinations being far more common than previously recognized. See Judith Shapiro, *Body Guards* (New York: Routledge, 1991).
5. Jean Lipman-Blumen, *Gender Roles and Power* (Englewood Cliffs, N.J.: Prentice-Hall, 1984).
6. Janet Yoder, "Rethinking Tokenism: Looking beyond Numbers." *Gender and Society* 5 (2) (1991): 178–93.
7. Wendy Brown, *Manhood and Politics: A Feminist Reading in Political Theory* (Totowa, N.J.: Rowman and Littlefield, 1988) was the first to gain prominence in this undertaking.
8. Christine DiStefano, *Configurations of Masculinity: A Feminist Perspective on Modern Political Theory* (Ithaca, N.Y.: Cornell University Press, 1991), 4.
9. William F. Whyte, *Man and Organization: Three Problems in Human Relations in Industry* (Homewood, Ill.: R. D. Irwin, 1959).
10. See Cathy Marie Johnson and Georgia Duerst-Lahti, "Public Work and Private Lives," in *Women and Men of the States,* ed. Mary Ellen Guy (Armonk, N.Y.: M. E. Sharpe, 1992) for an extended discussion of the ideological implications of this work.

11. Carolyn Wood Sherif, "Needed Concepts in the Study of Gender Identity," *Psychology of Women Quarterly* 6 (1982): 375–98.
12. Linda Nicholson, "Interpreting *Gender,*" *Signs: Journal of Women in Culture and Society* 20 (1994): 79–105.
13. See Carol Tavris, *The Mismeasure of Women* (New York: Simon and Schuster, 1992) for a thorough refutation of the idea of "the opposite sex" and the confounding influence of sex-role stereotypes in studies of gender.
14. Jane Flax, "Postmodernism and Gender Relations in Feminist Theory," *Signs* 12 (summer 1987): 621–43. According to Jane Flax, the concept gender relations is an analytic category and "a changing set of historically variable social process[es]" that encompasses a complex set of unstable social relations.
15. Teresa de Lauretis, *Technologies of Gender* (Bloomington: University of Indiana Press, 1987).
16. Brown, *Manhood and Politics.*
17. Kathleen B. Jones makes a compelling case that Butler essentially abandons women as subjects of feminist theory and politics, with "deeply troubling political implications," as "power refuses to disappear with the wave of the deconstructionist's magical wand." *Compassionate Authority: Democracy and the Representation of Women* (New York: Routledge, 1992), 9–10. We agree that Butler's work has numerous troubling political implications. Our point here is to stretch theorizing about gender, especially to illustrate its reified, normative, and expansive nature. Few real human bodies, male or female, escape the consequences of gender and its power.
18. Judith Butler, *Gender Trouble: Feminism and the Subversion of Identity* (New York: Routledge, 1990), 8.
19. See Judith Lorber in "Believing Is Seeing: Biology as Ideology," *Gender and Society* 7 (4) (1993): 568.
20. Butler, *Gender Trouble,* 6.
21. For a comprehensive overview of where gender has been used and applied, see Mary E. Hawkesworth, "Confounding Gender" (paper presented at the annual meeting of the Western Political Science Association, Albuquerque, N.M., March 10, 1994). As Judith Shapiro's study on sex change operations, *Body Guards,* reveals, in contemporary life biological sex may be more mutable than socially constructed gender.
22. See Jones, *Compassionate Authority,* 102; Virginia Sapiro, "The Political Uses of Symbolic Women: An Essay in Honor of Murray Edelman," *Political Communication* 10 (April–June 1993): 137–49.
23. Elaine Hall, "Waitering/Waitressing: Engendering the World of Table Servers," *Gender and Society* 7 (3) (1993): 329–46. Hall draws upon Candace West and Don Zimmerman. "Doing Gender," *Gender and Society* 1 (1987): 125–51.
24. Of course this problem itself hinges on a heterosexual starting point, and most women, regardless of color, would reconfigure the meaning of "lady" to incorporate the honor and respect accorded them without necessarily succumbing to the need for the gentlemanly protection inherent in "lady." See Toni Morrison, ed., *Race-ing, Justice, En-gendering, Power* (New York: Pantheon, 1992), for a number of writings about the Hill-Thomas hearings that touch upon the salience of this race difference in the construction of social reality.
25. Whether or not to criticize the concept of androgyny and all it entails figured as a prime intrafeminist dispute. Liberal feminists generally still hold this idea as central, while others see it as self-defeating (e.g., socialist or Marxist feminists) or largely irrelevant (e.g., postmodernist feminists).
26. Brown, *Manhood and Politics.* Also DiStefano, *Configurations of Masculinity,* and Jones *Compassionate Authority.*
27. Flax, "Postmodernism," 629.

28. This is not to suggest that women have no power within society. Rather, in terms of governance and leadership, women have been virtually absent.

29. Jeff Hearn, *Men in the Public Eye: The Construction and Deconstruction of Public Men and Public Patriarchies* (New York: Routledge, 1992): 48–53. He focuses on the period of 1870–1920 because he sees it as the prime time for the shift to "public patriarchies," although they occurred before and since as well.

30. Jones, *Compassionate Authority.*

31. Kenneth Hoover, *Ideology and Political Life,* 2d ed. (Belmont, Calif.: Wadsworth Publishing, 1994), 4.

32. See Murray Edelman. He introduced this idea most forcefully first in *The Symbolic Uses of Politics* (Urbana: The University of Illinois Press, 1964).

33. Christine DiStefano first wrote of this in 1983. "Masculinity as Ideology in Political Theory: Hobbesian Man Reconsidered," *Women's Studies International Forum* 6 (1983): 633–44.

34. Hoover, *Ideology and Political Life,* 5.

35. Brown, *Manhood and Politics.*

36. DiStefano, "Masculinity as Ideology."

37. Mark Kahn, "Fortune Is a Man" (paper presented at the annual meeting of the Western Political Science Association, Pasadena, Calif., March 1993). The allusion is to Hannah Pitkin's *Fortune Is a Woman* (Berkeley and Los Angeles: University of California Press, 1984), in which she identifies the presence of women in the writings of Machiavelli.

38. Letter from John Adams to Abigail Adams, April 14, 1781, in "Remember the Ladies," in *The Feminist Papers: From Adams to de Beauvoir,* ed. Alice Rossi (New York: Columbia University Press, 1973).

39. Hearn, *Men,* 9.

40. Robert A. Dahl, *Who Governs? Democracy and Power in an American City* (New Haven, Conn.: Yale University Press, 1989).

41. Virginia Sapiro, "Women's Studies and Political Conflict." In *The Prism of Sex,* ed. Julia A. Sherman and Evelyn Torton Beck, (Madison: University of Wisconsin Press, 1979).

42. Kenneth Clatterbaugh, *Contemporary Perspectives on Masculinity: Men, Women, and Politics in Modern Society* (Boulder, Colo.: Westview Press, 1990), 2.

43. Joseph Pleck and Jack Sawyer, *Men and Masculinity: Gender and Politics in the Thought of Niccolo Machiavelli* (Englewood Cliffs, N.J.: Prentice-Hall, 1974).

44. Michael Korda, *Male Chauvinism: How It Works* (New York: Random House, 1973).

45. Herb Goldberg, *The Hazards of Being Male: Surviving the Myth of Masculine Privilege* (New York: Signet, 1976) and *The New Male* (New York: Signet, 1979).

46. Jon Snodgrass, ed., *A Book of Readings for Men against Sexism* (Albion, Calif.: Times Change Press, 1977); Steven Goldberg, *The Inevitability of Patriarchy* (New York: William Morrow, 1974); George Gilder, *Sexual Suicide* (New York: Bantam Books, 1973).

47. Gilder, *Sexual Suicide.*

48. Joseph H. Pleck, *The Myth of Masculinity* (Cambridge, Mass.: MIT Press, 1981).

49. James Doyle, *The Male Experience* (Dubuque, Ia.: Wm. C. Brown, 1984).

50. Warren Farrell, *Why Men Are the Way They Are* (New York: McGraw-Hill, 1987).

51. Michael S. Kimmel, ed., *Changing Men: New Directions in Research on Men and Masculinity* (Newbury Park, Calif.: Sage, 1987).

52. Hearn, *Men.*

53. Harry Brod, *The Making of Masculinities* (Boston: Allen and Unwin, 1987).

54. Seymour Kleinberg, "The New Masculinity of Gay Men, and Beyond," in *Beyond Patriarchy,* ed. Michael Kaufman (Toronto: Oxford University Press, 1987).

55. Brown, *Manhood and Politics,* x.

56. Rosemarie Tong, *Feminist Thought: A Comprehensive Introduction* (Boulder, Colo.: Westview, 1989); and Alison M. Jaggar, *Feminist Politics and Human Nature* (Totowa, N.J.: Rowman and Allanheld, 1983).

57. *Otherness* is a broader concept than gender, incorporating all those (or aspects of those) who do not correspond to the prevailing dominant group. Dominant groups can make their characteristic "givens" as normal, and therefore those who do not share a set of characteristics become "other." This notion shifts depending upon the situation's salient characteristic. In the U.S. case, the "normal" characteristics that mark "others" include male, white, heterosexual, middle class, Christian, and to a lesser extent, college education and a professional occupation.

58. Brown, *Manhood and Politics,* 4.

59. Kellerman, *Political Leadership.*

60. Hoover, *Ideology and Political Life.*

61. Jones, *Leadership and Politics.*

62. Ibid., viii.

63. Ibid., 4 and 5 respectively.

64. Mughan and Patterson, *Political Leadership.*

65. Pippa Norris, "Electoral Systems and the Parliamentary Recruitment of Women," in Mughan and Patterson, *Political Leadership.*

66. Anthony King, "Margaret Thatcher: The Style of a Prime Minister," in Mughan and Patterson, *Political Leadership.*

67. Virginia Sapiro discusses the commonality of such gender-blind portrayal of Margaret Thatcher in "Political Uses."

68. Sandra Harding, *The Science Question in Feminism* (Ithaca, N.Y.: Cornell University Press, 1986), 15.

69. Judith Stiehm, ed., *Women's Views of the Political World of Men* (Dobbs Ferry, N.Y.: Transactional Publishers, 1984).

70. DiStefano, *Configurations of Masculinity,* 4.

71. Mary E. Guy, in this volume.

72. DiStefano, *Configurations of Masculinity,* 2.

73. Pamela Johnson, "Women and Power: Towards a Theory of Effectiveness," *Journal of Social Issues* 32 (1976): 99–110.

74. Marilyn Loden, *Feminine Leadership, or How to Succeed in Business without Being One of the Boys* (New York: Times Books, 1985).

75. Sally Helgesen, *The Female Advantage: Women's Ways in Leadership* (New York: Doubleday Currency, 1990); H. Mintzberg, *The Nature of Managerial Work* (New York: Harper and Row,1973).

76. Rita Mae Kelly, Mary M. Hale, and Jane Burgess, "Gender and Managerial/Leadership Styles: A Comparison of Arizona Public Administrators," *Women and Politics* 11 (2) (1991): 19–39.

77. Georgia Duerst-Lahti and Cathy Marie Johnson, "Gender, Style and Bureaucracy," *Women and Politics,* 10 (4) (1990): 67–120, and, "Management Styles, Stereotypes, and Advantages," in Guy, *Women and Men.*

78. Ann M. Morrison, R. P. White, and E. Van Velsor, "Executive Women: Substance Plus Style," *Psychology Today,* August 1987: 18–26; Belle Rose Ragins and Eric Sundstrom, "Gender and Power in Organizations: A Longitudinal Perspective," *Psychological Bulletin* 105 (1) (1989): 51–88.

79. Rita Mae Kelly, *The Gendered Economy* (Newbury Park, Calif.: Sage, 1991); and Duerst-Lahti and Johnson, "Management Styles."

80. See Duerst-Lahti and Johnson, "Management Styles" for more discussion on what the concept of the transgendered implies for women in management. The term *transgendered* has also been used by those who try to disrupt conventional categories of gender through self-presentation that

makes reading their "given" sex difficult. They attempt to cross (or trans) genders by being both and neither. Such activity, and a common reaction of strong desire to see what they "really" are, supports Judith Shapiro's contention that gender is less mutable than sex since sex change operations have become possible ("The Empire Strikes Back: A Post-Transsexual Manifesto," in *Body Guards*).

81. Georgia Duerst-Lahti, "Gender Power Relations in Public Bureaucracies" (Ph.D. disser., University of Wisconsin, 1987).

82. Ibid.; and Mary E. Guy and Georgia Duerst-Lahti, "Agency Culture and Its Managers," in Guy, *Women and Men*.

83. Nancy E. McGlen and Meredith Ried Sarkees, *Women in Foreign Policy: The Insiders* (New York: Routledge, 1993).

84. Ragins and Sundstrom, "Gender and Power."

85. The useful concept of doing gender comes from West and Zimmerman, "Doing Gender."

86. Hall, "Waitering/Waitressing," esp. 332–35 for quotations. For her ideas of "gendered modes of behavior," Hall draws heavily upon Carol Hagemann-White, "Gendered Modes of Behavior—a Sociological Strategy for Empirical Research" (paper presented at the Third International Interdisciplinary Congress on Women, July 1987, Dublin, Ireland).

87. Christine Williams, *Gender Differences at Work: Women and Men in Nontraditional Occupations* (Berkeley and Los Angeles: University of California Press, 1989).

88. Lorber, "Believing Is Seeing."

89. S. B. Bachrach and E. J. Lawler, *Power and Politics in Organizations* (San Francisco: Jossey-Bass, 1981), 2.

Chapter 2

The Study of Gender Power and Its Link to Governance and Leadership

Rita Mae Kelly and Georgia Duerst-Lahti

Gender power brings together two words historically treated as unrelated, particularly in the discipline of political science. Literature to date has primarily focused on the differences between men and women in the way they develop leadership careers and exercise power in organizations and in politics. Consideration has seldom been given per se to the ways power manifests itself in the interactions between men and women in public leadership roles. Rather, studies focus typically on male-female differences—in terms of *numbers* of women voting or elected to office, purported style differences, or of the *trends and patterns* of any changes (or lack thereof) occurring in these areas. An examination of the gendered nature of political power, of political philosophy, and of politics itself has been slow to develop. The examination of gender power has been even slower. In part, the lack of attention to gender power stems from its lack of visibility compared to sex differences, the erroneous interchangeable use of the terms *sex* and *gender,* and the general focus within the social sciences on sex as a variable rather than on gender as a conceptual frame of reference. To study gender is also to study men as gendered beings, and more.

The focus on gender power as an aspect of leadership draws quick attention to the fact that we need to know the sources of power available to individuals, how structurally based power accrues, as well as to the fact that we need to know more about how to study gender and gender power. Types of power interlink at the individual, organizational, interpersonal, and symbolic levels. Moreover, the characteristics and the sources of power develop longitudinally, over a person's lifetime. In some contexts and arenas, gender power will be in women's favor; in politics and most governance contexts, the gender power balance has been in men's favor. Our task is to analyze why this is so and to determine what factors are contributing to this gender power imbalance in leadership and governance.

In this chapter, we seek to accomplish four aims. The first is to compare and contrast basic analytical issues related to using gender rather than sex as a variable and as a conceptual frame of reference, highlighting the relevance of this difference for the study of public leaders and leadership. The second is to explicate more fully how power and gender are linked together. The third is to present a model of the broad categories of variables that contribute to the development of a public leader. This model articulates the impact gender, sex, and gender power have on ascension to public leadership. The fourth is to articulate as graphically as possible how the components of gender identified for analysis in a gender power context can be used. Within this discussion we explicate particular models of the various components of gender power that provide guidelines and hypotheses for exploring its reality. Throughout, we examine differences in the way men and women develop public-leadership careers and obtain and exercise power in organizations. We now turn to summarizing and comparing the basic assumptions that underlie this move from studying *sex* within a traditional positivist, classical research worldview to studying *gender* within a critical realist, relationalist worldview.

A Comparison of Assumptions and Definitions Used When Studying Gender and Gender Power versus Sex and Sexism in Social Analysis

As specified in the introduction and chapter 1, sex denotes biological and physiological differences between males and females. These, as Chafetz[1] notes, include chromosomal, hormonal, and morphological differences. Historically, the concept of sex roles encompassed all the related social and physical behaviors linked to each sex, but since the mid-1980s scholars—and to a lesser extent U.S. popular culture—have defined sex roles as more narrowly limited to "behaviors determined by an individual's biological sex, such as menstruation, pregnancy, lactation, erection, organism, and seminal ejaculation."[2] This narrower definition more clearly associates sex-linked biological processes to socially prescribed roles. Gender, in contrast, has come to "encompass all those cultural expectations associated with masculinity and femininity that go beyond biological sex differences.... As such, gender roles involve that intricate blend of social and psychological behaviors, attitudes, norms, and values that society designates 'masculine' and 'feminine.'"[3] One common confusion follows from the fact that much quantitative research uses sex as a variable to study social constructions. Researchers then are faced with knowing only the ostensible or stated sex of the respondent—but extrapolating to gender.

We agree with these broad-based distinctions but believe additional clarifications are needed. First, the strong relationship between structural functionalism, an essentialistic worldview of sexed beings, and the social-science concepts of sex, sex roles, and sex-role socialization needs to be recognized. At its starkest, the concept of sex roles has had the following normative overlay: If you were a biological female, then you would naturally be socialized to female-feminine sex roles. If you were a biological male, then you would naturally be socialized to male-masculine sex roles. Note that the biological category male or female collapses into the social categories of masculine/feminine under this model. If particular human beings opted for roles of the "opposite" sex, they were considered at best *sex-role crossovers;* more typically, they were considered social deviants. In part this rigidly follows from the dualistic logic that creates opposites.

This way of looking at how human beings become men and women generally ignored the process of engenderment. Engendering of roles, concepts, behaviors, and normative expectations occurs apart from the sex-role socialization of particular people. The roles either sex is expected to play also need to be conceptualized and developed. They are not decreed by nature. This conceptualization and development constitutes the process of engenderment. In contrast, the process of socialization proceeds by facilitating individuals to adopt particular roles. When societal consensus exists that we have only two sexes and that each should perform certain roles, then sex-role socialization is likely to be fairly uniform—probably even narrowly constricted and rigid. However, as more moments and behaviors are *transgendered,* that is, can be seen as appropriate performances by both sexes, then sex-role socialization will be less uniform.

As Karin Tamerius stresses in chapter 4 below, sex differences in politically relevant experiences are readily detected from four highly visible phenomena with important consequences for gender: (1) the very *content* of the sexual divisions in society, which are pervasive and directly measurable; (2) the *perspectives* of males and females that vary due to the subjectivity inherent in any interpretation; (3) the *mutuality* each sex develops based on commonality of experience; and (4) the *associations* formed from similar socialization of a same-sex group or from performing similar work. In other words, because humans are men or women, they experience the world in importantly different ways.

In contrast to sex differences, gender is more abstract, although it too has four analytical dimensions: (1) it is a *variable* with two, possibly more, categories, having some comparability to sex as a variable and thus able to facilitate exploring gender differences as well as sex differences; (2) it is *a property of an individual or an organization,* reflecting a person's identity or an organization's structural arrangements or ethos; (3) it is *a set of practices* revealing masculinity and femininity in interactive behavior; in this sense an emergent factor of social settings and an action occurring among and between people; and (4) it is *a normative stance regarding appropriate behavior, a prescribed or assumed way of behaving* within societal roles and structures. As such, it undergirds sociopolitical concepts, theories, and institutions. In this latter sense, gender embeds norms into concepts of governance and leadership as well as in our understandings of bureaucracy,[4] accountability, and innumerable other phenomena. It is obvious that we need to use a variety of tools and methods to understand gender and gender power.

The move to study gender rather than sex in the social sciences has considerable significance. Table 1 summarizes the major changes in assumptions one makes when one moves from the traditional classical notions of sex within the positivist or postpositivist worldview to a relational worldview linked with gender as a conceptual framework for studying sociopolitical phenomena.

The relational perspective of reality[5] posited by gender assumes a universe interconnected by a web of relations that are intrinsically dynamic, yet constrained. From the classical positivist perspective the real world is the sum of its observable parts. Typically the causal flow is linear, additive, and unidirectional. The parts determine the whole. From this perspective reality can be separated into dichotomous units and mutually exclusive, separated categories. The relational perspective undergirding the use of gender assumes an interactive, causal flow. Although males and females can be pooled together to form a unit of the

TABLE 1. A Comparison of the Attributes and Assumptions Underlying the Use of Gender versus Sex in Analyses

Sex	Gender
Parts determine the whole	Social construction of reality
Separation based on essential differences	Whole affects parts
	Parts affect whole
Conceptual dichotomies	Complementarity
Mechanical linear causality	Overlapping similarities
Absolute law of cause/effect	Participatory collusion in interactions
	Recursive interactions
Absolute bias toward one dichotomous pole	Balance
Truth as fixed	Indeterminance
Life as determined	Human agency impacts direction/movement
	Change
	Opportunity
	Choice
Truth as ahistorical	Transformation
Present structured by past	Purpose
Focus on individual	Focus on interaction
Isolated and atomized	Vertical and horizontal relationships
Self-interest primary	
No limits	Limits

Source: Reprinted by permission from Peter Gregware and Rita Mae Kelly, "Relativity and Quantum Logics: A Relational View of Policy Inquiry," in *Policy, Theory, and Policy Evaluation: Concepts, Knowledge, Causes, and Norms,* ed. Stuart S. Nagel (New York: Greenwood Press, 1990, an imprint of Greenwood Publishing Group, Inc., Westport, Conn.), p. 30, table 3.1.

family or be separated to refer to sexed dichotomous units, the resulting findings would reflect only the particular understandings (often reifications) of a historical moment in time. The gender framework does not accept the notion that maleness or femaleness and masculinity or femininity are essentialistic phenomena. Rather, the relationally based gender framework posits the social construction of reality and a recursive causal interaction among the parts of an entity and the whole, whether the entity be an individual, organization, or society. It also assumes complementarity, overlapping similarities, and human participation in the determination of outcomes.

The gender framework features human agency consciously in social and historical settings and contexts. Truth is not assumed to be fixed and comprehensible through onetime cross-sectional studies. Rather, reality becomes an interaction of human agency and physical phenomena. It is not denied that human beings or physical phenomena have shape, size, form, and substance; rather, it is asserted that human agency combines with these physical phenomena in constant movement. Options for change and choice are ever present. Human beings, in particular, can exercise such choices. When they do, the possibility for movement and change occurs. When social movements are active and strong, the probability of change is greater than when they are not. This fact, however, does not counter the notion that change, not stability and the status quo, is the constant of life and reality.

Just as the focus on gender helps us recognize that truth about physical beings and reality is not ahistorical, it also helps us understand the role of purpose and visions of the future have on transformation of the present and the past. Because this is so, we as scholars also have limits on what we can learn about the "nature" of reality. We too are constrained by our time and place in history. We can learn what has unfolded to the present. We cannot decipher Truth from here to eternity.

In establishing a conceptual frame of reference for studying gender and gender power, we continually highlight the need to do relational analyses rather than categorical or linear analyses. We also emphasize the need for multilevel, multidisciplinary, and interdisciplinary analyses. The use of the individual level of analysis seems invariably to reduce the study of gender to examinations of sex or gender differences between two mutually exclusive categories. Although some sex and gender differences of a categorical nature can be identified, they often offer little to our understanding of why men and women still tend to play different roles in political and economic systems. They also all too often lead to rather futile and perhaps useless and endless debates as to which version of the differences—the male or the female—are more valid or better than the other. Given the imbeddedness of masculine norms in politics, this literature tends to perpetuate the gender power advantage to men by diverting attention from fundamental dynamics.

The switch to a gender conceptual frame of reference also allows us to explore what distinguishes institutional sexism and its analysis from a gendered organizational analysis. To a large extent these distinguishing dimensions revolve around the latter's greater emphasis on relational and symbolic analysis rather than on categorical and difference analysis. It moves beyond documenting sex imbalance and sexism written into the practices of an institution to assumptions and "givens" that underpin the institutionalized advantages and disadvantages.

The relationship among gender, power, and leadership can only be studied in an interdisciplinary way. Psychological and political-science theories as well as theories of the sociology of culture and of organizations have critical perspectives to bear. The contributions of any one of them in isolation, however, can distort the perception of reality, leading us to uninformative, if not detrimental, conclusions. In our explications of how gender and gender power can best be studied, we will repeatedly highlight both relational and interdisciplinary research perspectives.

Our emphasis on gender power in this volume and on gender as a conceptual frame of reference marks the reconceptualization of the study of sex, sex differences, and sexism as it is linked to governance and leadership. Gender as a conceptual frame of reference and gender power as a particular concept and analytical tool need to be systematically added to the discipline of political science. We contend that greater comprehension of political and social life will result when we make this change.

On Power and Its Link to Gender

Traditional notions of power are heavily laden with gendered assumptions and connotations.[6] Power is a critical element of both governance and leadership and varies between men and women as individuals and within groups. As we will demonstrate, power also has a gender component, and therefore the gendered nature of power must be understood. In order to study gender power we need to understand how it is similar to and different from other types of power.

According to most political scientists and political psychologists, power is a property of individuals, institutions or organizations, and it is linked to interpersonal relationships. Sociologists and political scientists have typically viewed power as the ability of one person to influence or change the behavior of others.[7] Psychologists have viewed power as an acquired skill and a trait of the individual.[8] This perspective inspired numerous studies examining the variation in personality traits between individuals; exploring who among them has the greatest score on a power orientation or on the power trait scale. McClelland expanded this perspective, identifying power as an element of interaction. He highlighted the connections, behaviors, and perceptions among individuals, rather than viewing the ability to wield power as a personality trait possessed by individual persons.[9]

Others argue that power principally emanates from organizations to which people align themselves.[10] Organizations allow individuals access to and control over information and resources. Thus, the amount of power a person has depends on that individual's position in an organization. Power has also been treated as the capacity to effect outcomes or goals in organizations, and as a "structural phenomena created by the division of labor."[11]

Proponents of this perspective argue that position power is usually related to legitimate power, the position one has in a particular organization or a particular political entity.[12] It typically rests on the formal authority an entity grants an individual to reward and punish others and to set and control agendas. One accesses position power when participating in social, economic, and political systems. Position power, in turn, has historically been linked to the sex roles that a society assigns to men and to women through sex-segregated job structures. Position power delegates control over resources and establishes authority to reward and punish. It determines the types and quantities of information one is likely to have, be able to obtain, or legitimately use. It also impacts one's ability to operate in work environments.

These approaches to the study of power and its sources can mesh coherently. It is possible that the various types of power are cumulative, that they have a geometric rather than a simple additive or linear impact on each other, or that they constitute various aspects of a complex power source. For example, it may be that a person with charisma needs position power in order to be able to capitalize on a personality advantage, or, alternatively, it is feasible that once an individual is in power, he or she might (in a cumulative fashion) develop latent charismatic potential because followers look for charisma in a leader. It is also possible, as Ragins and Sundstrom contend,[13] that some types of power can compensate for the lack of other types. Ragins and Sundstrom illustrate this point by noting that informal networks might compensate for a lack of formal training if others in key positions know and commend one's abilities.[14] Personal contacts then can vouch for an individual in substitution for credentials. It is also possible that some sources of power change in value over time. To illustrate, expert knowledge rendered obsolete by new technology or research can diminish the worth of an expertise. We have scant call for blacksmiths today, for example.

We agree with Ragins and Sundstrom that power is cumulative,[15] and that, therefore, we need to develop a conceptual frame of reference that will enable us to explore how each of these properties of power come to reside differentially in men and women and to understand why women and men continue to be so differently enmeshed in the composite power context. But we wish to be very clear that our main focus is the gendered conditions of leadership and govern-ance, not just variations among individuals' capacity to get and exercise power. To understand this distinction better it is helpful to compare our gendered focus to previous feminist critiques of sexism and sexuality inherent in organizations and positions of power.

The approaches that have set most social scientists' frames of reference about women, governance, and leadership within organizations are *(a)* the utilitarian instrumental model of bureaucracies à la Max Weber, which assumes masculine norms as the standard for behavior; *(b)* the patriarchal, feminist standpoint model of Kathy Ferguson, which challenges the Weberian assump-tions and lays bare the masculine/patriarchal assumptions of bureaucratic struc-tures; and *(c)* the organizational sexuality model of Rosemary Pringle or Jeff Hearn and his colleagues, which demonstrates that private sphere of sexual relations permeates the public workplace and all organizations.

As Anne Witz and Mike Savage note,[16] these approaches lead us to think about and to conclude dramatically different things about women, women in organizations and governance, and women as leaders. The instrumental We-berian models lead us to be concerned, as Rosabeth Moss Kantor was in *Men and Women of the Corporation,*[17] with issues of equal opportunity, access, equality, and equity in the existing workplace. This perspective leads us to stratification theories from sociology and assumptions about sex differences to develop our hypotheses and to give context to our conclusions. Power and sex are sharply differentiated concepts, not viewed as particularly related. In con-trast, from Ferguson's perspective (in *The Feminist Case against Bureauc-racy*),[18] gaining access and equality within bureaucracies is not the issue; rather, transforming bureaucracies to a nonpatriarchal form is. Relying on Foucault more than Weber and on feminists' experience with self-organizing, Ferguson would have women develop their own ways of organizing and leading. Torn between social constructionism and sexual essentialism, Ferguson does not provide a clear guide to how women can or should deal with bureaucracies or behave in leadership positions; nonetheless, it is clear that getting access to and becoming equal with men within existing Weberian-type bureaucracies is not a worthy goal for her. Pringle also relies on Foucault and poststructuralism in *Secretaries Talk.*[19] Even more than Ferguson, Pringle sees power and sexuality as foundations for modern organizations. She argues that women's sexuality and emotions need to be reintroduced into modern organizations in a way that will enhance women's power. Bureaucratic discourses about sexuality, about ration-ality, and about sex differences need to change. Similarly, Hearn et al. demon-strate that sexuality permeates production in organizations as well as the reproduction of organizations.[20] Importantly, they identify and analyze the centrality of a masculine (hetero)sexuality of dominance as the prevailing paradigm in the organization of social process. Power, sex, and sexuality are not separated, as in Kantor's view. Women cannot simply use power of a higher position to counter males' traditionally greater gender power precisely because the form of sexuality itself—masculine (hetero)sexuality of dominance—prescribes women's subservience. Power and sexuality conjoin to create gender power conditions highly disadvantageous for women.

We agree with Pringle and Hearn et al. on this last point. In contrast to Rosabeth Moss Kantor's theory of positional power, we do not believe that simply attaining a position of power is sufficient to achieve either equality between the sexes or gender equality. Because we believe the gender power and leadership nexus is much more complex, we opt for a paradigm that acknowledges gender and the power that accompanies it. As Witz and Savage note, "Gender is embedded in the power relations of bureaucracy, just as power is embedded in gender relations in the form of male dominance and female subordination."[21] We extend their thinking to the organization of government more broadly. To address the range of issues involved in studying sex differences, sexuality, and the embeddedness of gender in organizations and governmental entities and concepts, as well as in persons, we need this broader paradigm.

How does one accumulate power and access the sources of power? And how does this accumulation and access become gendered? If we consider power to be a property of an individual, of individual's interpersonal relationships, and of organizations in a variety of ways, then it is clear that the sources of power come from these particular entities. How individuals combine these various components of power and the ongoing ease with which they access these sources will determine overall power. Because power beyond brute force is socially constructed, thought up, and reified, what we believe and how we think about power can determine power. Figure 2 depicts the various sources of power relevant to becoming a public leader. These sources of power are best analyzed at multiple levels ranging from the individual to the interpersonal to the power from position within an organization or society. All operate on and shape any individual's capacity to move into public leadership.

At the individual level, people can vary in terms of standard background characteristics that generate power in society—education, race, income, occupation, control over time and space, biological sex, age, and disability. Each of these characteristics can obviously influence the amount of power one has or is likely to obtain in a given moment in history in a given society. The list, however, fails to delineate the nature of the differences that result from sex-role socialization and differences in the attainment of education, the predisposition or drive

Career transitions	Level of analysis		
	Organizational	Interpersonal	Individual
Promotion to powerful position ↑	Performance appraisal Selection and tracking Training	Interpersonal perceptions Work relationships: Mentors Coalitions and networks Subordinate support	Self-selection Background Skills Personality traits Career aspirations Nonwork roles
Entry into organization Entry level Department Position power ↑	Publicity of job openings Recruitment practices Selection and hiring practices	Interpersonal perceptions: Stereotypes Prototypes Attributions Networks	Self-selection Background Skills Personality traits Career aspirations Nonwork roles
	Organizational boundary		
Entry into job market Job vs. career Occupation Specialty	Social-Systems Sex-role socialization	Sex roles and stereotypes	Self-selection Role conflict Training/education Economic pressures

Fig. 2. Relationship between path to power and levels of analysis. (From Belle Rose Ragins and Eric Sundstrom, "Gender and Power in Organizations," *Psychological Bulletin,* 105, no. 1 [1989]: 75. Copyrighted 1989 by the American Psychological Association, Inc. Reprinted with the authors' permission.)

and motivation to get and hold power, and the development of the particular personality traits, characteristics, and skills associated with the manifestation of power. Neither does it describe the gender constructions that facilitate or hinder individual advancement on the path to power. Figure 2 delineates the interconnections among levels of power in careers, pointing to the effect social systems have on them. On most of these dimensions sex power differences have been adequately analyzed and described by others. We need now to study the ways gender power is created by and manifested within each of these types of power. Through these analyses we will be better able to understand the gendered conditions of leadership and governance as well as gender variations in individual leaders' performance and success.

Integrating these aspects of gender, power, and leadership together means we need to bring into our conceptual framework a model of political leadership that links to organizations.

A Gender-Expanded Model of Be(com)ing a Public Leader

A framework for gender analysis of public leadership and power requires an encompassing overview of societal, organizational, interpersonal, and individual factors that pertain to the search for power, the pursuit of a career, and then the performance within a public-leadership context.[22] This means the framework must be longitudinal in perspective, and dynamic and relational in its understanding of reality.

Figure 3 depicts the basic model from which we are working. As can be seen, the individual public leader is at the center of focus. The gendered individual, a male or female person embedded in a cultural context with gendered dimensions, occupies the model's core. When analyzing gender power, it is critical to note two things in addition to the sex of the individual and the gender s/he projects: (1) the gendered nature of interpersonal interactions and practices; and (2) the gendered overlay within each of the other categories of variables.

The definitions of each of the major categories within this model are standard. An internal career is the "psychological term for the self-development, motivation, enhancement of personal capital, and development of mentoring and anchor networks undertaken by an individual in pursuit of a career."[23] An external career is the "sociological focus on career development [that] examines the career paths in organizations, career stages recognized by employers, and the career types recognized by society."[24] Organizational culture consists of the mores, values, beliefs, attitudes, and practices within an organization, including the contradictory ones that exist often between overt values and actual practices. This culture is permeated with gender overlays, or gender ethos, often resulting in distinctive gender cultures within different organizations—an elementary school compared to a construction company, for example.[25] National culture is broader but also consists of broad mores, values, beliefs, attitudes, and practices. This culture has a strong sex-role ideology and gendered assumptions imbedded within it. For example, an Arab woman in a Moslem culture will have a very different set of mores, values, beliefs, and interpersonal practices with which she will need to deal than an American atheist woman living in the United States. Women working and living within each national culture will be shaped by and will need to cope with this national culture and the particular organizational culture in which they are working. So will men.

The purpose of this particular model is to help us understand and explore the sources and manifestations of gender power. Use of the model will assist in comprehending how gender and gender power promote or impede the public-leadership capacities of individual men and women. It will facilitate understanding the gendered conditions of leadership and governance as well as the

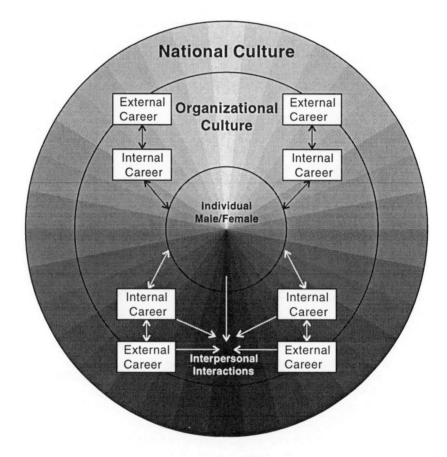

Fig. 3. A gender-based model for becoming and being a public leader

reasons why variations exist among individuals in terms of their capacity to get and exercise power.

Using the Gender Paradigm to Analyze Gender Power

We now turn to the more concrete matter of how to use the gender conceptual framework to study gender power. To keep the following methodological presentation as simple as possible, we will organize the discussion around the four different dimensions of gender. Within each dimension we will examine how the study of gender illustrates the need for a relationalist rather than a more classically based positivistic or postpositivistic understanding of reality.

Gender as a Variable or Category

Liberalism is dedicated to individualism, freedom from state interference into private matters and the liberal rights that promote freedom of self-image, lifestyle, and behavior. The liberal values of equality of opportunity, freedom of expression, and tolerance have served a nation of immigrants well, enabling diverse ethnic and nationality groups to pursue life, liberty, and happiness as each saw fit to do.

In the last half of the twentieth century both the women's movement and the civil-rights movement used the rhetoric of liberalism to try to change the status and position of people of color and women of all races. The intent was, in essence, to change the universal norm undergirding the popular saying signifying a free citizen—from "He's white, male, and twenty-one (and therefore ought to be free to do as he pleases)" to "He or she is human, over eighteen, and therefore free." Using a universal norm of citizenship, women and men of color in the United States were able to use analyses of differential treatment of men and women and of whites and people of color to promote greater social and political equality. In the process, however, they discovered severe limits in the utility of *sex* as a basic unit of analysis and of using sex differences as the conceptual frame of analysis.

The equal opportunity and affirmative-action laws of the 1950s, 1960s, and 1970s made substantial progress toward eliminating barriers in access to jobs, schools, and public participation. This very progress, however, lay bare several dilemmas about the liberal approach to the world and the dominant paradigm of reality derived from it. One of these major dilemmas involves the vexatious situation of having an empirical reality of highly diverse individuals living in varied contexts coupled with a political philosophy and analytic tradition that asserts individuals are universally the same, having no context and no physical bodies. Philosophically, the liberal individual is an abstracted person without context—an individual with rights but without sex, race, age, or disabilities and situated outside geographical and social boundaries. The ideal liberal society is color-blind and sex-blind. The liberal society is supposed to preclude the need for state intervention to facilitate "positive liberty." But this image of the disembodied liberal individual derives from ideas and circumstances most relevant to those who have held positions to most determine the assumed individual—a white male situated in middle-class Western Europe, the United States of America, and Canada. It has not aided women (or men of color) seeking equality and freedom as effectively as it has aided white men precisely because embedded notions require others to assimilate to assumptions given to us by those who see them as givens.

Women and men have been treated unequally throughout most of the history of the United States because people promoted separate classifications, based on biological-physiological sex differences, and because those holding public leadership posts—men—made marital family ties the basis for males to be designated as the legal, political representatives of women within the social unit of the family.

This classification separated society into a private female and a male public sphere. The private sphere dealt with domestic, household concerns requiring caring and nurturing. The public sphere dealt with the political, visible, and economic life, comprising heavy labor, military activity, and deliberation over the protection and livelihood of society. As Eisenstein has stressed, the rights of liberal democracies have been grounded and structured on the differences between men and women.[26] The liberal rights of men in the public sphere rested on the exclusion of women, that is, on the political, economic, and legal inequality of the sexes. In the 1980s we learned that the claim of women to the same liberal rights "offers a threat to the fabric of interdependence on which men's rights depend."[27] Efforts to simply add women to the political and economic systems and stir have not been successful. For women to be treated the same as men—for one woman to be added to one man, and to come up with two equal citizens, two equal soldiers, two equal employees, two equal leaders—has not been so simple as adding the abstract numbers of one plus one.

This societal and political problem stems to a very large extent from the contradiction between our understanding of empirical reality and our liberal universalistic assumptions about political actors. In the twentieth century, social scientists with behavioralist and positivistic bents have assumed that empirical reality consists of mutually exclusive and distinctive, separable units of analyses, males being one unit and females another. Political theorists and activists until recently, however, have simultaneously generally tried to maintain a nongendered universalistic understanding of this same reality. The analytical variable of sex from both a classical and positivistic worldview posits males and females as being within mutually exclusive categories based on biological and physiological differences revolving around reproductive capacities. The upper diagram in figure 4 illustrates this dichotomized view of the sexes and the notion of androgyny, which for a time was presented as a way of recognizing that males and females could behave similarly. The following quote from the 1863 U.S. Supreme Court majority ruling in *Bradwell v. Illinois* reflects the dichotomous view of women as political, economic, and social beings.

Man is, or should be, women's protector and defender. The natural and proper timidity and delicacy which belongs to the female sex evidently unfit it for many of the occupations of civil life. The constitution of the

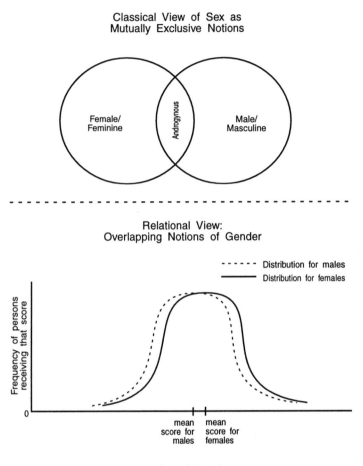

Fig. 4. Notions of sex differences. (From Rita Mae Kelly, *The Gendered Economy: Work, Careers, and Success* [Newbury Park, Calif.: Sage, 1991], p. 63. Reprinted by permission of Sage Publications, Inc. Copyright © 1991 by Rita Mae Kelly. The bottom figure depicting overlapping notions is adapted from J. S. Hyde, ed., *Half the Human Experience: The Psychology of Women,* 3d ed. [Lexington, Mass.: D. C. Heath, 1985], p. 140. Reprinted by permission.)

family organization which is founded in the divine ordinance, as well as in the nature of things, indicates the domestic sphere as that which properly belongs to the domain and functions of womanhood. The harmony, not to say identity, of interests and view which belong, or should belong, to the family institution is repugnant to the idea of a woman adopting a distinct and independent career from that of her husband.... The paramount destiny and mission of woman are to fulfill the noble and benign offices of wife and mother. This is the law of the Creator.[28]

With this opinion the U.S. Supreme Court denied Myra Bradwell equal citizenship with men by denying her the right to practice law, asserting categorical sex differences and roles, even though she had attained the requisite legal training and experience to be a lawyer. Her status as a married female overrode her status as a citizen, her intellectual abilities as a person, and her rights as either a businessperson or as an employee. This view of women and women's roles prevailed in legal rulings and in the national sex-role ideology largely until the women's movement in the 1970s.

Gender as a variable offers not only an alternative way of conceptualizing the reality of maleness/femaleness and masculinity/femininity, it also rests on a different understanding of reality. The word *gender* highlights the social construction of reality. It draws attention to how sex roles and behavioral patterns of men and women change over time and how they are interdependent. Resting on a relational perspective of reality, the focus on gender facilitates exploring how each sex has the characteristics of the other and how the relations between and within the sexes shape each, indeed the whole context within which each sex exists and manifests itself in particular historical contexts. The bottom part of figure 4 graphically depicts gender as a variable and reveals the contrast between this understanding of the gender continuum and the dichotomous notion undergirding sex as a category. Building on and expanding on the insights gained from explorations of sexuality, this gender view offers the possibility of three or more genders rather than two; it also recognizes the strong cultural (re)imposition of dichotomous and oppositional categories. This relational perspective does not ignore exploration of categories or the possibility of categorical differences. It recognizes distinctiveness and individuality when they do exist in given moments of time, but it also simultaneously posits relational bases of identity and community. In contrast to an essentialistic approach to sex as a unit of analysis, the relational perspective of gender questions the "given-ness" of such categories and asserts that reality does not consist only of "either/or-ness" but also involves "both/and-ness."

Gender as a variable has some similarities to sex as a variable. It too can be used to focus on differences. The exploration of differences between the sexes in percentages voting and offices held, for example, can be placed within the frame of "gender gaps" and proportions of individuals (regardless of their biological sex) with various types of masculine and feminine sex-role ideologies (see chap. 3). With an empirical focus, data on gender as well as sex can be observed, measured, and manipulated statistically. The move from sex as a categorical variable to gender as a continuum does not at first blush appear to be as radical epistemologically as it in fact is.

In part 2, Cheryl King and Karin Tamerius illustrate in their respective analyses the considerable difference the use of gender rather than sex as a variable makes. King demonstrates the need to distinguish between the sex (male/femaleness) of an individual and the gender (masculinity/femininity) of behavior and roles played by male and female decision makers or leaders. Using gender rather than sex as a variable, King is able to show that gender can be a property of a role or an organization as well as of a sexed individual and that the sex of the individual need not necessarily correspond with the role or organization. It is the negative interplay between the "genders" of the person, the role, and the organizational norms that produce biases, burdens, and barriers for each sex. However, gender power makes these biases, burdens, and barriers particular problems for women. Such analyses reveal how a traditional focus on sex simply distorts reality and creates myths about both the capacities and actual behavior of men as well as of women.

In chapter 4, Tamerius examines the influence of sex on legislative behavior and shows how the simple examination of the sex of a legislator and the results of roll call votes do little to help us understand the impact elected women have on the advance of a feminist agenda at this level of government. By using a gender focus, she is able to depict clearly how gender development and experience lead to greater commitment, support, and energy by most women legislators of all parties to feminist concerns. By going beyond the physical identification of legislators' sex, Tamerius uses knowledge about general differences in men's and women's private lives to explain new realities in political life, demonstrating the more profound affects that gender difference, as opposed to sex difference, has on gender power. In the process, she presents an excellent illustration of the need to focus on gender rather than sex if we are to understand political processes in this and future decades.

Gender as an Identity or Property

The relational perspective of gender demands a methodology that will help identify, describe, understand, and explain long-range interconnections between changes in sex roles and gendered patterns of behavior, and the relative gender power that follows to reinforce these patterns. It leads us to question whether men are or must be masculine or women are or must be feminine, and whether what we have assumed to be sex-linked traits and behaviors according to our present social prescriptions are indeed that. By focusing on gender we are continually encouraged to test the validity of presumed sex-based differences in personality. Gender as a property of an individual, organization, or other entity suggests that the sexes have highly variable, dynamic, and interconnected potentials and are not mutually exclusive human categories. While males and females might be part of a whole, and while the traits and behaviors of humans might be measurable at a moment in time, each person is highly likely to change as the whole unfolds and interacts. In human relations and social interactions, physical reality is often (but not always) more constant than our interpretations of that reality. Even social reality is not totally dependent on how we define and interpret it. Nonetheless, what appears to be real in physical terms in the social world is often only a reification of a particular historical interpretation of physical entities justified by the politics of the time.[29] Definitions, the social construction of entities and physical reality, clearly change over time. Gender within a relational perspective helps us recognize that the moment we define and identify a particular category for analysis we in some way change it and give it a particular direction. In the case of human beings our definitions help to give or deny potentiality for human agency. The analysis of our was-ness and being-ness help determine our becoming-ness.

Gender as a property or identity characteristic can refer to masculine and feminine traits of individuals, or it can refer to the gendered overlay on particular societal roles and institutional structures. As noted throughout this book, most work roles still are highly gendered. When one thinks of a soldier, a surgeon, or physicist, typically the image of a man comes to mind. When one thinks of a homemaker, a nurse, or elementary-school teacher, typically the image of a woman comes to mind. These roles have gendered dimensions that are usually part of the individual who performs these roles identities. Even entire industries have come to be gendered.[30] The service industries proportionately employ more women than men, whereas the manufacturing and heavy industries employ men more often than women. Those who work in these sectors, regardless of sex, then perform their work role according to the gendered norms of the sector. Work itself is gendered, so this gendered nature of work roles—public-leader roles for example—require gender analysis. In the complex world of the 1990s, both sexes need to manage gendered roles and expectations at work with their gendered activities in their lives outside their place of employment. Many people, especially women, find elements of their working and personal lives in conflict, and this conflict likewise has a gendered dimension. Moreover, incongruity between the gendered work role and the worker's gender can lead to psychological trauma, career failure, and considerable hostility in the workplace.

Figure 3, modeling career dynamics,[31] illustrates the necessity of understanding not only one's own internal career aspirations but also the concept of the external career and suggests how organizational culture and national sex-role and other ideologies interact either to promote or impede career success for some individuals. Women frequently find friction between male-oriented workplaces and traditional sex-role ideologies that severely limit their career options. Men too are shaped by such gender overlays. Nonetheless, as we noted earlier, the gender power advantage generally favors men and masculinity.

A major implication of the model of careers and public leadership presented in figure 3 is that hard work and individual self-improvement, though necessary for success, cannot independently enable most women to overcome most of the male-preferencing obstacles present in today's workplaces. Attention must also be paid to the gender overlays on the external career (including leadership roles and positions) that one seeks to pursue. To the extent that gender, power, and leadership interact in a gender-biased fashion in particular ways within careers, to that same extent the identity of that career will be gendered and the organizational structure will be gender biased. Greater gender power will go to one sex or another and to one sex-linked behavioral style (masculinity or femininity) versus the other. Cheryl King in chapter 3 illustrates the gendered nature of most high-level management or leadership positions in state government and articulates the difficulties women face as a result of "compulsory masculinity."

In the 1970s and 1980s academics and journalists alike paid considerable attention to institutional sexism. Much of this literature revolved around themes of how patriarchy led to sex differences in socialization and in sex roles in the private and public sectors. This in turn led to sex-segregated occupations and hence to a sex-segregated workforce. Sexism was institutionalized through differential valuation of occupations along sex lines and rules and practices that made women's entry into men's occupations difficult at best. Partly because of the heavy behavioral emphases in the social sciences, much of the research on institutional sexism consisted of counting the number of men and women in different positions and occupations. Over time, these analyses became more sophisticated, incorporating the impact of tokenism, of various percentages of women on behavior and policy, of job classification systems, and of sex segregation.[32] Institutional sexism clearly operates inside organizations. Barriers to job entry and promotion, varying access to career ladders, the role of mentors, and the empirical identification of pay inequities were identified using this approach. Introducing the variable of sex into studies of institutions made the frequent practice of sex segregation visible. When we look at legislatures, bureaucracies, and other governmental agencies, we can see the locus of such institutional sexism. Such sexism shapes and curtails the ability of women to act as they might choose and to rise to leadership positions within institutions.

Gendered organizational analyses and studies of institutional sexism begin by covering much of the same ground;[33] however, a gendered analysis goes beyond exploring the symbolic ascription of masculine or feminine qualities to the expectations held for positions; and then it links these expectations with power and opportunities available in career paths, line and staff positions, and organizational segmentation according to gender. Gendered organizational analysis also addresses the consequences of various percentages of each sex in an organization and on an organization, the relative openness to "other" styles and behaviors, and the impact respective styles and behaviors have for creating or breaking the glass ceiling. The very idea of the glass ceiling is itself rooted in gender power. The gendering process, that is, "the creation of symbols, images, and forms of consciousness that explicate, justify, and more rarely oppose gender divisions," becomes a focal point.[34]

A gendered organizational analysis pays attention to these processes and also examines the cognitive and psychological means individuals use as they attempt to make sense of the gendered nature of their workplace and of the gendered nature of their interrelationships, interactions, and attitudes. Such an analysis also explores the ways "advantage and disadvantage, exploitation and control, action and emotion, meaning and identity"[35] are gendered and impact individual and organizational behavior.

Joan Acker has summarized how a gendered theory of organizations would change our conceptual frame of reference by producing better answers to questions about organizational production and reproduction:

> Gendered processes are often resources in organizational control and transformation. Underlying these processes, and intimately connected with them, is a gendered substructure of organization that links the more surface gender arrangements with the gender relations in other parts of society. Ostensibly gender neutral, everyday activities of organizing and managing large organizations reproduce the gendered substructure within the organization itself and within the wider society.... [T]his is the most important part of the process to comprehend, because it is hidden within abstract, objectifying, textually mediated relations and is difficult to make visible. The fiction of the universal worker obscures the gendered effects of these ostensibly gender-neutral processes and helps to banish gender from theorizing about the fundamental character of complex organizations. Gender, sexuality, reproduction, and emotionality of women are outside organizational boundaries, continually and actively consigned to that social space by ongoing organizational practices. Complex organizations play an important role, therefore, in defining gender and women's disadvantage for the whole society.[36]

Gendered organizational analysis facilitates understanding how individual acts of sexism (and sometimes ostensibly neutral acts) lead to gender-biased institutional structures that reflect substantial gender power differentials. Gender and sex differences, in uses of space and time, in scheduling, arrangements, and behavior in the workplace become concerns for research. For example, prior assumptions about processes used in allocating jobs and pay, such as the neutrality of the supply-and-demand forces of the labor market, need to be challenged and rethought. The comparable-worth movement sought to recon-struct formulas and processes used to determine salaries and the criteria to define gender equity. Reliance on old masculine-imbued structures, assumptions, rules, and procedures does not readily support either exploring or resolving gender biases.

In part 3, Noelle Norton illustrates how a gendered organizational analysis of committee and floor interactions in the U.S. Congress helps us understand the ironic exclusion of women's voices from abortion and reproductive policies in the United States. Women have been winning congressional elections, yet to date they have exerted little influence in congressional hearings on such matters. A gendered organizational analysis shows the circuitous paths to power and influence on these policy issues. A more simple analysis of institutional sexism and roll call voting differences between the sexes would miss what becomes highly visible when focusing on gender power and its interaction with organiza-tional structure.

Meredith Newman presents another gendered organizational analysis; this one is of the gendered nature of Theodore Lowi's typology of policy types of governmental agencies. Instead of simply reporting where men and women are, Newman explores how the infusion of gender expectations into the agency's work and the policy type are related to the sex composition of policy clientele and the agency workforce, especially its upper-level managers. It also shapes the quality of the workplace, rewards, opportunities, and assumptions in how we analyze related dynamics. She reveals gender power in action. The results again reveal how gender power permeates even the broad contours of govern-mental structures and the selection of managers for these structures.

Gender as a Set of Practices,
Gender Power in Interpersonal Relations

Gender permeates many analytical categories we use to make sense of our personal relationships. When institutions support and reinforce gender power imbalances, the effects of those imbalances can spill over to create power imbalances in our personal interactions.

The focus on interpersonal relationships as a source of power draws direct attention to a particular type of gender power. This is person power, infused with sex-role ideology, sex-role socialization, and stereotypes about which behav-iors, styles, and attitudes and beliefs each particular sex will manifest. The interpersonal relationships grounded in these differences will obviously impact how women and men define their areas of expertise, how they will interact with others, and whom they will respect as leaders. It also is linked to the extent to which one sex will listen to a member of the other sex's efforts at rational persuasion and the extent to which they will be able to identify personally with a leader. In other words, the interpersonal relationships and our ideologies about how men and women are to interrelate impact directly French and Raven's ideas about "referent power."[37]

Referent power is used as a basis for identification and is critical to enhance one's ability to lead because it shapes how others refer to a person, whether or not they want to defer, or to follow along because others like the person. As noted in chapter 1, leaders need followers to lead. Sex-role ideologies typically have defined women as the followers and discouraged a sense that others should follow her, even if the woman is well liked and respected.

Gender as a set of practices highlights what Anna Jonasdottir calls the patriarchal sociosexual structure,[38] that is, those structures such as marriage and other sociosexual practices, habits, and traditions that shape, order, and regulate, the sociopower relations of sexed persons and the means of producing "life and living." Gender power differentials are heavily linked to these interpersonal sets of practices. Those practices linked to communication between the sexes, mating, reproductive differences, and the maintenance of social relations between the sexes constitute another "kind of power [love power] which moves history."[39] These sets of practices are certainly interpersonal, interconnected, dependent on social context, and dynamic. They also often become intimately implicated in work and personal relationships, as evidenced most notably in the Clarence Thomas confirmation hearings when he was a candidate for the U.S. Supreme Court, the Senator Packwood scandals, and the Navy Tailhook scandal.

Identifying the intersexual and gender-linked sets of practices that undergird male-female interactions and relationships is an important step in the study of gender power. Van Nostrand in *Gender-Responsible Leadership* argues that much of the gender power issues underlying male-female relationships stem from the effort of men to claim or keep "privilege and entitlement."[40] In this process efforts are made to "*dominate* discussions" or "*detach* and distance themselves from the group."[41] Females, in response, react by deferring or "playing 'diagnosing detective.'" The four behaviors—dominating, detaching, deferring, and diagnosing—become the basis for much of the male-female interactions that manifest gender power. In Anna Jonasdottir's perspective these are among the more empirically observable facts that validate the reciprocal—but unequal—empowerment process through which women and men create and re-create themselves as gendered, sociosexual beings.[42] Some of these interactions rely on both verbal and nonverbal communication, some on the use of space, time, and physical differences (e.g., size and body movements). All are heavily overlain with sex-role stereotyping and cultural interpretations of sexuality within and without the workplace.

Part 4 illustrates how a concern for gender power can illuminate these gendered sets of practices and how males can use interpersonal gender power to overcome or circuit the leadership and position power women have achieved in governance. In chapter 7, Kathlene examines how the election of women to state legislatures challenges the power assumptions of the sex status quo and, in turn, leads to the intensification of verbal gender power interactions. The dynamics of male feelings of entitlement in holding the legislative positions of authority obviously have been dented. One response is to dominate communication, historically another area of entitlement for males,[43] to counter the new positions of power women have attained.

In chapter 8 Kelly examines how sexual harassment is used to put women on the defensive in leadership positions. Although they hold equal positional power with their male counterparts in the upper echelons of state government, gender power derived from historical patterns of male entitlement and dominance, including sexual harassment, reduces women's power and limits their potential, especially as leaders. This type of negative gender power is amply illustrated by the consequences of sexual harassment in the workplace. The fact that women at the highest levels of state government receive the brunt of higher amounts of such harassment add weight to the assertion that gender power, not sexuality, undergirds these types of interpersonal interactions.

Gender as a Normative Stance or Value: Gender Power in Ideas, Names, and Concepts

Gender as a value permeates many concepts, entities and "givens" in the way we understand the world. Many of these givens can be found in prominent explanations and theories generated by opinion influencers in academe and the popular press. This gender valuing gives power to one sex or the other, whether the valuing is done explicitly or implicitly within the reasoning behind definitions or way in which structures or concepts are constructed and construed. As discussed in chapter 1, numerous political theorists[44] have explored the masculine-oriented and sexist assumptions of traditional political philosophy. Scholars such as Kelly, Guy et al., Stivers, and Ferguson, have documented how masculine bias permeates the economy and bureaucracies.[45] Although these and other scholars have moved our understanding of the gendered nature of concepts and the interplay of gender in organizations, they have only made a dent. One area currently receiving attention in studies of organizations is how the very concepts we use in our studies are permeated with gender bias. Mumby and Putnam,[46] for example, examine how the literature on "bounded rationality," assumed to be a gender neutral concept, actually reflects a gender politics of emotion. They show how a feminist reading of bounded rationality calls forth a concern for bounded emotionality and how the concern for rationality becomes a means of gender control as well as general control. Clearly comparable intellectual challenges to other concepts, such as accountability, bureaucracy, and leadership, need to be completed. The texts grounding our discussions shape our reality. We cannot reconstruct our realities unless we address the gender biases undergirding such concepts, texts, and theories. Gender as a normative stance reaffirms that gender analysis and gender power are concepts and realities grounded in value analysis and valuing. Using gender as a conceptual frame of reference is much more likely to draw attention to this type of issue than a reliance on sex as a variable or sexism as a conceptual focus.

In chapter 9, Duerst-Lahti and Verstegen feature the symbolic use of the "Year of the Woman" slogan and examine its place in women's representation. Importantly, they question why descriptive representation became so divorced from substantive representation and the way "the year" mitigated the gulf between them. As the media use and control symbols and language, they impact gender power. Although such power could favor women as well as men or could be neutral, to date it largely has been male biased. The Year of the Woman in Politics is in many regards the exception that proves the rule of masculine advantage in gender power.

In chapter 10 Mary Ellen Guy brings together an analysis of Hillary Rodham Clinton as a First Lady using all levels of analysis. Guy shows that this First Lady's personal attributes of power, her education, experience, competence, training, and charisma conflict with the role expectations for First Lady, wife and mother. Guy also demonstrates how symbolic notions of gender-appropriate behavior foster the continued questioning of Ms. Clinton's public standing. Her legitimacy as a presidential advisor and assistant clash with wifely role expectations. The interaction of gender contradictions in the First Lady's personal roles are exacerbated by the gender conflicts embedded in the U.S. health care system, the major policy arena concerning Ms. Clinton in 1993 and 1994. This chapter reveals both how far women have come in society and how much farther we need to go.

Summary

Women's efforts to advance their political and professional careers in the political system have only recently led to an intense study of the gendered nature of bureaucracies and organizations. Until the past decade, feminist theory and organizational theory have not informed each other. Indeed, the paradigms used for analysis within these subfields have spoken past each other. The study of women in governance and leadership has also tended to dwell on sex differences and sexism of various sorts. In this chapter we have *(a)* articulated how gender as a conceptual frame of reference fits within selected social-science assumptions about reality and human behavior; *(b)* explicated the concept of gender power, showing how gender and power are intimately linked; *(c)* presented a gender-based model for becoming and being a public leader; and *(d)* compared and contrasted basic analytical issues related to using gender rather than sex as a variable and as a conceptual frame of reference, highlighting the relevance of this difference for the study of public leaders and leadership. In doing so, we also have provided a conceptual frame of reference for reading the rest of this book.

Notes

1. Janet Saltzman Chafetz, *Gender Equity* (Newbury Park, Calif.: Sage Publications, 1990), 28.
2. Jean Lipman-Blumen, *Gender Roles and Power* (Englewood Cliffs, N.J.: Prentice-Hall, 1984), 2.
3. Ibid., 3.
4. Kathy Ferguson, *The Feminist Case against Bureaucracy* (Philadelphia: Temple University Press, 1984).
5. Peter Gregware and Rita Mae Kelly, "Relativity and Quantum Logics: Relational View of Policy Inquiry," in *Policy Theory and Policy Evaluation,* ed. Stuart S. Nagel (Westport, Conn.: Greenwood Press, 1990).
6. Belle Rose Ragins and Eric Sundstrom, "Gender and Power in Organizations: A Longitudinal Perspective," *Psychological Bulletin* 105 (1) (1989): 51–88.
7. Robert A. Dahl, "The Concept of Power," *Behavioral Science*, 2 (1957): 201–15; Amatai Etzioni, *A Comparative Analysis of Complex Organizations* (New York: Macmillan, 1975).
8. David C. McClelland, *Power: The Inner Experience* (New York: Irvington, 1975); David C. McClelland and D. H. Burnham, "Power Is the Great Motivator," *Harvard Business Review* 54 (2) (1976): 100–110.
9. D. Cartwright, *Studies in Social Power* (Ann Arbor: University of Michigan, Research Center for Group Dynamics, Institute for Social Research, 1959); Ragins and Sundstrom, "Gender and Power," 51–53.
10. D. Mechanic, "Sources of Power of Lower Participants in Complex Organizations," *Administrative Science Quarterly,* 7 (1962): 349–64.
11. Ragins and Sundstrom, "Gender and Power," 52.
12. Gary A. Yukl, *Leadership in Organizations* (Englewood Cliffs, N.J.: Prentice-Hall, 1981).
13. Ragins and Sundstrom, "Gender and Power," 52.
14. Ibid.
15. Ibid., 75.
16. Anne Witz and Mike Savage, "Theoretical Introduction: The Gender of Organizations," in *Gender and Bureaucracy,* ed. Mike Savage and Anne Witz (Oxford: Blackwell Publishers, 1992).
17. Rosabeth Moss Kantor, *Men and Women of the Corporation* (New York: Basic Books, 1977).
18. Ferguson, *Feminist Case against Bureaucracy.*
19. Rosemary Pringle, *Secretaries Talk: Sexuality, Power, Work* (London: Verso, 1989).

20. Jeff Hearn, D. L. Sheppard, Peta Tancred-Sheriff, and G. Burrell, *The Sexuality of Organization* (London: Sage, 1989).
21. Witz and Savage, "Theoretical Introduction," 31.
22. For an earlier approach to this framework, see Rita Mae Kelly and Mary Boutilier, *The Making of Political Women* (Chicago: Nelson-Hall, 1978).
23. Rita Mae Kelly, *The Gendered Economy* (Newbury Park, Calif.: Sage Publishers, 1991), 246.
24. Ibid.
25. Chafetz, *Gender Equity,* 28.
26. Zillah Eisenstein, *The Radical Future of Liberal Feminism* (New York: Longman, 1981), 344.
27. Ibid.
28. 83 U.S. (16 Wall) 130, 141.
29. Gregware and Kelly, "Relativity and Quantum Logics."
30. Kelly, *The Gendered Economy,* chap. 3.
31. See also C. B. Derr and A. Laurent, "The Internal and External Career: A Theoretical Cross-Cultural Perspective," in *Handbook of Career Theory,* ed. Michael B. Arthur, Douglas T. Hall, and Barbara S. Lawrence (New York: Cambridge University Press, 1989).
32. E.g., Kantor, *Men and Women;* Barbara F. Reskin and Heidi Hartmann, eds. *Women's Work, Men's Work: Sex Segregation on the Job* (Washington, D.C.: National Academy Press, 1986); Rita Mae Kelly and Jane Bayes, eds. *Comparable Worth, Pay Equity, and Public Policy* (Westport, Conn.: Greenwood Press, 1988).
33. Albert J. Mills and Peta Tancred, *Gendering Organizational Analysis* (Newbury Park, Calif.: Sage Publications, 1992).
34. Joan Acker, "Gendering Organization Theory," in Mills and Tancred, *Gendering Organizational Analysis.*
35. Joan Acker, "Hierarchies, Jobs, Bodies: A Theory of Gendered Organizations," *Gender and Society* 4 (1990): 146.
36. Acker, "Gendering Organization Theory," 259.
37. J. R. P. French and B. H. Raven, "The Bases of Social Power," in *Studies in Social Power,* ed. Dorwin Cartwright (Ann Arbor: University of Michigan Press, 1959).
38. Anna Jonasdottir, *Power, Love, and Political Interests* (Sweden, 1990). Reprinted as *Why Women Are Oppressed* (Philadelphia: Temple University Press, 1994).
39. Ibid.
40. Catherine Van Nostrand, *Gender-Responsible Leadership: Detecting Bias, Implementing Interventions* (Newbury Park, Calif.: Sage Publications, 1993), 8.
41. Ibid.
42. Jonasdottir, *Why Women Are Oppressed.*
43. Deborah Tannen, *You Just Don't Understand: Women and Men in Conversation* (New York: Morrow, 1990).
44. Carol Pateman, *The Sexual Contract* (Stanford, Calif.: Stanford University Press, 1988); Christine DiStefano, *Configurations of Masculinity: A Feminist Perspective on Modern Political Theory* (Ithaca, N.Y.: Cornell University Press, 1991), 4; Judith Butler, *Gender Trouble: Feminism and the Subversion of Identity* (New York: Routledge, 1990); Judith Butler, *Bodies That Matter: On the Discursive Limits of "Sex"* (New York: Routledge, 1993).
45. Kelly, *The Gendered Economy*; Mary Ellen Guy, ed., *Men and Women of the States* (Armonk, N.Y.: M. E. Sharpe, 1992); Camilla Stivers, *Gender Images in Public Administration: Legitimacy and the Administrative State* (Newbury Park, Calif.: Sage Publications, 1993); Ferguson, *Feminist Case against Bureaucracy.*
46. Dennis K. Mumby and Linda L. Putnam, "The Politics of Emotion: A Feminist Reading of Bounded Rationality," *Academy of Management Review* 17 (3) (1992): 465–86.

Part 2: Gender versus Sex as an Analytic Category: Gender Power and Sex Differences

Throughout the history of political science, when women have been the focal point of study, analyses have usually focused on differences between the sexes. All too often these analyses have used an essentialist approach to men and women and in so doing have obfuscated gender power differentials and given the impression that women are less interested, less capable, and less active political actors than men. It has also encouraged a focus on differences between men and women, often locating these differences in individuals, rather than on understanding and explaining those differences. The chapters in part 2 address the issues of gender, governance, and leadership in a new way, demonstrating how the use of gender as a conceptual frame of reference and as a variable enhances our understanding of power by identifying and clarifying gender power. These articles also articulate why the more traditional use of sex as a dichotomous variable in statistical analyses outside of a gendered conceptual frame of reference deceives and distorts our understanding of political phenomena.

In "Sex-Role Identity and Decision Styles: How Gender Helps Explain the Paucity of Women at the Top," Cheryl King begins with knowledge of the masculinism inherent in public bureaucracies and then integrates it with sex-role identity and gender predispositions among male and female high-level civil servants to illustrate the effects of gender power. She shows how "compulsory masculinity" operates underground as the first form of evaluation for public executives, regardless of the biological sex of individuals. King also points to the troubling paradox that women who succeed as executives under current gender power circumstances help to legitimize masculinist arrangements. Throughout her analysis, she reveals the complexity of gender and how it permeates governance and leadership.

Karen L. Tamerius in "Sex, Gender, and Leadership in the Representation of Women" develops a simple but forceful explanation of why we should expect gender to affect the quality of representation due to sex-based differences in life experiences. She shows how a feminist and gendered conceptual framework can clarify why women, regardless of political party, do consistently tend to represent women's interests in a way that men cannot and do not. In a parsimonious but potent model for understanding legislative leadership on any policy issue, she documents the differential resources women in congress expend on feminist legislation compared to men. In the process she reveals the inadequacy of roll-call votes, that is, data based on sex as a dichotomous variable, as a measure of gender representation and calls into question research that relies on simplistic assessments of gender. Tamerius links sex-role identity and one's gendered resources to legislative leadership and representation. In the process both King and Tamerius expand our knowledge of gender and gender power.

Chapter 3

Sex-Role Identity and Decision Styles: How Gender Helps Explain the Paucity of Women at the Top

Cheryl Simrell King

As the editors of this volume have indicated in the first two chapters, how our society constructs gender and is constructed by gender permeates all aspects of life, including those elements that influence how organizations are constructed and managed. Research done to investigate the reasons for the paucity of women at the top of public organizations supports these theoretical perspectives, as will be seen in this chapter. Contrary to popular belief, the fact that some women have "made it" has not significantly changed the nature of gender power in public organizations. While it is encouraging to see more women in leadership positions than in the past, many women are required to "act like a man" in order to succeed.[1] The mere presence of women does not necessarily reduce the reliance upon and power of the dominant mode, especially if the successes of these women is predicated upon the notion of assimilation. In fact, women's assimilation reinforces the gendered power differentials instead of contributing to their demise. In other words, if women are willing to play the game and, in some cases, play the game even harder than their male colleagues, their acceptance of the rules legitimizes the rules. After all, if women can be successful, why question the means by which success is attained?

What is often not questioned is the price one has to pay to be successful, and whether that price is the same for all people playing the game. People interested in changing the nature of public bureaucracies such that they are more reflective of the diversity of the general population need not only to look at the numbers as a measure of success but must also examine the construction of the processes by which success must be attained, the costs implied, and the effectiveness of these processes and costs in reaching the eventual goal of a more diverse bureaucracy. In other words, it is not enough to simply look at the numbers; you must also examine the basic construction of the domain that produces the numbers.

In addition, one cannot only study women in leadership positions in order to understand the paucity of women at the top. Wendy Brown convincingly argues that a feminist study of politics and political theory is like Evelyn Fox Keller's groundbreaking book on gender and science: "the widespread assumption that a study of gender and science could only be a study of women still amazes me: if women are made rather than born, then surely the same is true of men. It is also true of science."[2] Brown argues that feminist political theory is not just a study of women in politics. Rather, it is an examination of the gendered construction of the theory and theoretical constructs and the impact of those constructions upon the discipline (which includes the exclusion of women from politics). Brown argues that "political theory, a genre of theory concerned with Western's history's most exclusively masculine purview, is fairly saturated with various modalities of masculinity." She contends that the literature of political theory not only fails to include examples of the exclusion of women from politics and the relegation of women to subordinate status, it also "comprises a rich articulation of masculinist public power, order, freedom and justice."[3]

What is true for science and political theory is also true for the study of political leadership and governance. A feminist analysis of leadership in public organizations is not simply a study of women in leadership positions in public management. Surely the number and prevalence of women in executive management positions are important analytical parameters. However, just as comprehensive studies of science and political theory that only focus on women are insufficient, so also is it insufficient for the study of leadership and governance in public organizations.

Brown argues in her book that "more than any other human activity, politics has historically borne an explicitly masculine identity."[4] Public leadership and governance, as an integral part of politics, also bears an explicit masculine identity. This masculinity pervades most of public-management theory, research, and practice, particularly at the executive level. Women and men who "make it" to the top are expected to behave in ways that are explicitly and implicitly culturally masculine in nature. In addition, beyond requirements for specific behavior, the structures and institutions upon which executive-level public management are formed are gendered in their basic construction.

At the core of this gendered construction is the key notion of gender and gender power. At the core of gender and gender power, as the editors of this volume describe, are the normative underpinnings of our cultural belief systems, that is, cultural masculinism. The social construction of gender in our society, the resulting gender roles, and the distribution of resources and power both underlying and resulting from the construction of this concept *determine* public life. Gender and gender power are, in program evaluation terms, the *inputs* (how policy gets made), *outputs* (how policy is implemented), and *outcomes* (the impact of policy) of public leadership and governance.

In this chapter, I examine these inputs, outputs, and outcomes to help us understand the paucity of women in leadership positions in public organizations by reporting on recent research on this topic. In addition to examining the representation of women (e.g., the numbers), I also address the various domains that contribute to the explicit masculine identity that many believe is embedded in leadership and governance in our society. Research and theoretical literature in this area lead me to think that there are a number of key factors, or variables, that contribute to the strong masculine identity of leaders and leadership positions:

1. *Organizations are a male domain*—men are more likely to be leaders in public and private organizations than are women.
2. *Our culture is a masculine domain*—expectations about gender or sex roles embedded in our culture lead to a preference for masculine over feminine.
3. *The state is a masculine domain*—governance, politics, and the administrative state reflect the cultural preference for masculine over feminine.
4. *Leadership-management is a masculine domain*—our cultural preferences for masculine can be seen most clearly in our definitions of leadership and preferences for certain types of leaders.

Using this analytical framework, this chapter proceeds with a look at organizations as a male domain, moves on to describe a research project to test some theories about this framework, and then returns to the discussion of the other gender power domains implicit in leadership and governance.

Organizations as a Male Domain

The data on the distribution of women in organizations seem a bit like old news because of the recent attention given to these numbers, especially in the environment after the "year of the woman." However, old news or not, the results are clear. Although women are represented to a greater degree in most organizations than they have been in the past, women have not been entering executive offices at the same rates of entry into lower levels of management. Scores of studies, books, and articles have been published in the last few years investigating this phenomenon. The term *glass ceiling* was coined in 1987 as a metaphor for women's inability to break into executive offices, despite the proliferation of women at other levels in organizations.[5] The glass ceiling describes a "barrier so subtle that it is transparent, yet so strong that it prevents women and minorities from moving up in the management hierarchy."[6]

As table 2 indicates, in the private sector, women (primarily white women) have made substantial leaps into management positions over the last ten to fifteen years. However, proportionally fewer women hold senior or executive positions. Although women account for 46 percent of the private sector work-force, they account for only 3 percent of the executive level. Furthermore, in 1992, women accounted for only 5 percent of the enrollment in executive-train-ing seminars run by top business schools in the U.S. (e.g., Harvard, Sloane, Stanford), down from a peak of 8 percent in the late 1980s.[7] These executive-training programs are considered by most major private sector organizations to be an indispensable credential for future executives and officers. If only 5 percent of the people attending this crucial credentialing process are women, the promise of increased representation at executive levels in the private sector, at least in the near future, is pretty bleak.

In the public sector, the numbers are a bit more heartening. Women increasingly hold a greater proportion of total and management jobs but continue to have a proportionally low representation at top levels. Although women represent 48 percent of the workforce of the U.S. federal civil service (1990 data), they hold only 11 percent of the executive positions.[8] In state governments, the numbers are slightly better. A series of studies of state governments in the United States found that women make up almost 50 percent of the state government workforce in each state studied but hold only from 13 to 26 percent of the senior-level jobs.[9]

Although it would be nice to simply chalk up the representation differences to sex differences that show that men are, constitutionally, better managers and leaders than are women, this cannot be verified in research or in practice. Studies

TABLE 2.   Women in the Workforce (% of total)

	Public Sector		Private Sector	
	State level	Federal level	1981	1991
Labor force	50	48	43	46
Managers			27	41
Senior executives	13–26[a]	11	1	3

Sources: Mary Ellen Guy, *Men and Women of the States* (Armonk, N.Y.: M. E. Sharpe, 1993); Mary M. Hale and Rita Mae Kelly, *Gender, Bureaucracy, and Democracy* (Westport, Conn.: Greenwood Press, 1989), and Cheryl Simrell King, "Gender and Administrative Leadership in Colorado" (paper presented to the Western Political Science Association, Pasadena, Calif., 1993) (for state level); United States Merit Systems Protection Board, *A Question of Equity* (Washington, D.C.: Government Printing Office, 1992) (for Federal level); Data Bureau of Labor Statistics of Ferry International, cited in *Business Week,* June 8, 1992 (for private sector).
[a] Category may be more broadly defined than in private sector.

ranging from the classic literature review of sex differences by Maccoby and Jacklin to research on sex differences in management consistently report that there are few, if any, true managerial and leadership differences between men and women.[10] Additionally, research has failed to find consistent results that explain these representation differences by attributing the causes to the more concrete, measurable variables such as age, experience, education or time in career.[11] In fact, some studies indicate that, even when we hold all of these variables constant, women will not be proportionally represented at executive levels until sometime in the middle of the next century.[12]

These studies indicate that bureaucracies are a male domain. The power, particularly the decision-making power, still predominantly rests with men. Because we cannot explain this representational imbalance (and resulting power imbalance) using traditional meritorious variables (i.e., if only women had the education, experience, time in career, and leadership skills of men, then they would be represented), the trend in current research is to focus on the *perceptions* of differences (as compared to *real* differences) as defined by the cultural norms and expectations for management and sex-typed (or gendered) behavior. In other words, as the editors of this volume indicate in chapter 2, we move from sex as an analytical category to gender as a variable.

What Is Valued in Public Upper Management?
What Does It Take to Cut It?

What follows is a brief description of a research study I conducted of executives in a state government in the Western United States.[13] The research was designed to investigate the differences and similarities between men and women executive managers. The key constructs studied were executive style of leadership as defined by sex/gender-role identity and decision style. I expected, based upon previous research, that there would be minimal differences between men and women in these positions and that all would, for the most part, manifest culturally masculine styles. I was more interested in the presence or absence of dominant gender styles and the relationship between gender styles and the representation of women than I was interested in the differences and similarities between the sexes. I hypothesized that a preference for cultural masculinity creates a barrier to advancement for women. I expected that organizations within this state government that had few women in executive positions would have a higher preference for cultural masculinity than did those organizations that had higher representation of executive women. In short, I was asking the question of whether the paucity of women in executive management positions in a public bureaucracy could be due to a preference for cultural masculinity as defined by individual sex-role identity and decision-making style.

Sex-Role Identity

Sex-role identity is thought to be one of the most powerful determinants of human behavior. Whether one identifies as a masculine personality, a feminine personality, or a mix of both is due, for the most part, to childhood socialization and cultural expectations about roles as adults. In fact, when it comes to general behavior, sex-role identity or gender role may be the more powerful determinants of behavior than are biologically determined, sex-related characteristics. In other words, social constructions of gender and the inculcation of societal expectations about roles appears to be more important in determining behavior than is sex itself.

The foundations for sex-role identity as well as most other behavioral elements, are built at early ages through interactions with parents and peers. Sex-role identity begins early in life and continues to adjust and change throughout development. For example, Nancy Chodorow states that, from early on, "feminine personality comes to define itself in relation and connection to other people more than masculine personality does."[14] Because they are usually primarily parented by a same-sex parent, girls come to experience themselves as less differentiated than boys. As a result, feminine personalities define themselves in relation to others around them, not as separate.

Although with most complex and psychological issues determining whether biological or sociological factors are most influential is difficult, sex-role identity is thought to be primarily a factor of socialization. Therefore, it is important to differentiate between sex-related characteristics that are biologically determined and sex-role characteristics that are culturally influenced and determined:

> The words masculine and feminine do not refer in any simple way to fundamental traits of personality, but to learned styles of interpersonal interactions which are deemed to be socially appropriate to specific social contexts, and which are imposed upon, and sustain and extend, the sexual dichotomy.[15]

Traditionally, feminine traits have been associated with girls and women while masculine traits have been associated with boys and men. This is especially true in cultures that place a high value upon masculinity and men and a lower value upon femininity and women.[16] Although sex roles vary across cultures, clear, dominant sex-role patterns emerge cross-culturally that, for example, reflect an association of assertiveness and aggression with masculinity and nurturance and submissiveness with femininity.

Sex-role identity has been found to be related to a number of personality constructs, including competency. In a study of female competency, Sherman found that the goals of traditional femininity and competence are diametrically opposed.[17] Sherman concluded that feminine personalities are socialized to be passive and dependent and not socialized to be independent in problem solving or to achieve.

In a study examining the differences in children's play, Janet Lever reported that girls were more likely to avoid conflict in play than were boys.[18] Boys were able to resolve disputes more effectively, whereas girls avoided disputes; a dispute during a girls' game would most likely end the game. Lever concluded that boys are better at handling conflict than girls, a trait that she assumes translates into adulthood. Carol Gilligan evaluates Lever's findings as being bounded by traditional (masculinist) models of success:

> [The] assumption that shapes her discussion of results is that the male model is the better one because it fits the requirements for modern corporate success. In contrast, sensitivity and care for the feelings of others that girls develop through their play have little market value and can even impede professional success.[19]

There have been some criticisms of theorists like Gilligan and Chodorow focusing upon the generalizations made about behavior based upon limited studies of only women or girls.[20] In essence, these theorists have erred (like past studies in politics and leadership) because they focused on cultural sex differences (i.e., the differences between women and men) rather than focusing on gender differences (i.e., the differences between masculine and feminine personalities, regardless of sex). In addition, in their sex-differences studies, they examined only women or girls, instead of examining both sexes. They have, essentially, committed the error that Keller cites of examining a concept by only studying women.[21] Of course, it is ludicrous to assume that all women and no men are passive and nurturing, just as it is ludicrous to assume that all men and no women are aggressive and achievement-oriented. Therefore, researchers are beginning to look at sex-role identification separate from sex in the hope of understanding the relationships (or lack of) between sex roles and sex. For example, a man who has strong feminine characteristics will approach a situation differently than a man who has strong masculine characteristics. Similarly, a woman who has strong masculine characteristics will approach a situation differently than a woman with strong feminine characteristics. The people who are most likely to approach the situation similarly are the people who share the same sex-role identity or style rather than the same sex. In other words, gender identity, more so than sex, determines one's approach, although there is a strong correlation between sex and gender identity.

For example, in a study that challenges the stereotypes of traditional roles, Nona Lyons found that there are two orientations of identity that do not necessarily split along gender lines: a *responsibility* orientation, where the concept of self is rooted in connection and relation to others, and a *rights* orientation, where the concept of self is rooted in separation and autonomy.[22] Women tend, more than men, to identify with the responsibility orientation of self. Men tend, more than women, to identify with the rights orientation of self. These tendencies are, most likely, not related to sex differences but rather to differences in how each sex is socialized or to gender.

In another study, Carolyn Desjardins took Lyon's model and developed a two-dimensional theory of leadership based upon identity and moral orientations.[23] Her theory encompasses a *morality of rights* dimension that is traditionally masculine and a *morality of response* dimension that is traditionally feminine. The rights dimension embodies a leader who has a moral orientation toward justice and an analytical learning style and interacts best in a competitive mode. The response dimension has a moral orientation toward relationships and has a synthesizing/cooperative learning style and interaction pattern. Desjardins found that some men and women exhibited behavior within both dimensions, while the rights dimension tended to be exhibited by men and the response dimension tended to be exhibited by women. Like Lyon's study, Desjardins's work indicates that sex and gender style are correlated, but not causal.

Decision-Making Style

One of the most important things that managers and leaders do is to make decisions. As one would expect given the information presented above, management decision making, like all other aspects of management behavior, is gendered. Our expectations about how leaders should make decisions and, therefore, leadership behavior, tends to value the masculine over the feminine. Indeed, some research indicates that gender, sex roles, and management decision-making behavior are inextricably linked.[24]

Early research on gender and decision making focused upon the differences between men and women in moral development and cognitive processing. This focus was important because, prior to the 1970s, most work in this field systematically excluded sex as an analytical category.[25] Carol Gilligan's controversial work investigating moral development in women is considered by most feminist scholars to be one of the first important works applying the gender lens to cognitive processing and moral reasoning.[26] Gilligan's work spawned many other evaluations of feminine tendencies to organize events and information around connections. Foremost among these is Belenky et al.'s work on women's styles of knowledge acquisition.[27] Using William Perry's model of intellectual and ethical development of college-age men as their base model,[28] Belenky et al. posited that cognitive processing and decision making are gendered and that women operate from a different "voice" than do men.

Like Gilligan, Belenky et al. found that the most common intellectual perspective for women is the perspective that would be least valued by a masculine model of cognitive style. They state:

> In a world that emphasizes rationalism and scientific thought, there are bound to be personal and social costs of a subjectivist epistemology. Women subjectivists are at a special disadvantage when they go about learning and working in the public domain.[29]

Although, as mentioned before, these studies were methodologically limited, the results highlighted the limitations of the traditional moral-development, cognitive-processing, and decision-making models. This work made the field stand up and take notice of the fact that traditional models did not include the possibility of different voices or different approaches to decision making. Rather, based as they are on masculinist principles, the models assumed that women and men who were different from the masculinist norms were simply not as highly developed.

As in other fields, research on sex differences in decision making has shifted from using sex as the analytical category to using gender as the analytical category. Some examples of this research use Carl Jung's classic theory of psychological type as their key theoretical framework.[30] Jung believed that there are a limited number of fundamental ways in which people react to various situations, all of which can be classified into behavioral tendencies along four key dimensions. Two of these dimensions of psychological type represent cognitive functions related to the acquisition and evaluation of information, the two basic constructs of decision making. The *perception* functions divide the acquisition of information into either a sensing function (acquiring information from external sources, the five senses) or an intuitive function (acquiring information from internal sources). The *judgment* functions divide the evaluation of information into either a thinking function (the use of logic and analysis) or a feeling function (the use of emotions and connections). Of the four Jungian functions, the judgment function is the only one that indicates any sex differences, with, as one would expect, more women tending to be *feeling* evaluators and more men tending to be *thinking* evaluators.

Otis and Quenk used Jung's framework in a study of moral reasoning that used gender, rather than sex, as an analytical category.[31] Their findings question the assumptions of studies that used sex as the analytical framework. Otis and Quenk found that sex differences in moral reasoning are not necessarily related exclusively to sex, but rather are related to an aspect of individual style. In other words, sex is *related* to a preference for using a particular style but does not *cause* a preference for a particular style. The gendering of decision making, therefore, is not a function of one's sex as much as it is a function of cultural roles, expectations, socialization, and stereotypes.

The Research

The population of department heads, division heads, and section heads in the administrative organizations of a state government in the Western United States were sent a survey battery that included the Bem Sex Role Inventory (BSRI) and the Decision Style Inventory (DSI).[32] The BSRI measures one's preference for one of four dimensions of sex-role identity; masculine (high masculine, low feminine), feminine (high feminine, low masculine), androgynous (high masculine and feminine), and undifferentiated (low masculine and feminine). As one would expect, women generally tend to identify with a feminine sex-role identity, men with a masculine identity, and a small percentage of both women and men as androgynous.

The DSI measures one's preference for four styles of decision making: directive, analytical, conceptual, and behavioral. *Directive* types tend to be highly task related, are often control oriented, are realistic and direct when dealing with problems, and tend to be pragmatic and decisive. Directive types are the General Pattons of the organization. *Analytical* types are also task related but tend to be more focused on problem solving and can deal with a great deal of ambiguity. Analytical types are the researchers and analysts of the organization. *Conceptual* types are like analytical types but tend to be more people oriented, rather than task oriented, and are the dreamers of the organization. *Behavioral* types are highly people oriented, yet pragmatic. Behavioral types are the people managers of the organization. In large tests of this instrument, women have been found to have a greater tendency than men to have a dominant behavioral or conceptual style and are more likely to be in careers that value this style. However, when sex differences are tested within career fields (i.e., within engineering, within executive management, within nursing), there are no consistent difference between the sexes. In other words, the identity of the organizational or professional group is more likely to predict the decision style of the people involved than are any individual differences.

Demographic comparisons between the men and women executives who returned the survey battery yielded results that are consistent with other studies;[33] the women respondents were younger, had been in their careers for fewer years, and had more education, on average, than the men. Fewer woman respondents were married (88 percent of the men were married; 59 percent of the women) and more women lived alone (8 percent of the men lived alone; 24 percent of the women).

I hypothesized that the dominant sex-role identity of these executive managers would be masculine. This hypothesis was not confirmed by the research. In fact, the distributions of preference for the four sex-role identities was fairly equal; approximately 25 percent of the managers in each of the four categories. I also hypothesized that the dominant decision style would be a combination of directive and analytical. In reality, there was a mix of decision styles manifested, with about one-half of the executives dominantly analytical or directive (directive was the smallest individual categories; there are few General Pattons in this state government) and about one-half of the executives dominantly conceptual or behavioral.

Although there was little evidence to uphold my hypotheses about dominant styles, there were differences between the men and women in this sample. A greater proportion of women (34 percent) identified with a masculine sex-role identity than did the men (22 percent). Conversely, a greater proportion of the men (30 percent) identified with a feminine sex-role identity than did the women (20 percent). Women and men were the same with regard to decision style, with one exception. A greater proportion of the women than of the men did *not* rely upon a *behavioral* style of decision making, indicating a strong avoidance of traditional feminine decision styles in the women.

These results indicate two important things about these managers: (1) they are more diverse than originally thought, manifesting a wide range of styles as measured by sex-role identity and decision styles and (2) some of the men are more likely than the women to identify with traditionally feminine approaches, whereas some of the women are more likely than the men to identify with traditionally masculine approaches (and, conversely, the women are less likely to identify with traditionally feminine approaches).

Finally, these data, as discussed before, were used to try to predict the representation of women. Using discriminant analysis, several statistical models were tested. As it turns out, the only variables that discriminated between those departments with more women and those with less were those demographic variables mentioned earlier (age, education, time in career) and the kind of work that the organization does (e.g., sex-segregated occupations—women are in social services and education, men in law enforcement and general administration). Sex-role identity and decision making, as we would predict given the lack of a dominant model, were not good predictors of representation. Furthermore, the models were weak and were limited in their ability to predict representation.

What Do These Research Results Mean?

Demographic Differences

The women and men managers represented in this study resemble managers from other state bureaucracies and from the private sector.[34] On the average, women executives are less likely than men to be married or to be living with others. Conversely, almost all of executive men are likely to be married. At the same time, women are as likely as the men to have dependents. Men and women in these positions have different life situations. Why is this so? Why don't women and men in these positions have similar life situations? Some of the answers are found in personal choices and individual differences. Structural inequalities also provide answers.

The life of an executive is demanding, and the road that one must take to get there is long and arduous. Climbing the career ladder, especially quickly, coupled with managing the domestic sphere could be a monstrous burden to a manager.[35] Women who choose to put their careers first may not have the same life choices as men who put their careers first. This has little to do with ability and skills and everything to do with the way that careers and private life are structured.

Sex-Role Identity and Decision Style

Contrary to all of the original hypotheses, sex-role identity and decision style, in this sample, did not seem to be related to sex nor to the representation of women in these offices. Indeed, these findings are encouraging because they seem to indicate, for one state government, that all managers are not "required" to be masculine. Instead, a good mix of styles are manifested. However, there are interesting differences between men and women. Interpretations of these findings must be cautious, as these finding are merely trends, and the majority of the men and women in this sample are very much like one another with regard to sex-role identity and decision style. However, these women, like other women executives, are more likely than the men to be masculine and to avoid feminine decision styles; the men are more likely than the women to be feminine and less likely to avoid feminine decision styles.

These results may validate, and be validated by, other findings that hold that executive women must surrender, or accommodate, their femininity in order to be successful.[36] If this is true, then given that there may be no dominant masculine culture in this state government as measured by the instruments used in this study, the results of this study are even more disturbing; these results may indicate that masculinity is valued for women even when it is not a dominant or required style for all managers. Of course, we cannot infer the direction of causality here; one does not know if these women are in their positions *because* of their masculinity (e.g., these organizations prefer masculine behavior in women more than in men and choose women to fit this preference, the selection hypothesis) or if masculine tendencies are displayed *because* of their positions (e.g., in order to survive at this level, women must display more masculine characteristics than do men, the assimilation hypothesis).

Georgia Duerst-Lahti and Cathy Johnson, in a study of sex roles in three state governments, found somewhat similar results.[37] Women and men managers in their studies were asked to indicate the degree to which a series of character traits described their style. Their findings indicate that, overall, the men and women of those states described themselves similarly. When asked to describe a good public manager, masculine traits did not dominate the list. In addition, feminine traits were valued by all respondents. As the authors state: "if those who manage bureaucracies ever preferred predominantly masculine traits, they no longer do, at least by this measure."[38] However, men in their study were more likely than women to prefer stereotypical feminine traits, while women were more likely to hold administrators to a masculine standard. Could it be that the new "feminine" leadership models are acceptable as long as one is a man but that women are still required, or think that they are required, to conform to cultural masculinity? Is it possible that there is a double standard in leadership? Such double standards constitute the double binds that women in leadership positions must continually surmount.[39]

Other research that investigated the interaction of position, gender, and sex-role identity in private organizations found no relationship between sex and the possession of masculine traits.[40] In Ellen Fagenson's study of women and men at all levels of an organization, she found that: (1) perceived masculinity is related to position (the higher the position, the higher the perception of masculinity), (2) there was no relationship between sex and masculinity, yet there was a relationship between sex and femininity, (3) masculinity is positively related to the perception of power, (4) men and women at upper levels see themselves as similarly masculine, and (5) position is related to sex-role identity. Fagenson suggests that the nature of hierarchy in organizations is gendered, with those at the upper level in an instrumental power position (masculine) and those at lower levels in supporting or nurturing roles (feminine) to those in power. Therefore, Fagenson suggests that the masculinity of executive traits has little to do with the dominant sex and more to do with the labeling of these qualities as masculine or the tendency of masculinist cultures to label power as masculine. Fagenson suggests that these qualities should be called "upper-level" qualities, rather than masculine qualities.[41] Duerst-Lahti and Johnson also found that masculine traits were more likely to distinguish those at the top from those at middle-management ranks than they were to distinguish men from women.[42] Duerst-Lahti and Johnson and Fagenson's findings suggest that executive management may be gendered, while other levels are more neutral. Fagenson's findings additionally suggest that little neutrality exists at lower levels of management, where a feminine role is more valued than a masculine one. My findings suggest that masculinity and femininity are equally valued in upper management but that they may be unequally valued, or perceived as unequally valued, for men and women. In other words, masculinity may no longer be compulsory for all leaders, particular men. However, women may be judged under different standards.

Using Sex Role and Decision Style to Predict Representation

The fact that, in my study, sex role and decision style were not good explanations for the paucity of women in top management and that organization function and demographics were good explanations are bittersweet findings. The good news is that the findings may indicate that, at least for this organization, things are changing. The bad news is that the findings do not move us any further along in explaining why women are not proportionally represented at upper levels. At first blush, it is encouraging to think that the lack of a dominant masculine model may not be keeping women out of executive management positions. However, the ability for the statistical models developed in my study to predict representation was limited. Indeed, other research has found that the only consistently statistically predictive variables that explain the progress of men and women managers into executive positions are demographic variables like age, education, and experience.[43] Unfortunately, these models, like the models used in my study, could explain only a small portion of the variance in representation; these demographic variables are explanatory, but only to a small degree. In other words, these scientific, easy-to-measure variables can explain only some of the differences. Furthermore, as some research has found, these demographics simply state the obvious; the only statistical differences between men and women in top management is age, experience, and education. Women are younger, have been in their careers for less time, and tend to be more educated than the men. It follows then, some say, that as soon as women have been around as long as men and the numbers in the "pipeline" increase, women will be represented at upper levels to the same degree as men. However, research has indicated that this is not likely to happen.[44] At the current rates of appointment and promotion, it is estimated that it will take anywhere from thirty to forty-five years for the representation at upper levels to equal the representation of women in the workforce, regardless of how equal men and women become with regard to age, education, and experience. These demographic variables help us understand the differences between men and women at the top but do little to further our understanding as to why women are not proportionally represented at the executive level.

In short, researchers have had to concede that we cannot seem to explain the paucity of women at the top through our complicated statistical models. Try as we may, there are too many things out there working together to make it harder for women to reach these levels. The U.S. Merit System Protection Board's recently released comprehensive glass ceiling study is a good example of this.[45] They found that a glass ceiling does exist for women in the federal government that consists, in part, of factors that women can control (and researchers can measure) and of factors outside of a woman's control, such as unfounded judgments about job commitment and their ability to do their jobs well. Women have some control over their education and experience but very little control over perceptions of their work and structural barriers that keep them from moving up.

Another limitation of our studies of this phenomenon is the primary method of research used. For a variety of reasons ranging from a desire for simplicity to disciplinary norms, we researchers tend to use simple individual-level quantitative measures (usually surveys or economic data) as estimates of organizational measures. In other words, in my study, instead of going into the organizations and observing behavior and interviewing people about their perceptions of dominant styles in their organizations, I asked individuals to respond to pencil and paper measures of their individual style and used these as a proxy measure of organizational culture. It may well be that the individuals manifest different styles from what we find when we aggregate the data, so for groups these data produce misleading results. It may also be that one's perceptions of one's own behavior does not match other people's perceptions. In any case, individual-level data are not always good estimates of group-level data. Virtually all studies done in this area use individual-level data, a fact that may be hampering our abilities to understand representation at a higher level.

The limitations of survey research, the tendency for women to display more masculine styles, the tendency for women and men to be in sex-segregated organizations, as well as the results of other studies makes people doing research in this area hesitant to back away from the thesis that the compulsory masculinity of organizations ensures that only a select, and small, number of women populate the upper echelons. If the paucity of women at executive levels cannot be satisfactorily explained by demographics, what then is keeping women out? Unfortunately, the answer to that question is not simple and cannot be unearthed in any simple study that looks at representation as a result of discrimination theories or individual-level characteristics. Instead, the barriers are multiple in level, are related to a masculinist society that judges roles and behaviors differently due to sex and gender, are experienced almost exclusively by woman regardless of their color (although women of color experience these barriers differently than do white women), and are often impermeable. As Felice Schwartz indicates, the glass ceiling might actually be a "misleading metaphor … a more appropriate metaphor is kind of a cross-sectional diagram used in geology [where] the barriers occur when potentially counterproductive layers of influence on women—maternity, tradition, and socialization—meet management strata pervaded by unconscious preconceptions and expectations."[46]

These barriers that Schwartz describes are most likely related to the complicated layers of expectations and preconceptions that preclude and prescribe the preference for masculinity in organizations. We have already seen that organizations are a male domain. Now let's examine the other domains of masculinity that may be impacting and leading to the scarcity of women in leadership positions in public organizations.

Culture as a Masculine Domain

Sex roles and gendered behavior are important and powerful behavioral elements, but their power is not limited to individual-level behavior alone. Indeed, sex roles and gendered behavior are institutionalized as part of a culture and reflect important aspects of the culture itself:

> In all societies, gender roles and sex roles intertwine in a dynamic double helix that feminist theorists has labeled the sex-gender system. The threads of sex and gender roles are so intricately interwoven that most observers believe the current patterns have always existed. The threads of sex and gender roles are tied to filaments of age, class, religion, race and ethnicity as well.[47]

Sex and gender roles are interlaced within every avenue of life in a given culture. The definitions and bounds of private and public life are determined by cultural views of sex and gender roles. And, like it or not, in any given culture, one of the two sex or gender roles tends to be dominant and is valued more than the other. In most developed industrial countries, including the United States, masculinity is the dominant sex role and is valued more highly than femininity.[48] In a comprehensive study that encompassed surveying over 116,000 people in forty countries, Geert Hofstede found that one of the four key cultural differences between the countries was the centrality of masculinity in the culture. He found very interesting relationships between the respondents' views of traditional masculine goals and the organization of social life in their country. In his study, a country was classified as high masculinity (e.g., the United States,

Japan) when respondents tended to highly value traditionally masculine goals that are usually more popular with men. Countries with low masculinity (e.g., Denmark, Sweden) are ones in which traditional masculine goals were less highly values by respondents and respondents tended to positively endorse goals usually more popular among women. Countries with high masculinity tend to have fewer women in higher-qualified and better-paying jobs, fewer men who are positive toward the idea of seeing women in leadership positions, more segregation of the sexes in higher education, and an ethic that it is legitimate for organizations to interfere with private life (e.g., work interfering with family). Countries with lower masculinity tend to have more women in better jobs and more positive attitudes about women and leadership and believe that organizational and private life should be separate. In other words, the valuing of one gender role over the other seems to be significantly related to the constellation of social and organizational life. If masculinity is highly valued, certain conditions tend to exist, conditions that may be less positive for women than for men. If masculinity is less valued, conditions for men and women may be more equal.

The impact of the valued gender goes beyond the simple representation of women and the attitudes of a culture about that representation to form the underpinning of the tension underlying the distribution of power in a culture. Or, as the editors of this volume state, the ideological manifestation of the valuing of masculinity, masculinism, determines how power in a society is organized. And even if the events or situations that allowed masculinism to develop have changed, there is little opportunity to change the cultural preferences and gender power relationships. Jean Lipman-Blumen draws our attention to the fact that the basis of gender power and the differentials manifested in modern relationships and institutions seems to stem from the necessity of role behavior in more primitive times.[49] The fact that women bore and nursed children led to the

> active versus passive, independent versus dependent dichotomy that shapes sexual stereotypes form which civilization is struggling to emerge.... Once such patterns are established, those who have become accustomed to greater privilege and power find it both natural and imperative to defend the status quo.... Later generations accept the structures as a given ... even when the original conditions that gave rise to the social structure have changed, institutional arrangements perpetuate the system.[50]

State-Institutional Arrangements as a Masculine Domain

As more attention is centered upon the issue of representation in public organizations, some theorists and practitioners are focusing their criticisms of the inability of public organizations to achieve social equity around structural, philosophical, and professional issues. Some criticisms focus upon the limitations of our training methods and address the cultural preference in the social sciences for masculine characteristics over feminine characteristics.[51] This preference is translated into professions and the practice of professions through educational processes.

The groundbreaking feminist criticism of the profession of public administration is Camilla Stivers's work.[52] Stivers's thesis focuses around the dilemmas of gender contained in the images of expertise, leadership, and virtue that mark defenses of administrative power in public-administration theory. As Stivers states:

> [These images] not only have masculine features but help to keep in place or bestow political and economic privilege on the bearers of culturally masculine qualities at the expense of those who display culturally feminine ones. Far from being superficial window-dressing or a side effect, the characteristic of masculinity of public administration is systemic: it contributes to and is sustained by power relations in society at large that distributes resources on the basis of gender and affects people's life chances and their sense of themselves and their place in the world.[53]

Although Stivers investigates several of the major underpinnings of the theory and legitimacy of the administrative state, a key focus of her analysis is on administrative power and the gendered nature of power distribution. She argues that public administrators have a significant amount of discretionary power in their exercise of authority over the activities of individuals and corporations. The use and distribution of this power, in her view, is gendered, with a preference given to distributing the power within masculine guidelines. A feminist approach to public-administration theory, Stivers argues, entails "calling the [existing paradigms] into question and exploring their implications, which include the material differences in access to resources and power they sustain and the perceptions of self and world they generate."[54]

Other feminist scholars investigating the nature of public organizations focus not on the discipline of public administration, but instead on the basic construction of public bureaucracies themselves. From this perspective, representation and the construction of public bureaucracies are closely tied to structural conditions and historical patterns of sex- and gender-role interactions.[55] Legal doctrine, cultural definitions of gender differences, a sex-segregated occupational structure, and bureaucratic forms of decision making and control have been inextricably interwoven with notions of male and female sexuality. Interaction among these variables gives rise to the possibility, indeed the likelihood, of differential treatment of women in organizations, and the dominant mode of cultural masculinity in public organizations.

One of the more comprehensive and accessible reviews of the important literature on the nature of gender and bureaucracy is Anne Witz and Mike Savage's introduction to their recent edited volume.[56] The authors artfully outline and discuss three of the groundbreaking feminist works in the field of gender and bureaucracy: Rosabeth Moss Kantor, Kathy Ferguson, and Rosemary Pringle.[57] Witz and Savage argue, using these three theorists as their base, that "in order to understand gender inequality, it is essential to see how organization forms *structure* and are themselves *structured* by gender."[58]

As Wendy Brown states: "the quest for manhood ... as domination of men and the environment; as thought and action liberated from sensual and emotional aspects of being, results in a bureaucratic and capitalist machinery in which man is utterly ensnared, unfree, and by Weber's own account, inhuman."[59] Public bureaucracies, by their definition of rational, controlled organizations, are gendered. Max Weber's basic account of rationality in organizations is premised upon the recognition of bureaucracy's masculine, masculinist, and patriarchical overtones.[60] Catherine MacKinnon asserts that the state is male because it adopts the standpoint of men, or the male view of the world, which it then calls objectivity (and rationality).[61]

Leadership/Management as a Masculine Domain

The gendered construction of organizations, the masculinity of public bureaucracies, and the cultural preference for masculine behavior translate well into our cultural expectations and attitudes about leadership and management. Our perceptions of what traits and/or characteristics make a good manager or leader are gendered with a preference for masculinity.

In 1977, Powell and Butterfield investigated perceptions of effective managerial traits.[62] The results of their research indicated that effective managerial traits tend to be those traits that are traditionally associated with masculinity (e.g., aggressive, decisive, rational). In fact, management traits that can be classified as traditionally feminine or androgynous (e.g., caring, connected, supportive) were seen as detracting from perceptions of managerial effectiveness.

One might argue that perceptions of management behavior have changed significantly since the late 1970s. However, a replication of Powell and Butterfield's original study indicates that perceptions about effective management traits have not changed over time.[63] In the 1977 study, 60 percent of respondents viewed a good manager as masculine; in a 1985 study 66 percent of respondents viewed a good manager as masculine. Regardless of strides made by women in management over the last twenty years, regardless of research that indicates that better managers tend to be androgynous, and the popular opinion that more feminine approaches to leadership have a great deal of value,[64] stereotypes or beliefs about what constitutes good management traits seem to not have changed: good management equals masculine management.

Given the dominant stereotypes about good or effective management behavior, it follows that people who have *not* been socialized to behave in ways that are consistent with a masculine gender identity may be handicapped with regard to their ability to succeed in a management situation. This may be particularly true for women. Indeed, a plethora of popular and scholarly work has recently surfaced that address the conflicts that executive women face given the tension between their gender role socialization and the norms of the management workplace.[65] Research and interviews with private-sector female executive managers communicate a clear message: being feminine is counterproductive to being an executive manager.[66] As Rita Mae Kelly indicates in her description of the masculine nature of bureaucracies:

> women who become managers and have successful careers must become like men, not only in their training but also in their behavior ... fewer women [than men] will have the power, achievement and leadership motives [necessary to advance], given sex role socialization and ideologies, but those that do have these motives will behave similarly to men.[67]

Stivers also believes that the negative relationship between femininity and executive management exists in public bureaucracies:

> women who pursue careers as professional public administrators are faced with a dilemma—the fundamental dissonance between what is expected of them as professional women and what is expected of them as professional experts.... Thus, it is fraudulent to offer women an [opportunity] to rise through the ranks of bureaucracy while the requirements and exemplary qualities for that sort of career remain inconsistent with what is expected of them as women. To point out that a number of women have done it successfully is to miss the point. They have virtually never done it without constant effort to manage their femaleness on the job and without the continuing struggle to balance work and home responsibilities.[68]

Traditional masculinist images of leadership focus upon rational models of decision making, emphasize taking charge, and rest upon authority and control. As it happens, the new leadership styles that emphasize more cooperative, consensual, and connected leadership can be described as traditionally feminine characteristics.[69] As the desire for these new methods of leading and managing becomes more acute, the need to investigate the gendered underpinnings of our cultural expectations about management behavior and the gendered nature of organizations becomes more important. However, it is extremely important to keep the level of criticism at the structural level, that is, focused at the organizational or institutional rather than at the individual level. One must be cautious, for example, to assume that women naturally manage or lead in a different way than men. This does a grave disservice to the diversity that exists between and among women and men and serves to perpetuate the masculine/objective/rational myths of determinism in behavior. In addition, we need to be wary of advocating another model (e.g., a feminine model) as the one best way of managing or leading. Femininity is developed, in our culture, in opposition to masculinity. In other words, feminine is feminine *because* masculine is masculine. Therefore, if one is truly critical of the gendered basis of behavior, structures, and institutions of our society and unwilling to accept masculinity as a model, one must also be critical of and unwilling to accept femininity as a substitute.

Some Closing Thoughts about Masculinity and Public Organizations

Regardless of the small ray of hope (and the ray is even smaller given the differences between men and women) that the results of my study may indicate, a cultural preference for certain behaviors within and outside of organizations is alive and well. The good news is that there may be greater acceptance of diversity in styles and behavior at the executive levels of bureaucracy. In fact, a quick glance at Bill Clinton's cabinet and staff would indicate that diversity is more highly valued now than ever before. However, the bad news for women is that, even though the trends may be changing, they may not be changing for women. While there may be greater latitude for different styles and behaviors in general, women may still be expected to act like a man, or act more like a man than men, in order to be successful. The numbers are misleading. We are lead to believe that the increasing numbers of women in executive positions in our public bureaucracies means organizational change. However, as Witz and Savage explain:

> Women in state bureaucracies are strangers in a male world.... Simply recruiting women to the higher echelons of bureaucratic organization does not necessarily mean that the character of the organization will become less masculinist and more feminized and woman-friendly. On the contrary,

individual women in senior bureaucratic positions may perforce have to learn to act like men in order to function effectively at these levels.[70]

The power of individual behavior or individual differences is not enough to change the institutionalization of gender relationships as reflected in the structures and processes of modern public bureaucracies. Regardless of who one is as an individual, existing as an individual within organizations is a challenge, particularly if one is a woman, person of color, or a member of another "other" group. In a sense, bureaucratic organizations require forms of compulsory behavior of all of its participants, particularly if one chooses to rise beyond the support positions of the lower levels and into the instrumental positions of power at the upper levels. Masculinity is one form of compulsory behavior required by bureaucracies. Like the power relationships in general society, the power distributions of organizations are gendered because bureaucratic power is traditionally defined as masculine.

The results of the numerous studies to date have lead me to hypothesize that masculinity is, and continues to be, the first level of evaluation at the executive level of management. It may well be in modern times that this compulsory masculinity is subconscious or underground. As a culture, we may be loathe to admit that the first thing a leader must be is masculine. However, this may well be the case. In addition, a leader may not be able to show feminine characteristics until *after* they have proved their masculinity. Unfortunately, for women, proving one's masculinity is not as easy as it is for men. Because of the deep cultural foundations of sex or gender roles, men prove their masculinity almost by default (I am man, therefore you expect that I am masculine—I need to prove to you that I am feminine). Likewise, women prove their femininity almost by default (I am woman, therefore you expect that I am feminine—I need to prove to you that I am masculine). Women who want to be organizational leaders may be handicapped from the beginning by the expectation that they prove their masculinity. In addition, women may be faulted more for their femininity than are men. As long as they are appropriately heterosexual (which the concomitant compulsory heterosexuality of bureaucracies demands),[71] men may get the luxury of greater latitude in roles because they don't have to work so hard to prove their masculinity.

This "proving one's masculinity" thesis may also account for the unexplained differences between men and women executive's life situations. If women have to prove their masculinity and manage their femininity at work in addition to managing the complicated roles and duties of partner and/or wife and mother outside of work, is it any wonder that fewer executive women are in traditional life situations than men? With all of this role management, it makes sense that more executive women than men would opt out of traditional life situations.

To fault women for overcompensating their masculinity and undercompensating their femininity would be fruitless; what choice does a woman have if she chooses to be successful within these constructs? Unfortunately, the conformity of women to these constructs does little to change the nature of gender power in public organizations. Instead women's conformity to masculinized norms reinforces gender power relationships rather than weakening them. For if women are capable of and willing to prove their masculinity in the masculine bureaucracy, there is little impetus for criticism and change. Women confront a double bind that bolsters masculinism regardless of their choice.

From where, then, will this impetus for criticism and change come? Certainly it is coming to some degree from the academy, with the plethora of work like this edited volume that examines the masculinist nature or bureaucracies, governance, and power relationships. Certainly it is coming, to some degree, from practitioners who are challenging the assumptions and refuse to conform to all of the compulsory behaviors required of those who work in public organizations. To no one's surprise, these nonconformist practitioners and scholars tend to be on the margins in their respective areas, rather than in the mainstream. Until these criticisms enter the mainstream both in scholarship and practice, we will continue to face the many thorny issues of gender power in leadership and governance discussed in this text. Our organizations, like the disciplines that define them, are made, not born. It is time to make them different.

Notes

1. Jaclyn Fierman, "Why Women Still Don't Hit the Top," *Fortune,* July 30, 1990, 40–62.
2. Wendy Brown, *Manhood and Politics* (Totowa, N.J.: Rowman and Littlefield, 1988); Evelyn Fox Keller, *Reflections on Gender and Science* (New Haven, Conn.: Yale University Press, 1985).
3. Wendy Brown, *Manhood and Politics,* ix.
4. Ibid., 4.
5. Anne M. Morrison, Randall P. White, and Ellen Van Velsor, *Breaking the Glass Ceiling: Can Women Reach the Top of America's Largest Corporations?* (Reading, Mass.: Addison-Wesley, 1987).
6. Anne M. Morrison and Mary Ann Von Glinow, "Women and Minorities in Management," *American Psychologist,* 35 (2) (1990): 200–208.
7. Anne B. Fisher, "When Will Women Get to the Top?" *Fortune,* September 21, 1992, 44–56.
8. United States Merit Systems Protection Board, *A Question of Equity: Women and the Glass Ceiling in the Federal Government* (Washington, D.C.: Government Printing Office, 1992).
9. Mary Ellen Guy, ed., *Women and Men of the States* (Armonk, N.Y.: M. E. Sharpe, 1993); Cheryl Simrell King, "Gender and Administrative Leadership in Colorado" (paper presented at the Western Political Science Association, Pasadena, Calif., 1993; and Mary M. Hale and Rita Mae Kelly, *Gender, Bureaucracy and Democracy* (Westport, Conn.: Greenwood Press, 1989).

10. Eleanor Emmons Maccoby and Carol Nagy Jacklin, *The Psychology of Sex Differences* (Stanford, Calif.: Stanford University Press, 1974); Susan M. Donnell and Jay Hall, "Men and Women as Managers: A Significant Case of No Significant Differences," *Organizational Dynamics* 8 (4) (1980): 60–77.

11. E.g., J. Edward Kellough, "Integration in the Public Workplace: Determinants of Minority and Female Employment in Federal Agencies," *Public Administration Review* 50 (5) (1990): 557–66; and Gregory B. Lewis, "Progress toward Racial and Sexual Equality in the Federal Civil Service," *Public Administration Review* 48 (3) (1988): 700–707.

12. Kellough, "Integration in the Public Workplace"; and Lewis, "Progress toward Racial and Sexual Equality in the Federal Civil Service."

13. For more details see King, "Gender and Administrative Leadership"; and Cheryl Simrell King, "Gender and Management: Men and Women and Decision-Making in Public Organizations" (Ph.D. diss., University of Colorado at Denver, 1992).

14. Nancy Chodorow, "Family Structure and Feminine Personality," in *Women, Culture and Society,* ed. Michelle Zimbalist Rosaldo and Louise Lamphere (Stanford, Calif.: Stanford University Press, 1974).

15. John Newson, Elizabeth Newson, Diane Richardson and Joyce Scaife, "Perspectives in Sex Role Stereotyping," in *The Sex Role System,* ed. Jane Chetwynd and Oonagh Hartnett (London: Routledge and Kegan Paul, 1978).

16. Geert Hofstede, *Culture's Consequences: International Differences in Work-Related Values* (Newbury Park, Calif.: Sage Publications, 1984).

17. Julia Sherman, "Social Values, Femininity and the Development of Female Competence," *Journal of Social Issues* 32 (3) (1976): 181–95.

18. Janet Lever, "Sex Differences in the Games Children Play," *Social Problems* 23 (1976): 478–87.

19. Carol Gilligan, *In a Different Voice: Psychological Theory and Women's Development* (Cambridge, Mass.: Harvard University Press, 1982), 10.

20. E.g., Katha Pollitt, "Are Women Morally Superior to Men?" *Nation,* December 28, 1992, 799–807.

21. Keller, *Reflections.*

22. Nona Plessner Lyons, "Two Perspectives on Self, Relationships, and Morality," *Harvard Educational Review* 53 (1983): 125–45.

23. Carolyn Desjardins, "Gender Issues in Community College Leadership," *American Association of Women in Community and Junior Colleges Journal* 25 (1989): 125–37.

24. Mary Field Belenky, Blythe McVicker Clinchy, Nancy Rule Goldberger, and Jill Mattuck Tarule, *Women's Ways of Knowing: The Development of Self, Voice and Mind* (New York: Basic Books, 1986); and Gilligan, *In a Different Voice.*

25. Indeed, women were even excluded as subjects. See William Graves Perry, *Forms of Intellectual and Ethical Development in the College Years* (New York: Holt, Rinehart and Winston, 1970); and Lawrence Kohlberg, *The Philosophy of Moral Development* (San Francisco: Harper and Row, 1981).

26. Gilligan, *In a Different Voice.*

27. Belenky et al., *Women's Ways of Knowing.*

28. Perry, *Forms of Development.*

29. Belenky et al., *Women's Ways of Knowing,* 55.

30. Carl Jung, *Psychological Type* (New York: Pantheon Books, 1923).

31. Gerald D. Otis and Naomi L. Quenk, "Care and Justice Consideration in 'Real Life' Moral Problems," *Journal of Psychological Type* 18 (1989): 3–10.

32. Sandra L. Bem, *The Bem Sex-Role Inventory* (Palo Alto, Calif.: Consulting Psychologists Press, 1981); Alan J. Rowe and Richard O. Mason, *Managing with Style: A Guide to Understanding, Assessing and Improving Decision-making* (San Francisco: Jossey-Bass, 1987).

33. Overall, a total of 309 (70 women, 238 men) out of the population of 506 managers returned usable surveys, representing an overall response rate of 61 percent. The proportion of men to women in the sample (77 percent to 23 percent) almost exactly matched the proportion of men and women in the population (78 percent to 22 percent).

34. Edith Gilson and Susan Kane, *Unnecessary Choices: The Hidden Life of the Executive Woman* (New York: Paragon Press, 1989); Hale and Kelly, *Gender, Bureaucracy, and Democracy;* Rita Mae Kelly, Mary Ellen Guy, Jane Bayes, Georgia Duerst-Lahti, Lois L. Duke, Mary M. Hale, Cathy Johnson, Amal Kawar and Jeanie R. Stanley, "Public Managers and the States: A Comparison of Career Advancement by Sex," *Public Administration Review* 51 (5) (1991): 402–12; and Beth Milwid, *Working with Men: Professional Women Talk about Power, Sexuality, and Ethics* (Hillsboro, Oreg.: Beyond Words Press, 1987).

35. Arlie Hochschild, *The Second Shift* (New York: Avon Books, 1989).

36. Gilson and Kane, *Unnecessary Choices;* Rita Mae Kelly, *The Gendered Economy: Work, Careers, and Success* (Newbury Park, Calif.: Sage Publications, 1991); Milwid, *Working with Men;* and Camilla Stivers, *Gender Images in Public Administration: The Dilemmas of Expertise, Leadership, and Virtue* (Newbury Park, Calif.: Sage Publications, 1993).

37. Georgia Duerst-Lahti and Cathy Marie Johnson, "Management Styles, Stereotypes, and Advantages," in Guy, *Women and Men.*

38. Ibid.

39. Kathleen Hall Jamieson, *Beyond the Double Bind: Women and Leadership* (New York: Oxford University Press, 1995), esp. ch. 1, p. 8.

40. Ellen Fagenson, "Perceived Masculine and Feminine Attributes Examined as a Function of Individual's Sex and Level in the Organizational Power Hierarchy: A Test of Four Theoretical Perspectives," *Journal of Applied Psychology* 25, (2) (1990): 204–11.

41. Ibid., 209.

42. Duerst-Lahti and Johnson, "Management Styles."

43. Kellough, "Integration"; and J. E. Kellough, "The 1978 Civil Service Reform Act and Federal Equal Opportunity Act," *American Review of Public Administration* 19 (1989): 313–24.

44. U.S. Merit Systems Protection Board, *A Question of Equity,* 37; Kellough, "Integration in the Public Workplace"; Gregory B. Lewis, "Progress toward Racial and Sexual Equality in the Federal Civil Service," *Public Administration Review* 3 (1988): 700–707; and Gregory B. Lewis, "Changing Patterns of Sexual Discrimination in Federal Employment," *Review of Public Personnel Administration* 7 (1987): 1–13.

45. U.S. Merit Systems Protection Board, *A Question of Equity,* 37.

46. Felice N. Schwartz, "Management Women and the New Facts of Life," *Harvard Business Review,* 67 (1) (1989): 68.

47. Jean Lipman-Blumen, *Gender Roles and Power* (Englewood Cliffs, N.J.: Prentice-Hall, 1984).

48. Hofstede, *Culture's Consequences.*

49. Lipman-Blumen, *Gender Roles and Power.*

50. Ibid., 4–5.

51. Sandra G. Harding, *The Science Question in Feminism* (Ithaca, N.Y.: Cornell University Press, 1986); and Keller, *Reflections.*

52. Stivers, *Gender Images.*

53. Ibid., 4.

54. Ibid., 126.

55. Kathy E. Ferguson, *The Feminist Case against Bureaucracy* (Philadelphia: Temple University Press, 1984); and Frances L. Hoffman, "Sexual Harassment in Academia: Feminist Theory and Institutional Practice," *Harvard Educational Review* 56 (2) (1986): 105–21.

56. Anne Witz and Michal Savage, "Theoretical Introduction: The Gender of Organizations," in *Gender and Bureaucracy,* ed. Mike Savage and Anne Witz (Oxford: Blackwell Publishers, 1992).
57. Rosabeth M. Kanter, "Some Effects of Proportions on Group Life: Skewed Sex Ratios and Responses to Token Women," *American Journal of Sociology* 82 (1977): 965–90, and *Men and Women of the Corporation* (New York: Basic Books, 1977); Ferguson, *Feminist Case against Bureaucracy;* and Rosemary Pringle, *Secretaries Talk: Sexuality, Power and Work* (London: Verso, 1979).
58. Witz and Savage, "Theoretical Introduction," 8.
59. Brown, *Manhood and Politics,* 5.
60. Max Weber, *From Max Weber: Essays in Sociology,* ed. and trans. Hans Gerth and C. Wright Mills (New York: Oxford University Press, 1946); Rosalyn Wallach Bologh, *Love or Greatness: Max Weber and Masculine Thinking: A Feminist Inquiry* (London: Unwin Hyman, 1990); Fergusen, *Feminist Case against Bureaucracy;* and Brown, *Manhood and Politics.*
61. Catherine MacKinnon, *Towards a Feminist Theory of the State* (Cambridge, Mass.: Harvard University Press, 1987).
62. Gary N. Powell and D. A. Butterfield, "The Good Manager: Masculine or Androgynous?" *Academy of Management Journal* 22 (1979): 395–403.
63. Gary N. Powell, *Women and Men in Management* (Newbury Park, Calif.: Sage Publications, 1988).
64. Donnell and Hall, "Men and Women"; Duerst-Lahti and Johnson, "Management Styles"; Marilyn Loden, *Feminine Leadership, or How to Succeed in Business without Being One of the Boys* (New York: Times Books, 1985); and Judy B. Rosener, "Ways Women Lead," *Harvard Business Review* 68 (6) (1990): 119–25.
65. Gilson and Kane, *Unnecessary Choices.*
66. Milwid, *Working with Men.*
67. Kelly, *The Gendered Economy,* 97–100.
68. Stivers, *Gender Images.*
69. Harding, *Science Question in Feminism;* Harlan Cleveland, *The Knowledge Executive: Leadership in an Information Society* (New York: Dulton Books, 1985); and Loden, *Feminine Leadership.*
70. Witz and Savage, "Theoretical Introduction," 43.
71. E.g., Pringle, *Secretaries Talk.*

Chapter 4

Sex, Gender, and Leadership in the Representation of Women

Karin L. Tamerius

The face of American government is undergoing a dramatic transformation. After more than two centuries as almost exclusively male purviews, our nation's major political institutions are moving surely, if not exactly swiftly, toward sexual integration. The Center for the American Woman in Politics reports that since 1983 the percentage of official government positions held by women has increased from 4 percent to 10 percent in Congress, from 13 percent to 20 percent in state legislatures, and from 11 percent to 22 percent in statewide elective offices. Although nationwide women still hold no more than a quarter of the seats at any level of government, changes over the last decade indicate real movement toward parity.[1]

Recent advances by women in the political arena have attracted new attention to a number of old but important questions about the relationship between sex, gender, and representative governance: Are the women in public office more supportive of women's issues than their male counterparts? Are they more attentive to the needs and concerns of the women in their constituencies? Do they work harder to enact policies for women into law? In short, does the sexual integration of our political institutions lead to greater representation of women's interests?

For most feminists there is little doubt about the answers to these and related questions. From our perspective the current sexual conversion in American politics is not simply an alteration of the countenance of government. As women ascend the steps of the Capitol, assume their places in the president's cabinet, and take their seats on the bench of the Supreme Court, they alter the political landscape in ways that cannot be captured by photographs or physical descriptions. More than just the symbolic representatives of women's growing political clout, female public officials afford substantive representation of women's political interests; in the language of Hanna Pitkin, they are "standing for" and "acting for" women simultaneously.[2]

Indeed, the change before us is not an accident nor the consequence of natural political evolution; rather, it is a revolution brought about by feminists seeking to alter the content of government decision making. For two decades organizations like the National Women's Political Caucus (NWPC), Early Money Is Like Yeast (EMILY's List), and the Women's Campaign Fund have labored tirelessly to get more women elected and appointed to public office in the hope of making government more responsive to women's wants. And now, with fifty-four women in Congress, two women on the Supreme Court, six women in the president's cabinet, and countless more in state and local offices around the country, these organizations and their supporters look forward to fundamental improvements in the status of women in the United States.

But even as feminists celebrate these long-awaited political victories, there are those who say that the transformation taking place before us is mere metaphor; a sign of how far we have traveled perhaps, definitely a sign of our distance yet to go, but a poor harbinger of things to come. In their view, recent elections have achieved greater numerical representation for women while leaving the substance of politics untouched. Institutional scholars tell us that government is largely unaffected by the individuals who populate it. Others, endorsing feminism but misconstruing its meaning, insist that women are the same as men and therefore will not affect the administration of government at all.[3] Male politicians, conveniently forgetting centuries when maleness was a primary prerequisite for public office, complain bitterly about having their representativeness judged on the basis of their sex.[4]

Even more significant than the rhetoric, however, are the statistics naysayers use to buttress their claims. Ever since women first began to achieve public office in significant numbers, researchers have been attempting to assess their impact on the "feminist" content of policy. The general conclusion to emerge from these studies—located primarily in state legislatures and Congress—is that women matter, but they do not matter much. The main indicator used to gauge sex differences in the representation of women in government institutions is the roll call voting of elected officials on "women's issues." All else being equal, sex has not been shown to be an important determinant. Although women at all levels of public office tend to vote in a slightly more feminist direction than their male colleagues, these differences rarely have been substantively significant.[5] Moreover, in the rare instances when meaningful differences have been found—in roll call voting on women's issues in the California Assembly,[6] for example—it still appears that electing women to public office is at best an inefficient way of enhancing the representation of women's interests. Since inevitably the most powerful predictor of feminist voting is party membership, it follows that organizations seeking to promote women's welfare through government action would be best advised to direct their electoral resources toward Democratic candidates of either sex.

While nonfeminists have used these studies (with some justification) to declare vindication, there has been an understandable, yet ultimately unfortunate, tendency among feminist scholars and activists to mildly overclaim results, to report that which is only statistically significant as substantively significant, and to declare meaningful difference where the evidence supports little more than distinction. I am convinced that this inclination arises from a fundamental and troubling disjunction between what we have found as researchers and what we "know" as individuals. While the facts of indifference in these studies approaches incontrovertibility, a conclusion of no difference defies our understanding of the world. It does not jibe with what we know about ourselves as politically aware and active women in American society, women who in our daily lives are more apt to notice and draw attention to sex inequities than are men; it does not fit with what we know about the history of the feminist movement, a movement that women have always led; and it does not accord with what we know about most of the women serving in public office today, women who are personally committed to promoting women's welfare through government action. Women in public leadership posts *seem* to make a difference. Faced with a seemingly dichotomous choice between seeing meaningful difference in results where there is little and challenging a basic component of feminist theory and experience, we have chosen the former course. But are our findings and our beliefs as truly incongruous as they appear?

On the contrary, I argue in this chapter that the largely negative findings of earlier studies are in fact perfectly compatible with a feminist worldview, even one that says that having more women in government will significantly enhance the representation of women's interests. It is my contention that previous work on this topic failed to uncover substantial sex differences not because the feminist project has failed or been misguided, but because difference was operationalized with scant regard to the stated and unstated theories of gender and politics that underlie feminist predictions. Rather than considering what we mean when we say that women will alter the substance of government and choosing tools well suited to investigating those propositions, researchers have simply appropriated traditional indicators of difference and applied them to the study of gender. Yet, as the work of a number of feminist epistemologists attests, such an approach is bound to provide a distorted image of the nature and consequences of women's political participation.[7]

The major shortcoming of previous studies from a feminist perspective is the failure to take into account the gendered nature of conventional measures. Regrettably, the stock research implements of modern political science did not arise untainted from the sexually divided environment of their origination.

Developed largely by men to answer questions of interest to men about the political behavior of men, many existing tools contain an inherent male bias. In the study of legislative behavior, for example, the traditional emphasis on roll call voting, which assumes that enactment is the most important stage in the legislative process, privileges majority and, therefore, male interests. Since policies of concern to the majority of members are bound to make it to the floor eventually, early maneuvers are unlikely to have a major impact on whether a policy is ultimately adopted. From the perspective of women and other legislative minorities, however, critical stages of the legislative process are more properly identified as agenda setting and policy formulation, since the vast majority of policies of interest to underrepresented groups, including feminist bills, never receive consideration on the floor.

While the existence of such male biases does not mean that conventional indicators such as roll call votes should never be used to study sex differences, these biases do mean that we need to seriously investigate their implications and appropriateness for assessing gendered constructs before employing them in our empirical research. At the same time, we should not hesitate to develop novel alternatives capable of providing more accurate depictions of "female-oriented" behavior when conventional measures prove unequal to the task.[8] Ultimately, fully comprehending women's (and men's) impact on governance requires the use of instruments that are informed by and fundamentally compatible with our theories of gender and politics.

Recognizing, then, that earlier efforts to document the representational contributions of female officeholders omitted a crucial step, we need to repeat the process, this time making an effort to formulate and test hypotheses that conceptualize difference in feminist terms. The study reported here is an attempt to do just that. Drawing on theoretical and empirical work in gender and politics, legislative politics, and a series of interviews with more than a dozen members of Congress,[9] I develop and evaluate a model of sex differences in legislative behavior that posits several ways in which being female may impel a representative toward legislative leadership on feminist issues.

Why Expect Sex Differences in Representation?

In striving to develop realistic and defensible predictions about the impact of female legislators on governance, I began by looking for ways in which being a woman or man structures a representative's relationship with women's issues. My investigation yielded a number of factors that, in theory, have the potential to produce gendered representation. Falling into two distinct yet causally related categories—sex differences in *experience* and sex differences in *attitudes* and *resources*—these determinants may conspire with the demands of representative institutions to produce sex differences in *feminist legislative leadership*—active involvement in the establishment and promotion of a feminist legislative agenda.

Sex Differences in Experience

A central notion of feminist standpoint theory is that women and men have different experiences in life that have consequences for how their interests are represented in politics. Although standpoint as an approach has come under criticism in recent years for its tendency to ignore politically relevant differences among women—especially those having to do with class, ethnicity, race, and sexual orientation—the model outlined here assumes no such homogeneity. Rather than supposing that all women's experiences are alike in type or meaning, my model assumes only that women's lives tend to differ in salient and systematic ways from those of men. In this study four gendered aspects of representatives' experiences—*content, perspective, mutuality,* and *association*—are expected to be particularly crucial in fashioning legislative involvement with women's concerns.

Content

The first feature that distinguishes the experiences of female and male legislators is their gendered content. Although the women and men who serve in public office tend to come from similarly privileged backgrounds, they are still likely to experience life in substantively different ways. Sex disparities in the types of experiences legislators have arise in part from fundamental biological distinctions (such as the capacity to become pregnant) but also from pervasive sexual divisions within society. Among the social factors that are likely to result in divergent experiences for women and men are sex differences in socialization, prejudicial treatment, occupation, socioeconomic status, domestic roles, and criminal victimization.

Perspective

A second distinction to be made about the experiences of female and male legislators is their gendered perspective. Simply put, women's experiences happen to women while men's experiences happen to men. This divergence in outlook limits the amount of insight either sex can have into what it is like to be the other since the interpretation, salience, and feeling of any experience is likely to be mediated at least in part by whether it is happening to us or someone else. While the "objective" experience—what happens—may be the same, we can only perceive it subjectively, through a gendered lens. Consequently, just about the only way men can experience womanhood or, conversely, women can experience manhood, is with the assistance of their imaginations.

Mutuality

A third factor that distinguishes the experiences of female and male legislators is gendered mutuality. In simple terms, women's experiences tend to be shared by other women while men's experiences tend to be shared by other men. Since the degree to which members of a social group identify with each other depends in large part on the commonality of their experiences, this divergence is likely to strengthen ties within the sexes while weakening bonds between them.

Association

A final aspect that differentiates the experiences of female and male legislators is their gendered association. Despite strong familial and emotional ties, women and men often work and socialize in sexually exclusive groups. Within the context of American politics, for example, male politicians historically have operated through political old-boys networks inimical to the participation of women. Partly in response to the male dominance of these informal associations, many female politicians have opted to work closely with political organizations for women. Not only do such groups often provide a starting point for women's political careers—affording much needed experience, encouragement, and funding—but they frequently continue to work closely with female legislators long after they are elected to public office.

Sex Differences in Attitudes and Resources

Although feminist standpoint theory has successfully focused attention on the political relevance of legislators' experiences, it has made little attempt to specify the mechanisms by which experience as a woman or man might be translated into gendered representation. In the model described here, it is hypothesized that experiences affect political engagement with issues of particular concern to women in two ways: first, by altering legislators' attitudes—*support* and *commitment*—toward women's issues, and, second, by providing legislators with resources—*awareness* and *expertise*—that facilitate feminist activism.

Support

One consequence of sex disparities in experience is that female legislators may be especially supportive of policies for women. Women's experiences may shape their policy attitudes by providing compelling evidence of the need for government action on feminist concerns. A female legislator who has suffered discrimination in hiring, for example, has personal confirmation that the problem of sex discrimination exists, while a male legislator who has had no such experience may remain skeptical. At the same time, because a female legislator who has experienced discrimination is afforded unique insight into its emotional and financial ramifications, she may be inclined to judge the problem more severe than do her male counterparts.

Women do not need to confront problems directly, however, to have their policy attitudes shaped by their experiences. Female legislators may become convinced of the need for feminist policies simply through their frequent association with other women. For example, a legislator may be persuaded to support an antidiscrimination policy because she has had the opportunity to speak with victims of sex discrimination about their experiences. Similarly, being involved with organizations that possess substantial information about the severity and extent of prejudice may encourage a female legislator to alter her assessments of the need for policies designed to fight sex bias in the workplace.

That the gendered experiences of female legislators play a role in their attitudinal support for feminist policies was a point frequently made in my interviews and, now, increasingly on the floors of Congress. In a recent debate over the Family and Medical Leave Act, for example, two newly elected Democratic senators, Dianne Feinstein from California and Patty Murray from Washington, discussed the need for the legislation in light of their own experiences as female employees and family caretakers. Said Senator Feinstein explaining her support of the policy:

> Thirty-five years ago, when I gave birth to my daughter Katherine, there was no maternity or family leave. I left my job to have my child.... From personal experience, I have also seen how difficult it is to concentrate on work when a parent or family member is critically or terminally ill.[10]

Senator Murray discussed a related experience:

> When I was 26 years old and worked as an executive secretary in Seattle, I became pregnant with my first child. At that time, even though I was working out of economic necessity, there were no options for working

mothers. A family leave policy would have enabled me to devote my attention to the changes in my family.[11]

Commitment

A second consequence of sex disparities in experience may be that female legislators are especially committed to policies for women. Gendered experiences may cause female legislators to make feminist issues a priority for two reasons. First, as noted above, their unique perspective on women's issues may enhance their assessments of problem severity, making them more inclined to place women's issues high on the list of national concerns. Second, female legislators may feel a special responsibility for helping women with their problems as a result of their common experiences and group membership. Indeed this was a recurring theme in my interviews, since many of the women felt very strongly that as women they have special obligations to represent women's interests. In their words:

> Women in Congress have a responsibility to be leaders on women's issues. If women don't point out women's problems, no one will. (Republican)

> Women in Congress have special responsibilities because there are so few of us. We try to represent all women to the best of our ability. I have a special responsibility because how policy impacts women has been neglected. (Democrat)

> I think that each of us feels very much that in addition to representing our own districts [we have a responsibility to represent women across the country] who look to us with some hope that their voices will be heard in terms of issues they care about. (Democrat)

Awareness

A third consequence of sex disparities in experience is that female legislators may be especially aware of issues of concern to women. Theoretically, gendered experiences give female officials an advantage in identifying the problems facing women in two respects. First, female legislators may be more aware of women's problems because they have encountered those problems in their own lives. A congresswoman who has been the victim of spousal abuse, for example, is apt to be more cognizant of crimes against women than are her male colleagues who have never suffered domestic violence. Second, female legislators may learn about women's problems through their association with other women. For example, one of the primary goals of feminist organizations is to bring problems of particular concern to women to the attention of female legislators.

That women in Congress are more aware of women's issues than their male counterparts was strongly suggested in the interviews. To begin with, when asked to identify women's issues, congresswomen cited a much broader range of concerns than their male counterparts. While the men tended to associate women's issues only with those areas of discrimination and devaluation that have been identified and articulated in the mainstream media's coverage of the women's movement, such as, abortion, child care, and family leave, the congresswomen recognized a wide range of additional concerns, including the economy, health care, and the Gulf War.

Sex differences in awareness also emerged in members' responses to questions about their committee activities on behalf of their female constituents. Many of the congressmen were hard pressed to see any connection between their committee assignments and women's concerns. According to a Democratic congressman on the Public Works and Transportation Committee, for example, he had not undertaken any activities specifically for women in committee sessions because "my committees don't have jurisdiction over women's issues." Similarly, a Republican congressman said his activities on the Banking, Finance, and Urban Affairs Committee had not involved women's issues, explaining, "[W]omen do not surface in these discussions." In contrast, the congresswomen saw committee sessions as a prime opportunity to engage in what they referred to as "consciousness-raising" on women's issues—efforts to educate male members about women's problems and ensure that policies are written in a manner responsive to women's concerns. In their words:

> In committees I raise questions about how programs affect women, what is being done for women. I have a consciousness-raising role. As a result, men in my committees have become more responsive. They make sure more women testify during hearings. (Republican)

> My committee assignments are not focused in any way or another on women, but I always ask about women, whether its a banking issue, women in development, whether it's health issues, whatever it happens to be.... I want to know about what are they doing for women.... When I was on the banking committee, [I made] sure women were always given some priority or some regard in terms of their ability to be part of the financial scheme of things. (Democrat)

Expertise

A final consequence of sex disparities in experience is that female legislators may be especially expert on women's issues. In addition to imparting information about the types of problems women confront, experiences may also afford information about how those problems can best be resolved. To begin with, female legislators may acquire policy information by facing gender-based problems in their own lives. For example, a female legislator and mother who has had difficulty securing reliable and affordable day care for her children may be more apt to recognize that a jobs program for unemployed women will not succeed unless it makes adequate provisions for child care. At the same time, female legislators may acquire policy expertise from their associative experiences with other women. Feminist organizations are particularly important in this regard, since they often act as clearinghouses for information relating to women and women's concerns.

In the interviews both female and male representatives felt that women in elected office have a better sense of how to develop and implement feminist policy as a result of their life experiences. As a Democratic congresswoman explained:

> It's just natural [for congresswomen to be more active on women's issues]. I mean, it's something we know more about, so you're inclined to work on issues you know more about.... For too many years men who have called all these shots have not ever decided for us that there should be more research for women on breast cancer, for example, or any issues that are strictly a women's health issue. And so I think that it is just that we know more about those subjects and have some additional sensitivity about why there have to be changes and how that change should take place.

Congressmen expressed similar sentiments:

> If you view government as an engine of social change, I think women have a better understanding of some issues that need change in this society and they should use that better understanding to the betterment of society. (Republican)

> Congresswomen learn more [about women's issues] because they are women. (Democrat)

Sex Differences in Feminist Legislative Leadership

As noted earlier, one consideration that has been lost in the debate over the impact of female officeholders on the representation of women is that gender is likely to interact with legislative institutions in ways that are not captured by conventional conceptions of political difference. For this reason, before attempting to measure the effect of women's gendered attitudes and resources, it is important to examine the roles support, commitment, awareness, and expertise play in the legislative process. In the model delineated here, it is hypothesized that because of the widely varying demands of legislative activities, gendered attitudes and resources will result in sex differences in legislative leadership on feminist issues.

A widely known, but little heeded, fact of legislative politics is that different activities demand different things from the representatives who engage in them. Among the factors that distinguish among legislative activities is the amount of attitudinal support they require. In simple terms, there are some activities representatives are willing to undertake when their support for a policy is low, others they are willing to undertake when their support for a policy is moderate, and still others they are willing to undertake only when their support for a policy is high. For example, roll call voting is one activity that does not require high levels of policy support since a legislator need only prefer a policy to its alternative to cast a vote in support of it. In contrast, activities like cosponsorship, speechmaking, and sponsorship imply high levels of policy endorsement.

A second factor that distinguishes among legislative activities is the level of commitment they require from representatives who engage in them. Legislative sponsorship, for example, is a high-commitment activity because it requires large outlays of a legislator's time and energy. Not only does the sponsor of a bill tend to play a primary role in drafting the legislation, but she or he is usually also responsible for soliciting support from other legislators in order to build a coalition that will carry the bill to passage. Alternatively, activities such as voting, cosponsorship, and, to a lesser degree, speechmaking are low-commitment activities because they require legislators to expend comparatively few resources.

A third factor that distinguishes among legislative activities is the amount of issue awareness they require. Put simply, legislators must be highly conscious of an issue of concern to the public in order to engage in certain activities, but may engage in others while relatively unaware. For example, in order to sponsor legislation, a legislator must first know that a problem requiring government attention exists. In contrast, voting requires little awareness of issues because by the time legislation has gone to the floor for a vote, a problem has already been identified and the task before legislators is simply to accept or reject a proposal for solving it. At the same time, activities such as speechmaking and cosponsorship fall somewhere between these two extremes because neither demands that a legislator initiate action on a problem and yet both activities are often undertaken before an issue has been subject to much public debate.

A final factor that distinguishes among legislative activities is the amount of policy expertise they require. As Kingdon's study of voting decisions in Congress makes clear, voting is one legislative activity that requires little substantive knowledge since representatives are able to rely on cues from a variety of sources when making their voting decisions.[12] In contrast, legislators must be relatively well informed to sponsor a bill and guide it through the legislative process. Other activities such as cosponsorship and speechmaking require legislators to be reasonably informed, but do not demand that they be experts.

Given these systematic differences in the attitudinal and resource burdens imposed by legislative activities, and given the expectations about sex differences in attitudes and resources discussed earlier, the potential consequences of gender in representative institutions are now readily apparent. Specifically, activities that require the greatest amount of support for, commitment to, awareness of, and expertise on women's issues should elicit the largest sex differences, while activities that require the least amount of support, commitment, awareness, and expertise should elicit the smallest differences. By taking a look at some of the most common legislative activities and the attitudinal and resource demands each imposes, several clear predictions for sex differences in feminist legislative behavior emerge. As shown in table 3, when activities are ranked according to predicted sex differences, the resulting order of magnitude is as follows: roll call voting (smallest), cosponsorship, speechmaking, and sponsorship (largest).

In light of these predictions, conceptualizing difference in feminist terms appears to mean more than simply thinking of female legislators as more feminist in orientation than men. It also means thinking of women as leaders on

TABLE 3.   **Predicted Sex Differences by Activity Type: Feminist Legislative Leadership**

Activity Requirements	Roll Call Voting	Co-Sponsorship	Speeches	Sponsorship
Support	Moderate	High	High	High
Commitment	Low	Low	Moderate	High
Awareness	Low	Low	Moderate	High
Expertise	Low	Low	Moderate	High
Predicted Sex Differences	Small	Small/Medium	Medium	Large

feminist issues—the people who assume responsibility for shaping the legislative agenda and doing the work necessary to get feminist policies enacted into law. From this perspective, the reason previous studies of sex differences in governance failed to uncover compelling evidence of female legislators' impact on politics is because they relied on roll call voting—the indicator theoretically associated with the least dramatic aspect of gendered representation.

Measuring Difference

Assessing the influence of sex on feminist legislative behavior is a difficult task. Like most political terms, the feminist label refers to a highly subjective and mutable concept that shifts in meaning depending on how and by whom it is used. While few would deny that in general feminism seeks to advance the well-being of women, there are conflicting notions about what constitutes women's welfare and about how that welfare can be best advanced. Thus, researchers on this topic confront an inescapable tension between the need to specify *feminist* for purposes of measurement and the desire to define feminist in a manner that is reflective of the full diversity of attitudes that the term represents. If we say, on the one hand, that feminism consists of all efforts to advance women's well-being, the concept in its broadness may cease to be meaningful. But if, on the other hand, we equate feminism with a particular set of policies, then our definition may speak to the interests and politics of a few stereotypical women rather than to us all.

Sadly, there is no satisfactory resolution to this dilemma. My own admittedly imperfect answer was to employ a definition of feminist that is consistent with liberal feminism, the most common form of feminism in American politics and the version most strongly associated with such groups as the NWPC and the National Organization for Women (NOW). Under this definition, legislators' behaviors were defined as feminist if their primary purpose was to promote the well-being of women through one or more of the following: eliminating discrimination on the basis of sex, redressing grievances of women who have suffered discrimination on the basis of sex, addressing needs arising from women's unique physiologies or socioeconomic conditions, or achieving public recognition of women's contributions to society.

The major advantage of this definition is sufficient precision to permit meaningful measurement while still capturing a significant number of the activities found under the broadest interpretation of the feminist label. The major disadvantage is its reliance upon a form of feminism long criticized for its white, upper-middle-class, and heterosexual biases. Though some will no doubt argue that this compromise exacts too great a price in representativeness, my own sense is that the definition sacrifices little generalizability not already relinquished by the decision to study legislative behavior in the first place. After all, legislatures are not themselves bastions of diversity. There are very few nonwhite, non-upper-middle-class, or openly homosexual representatives, and, as rare as it is to hear feminist demands in government, it is even rarer to find a form of feminism in these bodies that falls outside traditional liberal feminist bounds. The definition adopted here, then, subtracts only incrementally from the present low variance within the institution.

The locus of this study was the U.S. House of Representatives during the 101st Congress (1989–90) . The sample included all twenty-four women and a matched group of twenty-four men who served in the House during this entire period. The matching procedure selected those men who shared the same party, seniority, and ideology as the women.[13] When possible, men were also paired with women on the basis of region and age. The purpose of using a matched sample was to measure the independent effect of sex on feminist legislative leadership. In accordance with the typology developed earlier, four types of legislative activities were examined: feminist roll call voting, feminist speechmaking, feminist cosponsorship, and feminist sponsorship.

Findings

The first dependent variable I examined was feminist roll call voting. The votes included in this measure were drawn from the NWPC's *Voting Record on Women's Issues* for the 101st Congress. Of the twenty-four votes included in the *Record* seventeen fit the definition of feminist outlined above and were incorporated into the feminist voting index. For each legislator, the value of the roll call voting variable was equivalent to the percentage of all the votes she or he cast on women's issues that were feminist.

As in previous research, there was a measurable sex disparity in the voting behavior of the representatives. Seventy-seven percent of the votes congresswomen cast on the seventeen issues were feminist, compared with 70 percent of the votes cast by the congressmen. In accordance with predictions, however, this difference was far from large, equivalent to about one more feminist vote per congresswoman, indicating that sex is not a major determinant of roll call voting on women's issues. In addition, party was a better predictor of feminist voting than sex, with 78 percent of the Democrats' votes being feminist compared to just 65 percent of the Republicans' votes.

The second variable I examined was feminist bill cosponsorship. Bills were coded as feminist if they sought to improve the position of women in society by eliminating discrimination on the basis of sex; compensating women who have suffered discrimination on the basis of sex; addressing needs arising from women's unique physiologies and/or socioeconomic conditions; or formally recognizing women's contributions to society. The value of the cosponsorship variable for each legislator was the percentage of the total legislation she or he cosponsorerd that was feminist.

All told, the congresswomen cosponsored legislation 11,962 times. Of these instances, 1,088 (9 percent) involved feminist bills. In contrast, the congressmen signed their names to legislation 9,541 times, and of these cases, 569 (6 percent) involved feminist bills. Since in practical terms this difference amounts to about 23 more pieces of feminist legislation per congresswoman, legislative cosponsorship is clearly an area in which the behavior of women and men in Congress is substantially different. Moreover, sex was a more important determinant of cosponsorship than partisanship, which had no discernible impact on the dependent variable; both Democrats and Republicans dedicated about 10 percent of their cosponsorship activity to feminist bills.

The third dependent variable I examined was feminist speeches on the floor of the House. Sex differences in this area were also highly pronounced. Speeches were coded as feminist if they supported feminist legislation; opposed legislation specifically identified by the NWPC as adverse to the advancement of women; called attention to problems of particular concern to women; or recognized women's contributions to society. The value of the speech variable for each legislator was the percentage of speeches she or he made within Congress that were feminist.

Of the 2,841 speeches given by the congresswomen, 241 were feminist. During the same period, congressmen gave 1,941 speeches of which 81 were feminist. This means that on average the women gave about 6 more feminist speeches per person than did their male counterparts. As with feminist cosponsorship, the effect of sex on feminist speechmaking was greater than the effect of party, which accounted for less than a 1 percent difference between members. On average, about 8 percent of the speeches given by both Democrats and Republicans were feminist.

Sponsorship of feminist legislation was the final dependent variable, and was measured in the same manner as the cosponsorship variable. Overall, the congresswomen sponsored legislation 582 times, and in 69 of these instances the legislation they sponsored was feminist. In contrast, the congressmen sponsored legislation 328 times, and in only 6 of these instances did the legislation fall into the feminist category. In practical terms, this means that female members sponsored about 2 more pieces of feminist legislation per person than did the congressmen. As with feminist speechmaking and bill cosponsorship, feminist bill sponsorship variation by party was almost imperceptible; both Democrats and Republicans spent about 11 percent of their sponsorship activity on feminist bills.

TABLE 4.   Sex Distribution by Feminist Activity Type

Feminist Activities	Women	Men	Totals
Roll Call Votes	52%	48%	100%
Co-Sponsors	66%	34%	100%
Speeches	75%	25%	100%
Sponsors	92%	8%	100%

In order to determine whether these sex differences varied in magnitude depending on the types of activities in which the representatives were engaged, I compared the sex distributions of different feminist activities. As shown in table 4, the gap between women's and men's feminist legislative involvement increased consistently in the predicted direction: the greater the attitudinal and resource demands imposed by an activity, the larger the sex disparity. While in this study women cast just over half of the feminist votes, they constituted 66 percent of the cosponsors of feminist legislation, 75 percent of the profeminist speakers, and 92 percent of the sponsors of feminist legislation. This finding conforms closely to the model of feminist legislative leadership developed earlier. Although not definitive, the results are consistent with an interpretation that posits heightened support, commitment, awareness, and expertise among female members of Congress as primary determinants of sex disparities in feminist legislative leadership. While congressmen are not averse to feminist policies, congresswomen provide the bulk of the leadership on feminist issues.

Discussion

And so it appears that feminists were right to trust their political instincts, ignore the dictates of conventional wisdom, and abide the lessons of their own experience, for the women serving in public office today are significantly altering the content of legislative decisionmaking. While only slightly more inclined than their male counterparts to favor feminist legislation, congresswomen are considerably more likely to introduce it into congressional deliberation, affirm it with their signed endorsements, and promote it with their speeches. Accordingly, the most important distinction to be made about female and male members of Congress lies less in their desire to enact feminist policies than in their willingness and ability to initiate and guide those policies through the legislative process. Simply put, congresswomen tend to be leaders in feminist policy and congressmen do not.

No doubt these findings come as little surprise to those activists whose hard work on the front lines of the feminist movement made recent gains by women in the political arena possible. As their toils supposed, increasing the number of women in public office is an effective strategy for achieving greater representation of women's interests in governance. Moreover, the electoral efforts of women's groups are likely to have a greater effect on the representation of women's interests than would electing more Democrats alone, since as a group Republicans are no less likely than Democrats to provide leadership on women's issues.

Still, it would be a mistake to conclude on the basis of these data that only women are willing and able to represent women's interests in politics. Although living as a woman seems to provide a decided advantage in the representative process, men do not appear to be irretrievable captives of their experiences. This study, like others, found only a small difference in the roll call voting of female and male members on feminist issues, indicating that as a group congressmen are not hostile to policies for women. Whether this has come about because of the consciousness-raising efforts of female legislators and women's organizations, reelection pressures, or because male legislators have made an effort to understand and empathize with women's lives—or both—it is a reassuring sign that there is no unbridgeable disjunction between experience as a man and the representation of women. Thus, encouraging and helping men to become better representatives of women's interests is as useful a project as taking advantage of women's natural insights and proclivities in the representative process.

At the same time, it is important to note that living as a woman is not enough by itself to induce feminist legislative activism. Although as a group congresswomen are more feminist in orientation than congressmen, as individuals they are occasionally less supportive of feminist policies. Indeed, in this study the representative with the least feminist roll call voting record (0 percent votes feminist) was a woman. Hence, in addition to working to increase the number of women serving in public office, feminist organizations should continue to encourage those aspects of women's experiences that are likely to heighten activism on women's concerns. In particular, this research suggests that feminist organizations can increase legislative leadership on feminist issues by providing a means for female legislators to learn about the experiences of other women. Not only is such information likely to bolster women's support for and commitment to feminist causes by highlighting the extent and severity of women's oppression, but information from feminist organizations is also likely to impart the policy awareness and expertise that make legislative initiative possible.

Although the finding of large sex differences in feminist legislative leadership reported here is an important one, it is not the only major result of this study. Perhaps even more significant is the discovery that sex differences in legislative leadership were overlooked by researchers for so long. That time and time again feminists studying legislative bodies failed to investigate or document women's leadership roles says a great deal about the need for empirical work on gender and politics that is as feminist in theory and method as it is in intent. As this study demonstrates, deploying feminist theory in our observational studies affords the great advantage of allowing us to break out of dominant paradigms that may obscure gender's political consequences. Here, reliance on feminist standpoint theory facilitated the identification of measures of difference in Congress that were much better equipped than roll call voting to capture the contributions congresswomen are making to the representation of women's interests. Only through exploring the specific attitudinal and resource consequences of women's unique standpoints was I able to determine that large and meaningful sex differences in feminist behavior are more likely to be educed by highly demanding legislative activities, such as feminist bill sponsorship, than by less demanding activities, such as feminist roll call voting.

Admittedly, since in its current form much theoretical work is insufficiently specified for purposes of measurement, firmly grounding our empirical studies in feminist theory can be a messy and time-consuming process. Nonetheless, it would be a mistake to view its alternative as carrying fewer costs. Without such theoretical guidance, we will continue to resort to the very same methods and concepts that have historically rendered women politically "invisible" thereby perpetuating the invisibility.[14]

Despite the methodological shortcomings of earlier studies, however, feminist scholars ultimately bear little if any of the responsibility for the failure of contemporary political science to recognize the representational consequences of gender. To the contrary, that blame rests squarely with the political discourse that disappeared women in the first place, a discourse that even today perpetuates an artificial bifurcation between representatives' public and private lives. Under this vision of the political, women's legislative contributions have remained obscured because they originate in places outside the designated realm of politics: in women's bodies, in women's experiences, in women's identities, and in women's relationships. With no space for private lives in its conceptual framework, masculinized political science neither discerns nor appreciates the power of gender.

Conclusion

These findings result in two major conclusions that tell us about the broader relationship between gender and leadership in a governmental setting. First, contrary to conventional political wisdom, the power of gender is not restricted to a single, symbolic level of influence. At the same time that the sex composition of government serves as an important sign of women's and men's relative political power, the gendered political attitudes and resources of public officials condition institutional responses to women's concerns. While here we have only

seen empirical evidence of gender power in one domain—legislative politics—the underlying dynamic should operate in much the same way everywhere
government officials are in a position to shape the direction and content of public
policy.

Second, leadership, far from being the ungendered activity envisioned by
many standard political-science texts, is in fact a primary locus of gender power.
By motivating and facilitating political involvement, gender is a primary determinant of the types of issues around which leadership will successfully emerge.
For this reason, all scholars interested in the study of leadership are well advised
to consider the power of gender (and its concomitant, sex) in their own research.

Notes

1. Center for the American Woman and Politics, *Fact Sheet: Women in Elective Office 1993* (New Brunswick, N.J.: Eagleton Institute of Politics, Rutgers University, 1993).
2. Hanna F. Pitkin, *The Concept of Representation* (Berkeley and Los Angeles: University of California Press, 1967).
3. Joyce Purnick, "Women Stereotyping Women: The Risky Business of Gender Politics," *New York Times,* July 11, 1990, A16.
4. Bill Stahl, "Seymour Makes a Pitch to Women Voters," *Los Angeles Times,* July 8, 1992, A3.
5. Frieda L. Gehlen, "Women Members of Congress: A Distinctive Role," in *A Portrait of Marginality,* ed. Marianne Githens and Jewell Prestage (New York: McKay, 1977); Sheila Gilbert Leader, "The Policy Impact of Elected Women Officials," in *The Impact of the Electoral Process,* ed. Louis Maisel and Joseph Cooper (Beverly Hills, Calif.: Sage Publications, 1977); David Hill, "Women State Legislators and Party Voting on the E.R.A.," *Social Science Quarterly* 64 (1982): 318–26; Janet A. Flammang, "Female Officials in the Feminist Capital: The Case of Santa Clara County," *Western Political Quarterly* 38 (1985): 94–118; Sue Thomas, "Voting Patterns in the California Assembly: The Role of Gender, *Women and Politics* 9 (1989): 43–53; Samantha L. Durst and Ryan W. Rusek, "Different Genders, Different Votes? An Examination of Voting Behavior in the U.S. House of Representatives," paper presented at the annual meeting of the American Political Science Association, Washington, D.C., September 2–5, 1993.
6. Thomas, "Voting Patterns."
7. Kathleen B. Jones and Anna G. Jonasdottir, eds., *The Political Interests of Gender: Developing Theory and Research with a Feminist Face* (London: Sage Publications, 1988).
8. Ibid.
9. Sixteen interviews (nine with women and seven with men) were conducted in person during May, June, and July 1991. The sessions ranged in length from fifteen minutes to one hour, and, because of members' time limitations, not all questions were asked in every interview. To encourage members to speak freely about their attitudes and activities, respondents were promised anonymity and the sessions were recorded with written notes (taken during and immediately following the interviews) rather than with a tape recorder.
10. *Congressional Record* (1993), vol. 139, no. 12.
11. Ibid.
12. John W. Kingdon, *Congressmen's Voting Decisions,* 3d ed. (Ann Arbor: University of Michigan Press, 1989).

13. Ideology was measured with rankings from the Americans for Democratic Action (ADA) and the American Conservative Union (ACU) for 1987, 1988, and 1989.
14. Jones and Jonasdottir, *Political Interests of Gender.*

Part 3: Gender as a Property: Institutional Sexism and Gendered Organizational Analysis

Attributing masculinity/femininity—gender—to behaviors, physical entities, or roles is not uncommon in human discourse. Less commonly, we say that organizations or concepts have gendered aspects, and, even more seldomly, we analyze them as gendered. In part 3 the gendered nature of political organizations is explicitly analyzed. Institutional sexism is contrasted with a gendered organizational analysis. The grounding of the former in the sex-difference literature and conceptual frame of reference contributes to its narrowing of research foci. The latter incorporates insights of institutional sexism—acknowledging that men control most institutional resources and establish practices that reinforce that control—but moves beyond to reveal how this emphasis of the social sciences blinds us to a broader sociopolitical reality.

Noelle Norton, in "Women, It's Not Enough to Be Elected: Committee Position Makes a Difference," begins by documenting the institutional sexism of the legislative committee structure to the detriment of women's influence on reproductive policy. That is, sexism is institutionalized to keep women from addressing issues of tremendous importance to women. She then expands analysis of organizational power structures and joins it with a gendered organizational analysis enabling her to track how gender power impacts national U.S. reproductive policies. She demonstrates how the existing gender power arrangements of Congress's organizational structure interacts with masculinist ideology and the dominance of men in the legislative hierarchy to stymie women's efforts to exert leadership on policies vitally important to all women.

Meredith Newman in "The Gendered Nature of Lowi's Typology: Or Who Would Guess You Could Find Gender Here?" explores how the gendered nature of the U.S. economy carries over to the public bureaucracies and, most importantly, to our common understandings of how various policy agencies work. By examining the unspoken, but highly gendered, nature of explanations of variations across policy areas, Newman reveals the depth of masculinist influence on our thinking. Scholars who employ the common policy typology have apparently never noticed the correspondence between patterns of conflict, centralized control, claims of universal or specific benefits, and the gender of clientele and top managers. Newman shows the gendered opportunity structure of agencies through sex differences in pay, positional power, autonomy, conflict, and access that reflect wide gender power differentials.

Both Norton and Newman advance our knowledge of how gender power is embedded in the reality of governance and leadership, providing insights not only into how and where power differentials between men and women exist, but also into the way gender power influences and masks how we understand why these differentials exist.

Chapter 5

Women, It's Not Enough to Be Elected: Committee Position Makes a Difference

Noelle Norton

As more women are elected to political office each year, questions about whether women legislators can change public policy to improve the lives of individual women and to enhance perceptions of women's roles become increasingly important. Although recent empirical research indicates that women legislators are more interested in working on legislation concerning women, children, and the family than their male counterparts,[1] their election to public office does not guarantee their influence over policies that differentially affect the genders. A major obstacle to their success can be found in the institutional arrangements and avenues for crafting public policy—the structure of legislative committee systems and the power of the male committee and subcommittee leaders. A thorough analysis of how institutional roadblocks influence one set of national policies concerning women demonstrates that women must gain institutional position power before they can exert any gender power over policies of importance to women.

Since national reproductive policies—abortion, family planning, pregnancy, teenage pregnancy, surrogacy, and parental leave—closely touch the identities of all women, their formation at the institutional level provides a set of excellent examples with which to analyze the power and influence of women lawmakers over the lives of women. For biological reasons, individual women have more at stake than do men on questions about reproductive-policy legislation. Reproduction also determines how women participate in society and live their lives. Babies— products of reproduction—affect a woman's social role, social construction, and self-identity. Further, how we think about women and their capacity to make reasoned decisions about important issues is symbolically reflected in national legislation. Because this legislation codifies the amount of control we as a polity are willing to grant women, it is important to consider who holds the power to make policies with such differentially gendered effects on daily life, liberty, and happiness. Here I consider the implications of gender power at the institutional level, with a focus on the intersection of individual legislators and the institution of Congress at a policy type, reproductive policy, that affects both individual women and the symbolic construction of woman. The fact that empirical research shows women legislators have identified reproductive policies to be among those of special importance to female lawmakers makes the use of these examples even more compelling.[2]

Although women legislators have vocalized their interest in and support for various reproductive policies crafted by the United States Congress over the past two decades, these lawmakers rarely hold positions enabling them to participate in drafting the final legislation. To fully understand the lack of influence individual women lawmakers have over these policies, we must understand how the ability to design controversial national reproductive policies heavily depends upon an individual's specific institutional position in Congress. Then, we must consider whether women lawmakers have ever held the appropriate institutional position to make a significant policy difference: that is, whether they have been able to write a policy in subcommittee before it reaches the floor, amend a policy at a full committee meeting, manage a bill on the floor as a key member of the subcommittee, offer amendments on the floor without facing a series of restrictive amending rules attached by committee chairs, and exercise influence in the interchamber conference committee meetings between the House and the Senate. The institution selected for analysis is the United States House of Representatives because the House and its committee system are often used to describe the common functioning of democratic legislatures. A large part of the empirical research on the effects institutional position and structure have on policymaking comes from data collected about the House of Representatives. Thus, lessons learned about congressional avenues for influencing reproductive policies can be used to understand the avenues other democratic institutions follow for handling similar policies.

This chapter has been divided into three sections, all leading to the conclusion that if women do not sit on the committees with jurisdiction over reproductive policy, their influence in this area will probably not be significant. First, the importance of holding key committee positions in Congress will be examined. Although legislative scholars are involved in an ongoing debate about whether committee position confers more influence over policy than does non–committee membership, evidence will be presented showing that sitting on a committee is crucial for those interested in influencing reproductive policy. Second, once the importance of committee position has been established, the committee seats women legislators have held giving them jurisdiction over reproductive policy will be detailed. The scant number of women holding positions enabling them to make a difference over the past two decades is significant. Finally, a review of the scope of our national reproductive policy, which has been crafted primarily by a set of male congressional leaders with jurisdiction over reproductive policy, will be presented. The consequence of having male lawmakers with the institutional power and resources, but without the same kind of vested interest or dedication that women have, is apparent when we examine the current condition of our national reproductive policies, which are considered by many to be in disarray and focused almost entirely on restrictions of abortion funding. This study points to the probability that women lawmakers, who are more interested in these policies, might make a difference if they obtain institutional avenues to change women's lives.

Although avenues to influence legislation have been opening for women lawmakers, opportunities for formal leadership positions remain limited. Because of stereotypes and expectations about the roles women should play in society, women legislators have had difficulty gaining respect as political candidates and as policymakers.[3] Even though women candidates made tremendous strides by running for office in record numbers and winning in the 1990 election,[4] recent research on candidate evaluations shows that gender role attitudes still make a difference in the assessment of the skills of women candidates.[5]

As women legislators' numbers and seniority have grown inside legislative institutions, we have seen that their participation and success in individual and coalitional efforts to sponsor legislation of interest to women have increased.[6] Yet to see women holding the critical institutional positions of power is still rare, and for women to accumulate power and resources when those who have power are not willing to relinquish it remains difficult. To be able to exercise political leadership effectively, the use of both institutional and individual resources is important.[7] Thus, regardless of numerical representation, until women legislators obtain institutional power, their ability to make a difference will remain circumscribed.

Committee Power

In June 1993, yet another heated battle over the congressional restriction of Medicaid-funded abortions was fought on the floor of the House of Representatives. Concerned legislators, including some of the freshman women from the new 103d Congress, engaged in an unusually bitter debate with a contingent of abortion opponents led by Henry Hyde (R-Ill.), one of the original authors of the policy.[8] Despite passionate oratory from a group of women in coalition, the apparent preferences of the floor activists, the floor majority, and the president were set aside in favor of the policy preferred by the Appropriations Committee. Although the president's budget did not include the seventeen-year-old restrictions on Medicaid-funded abortions, the Appropriations Committee included these restrictions in their policy design for fiscal year 1994, and they were ultimately approved by the entire House. Frustrated with the maneuvering of the Appropriations Committee over this policy, Patricia Schroeder (D-Colo.), one of the floor activists, declared, "They changed the rules and left us hanging out there."[9]

This example reveals the power of a congressional committee to draft legislation despite the appearance that any representative can draft these policies on the floor. The twenty-three-year reproductive-rights debate on the floor of the House of Representatives has often been characterized as the most volatile and emotionally charged that members have faced in the modern Congress. The contentious floor debates and highly publicized floor amendments over these issues have helped fuel arguments that policymaking is no longer controlled by the once-powerful congressional standing committees. Many have argued that national issues such as abortion have encouraged participation by members of Congress on the House floor, where visibility is paramount, instead of in committee, where participation is more difficult to trace. Yet a thorough analysis of the way the House handles reproductive policies indicates that decisions about these volatile policies are not made primarily through floor amending activity, but rather remain for the most part within the purview of the committees of jurisdiction.

Measuring Floor Power

A superficial analysis of reproductive-policy floor amending over the years initially suggests that these policies provide a perfect example of the breakdown of the traditional institutional committee structure of the House. Three indicators of floor power suggest that committee position *may not* be important for those interested in designing reproductive policies.[10] First, a sample of reproductive-policy floor amendments made between 1973 and 1992 shows that there is a flurry of reproductive-policy amending on the House floor every time the abortion issue captures national attention,[11] which might indicate that our representatives draft this legislation on floor. For example, after the announcement of Supreme Court decisions in *Roe v. Wade*[12] and *Webster v. Reproductive Health Services,*[13] reproductive-policy floor amending activity increased substantially from previous years.[14] Because floor activity increases when these policies become publicly salient, this suggests that committees with jurisdiction may have little control over their own agendas. Second, bill managers from the subcommittee have not always been successful in fending off unwanted amendments. In fact, 50 percent of the reproductive-policy amendments opposed by the bill manager were successful, indicating that bill managers are not able to stop unfriendly reproductive-policy amendments.[15] Finally, a majority of reproductive-policy floor amendments have typically been made by representatives who do not hold seats on the committees with jurisdiction over that policy. In twenty years, non–committee members have offered 55 percent of all reproductive-policy actions. Moreover, there is evidence that non–committee member floor amendments have been more successful than have committee and subcommittee member amendments, indicating that committee members with jurisdiction are not always shown respect on the floor when reproductive policy questions are under consideration.[16]

These three indicators all point to a lack of committee influence over crafting reproductive policy. The depiction of committees as successful on the floor or even as central to policy outcomes[17] appears not to apply. Instead, the depictions of committees with eroded influence on the floor appear to provide more accurate descriptions.[18] This evidence suggests that committee position is not necessarily an important resource for women legislators attempting to make a difference in policy outcomes. If this is true, women legislators could develop their individual influence to draft legislation on the floor rather than fight for the appropriate committee positions.

Looking at Committee Power—Policy Origins and Floor Activists

Under more careful examination, however, it becomes apparent that committees and subcommittees do retain control over these policies, despite evidence of contentious floor debates and numerous floor amendments. Counting floor amendments and the success rates of bill managers provides only snapshots of reproductive policymaking and tells us nothing about the scope of institutional-position power. An alternative methodological approach that identifies the origin of key policy provisions and the specific identities of members of Congress involved in floor activity provides a more complete picture. The more in-depth approach I introduce shows that only a small percentage of reproductive policies designed in subcommittee either fail or are rewritten by the floor and remain unchanged by the conference committee. Moreover, this approach shows that a majority of all the floor activity comes from a very exclusive set of representatives who for the most part hold key congressional committee positions.

The first step in a more thorough analysis of reproductive policymaking includes tracing the origins of reproductive-policy legislation throughout the entire policymaking process. We need to find out where the final version of national reproductive-policy legislation actually originates—inside committees, on the floor, or in the conference committee. I use a sample of 126 bills,[19] identified as containing significant reproductive policies that originated between 1969 and 1992, to trace the origins of this legislation. Several sources were used to identify the origins of the final version of each of these reproductive policies.

First, summaries of the progression of the legislation through the House are provided by the *Congressional Quarterly Almanac*. These summaries gave the initial indication of where each policy provision originated. Second, the progression of legislation reported by the *Congressional Quarterly Almanac* was verified with the following set of primary sources: minutes from full-committee markup meetings;[20] the Committee on Rules' Legislative Calendars; floor debates from the *Congressional Record;* conference reports; and debates over conference reports from the *Congressional Record,* 1969–92.

When the results of activity are recorded at each portion of the policymaking process, it is relatively simple to pinpoint where an idea originated and garnered support. As the origin of a reproductive policy was identified, a code was assigned indicating which panel was responsible for the policy approach. The outcomes of both successful and unsuccessful legislation were coded as originating in one of the following House locations: the subcommittee/committee, the floor, or the conference committee.[21]

The analysis presented in table 5 indicates that only 16.7 percent (21 out of 126) of all House reproductive-policy legislation originated from the floor, while a total of 83.3 percent (105 out of 126) originated from subcommittees and committee activity at some point in the process. Furthermore, table 5 also

TABLE 5.   Origin of Reproductive Policy Legislation, 1969–92

Origin	% of Bills	Number of Bills
House floor design:	16.7	21
Successful (passed)		
Designed or killed on floor	11.9	15
Unsuccessful (not passed)		
Designed on floor, died after passage	4.8	6
Subcommittee/committee design:	83.3	105
Successful (passed):		
Subcommittee/committee design	34.1	43
Conference committee design	11.1	14
Unsuccessful (not passed):		
Stalled in committee	16.7	21
Died after floor passage	4.8	6
Vetoed by president	16.7	21

Sources: Congressional Record, 1969–92; *Congressional Quarterly Almanac,* 1969–91; *Congressional Quarterly Weekly,* 1992; Committee meeting minutes from Appropriations, Energy and Commerce, Judiciary, and Education and Labor Committees, 1975–92; Conference Committee Reports, 1973–92.
Note: Total $N = 126$.

shows that, of the 16.7 percent influenced by the floor in two decades, only 11.9 percent (15 out of 126) became law. Included in the 83.3 percent influenced by committees are policies that originated in the following House locations: 34.1 percent of the legislation was crafted by subcommittees and committees and successfully passed in the form it was originally designed;[22] 11.1 percent of the legislation was passed into law as committee-preferred compromises designed by a conference committee comprised almost entirely of subcommittee members;[23] 16.7 percent of the legislation was retained by the committees and never reached the House floor; another 16.7 percent of the legislation, although originally designed by subcommittees and committees, was vetoed by the president; and finally, 4.8 percent of the legislation, also originally designed by the subcommittees and committees, was killed by the Senate. Although committees are not always successful, these findings show that a substantial majority of reproductive-policy legislation was designed by the committee and subcommittee of jurisdiction.

Further, committees have also held responsibility for a substantial majority of the successful reproductive policies. The floor has been responsible for 21 percent (15 out of 72) of the reproductive policies passed into law, while the committees have been responsible for 79 percent (57 out of 72) of the policies passed into law. Table 5 provides a breakdown of the origin of both successful and unsuccessful policies under analysis.

Specific examples of committee and subcommittee involvement in the original design and support of reproductive policies abound. The Hyde amendment, prohibiting the use of federal Medicaid funds for abortion except when the mother's life was endangered, is perhaps the most controversial and important piece of federal legislative reproductive policy. Many might argue that the Hyde amendment provides a perfect example of floor power. Representative Henry Hyde offered an amendment to the Labor, Health, Education, and Welfare (LHEW) appropriations spending bill for fiscal year 1977. Hyde was not a member of the Appropriations Committee, and his amendment, which was offered on the floor in 1976, passed and has been attached to all Labor, Health, Education, and Welfare bills (Labor Health, Human Services, and Education after 1980) in one version or another since 1976. It appears that the Hyde amendment exemplifies noncommittee floor amending activity.

The story rarely told, however, is that the Labor, Health, Human Services, and Education subcommittee chairs and their Appropriations Committee chairs have always supported and actually fought for the language initially written by Representative Hyde. After the first amendment in 1976, the language of the Hyde amendment has been initiated, supported, and encouraged in the subcommittee.[24] Review of full-committee markup minutes and debate in the *Congressional Record* indicates that the two subcommittee leaders in charge of this legislation for the past 20 years, Daniel Flood (D-Pa.) and William Natcher (D-Ky.), supported the restrictive abortion language because of personal conviction. Even between 1989 and 1992, when a floor majority favored loosening of the restrictive language, Natcher and Jamie Whitten (D-Mo.), the Appropriations Committee chair, were both reluctant to fight for the more liberal language allowing Medicaid-funded abortions for victims of rape and incest. Furthermore, few realize that the actual language used for the Hyde amendment was designed by a LHEW subcommittee member.[25] Congress member Silvio Conte offered the language we are all familiar with during the conference committee meeting. The House ultimately accepted Conte's language, not Hyde's.

The second step in a more thorough analysis of reproductive policymaking includes identification of those who attempted to change reproductive policy from the floor. Although a majority of representatives attempting floor amendments are non–committee members, a more in-depth analysis of the floor amending activity[26] shows that a large percentage of these noncommittee members actually sit on another House subcommittee with jurisdiction over other kinds of reproductive policies.[27] These findings imply that committee members can anticipate participation from certain members with similar institutional positions.

During the entire period of floor activity studied, approximately 45 percent of all floor action was conducted by committee and subcommittee members with specific jurisdiction over some kind of reproductive policy; 27 percent of the amendments were made by members with subcommittee jurisdiction over other kinds of reproductive policies; and only 29 percent were made by noncommittee members who had no other reproductive-policy committee assignments. Thus, 71 percent of the floor action comes from authors who hold key reproductive-policy institutional positions. Table 6 emphasizes the decline of activity by non–committee members over the years and the increase in activity by committee members and members from other subcommittees with similar jurisdictions. By 1992, only 7 percent of the floor action was sponsored by non–committee members. Henry Hyde, for example, has been a member of the Judiciary's Subcommittee on Civil and Constitutional Rights. When Hyde was not able to convince his subcommittee to sponsor a human-life constitutional amendment that would prohibit abortions, he took action by sponsoring the Appropriations spending limitation amendment restricting the use of federal Medicaid funds for abortions. Like Hyde, a substantial number of the noncommittee activists actually serve on other subcommittees with important jurisdiction over reproductive-policy legislation.

Because congressional rules specify that the Rules Committee and committee leaders together have the authority to design restrictive rules allowing floor amendments from predetermined authors, the ability for non–committee

TABLE 6. Type of Author for Reproductive-Policy Floor Actions, 1973–92

Congresses	Committee[a]		Jurisdiction[b]		Non–committee[c]	
	Number of Actions	%	Number of Actions	%	Number of Actions	%
93rd and 94th (1973–76)	1	8.3	7	58.3	4	33.3
95th and 96th (1977–80)	18	45.0	8	20.0	14	35.0
97th and 98th (1981–84)	5	35.7	2	14.3	7	50.0
99th and 100th (1985–88)	11	57.9	3	15.8	5	26.3
101st and 102nd (1989–92)	15	55.6	10	37.0	2	7.4

Source: Congressional Record, 1969–92.
[a]Includes actions taken by standing-committee members.
[b]Includes actions taken by non–committee members who have similar reproductive-policy jurisdiction on other committees.
[c]Includes actions by non–committee members and members without reproductive-policy jurisdiction on another committee.

members to make change is further circumscribed by rules and structures.[28] This may explain why, despite their interest, women legislators, without committee position, are not seen among the names of reproductive-policy floor activists. A substantial number of all floor actions are done by a small group of males who are often given avenues for amendment and policy change on the floor by the committee leaders with reproductive-policy jurisdiction. Forty-three percent of *all* amending activity on the floor was done by six individuals between 1973 and 1992: Chris Smith (R-N.J.), Robert Dornan (R-Calif.), William Dannemeyer (R-Calif.), John Ashbrook (R-Calif.), Robert Bauman (R-Md.), and Mark Siljander (R-Mich.). Furthermore, the non–committee members who were able to make amendments on the floor are comprised of an even more exclusive group of male legislators. Seventy percent of all amending activity done by the non–committee members was done by four individuals: Chris Smith, Robert Dornan, Robert Bauman, and Mark Siljander. This evidence implies that committee leaders have the ability to grant floor access to whomever they chose through prefloor bargains and that women legislators have not been among those floor activists granted exclusive access—a clear indicator of their lack of institutional gender power.

Overall, these findings provide a more satisfactory explanation for the apparent increase in floor activity than findings that count only levels of committee and noncommittee amending activity. These results also help corroborate research by legislative scholars who argue that subcommittee membership provides influence to members of Congress.[29] A majority of the amending comes from subcommittee members with some kind of jurisdiction over the reproductive policy under debate or from floor activists who are granted floor access by the committee and/or subcommittee leaders. These results emphasize the conclusion that committees have significant influence over reproductive policy at various stages of the legislative process.

The ability of committee leaders to dominate both committee and floor reproductive-policy activity shows the pervasive control male gender power has at the institutional level over women's lives and over national policies that help create our images of woman. In the next section, we will consider the limited influence women legislators have had over these policies at the institutional level in the House of Representatives. If the locus of power shifted and more women had power to grant access and support for the design of reproductive-policy legislation, it is difficult to imagine that reproductive policies would not change in some fashion to reflect the vested interests of women, regardless of how varied those interests might be.

Women Legislators' Access to Position Power

What opportunities have women legislators had to make change in reproductive-policy legislation? Evidence to be presented here suggests that women legislators have not had the opportunity to significantly develop reproductive policies because they do not hold the leadership or committee positions enabling them to make change. Since we have seen that a substantial majority of reproductive policies are designed inside committees and floor amending is dominated by representatives with committee jurisdiction over reproductive policy, holding the appropriate committee positions is crucial for those interested in making change. Although there have always been opportunities for participation in contentious floor debates, avenues for crafting these policies are limited to those sitting in the right position. Much of the floor activity is meaningless, while the real action is conducted inside standing committees, the Rules Committee, and conference committees by the legislative leaders who are least affected by gendered policy outcomes. It is important to emphasize that evidence regarding the lack of participation by women legislators helps to illustrate how differential institutional power ultimately leads to differential gender power.

Women legislators have demonstrated their keen interest in forming national reproductive-policy legislation by their involvement in informal coalitions seeking change, membership in the Congressional Caucus on Women's Issues, sponsorship of legislation, and participation in floor debate. For example, some of the most passionate floor speeches on these issues over 23 years have come from women legislators such as Bella Abzug (D-N.Y.), Shirley Chisholm (D-N.Y.), Cardiss Collins (D-Ill.), Marge Roukema (R-Md.), Patricia Schroeder (D-Colo.) and Barbara Boxer (D-Calif.). Although these individual and coalition efforts are important, the sponsorship of legislation and participation in floor debate does not necessarily indicate an ability to influence the passage of legislation throughout the complex bill-making process. As noted, the freshman women legislators of the 103d Congress who attempted to remove the Appropriation Committee's Medicaid abortion-funding restrictions quickly found that floor debates did not lead to policy change. After the vote on continuance of the restrictions passed, Corinne Brown (D-Fla.) said, "It's still all white men in blue suits that know what's best."[30] Clearly, Brown's implication is that those with the institutional resources and power are still able to make policy decisions despite the fact that the policy does not touch their lives.

Measurement of policy influence must include an evaluation of the female legislators' involvement in all parts of the bill-making tree to be complete. We need to look at more than numerical representation and actions like bill sponsorship to see if women legislators have influence. A review of their participation in committee, subcommittee, and conference committee activity will show that women have simply not had the access to positions enabling them to influence reproductive policy. Since committees also control a substantial amount of amending on the floor,[31] the participation of women legislators has been limited to bill sponsorship and speeches that do not directly lead to alterations in policy design or to institutional power for individual women legislators. An examination of female legislators' floor amending activity will show how infrequent their floor participation has been over two decades.

First, women legislators have rarely held seats on the committees with reproductive-policy jurisdiction. Ironically, reproductive policies have been split among some of the most powerful committees in Congress, where women legislators are rarely found because they lack the prerequisites for appointment enjoyed by many male legislators—seniority and its concomitant prestige. Most of the reproductive-policy measures considered by the House floor have been handled primarily by the following House committees: Appropriations, Energy and Commerce, Judiciary, Education and Labor, Armed Services, and Foreign Affairs. Specifically, table 7 shows that nearly 60 percent of the policies were steered by the powerful Appropriations Committee and that the similarly powerful Energy and Commerce steered another 23 percent. Between 1973 and 1990, an average of five women per Congress sat on the key committees dealing with reproductive policy. The average number of women on each of these committees during this period are as follows: Appropriations, 2.1; Energy and Commerce, 1.1; Judiciary, 1.3; and Education and Labor, 1.2 (see table 7).

Moreover, a number of legislative scholars have argued that these particular committees with reproductive-policy jurisdiction continue to control their policy activity on the floor despite evidence of increased floor amending activity since the reform of Congress in the mid-1970s.[32] Therefore, an overwhelming number of reproductive policies are managed by the kind of committee that

TABLE 7.   Committee Jurisdiction over Reproductive Policies, 1969–92

Committee	Legislation under Jurisdiction ($n = 105$)[a]		Average Number of Committee Members[b]	Average Number of Womenc	% Women on Committee
	Number of Bills	%			
Appropriations	62	59.0	56	2.1	3.7
Energy and Commerce	24	22.9	42	1.1	2.6
Judiciary	5	4.8	33	1.3	3.9
Education and Labor	5	4.8			
Armed Services and Foreign Affairs	7	6.7			
Government Operations[d]	2	1.9			

Sources: Congressional Quarterly Almanac, 1969–91, Congressional Quarterly Weekly, 1992; Congressional Record, 1969–92.

  [a]Only policies considered on the House floor are included in this sample.

  [b]Average number of committee members recorded only for four committees with most important reproductive-policy jurisdiction.

  [c]Average number of women sitting on each committee, recorded only for the four committees with most important reproductive-policy jurisdiction.

  [d]Government Operations had jurisdiction over Nixon's National Commission on Population Growth.

typically commands respect on the floor and utilizes strategies at all parts of the bill-making process to usher through its version of the legislation.[33] It is unlikely that these committees will yield control to many non–committee members. This domination over reproductive policy by a single gender, seated on the most powerful congressional committees, clarifies the effects of gender power at all levels of analysis—individual, institutional, and symbolic. Women legislators are simply not politically powerful enough in Congress to gain the institutional advantages that will allow them to make a difference over the lives of individual women and over the symbolic construction of woman made through public policies.

    Yet, many scholars argue that there is an even more important institutional position to consider—subcommittee membership. In many respects, membership on a subcommittee with power over reproductive policy is a more important institutional resource than committee position. After the passage of the "subcommittee bill of rights" in the mid-1970s, many legislative scholars began to argue that Congress had become a subcommittee government.[34] Norton agrees that subcommittees are powerful, especially in their ability to influence reproductive policies.[35] Approximately 70 percent of the amendments offered in full-committee markup meetings are made solely by subcommittee members, and 85 percent of all reproductive policies reported to the floor from committee were entirely designed by the subcommittee of jurisdiction.[36] Thus, the subcommittee-designed version of a reproductive policy will likely be passed intact without alteration by the floor.

Unfortunately, in the twenty-three years under analysis only three women have held assignments on key reproductive-policy subcommittees, which again emphasizes that position power in this area is almost exclusively male. Between 1969 and 1992, no women sat on Appropriations subcommittees with specific jurisdiction over reproductive policy; only Cardiss Collins was seated for three Congresses on the Energy and Commerce's Subcommittee on Health and the Environment with jurisdiction over family planning programs; only Patricia Schroeder has been seated on the Judiciary's Subcommittee on Civil and Constitutional Rights with jurisdiction over constitutional abortion questions;[37] and, only Marge Roukema has consistently been involved in the Education and Labor Committee's deliberations over the family and medical leave acts with her position on the Labor Management Relations subcommittee. Furthermore, none of these women has held a position of leadership on these subcommittees or committees. Marge Roukema comes closest to a leadership position because of her ranking minority status on the Education and Labor subcommittee. In the 104th Congress, which is beyond the time frame of this study, Senator Nancy Landon Kassebaum serves as Chair of the Labor and Human Resources Committee.

Subcommittee membership confers valuable benefits beyond granting Congress members access to designing policy vehicles. Subcommittee leaders are typically the bill managers on the floor, giving these individuals privileges in crafting the floor rules and managing the floor debate; and subcommittee members usually are granted seats on the conference committee, giving these individuals a chance to influence policy at the final point in the policymaking process. Because women legislators have not held the subcommittee leadership positions, they have not had the opportunity to manage a bill;[38] they have not participated in crafting restrictive floor rules for their committees; and they have rarely been seated on the conference committees that hammer out House and Senate reproductive-policy disagreements. Bill managers used their influence to attach restrictive rules to approximately 82 percent of all legislation containing reproductive-policy elements between 1969 and 1992,[39] limiting the scope of reproductive-policy floor amending to individuals approved of by the committee leaders. Furthermore, out of ninety-two reproductive-policy bills that faced bicameral resolution between 1969 and 1992, only five of the conferences dealing with reproductive policy issues included women legislators.[40]

Finally, since committee and subcommittee membership has been affected by gendered arrangements and women have not held the necessary institutional positions in numbers to influence reproductive policy, we need to consider what they have been able to accomplish on the floor as individual legislators. As noted, however, a substantial number of the measures including reproductive policies have had restrictive rules attached by the committee of jurisdiction. Thus, women legislators have simply not had the opportunity to make real legislative changes as individuals on the floor. Four women between 1973 and 1992 offered amendments or procedural motions on the floor of the House of Representatives.[41] Only Patricia Schroeder (twice), Barbara Boxer, and Olympia Snowe (R-Mass.) took floor action. Unfortunately, only one of these actions was successful. During consideration of the fiscal year 1992 appropriations for the Departments of Labor, Health and Human Services, and Education, Patricia Schroeder was able to offer a point of order that dropped a parental-notification requirement from Title X of the Public Health Service Act.[42] It is interesting to note that Schroeder was not a member of the standing committee of jurisdiction, but she is a member of a *subcommittee* with reproductive-policy jurisdiction. In other words, she is one of the few women with an established institutional position and power on a committee handling reproductive policy, which may explain her ability to gain access to policy change.

The Policy Consequences

Linking women lawmakers' lack of institutional power to the quality of our national reproductive policies is a difficult task. There are too few women in national public office who have held appropriate committee positions to show an empirical correlation between their actions and the condition of our national reproductive policies. Recent research on women state legislators and two congressional case examples, however, indicate that women legislators can bring change to this policy area if given institutional avenues for influence. Berkman and O'Connor found that the increased presence of women state legislators significantly affected a set of state abortion policies.[43] Specifically, they found that women who sat on the appropriate committees were successful at blocking legislation they opposed from being reported to the floor (112). Similarly, at the national level, Patricia Schroeder holds a seat on the Judiciary Committee's subcommittee that has been responsible for blocking all human-life constitutional amendments from reaching the House floor; and Marge Roukema holds a seat on the Education and Labor Committee's subcommittee that was instrumental in ushering the Family and Medical Leave Act through Congress.

These pieces of evidence are not conclusive, yet they emphasize a need to consider our elected political leaders as those responsible for the shape of our current reproductive policies and the gendered nature of leadership over repro-ductive-policy formation. Although congressional leaders do hold responsibility over reproductive policy through their committee jurisdiction, Congress has been reluctant to provide decisive policy on anything but restrictions for Medicaid-funded abortion.[44] Much of the reproductive-policy literature places blame for poor policy on the interest groups responsible for framing the issues[45] or on the Judiciary for being either too active or inactive depending on perspective.[46] Research, however, must also focus on the effect that the lack of leadership has on reproductive-policy outcomes. The above evidence suggests that gender-based power plays an important role in how reproductive policy proceeds.

Our congressional leaders govern within a system that has traditionally considered reproduction to be outside the realm of politics. The writings of the great Western political theorists demonstrate that male leaders have historically defined pregnancy, birth, and raising children as "prepolitical."[47] These writings have translated into institutional practices we live with today. The lack of involved leadership, therefore, has deep institutional roots. Many legislators today would be happy to forget about "the abortion problem" or family-planning concerns because most only have a small personal stake in these issues and the tradition set by their male predecessors does not leave a pattern of interest requiring they pursue new policy directions with the resources at their disposal. *Still, despite the ancient claims that reproduction is of no concern to political leaders, these leaders are and have been involved in the framing of these policies with both their actions and inactions.*

State decisions to organize and regulate social and political relations between women and men dramatically affect the lives of individual citizens.[48] The decision to fund abortions for Medicaid recipients and grant family care leave for employees make a difference in individual lives, especially the lives of women. Specifically, members of Congress have used their authority to restrict funds for a poor woman interested in obtaining an abortion, unless that abortion would save her life; and, they have used their authority to allow employees—usually a woman—twelve weeks of unpaid family care leave to take care of a new baby or a sick relative. Each decision affects the turn of life's events for both the poor woman and the working woman alike.

When we look at the disarray of our national legislative policies designed to regulate reproduction, it becomes painfully evident that we are now facing the consequences of having a set of political leaders who are uninterested in, but inevitably responsible for, reproductive policies. Since 1969, congressional decision making for reproductive policy has been marked by a set of practices that indicate an abdication of leadership: the policies are fragmented into multiple committee jurisdictions; they have been handled as riders on other forms of legislation instead of as a single piece of legislation; they have been focused almost entirely on the single issue of abortion and not on the entire package of reproductive policies; and since 1981 there has been no policy innovation, only retrenchment of former policies. In other words, reproductive-policy legislation has received marginal treatment and lacks the coherence leading to a forward momentum that typically marks policy leadership. Each of these practices will be considered in turn.

First, there are at least ten House committees and nineteen House subcommittees that have claimed jurisdiction over reproductive policy during the past two decades. Although Congress is renowned for fragmenting policy into multiple or overlapping jurisdictions (e.g., environmental policy),[49] reproductive policies are fragmented in a uniquely decentralized fashion. Almost all reproductive policies have been handled by committees described by Smith and Deering as "highly fragmented" committees.[50] Hence, rather than being handled by committees that have more focused jurisdictions and medium to low levels of policy fragmentation, reproductive policies are handled within the purview of committees that deal with a wide variety of policy issues.

In the previous section, both the Appropriations and Energy and Commerce Committees were identified as holding jurisdiction over several of these policies. The Energy and Commerce Committee holds jurisdiction over family planning, contraceptive research, and surrogacy arrangements, while the Appropriations Committee holds jurisdiction over the funding of the entire range of these policies. But many more committees are involved. For example, the Judiciary Committee considers all reproductive-freedom bills and human-life constitutional amendments; the Education and Labor Committee considers pregnancy, family leave, and employment issues; the Foreign Affairs Committee handles global population planning; and the Ways and Means Committee works on prenatal care covered under Medicaid. One of the more intriguing jurisdictions has occurred at the subcommittee level—the Energy and Commerce Committee's Subcommittee on Transportation, Tourism, and Hazardous Materials claimed jurisdiction over surrogacy arrangements in 1987.[51] This kind of fragmentation and association with the highly fragmented committees shows the lack of coordination and the congressional reluctance to work on comprehensive national reproductive policies. Instead of coordinating policy direction, these policies are spread all over Congress. Although other issues are scattered among committees and multiple jurisdictions are growing,[52] few policies face such extensive fragmentation in committees with little time for focused attention.

Second, most reproductive-policy legislation has come in the form of riders on other legislation. When the proportion of reproductive policy made in the form of amendments or riders on other measures is compared to the proportion made as a single piece of legislation, coherent legislation appears rare. Approximately 77 percent of all reproductive policies included in the sample have been considered in the form of amendments to other legislation.[53] Abortion-funding bans for Medicaid recipients, Peace Corp volunteers, federal prisoners, overseas military personnel, and federal employee insurance plans have all come in the form of appropriation-limitation amendments. Similarly, bans on abortion services through the Legal Service Corporation, Civil Rights Commission, and fetal-tissue research have come in the form of legislative amendment. In over two decades, less than one-fourth (23 percent) of the policy has come in the form of a single policy. The few "whole" reproductive-policy measures we have, however, do exemplify more comprehensive forms of national reproductive-policy legislation: Title X of the Public Health Services Act (family planning), family-planning reauthorization measures, the Pregnancy Discrimination Act of 1978, Health Services Centers bills, and foreign-aid authorization measures, which include authorization for global family-planning programs.[54]

Finally, Congress has focused the substantial majority of its reproductive-policy effort on the single issue of abortion. The myopic attention to abortion indicates that our political leaders find little other than abortion policy as an important part of reproduction. This lack of coherence and forward thinking affects the daily lives of a number of women. Since the announcement of *Roe v. Wade* in 1973, the proportion of reproductive policies that have focused on abortion has steadily grown at the expense of other reproductive policy. A comparison of abortion policies to all other reproductive policies in the sample, shows that 75 percent of all reproductive policy made in two decades centers on abortion. Before 1980, however, over one-third (35 percent) of all reproductive policies considered by Congress included more comprehensive packages of reproductive-policy legislation like family planning, pregnancy disability leave, and abortion-related services. Not until after 1980 did congressional attention to a full spectrum of reproductive legislation drop to less than one-fourth (21 percent) of all reproductive-policy efforts.

Figure 5 shows the steadily growing proportion of abortion-related policies considered in Congress since 1969. The only apparent exception to the growing attention to abortion occurred between 1985 and 1988, but at the same time, note that 60 percent of the nonabortion policies considered during this time period failed. Thus, successful abortion legislation actually remained predominant between 1985 and 1988. After the announcement in 1989 of the Supreme Court decision in *Webster v. Reproductive Health Services,* many expected congressional leaders to take more reproductive-policy action because national attention was turned toward their decisions regarding these issues. Still, figure 5 shows that only 15 percent of the policies considered after 1989 were nonabortion policies, indicating a continued fixation on abortion instead of on all of the reproductive policies of special importance and interest to women who are affected by national reproductive-policy action or inaction.

In summary, the evidence of fragmented reproductive-policy committee jurisdictions, the lack of comprehensive legislation, and a narrow focus on

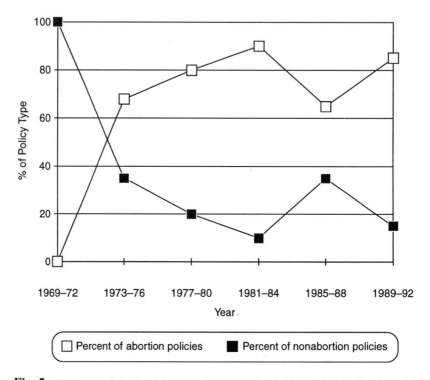

Fig. 5. Percentage of abortion and nonabortion congressional policies, 1969–92. Data is pooled in four-year increments. $N = 126$ (1969–72, $n = 6$; 1973–76, $n = 9$; 1977–80, $n = 25$; 1981–84, $n = 21$; 1985–88, $n = 25$; 1989–92, $n = 40$).

abortion all point to an absence of congressional direction in respect to reproductive policy. Leaders with the jurisdictional responsibility are apparently unwilling to work toward more coherent policy, regardless of moral convictions. Unlike many other nations, the United States is distinguished by its abdication from this policy area.[55] A few scholars have recently compared the national policies of inactive and active states and have suggested that for a nation allowing abortion, the United States is unique in its lack of comprehensive reproductive policy. States like France and Sweden, which are actively involved in crafting reproductive policy, have more comprehensive reproductive policies with abortion and nonabortion policy linked to state health plans.[56] The Alan Guttmacher Institute reports that in seventeen developed countries abortion services are available free of charge as part of an entire package of national health and reproductive-health insurance plans.[57]

The Future Outlook

Women's lack of influence over a policy that affects the lives of women sets up a spiral of consequences in a societal and political system based on gender power.[58] Although more women are entering public office, the routes open to women candidates are still more limited for women than for men, in part because they do not retain power over reproductive-policy legislation. Therefore, there are few women legislators and none with enough seniority or power in this area to accumulate the institutional resources to make a difference in legislative outcomes. Without the institutional resources, women lawmakers are then not able to make the kinds of policy changes that might help individual women gain more power and resources in their lives. Thus, the cycle continues, with male legislators accumulating the resources to perpetuate position power.[59]

In this paper we have seen that congressional position power includes the jurisdictional power over a policy that primarily affects women. The structure of the legislative committee system and the leadership participating in committee governance set up policy outcomes that are made by one sex for use by the other sex. Gender power at the institutional level not only arranges daily lives of individual women who debate family-planning, abortion, and pregnancy decisions, but also constructs the meaning of reproduction through public-policy definitions and legislation. Future questions about the meaning of motherhood itself will undoubtedly be tackled through public policy crafted inside legislative committees as surrogacy arrangements and biological motherhood are brought into the legislative arena. Already Congress has begun to hold committee and subcommittee hearings on these controversial issues, which differentially affect men and women to their core, but whether a coherent policy will come from a male-dominated Congress narrowly focused on abortion policies remains to be seen.[60]

A future with reproductive policy designed by interested women congressional leaders is difficult to envision within this current system. Since the rate at which women will increase numerical representation and secure the appropriate institutional position is unknown, there is no indication that our method of designing national reproductive policy will change. Still, we can consider alternative futures with two possible scenarios. One includes the formation of a single committee with reproductive-policy jurisdiction that would attract members keenly interested in framing clear policy goals; while the other includes encouraging women legislators, despite their numbers, to seek appropriate seats of power within the current institutional structure.

For several reasons, however, the first proposition is dangerous. A single reproductive-policy committee might be subject to control by extreme factions on either side of the policy debate. Moreover, a committee dedicated to women's issues and filled with interested women legislators would probably not gain congressional prestige and power. Historically, organizational resources and assets held by women do not have the same value as the same organizational resources and assets held by men.[61]

Thus, if women legislators wish to involve themselves in crafting different kinds of outcomes, the evidence about committee control over reproductive policy suggests that they must seek position power within the current institutional structure. The Congressional Caucus on Women's Issues has worked from 1981 to 1994 to assure that women legislators seek and receive committee assignments that aided in the achievement of their policy goals. Through appropriate committee assignment, interested women legislators may be able to make their mark on policy development. The 103d Congress has already provided more opportunities for women to influence reproductive policies. Each of the committees involved in this policy area had increased numbers of women assigned in 1993. Appropriations had six women; Energy and Commerce had four; Education and Labor had five; and Judiciary still had only one. Of more significance, however, for the first time four women from Appropriations sat on the Labor, Health, Human Services, and Education subcommittee, which has jurisdiction over the funding for many reproductive-policy programs.

Still, neither alternative—a single reproductive-policy committee or women's position power—is likely to overturn male institutional power for the next several years. Eventually, as women continue to work in coalition, develop seniority, and seek leadership posts on the appropriate committees, they will begin to develop their own tradition of interest regarding issues of concern to women. When women then finally do achieve committee power or position power, they will be able to use these resources at their disposal to make policy differences that affect the futures of those citizens with whom they share common interests.

Appendix 1

A. Reproductive-Policy Floor Amending Sample

This sample includes 112 amendments and procedural motions made to 105 bills on the floor of the House between the 93d (1973–74) and the 102d (1991–92) Congresses. Amendments made between the 91st (1969–70) and the 92d (1971–72) were not included in the sample because there were no floor actions taken on reproductive-policy legislation prior to 1973, except for the approval or passage of legislation. The bills and policies selected to collect amendment data were identified as significant pieces of reproductive-policy legislation by the *Congressional Quarterly Almanac* (1969–92) and four national interest groups dedicated to reproductive policy issues: the National Abortion Action Rights League, National Right to Life Committee, National Women's Political Caucus, and Planned Parenthood Federation of America. Use of all five sources assures that the sample represents a comprehensive, if not a complete, list of all reproductive policies considered by the House. Both amendments and procedural motions have been included in the sample of 112 floor actions. Procedural motions are considered in addition to primary and secondary amendments, because debate on the House floor indicates that the majority of these procedural motions had policy meaning. Procedural motions include the following types of actions: motions to rise, time limits to debate, and recommittal attempts. A vote for or against a procedural motion can lead to significant differences in reproductive-policy outcomes.

B. Reproductive Policy Legislation Sample

This sample is composed of 126 bills identified as those containing significant pieces of reproductive policy legislation, originating between 1969 and 1992 (91st through the 102d Congresses). These are bills that have been given serious attention in the House of Representatives, beyond simple assignment to the committee's of jurisdiction. The sample of reproductive-policy legislation was selected in the same way the sample of floor amendments was selected—the *Congressional Quarterly Almanac* (1969–92) and reports from four national interest groups helped identify all of the significant reproductive policies considered between 1969 and 1992. The difference between the sample A and sample B is the unit of analysis. In the sample of legislation (sample B), bills containing reproductive-policy legislation are the unit of analysis; while in the sample of amendments (sample A), amendments are the unit of analysis.

Appendix 2

Coding Scheme for Identifying the Origin of Reproductive-Policy Legislation

Legislation with a floor origin or floor defeat was coded 1; subcommittee/committee origin was coded 2; conference committee origin was coded 3; presidential veto of bill drafted in committee was coded 4; policy that died after leaving House floor, but with evidence of floor influence, was coded 5; policy that died after leaving House floor, but with evidence of committee influence, was coded 6; policy that never left committee was coded 7. Policies that were crafted in the subcommittee, were rewritten on the floor, and returned to original form in the conference committee were coded 2, while policies that were crafted in the conference committee were coded 3. The coding scheme assures that policies either originating or failing on the floor are coded as clear indicators of floor power. The policies killed by the Senate and the president are coded as bills with committee origins because they were not affected by floor actions—they originated in the committees and remained intact until they left House control.

Notes

1. Michelle Saint-Germain, "Does Their Difference Make a Difference? The Impact of women on Public Policy in the Arizona Legislature," *Social Science Quarterly* 70 (1990): 956–68; Sue Thomas, "The Impact of Women on State Legislative Policies," *Journal of Politics* 53 (1991): 958–76; Sue Thomas and Susan Welch, "The Impact of Gender on Activities and Priorities of State Legislators," *Western Political Quarterly* 1 (1991): 445–56.
2. Michael B. Berkman and Robert E. O'Connor, "Do Women Legislators Matter? Female Legislators and State Abortion Policy," *American Politics Quarterly* 21 (1993): 102–24; Susan J. Carroll, *Women as Candidates in American Politics* (Bloomington: Indiana University Press, 1985); Robert Darcy, Susan Welch, and Janet Clark, *Women, Elections, and Representation* (New York: Longman, 1987); Shelah G. Leader, "The Policy Impact of Elected Women Officials," in *The Impact of the Electoral Process,* ed. Joseph Cooper and Louis Maisels (Beverly Hills, Calif.: Sage. 1977); Thomas and Welch, "Impact of Gender"; Susan Welch, "Are Women More Liberal Than Men in the U.S. Congress?" *Legislative Studies Quarterly* 10 (1985): 125–34.
3. Carroll, *Women as Candidates;* Irene Diamond, *Sex Roles in the State House* (New Haven, Conn.: Yale University Press, 1977); Susan Gluck Mezey, "Does Sex Make a Difference? A Case Study of Women in Politics," *Western Political Quarterly* 31 (1978): 492–501; Irwin N. Gertzog, *Congressional Women: Their Recruitment, Treatment, and Behavior* (New York: Praeger, 1984).
4. Center for the American Woman and Politics, *Women in Elective Office 1990,* fact sheet, and *CAWP News and Notes* (New Brunswick, N.J.: Center for the American Woman and Politics, Eagleton Institute of Politics, Rutgers University, 1991).
5. Deborah Alexander and Kristi Andersen, "Gender as a Factor in the Attribution of Leadership Traits," *Political Research Quarterly* 46 (1990): 527–45.
6. Saint-Germain, "Does Their Difference"; Thomas and Welch, "Impact of Gender"; Karin L. Tamerius, "Does Sex Matter? Women Representing Women's Interests in Congress" (paper delivered at the annual meeting of the Midwest Political Science Association, Chicago, April 1993).
7. Bryan D. Jones, ed., *Leadership and Politics* (Lawrence: University of Kansas Press, 1989); Jean Lipman-Blumen, *Gender Roles and Power* (Englewood Cliffs, N.J.: Prentice-Hall, 1984); Belle Rose Ragins and Eric Sundstrom, "Gender and Power in Organizations: A Longitudinal Perspective," *Psychological Bulletin* 105 (1989): 51–88.
8. See "Abortion Funding Ban Added to Labor-HHS Budget," *Congressional Quarterly Weekly,* 103d Congress, 1st sess., June 26, 1993, 1657–58; "Abortion Funding Rebuff Shows House Divided," *Congressional Quarterly Weekly,* 103d Congress, 1st sess, July 3, 1993, 1735–39; "Abortion Funds Ban Retained in House Test," *Los Angeles Times,* July 1, 1993, A1; and "Rep. Hyde Still Likes Controversy," *Los Angeles Times,* July 6, 1993, A5.
9. "Abortion Funding Rebuff," 1739.
10. As examples of scholars who use similar kinds of indicators to measure floor and committee power, see Stephen S. Smith, *Call to Order: Floor Politics in the House and Senate* (Washington, D.C.: Brookings Institution, 1989); Barry Weingast, "Floor Behavior in the U.S. Congress:

Committee Power under the Open Rule," *American Political Science Review* 83 (1989): 795–815; Barry Weingast, "Fighting Fire with Fire: Amending Activity and Institutional Change in the Postreform Congress," in *The Postreform Congress,* ed. Roger Davidson (New York: St. Martin's Press, 1992).

11. See appendix 1A for description of the sample of reproductive-policy floor amendments.

12. 410 U.S. 113, 1973.

13. 492 U.S. 490, 1989.

14. Noelle H. Norton, "Committee Position Makes a Difference: Institutional Structure and Women Policy Makers" (paper delivered at the annual meeting of the Western Political Science Association, Pasadena, March 1993); and "Congressional Committee Power: The Reproductive Policy Inner-Circle, 1969–1992" (Ph.D. diss., University of California at Santa Barbara, 1994).

15. Noelle H. Norton, "Women Lawmakers, Reproductive Policy and Congressional Anomie, 1969–1992" (paper presented at the annual meeting of the American Political Science Association, Washington, D.C., September 1993), and "Congressional Committee Power."

16. Norton, "Committee Position," and "Congressional Committee Power."

17. James W. Dyson and John W. Soule, "Congressional Committee Behavior on Roll Call Votes: The U.S. House of Representatives, 1955–64," *Midwest Journal of Political Science* 14 (1970): 626–47; Richard F. Fenno Jr., *Power of the Purse* (Boston: Little, Brown, 1966); Richard F. Fenno Jr., *Congressmen in Committees* (Boston: Little, Brown, 1973); Barbara Hinckley, "Policy Content, Committee Membership, and Behavior," *American Journal of Political Science* 19 (1975): 543–57; Barry Weingast and W. Marshall, "The Industrial Organization of Congress," *Journal of Political Economy* 96 (1988): 132–63; Woodrow Wilson, *Congressional Government: A Study in American Politics* (Cleveland: Meridan, 1885).

18. Stanley Bach, "Representatives and Committees on the Floor: Amendments to Appropriations Bills in the House of Representatives, 1963–1982," *Congress and the President* 13 (1986): 41–53; Thomas Gilligan and Keith Krehbiel, "Organization of Informative Committees by a Traditional Legislature," *American Journal of Political Science* 34 (1990): 531–64; Keith Krehbiel, "Why Are Congressional Committees Powerful?" *American Political Science Review* 81 (1987): 929–35; Keith Krehbiel, *Information and Legislative Organization* (Ann Arbor: University of Michigan Press, 1991); Smith, *Call to Order.*

19. See appendix 1B for description of the sample of reproductive-policy measures considered by Congress.

20. Minutes of full-committee markup minutes are stored in the committee offices. Committees make these minutes available to interested individuals in their offices. The minutes are not verbatim transcripts of the full meeting, but they are minutes that summarize all debates and amending activity conducted in markup meetings.

21. See Appendix II for the coding used to determine the origin of the reproductive policy legislation.

22. Included are policies returned to original form by the conference committee, after floor alteration.

23. See Noelle H. Norton, "House Committees in Controversial Conferences Bicameral Politics of Reproductive Policy, 1969–1992" (paper presented at the annual meeting of the Western Political Science Association, Albuquerque, N.M., 1994).

24. For review of the initial debates over Hyde amendments and a review of Appropriations Committee support see "Veto of Labor-HEW Funds Bill Overridden," *Congressional Committee Almanac,* 94th Cong., 2d sess., 1976, 790–804; "Abortion Agreement Ends Funding Deadlock," *Congressional Quarterly Almanac,* 95th Cong., 1st sess., 1977, 295–313; and "Labor-HEW Funds: Abortion Compromise," *Congressional Quarterly Almanac,* 95th Cong., 1978, 105–15.

25. Robert Packwood, "The Rise and Fall of the Right to Life Movement in Congress: Response to the Roe Decision, 1973–1983," in *Abortion, Medicine, and the Law,* 4th ed., ed. J. Douglas Butler and David F. Walbert (New York: Facts on File, 1992).
26. See appendix 1A for description of the sample of reproductive-policy floor amendments.
27. Norton, "Committee Position," and "Congressional Committee Power."
28. Stanley Bach and Steven S. Smith, *Managing Uncertainty in the House of Representatives: Adaptation and Innovation in Special Rules* (Washington, D.C.: Brookings Institution, 1988); Smith, *Call to Order;* Weingast, "Fighting Fire with Fire."
29. Roger Davidson, "Subcommittee Government: New Channels for Policymaking," in *The New Congress,* ed. Thomas E. Mann and Norman J. Ornstein (Washington, D.C.: American Enterprise Institute, 1981); Steven H. Haeberle, "The Institutionalization of the Subcommittee in the United States House of Representatives," *Journal of Politics* 40 (1978): 1054–65; Richard L. Hall, "Participation and Purpose in Committee Decision Making," *American Political Science Review* 81 (1987): 105–27; Richard L. Hall and C. Lawrence Evans, "The Power of Subcommittees," *Journal of Politics* 52 (1990): 335–54; Steven S. Smith and Christopher J. Deering, *Committees in Congress,* 2d ed. (Washington, D.C.: Congressional Quarterly Press, 1990).
30. See "Abortion Funds Ban," A1.
31. Weingast, "Floor Behavior," and "Fighting Fire with Fire."
32. Roger Davidson, "The Emergence of the Postreform Congress," in Davidson *The Postreform Congress;* Lawrence C. Dodd and Bruce I. Oppenheimer, "Consolidating Power in the House: The Rise of a New Oligarchy," in *Congress Reconsidered,* 5th ed., ed. Lawrence C. Dodd and Bruce I. Oppenheimer (Washington, D.C.: Congressional Quarterly Press, 1992); David E. Price, "Policy Making in Congressional Committees: The Impact of Environmental Factors," *American Political Science Review* 72 (1978): 548–74; Smith, *Call to Order;* Smith and Deering, *Committees in Congress.*
33. The analysis of policy origins of bills indicate that only 16.5 percent of those handled by Appropriations originated on the floor. Similarly, the Energy and Commerce Committee, labeled by many as one of the more influential committees (Price, "Policy Making"; Smith, *Call to Order;* Hall and Evans, "The Power of Subcommittees"), has lost on the floor only 17 percent of the time (Norton, "Congressional Committee Power").
34. Davidson, "Subcommittee Government"; Haeberle, "Institutionalization"; Clifford M. Hardin, Kenneth A. Shepsle, and Barry R. Weingast, "Government by Subcommittee," *Wall Street Journal,* June 24, 1983; Smith and Deering, *Committees in Congress.*
35. Norton, "Congressional Committee Power."
36. Norton, in "Congressional Committee Power" and "Committee Position," uses a sample of 102 amendments made to 113 bills at full-committee markup meetings to conduct an analysis of subcommittee involvement in policy design between 1977 and 1992. The committee amendment data was collected from minutes of full-committee markup meeting. Data were collected only for bills and policies under the jurisdiction of four committees (Judiciary, Appropriations, Education and Labor, and Energy and Commerce) and not from all committees with reproductive-policy jurisdiction.
37. Patricia Schroeder also sits on the Armed Services Subcommittee on Military Personnel, which briefly held jurisdiction over one piece of reproductive policy in 1992. The Senate passed a bill that would have allowed overseas military personnel to obtain abortions with personal funds (S3144). When the bill moved to the House, it was considered in the Military Personnel subcommittee. The bill is an exception because typically this personnel issue has been handled in the Appropriations subcommittee on defense. The president pocket vetoed the bill in 1992.
38. Again, Patricia Schroeder presents the one exception to this statement. When the bill regarding abortions for overseas military personnel (S3144) was considered in the House, Schroeder managed the bill on the House floor as the subcommittee chair for the Armed Services

Subcommittee on Military Personnel. The example is not emphasized because this subcommittee typically does not hold jurisdiction over reproductive policy. Essentially, it was an rare exception that allowed Schroeder to manage this bill.

39. Norton, "Congressional Committee Power."
40. Norton, "Committees in Controversial Conferences," and "Congressional Committee Power."
41. See appendix 1A again for description of the sample of reproductive-policy floor amendments.
42. See "Abortion Dispute Derails First HHS Bill," *Congressional Quarterly Almanac*, 102d Cong., 1st sess., 1991, 501–12; or (HR-2707, 1991).
43. Berkman and O'Connor, "Do Women Legislators Matter?"
44. Barbara Hinkson Craig and David M. O'Brien, *Abortion and American Politics* (Chatham, N.J.: Chatham House, 1993), chap. 4; Sharon Block, "Congressional Action on Abortion: 1984–1991," in *Abortion, Medicine, and the Law*.
45. Nancy Aries, "Fragmentation and Reproductive Freedom: Federally Subsidized Family Planning Services, 1960–1980," *American Journal of Public Health* 77 (1987): 1465–71; Angela Y. Davis, *Women, Race, and Class* (New York: Random House, 1981), chap. 12; Susan Davis, ed., *Women under Attack: Victories, Backlash, and the Fight for Reproductive Freedom* (Boston: South End Press, 1988), pamphlet no. 7; Marlene Fried, ed., *From Abortion to Reproductive Freedom: Transforming a Movement* (Boston: South End Press, 1990); Joyce Gelb and Marian Lief Palley, *Women and Public Policies* (Princeton, N.J.: Princeton University Press, 1987); Thomas Shapiro, *Birth Control Politics: Women, Sterilization, and Reproductive Choice* (Philadelphia: Temple University Press, 1985).
46. Mary Ann Glendon, *Abortion and Divorce in Western Law: American Failures, European Challenges* (Cambridge, Mass.: Harvard University Press, 1987); Hyman Rodman, Betty Sarvis, and Joy Bonar, *The Abortion Question* (New York: Columbia University Press, 1987); Eva Rubin, *Abortion, Politics, and the Court* (Westport, Conn.: Greenwood Press, 1982); Lawrence H. Tribe, *Abortion, the Clash of Absolutes* (New York: Norton, 1990).
47. Wendy Brown, "Reproductive Freedom and the Right to Privacy," in *Families, Politics, and Public Policy: A Feminist Dialogue on Women and the State*, ed. Irene Diamond (New York: Longman, 1983); Wendy Brown, *Manhood and Politics: A Feminist Reading in Political Theory* (Totowa, N.J.: Rowman and Littlefield, 1988).
48. Wendy Brown, "Reproductive Freedom and the Right to Privacy," in *Families, Politics, and Public Policy: A Feminist Dialogue on Women and the State;* Zillah Eisenstein, "The State, the Patriarchal Family, and Working Mothers," in Diamond, *Families;* Rosalind Petchesky, *Abortion and Woman's Choice: The State, Sexuality, and Reproductive Freedom* (New York: Longman, 1984).
49. Roger Davidson and Walter J. Oleszek, *Congress and Its Members* (Washington, D.C.: Congressional Quarterly Press, 1990), 212.
50. Smith and Deering, *Committees in Congress,* 78–80.
51. See Committee on Energy and Commerce, House of Representatives, 100th Congress, 1st sess., serial no. 100–143; hearing before the Subcommittee on Transportation, Tourism, and Hazardous Materials on HR 2433, Surrogacy Arrangements Act of 1987, October 15, 1987.
52. Melissa P. Collie and Joseph Cooper, "Multiple Referral and the New Committee System in the House of Representatives," in Dodd and Oppenheimer, *Congress Reconsidered;* Davidson and Oleszek, *Congress and Its Members;* Davidson, "Emergence."
53. See appendix 1B again for description of the sample of reproductive polices.
54. See "Population Control: Increased Federal Concern," *Congressional Quarterly Almanac,* 91st Congress, 1st sess., 1970, 570–74; and the Family Planning Services and Population Research Act of 1970 (Title X of the Pubic Health Service Act), PL 91–572; Pregnancy Sex Discrimination Prohibition, PL 95–555, 92 STAT. 2076; and "Pregnancy Disability, Rights," *Congressional Quarterly Almanac*, 95th Cong., 2d sess., 1978, 597–99.

55. Block, "Congressional Action on Abortion"; Dorothy McBride Stetson, "The Abortion Politics Triad in Russia, France, and the United States" (paper delivered at the annual meeting of the American Political Science Association, Chicago, September 1992).

56. Donald P. Kommers, "Abortion in Six Countries: A Comparative Legal Analysis," in Butler and Walbert, *Abortion;* Glendon, *Abortion and Divorce;* Stetson, "Abortion Politics Triad."

57. Stanley K. Henshaw, "Induced Abortion: A World Review 1990," in Butler and Henshaw, *Abortion,* 426.

58. Lipman-Blumen, *Gender Roles and Power.*

59. Ibid., 81.

60. Again see Committee on Energy and Commerce, House of Representatives, 100th Congress, 1st sess., Serial No. 100-143, hearing before the Subcommittee on Transportation, Tourism, and Hazardous Materials on HR 2433, Surrogacy Arrangements Act of 1987, October 15, 1987.

61. Ragins and Sundstrom, "Gender and Power," 81.

Chapter 6

The Gendered Nature of Lowi's Typology; or, Who Would Guess You Could Find Gender Here?

Meredith Ann Newman

This chapter reexamines Lowi's typology of federal-agency types through the lens of state bureaucracies. It demonstrates how gender, organizational mission, and opportunity are inextricably linked. The general Weberian principle that bureaucracy is by nature objective or neutral and therefore unisex, treating all persons in terms of function and role without regard to gender, is called into question. By means of data generated during the author's study of 253 upper-level administrators in twenty-eight state agencies of Florida, Newman shows how gender power, sex-role expectations, and institutional dimensions interact with policy types and their accompanying prognostications, especially about the breadth of benefit distribution and level of conflict.

This chapter looks beneath the veneer of Lowi's typology to an examination of the organizational environment that might produce significant variations in work experiences across the three agency types, regulatory, distributive, and redistributive. The extent to which the degree of bureaucratization, professionalization, and the values inherent in the type of policy impact the work environment become clearer in the process. Interestingly, the general opportunity structure and organizational bases of power are far from equitable, with heavily male-dominated agencies seeming to enjoy far more amenable circumstances. The "fit" between the individual and the agency type, patterns of career advancement into leadership posts, and work experiences appear to be more than coincidental. Analysis of the benefits and opportunities available to individuals within various types of organizations reveal implicit masculinity and advantages accruing to those who work in heavily male-dominated agencies.

Organizations, Mission, and Gender Power

Organizations are not created equal. Organizational consequences flow from the peculiarities of mission. Such consequences are manifest as structures of opportunity that impact career success, especially women's advancement into positions of authority and power. The analysis in this chapter extends the current debate over the origin and composition of barriers to career advancement by examining the nature of state organizations and the extent to which the agencies themselves are gendered. We can locate gender power in opportunity structures that differ according to an agency's mission and in the way we have come to think about agencies, especially through Lowi's typology. The debate shifts from a focus on individuals in organizations as the unit of analysis to the characteristics of public organizations themselves and assumptions implicit in long-standing analyses of them. This focus allows us to uncover the gendered nature of these institutional structures, which reflect substantial gender power differentials.

Equity and Gender Power in Public Bureaucracies

Representative bureaucracy and female parity at all levels in public organizations are attainable, yet unrealized, goals. More than twenty years have elapsed since the passage of Equal Employment Opportunity and Affirmative Action legislation, yet women continue to be underrepresented at the top of the organizational hierarchy. Frederickson's compound theory of social equity delineates organizational equality into *block* and *segmented* categories.[1] Block equality is a holistic approach to the concept of equality that views overall representational concerns among groups within an organization. Segmented equality examines representation at various levels within the organization. Upper-level management positions in state governments represent one such level, or segment. While block equality has been achieved in terms of proportion of the total workforce, segmented equality remains elusive. Women continue to be compressed into the lower levels of public agencies and concentrated into traditionally defined female occupations, in other words, under glass ceilings and within glass walls.

Although women fill 46 percent of federal white-collar jobs, they hold only 15 percent of GM-13 to GM-15 positions.[2] At the top of the federal government hierarchy, women hold only 12 percent of the Senior Executive Service positions.[3]

Women fare somewhat better at the state government level. According to a recent study by Bullard and Wright,[4] 20 percent of executives in state governments are women. An ongoing empirical study organized by Kelly addresses a number of issues related to the integration of women into the managerial ranks of state government administrations.[5] To date, the study has been undertaken in seven states (Arizona, Texas, California, Alabama, Wisconsin, Utah, and Florida). The proportion of women in the upper-management levels of these seven state governments ranges from 13 percent in the Arizona civil service to 25 percent in Texas.

Top-level positions represent power generally because they offer positional power in terms of authority and legitimacy to influence public decisions. These posts also enable control of structural resources in organizations in terms of budget and supervision of personnel as well as through implementing public policy. These posts represent gender power in that men hold a minimum of three-fourths of these crucial public leadership posts.

Changing Gender Power of Public Agencies

In reviewing the current literature, a common theme emerges—a search for responses to the question, What variables should we manipulate to improve the status of women in public administration? Variables may be clustered into three categories: human-capital variables, sociopsychological variables, and systemic variables.[6]

Human-capital barriers are identified as insufficient education, dysfunctional choices, domestic constraints, limited financial resources, and insufficient experience. Psychological barriers include sex-role socialization, sex-role stereotypes/role prejudice, negative perceptions of women's capacity for managing, questionable motivation, and limiting self-concepts. Systemic barriers manifest themselves as sex segregation in the labor force, differential career ladder opportunities, sex segregation of domestic labor, limited access to professional training, limited access to informal networks, lack of mentors, veterans preference, lack of power, sexual harassment, perceived lack of compatibility, and the lack of (female) role models (for women). Notice that gendered aspects here operate from women's vantage point and focus on women's lack of fit with a system established by men, based upon masculine assumptions that suit men well. In other words, variables important to advancing into leadership posts in public bureaucracy create circumstances of gender power that advantage men and masculinity.

In each category—human-capital, sociopsychological, and systemic variables—the unit of analysis is the individual. Manipulation of these variables results in prescriptive policies aimed at lowering or removing these barriers. This approach is valid, yet incomplete. When we add the nature of organizations themselves into the analysis, we are able to approach the problems through a different lens. In the process, a more fundamental question arises, Are all organizations created equal? In other words, do opportunity structures differ, and if so, what produces these differences? Are some agencies more conducive to influence and status for women—organizational power generally—than others? Are some agencies more conducive than others for individual women within them to advance into leadership posts and opportunities to influence public policy? Are some agencies more conducive than others to women's career advancement, a key for moving into leadership positions?

In seeking a response to these questions, the nature of organizations is examined from a theoretical standpoint and the theoretical standpoint itself is examined for gendered dimensions. First, I summarize a popular theoretical approach to examining the linkages between policy types and organizations, that of Theodore Lowi and others who have extended his ideas. Next, I consider the assumptions within the theoretical approach for power implications, especially those related to gender power. Finally, I use a case study of the state of Florida Senior Management Service executives to examine the implications of theory in practice in terms of work experiences and structures of opportunity.

A Theoretical Approach

According to organizational theorists, the structure and behavior of institutions is determined, at least in part, by the character of the institution itself;[7] its predominant culture;[8] and the characteristics of the policies they administer.[9] Representative of this latter approach is Lowi's thesis of administrative structure, and his typology of agencies grouped by policy type.[10] Lowi's framework of administrative structure is based on four models, the Regulatory Agency Model, the Distributive Agency Model, the Redistributive Agency Model, and the Constituent Agency Model. Each model develops "its own characteristic political structure, political process, elites, and group relations."[11] The discussion that follows concentrates on the first three models, the latter model not being immediately relevant as it focuses on boundary and jurisdictional issues, such as reapportionment, rather than functional or policy content themes.[12] What is the organizational structure and behavior of each of Lowi's three agency types? Does the policy typology predict the work environment therein? Do opportunity structures differ according to the nature of these organizations? If so, can the Weberian principle of bureaucracy remain tenable?[13] Does Lowi incorporate gender-relevant interpretations into his model? A review of his work, as he and others have developed it, is a necessary starting point.

Regulatory Agencies

Regulatory agencies include those dedicated to insurance, environment, business, professions, legal affairs, commerce, corrections, law enforcement, and parole.[14] These regulatory agencies are responsible for implementing the classic control policies of government, formulating or implementing rules imposing obligations on individuals, and providing punishment for nonconformance.[15] Regulation is, by definition, a coercive process, part of administrative law, rule making, and enforcement. Regulatory policies and programs most often involve concentrated costs, with some interests losing, but benefits are marginal and widely dispersed, thereby limiting salience and diminishing sources of conflict.[16]

Regulatory agencies show distinctive organizational features. Such agencies, according to Lowi,[17] should be the most rule bound, with a tendency for lateral entry, that is, to recruit personnel from the outside directly into upper-management ranks; these lateral entrants would tend to be process-and-procedure specialists (e.g., lawyers); with large proportions of high-ranking managers, that is, with a flatter and more truncated hierarchy than in Weber's model of an ideal bureaucratic structure. These agencies also tend to be small, with relatively small budgets and few employees. Nonetheless, they have widespread influence in their particular sector of regulation.

Distributive Agencies

Distributive agencies include the Departments of Highway Safety and Motor Vehicle, Natural Resources, Agriculture and Consumer Services, Game and Fish Commission, and Transportation.[18] These distributive agencies are defined by Lowi as being almost the opposite of regulatory agencies in mission. That is, while both agency models are "responsible for policies that work directly on or through individuals, the relationship is one of patron and client rather than controller and controlled. Consequently, distributive agencies can operate in their political environment almost as though they had unlimited resources."[19] Such is a powerful basis of operation. As clientele agencies, they exist to foster and promote the interests of their clientele through field service and functional representation.[20] Distributive (or developmental) policies or programs have generally been said to produce only winners, not losers, and involve a high degree of cooperation and mutually rewarding logrolling.[21]

Distributive policies are commonly referred to as pork barrel programs. According to Lowi, "[T]he very imagery of the pork barrel is one of a collection of very discrete units that can be drawn out one at a time, each in isolation from each of the others."[22] Once a policy sets the pork barrel process in train, the behavior series is predictable. For example, "[T]he public works decision-making process is tantamount to a conspiracy to keep larger social questions from becoming issues of public policy."[23] Lowi and Ginsberg refer to distributive policies as patronage policies. Stated succinctly, patronage techniques of control are generally used in the service of "distributive policies."[24] The more powerful the client group, the more powerful the agency patron.

Because organizational consequences flow from the peculiarities of mission,[25] distributive agencies should be different from regulatory agencies on a number of important characteristics. Because such agencies have strong mutually supportive relationships with their clientele, these agencies strongly resist changes in power and authority.[26] Their functional decentralization means that more employees who are highly specialized in the substantive business of their particular agencies are likely to be promoted to top management positions than in other agencies.[27] According to Ripley and Franklin, these individuals are characterized by long service and usually by long-established patterns of personal interaction.[28] And their loyalties tend to be primarily institutional (to the agency itself). The hierarchy of a typical distributive agency is relatively flat, reflecting a reliance upon professional norms for cohesion and uniformity. That is, individuals within distributive agencies have considerable autonomy from agency control. Individuals in these agencies, then, have considerable leeway to give leadership to issues of concern to them.

Redistributive Agencies

Redistributive agencies include welfare, education, health and rehabilitative services, community affairs, veterans affairs, labor and employment security, and revenue.[29] Their redistributive policy and programs are explicitly intended to manipulate the allocation of wealth, property, or rights among social classes or racial groups in society. The redistributive feature enters because a number of actors perceive that there are "winners" and "losers" and that policies transfer some value to one group at the expense of another group.[30] Health, education, and social-welfare programs are commonly identified as redistributive in intent and impact.[31] Affirmative action in hiring to increase the employment of women and minorities is an example of a redistributive policy.

Redistributive agencies "maintain and manipulate categories of human beings."[32] Their rules are understood to affect society on a larger scale than any others. Redistributive agencies discriminate along broad class lines: between the money providers and the service demanders, for example, rich versus poor, young and employed versus old and unemployed. Because the actors perceive that there will be distinct winners and losers, the stakes are thought to be high, and this fact means the policymaking process will be marked by high degrees of visibility and conflict,[33] conflict that often upsets the status quo.

This responsibility for making or maintaining those rules is a determining factor in the organizational structure of redistributive agencies. "Great stress is placed on having the best management at the top, including people and professions of high social status."[34] These agencies place heavy emphasis on recruitment at the bottom, low lateral entry, internal promotion to top management, very narrow spans of control, and overhead controls. The hierarchy of redistributive agencies would resemble the classic, narrow, high-peaked pyramid due to the narrow spans of control, where one supervisor has a minimum number of subordinates.

Power, Opportunities, and Assumptions

Let us now examine this common typology to see what it implies about power generally and gender power more particularly. Special effort will be made to identify relevant implicit assumptions.

First consider the assessment of regulatory agencies. In fulfilling their purposes, regulatory agencies operate as the classic control portion of governance, the coercive arm of the state. In many regards regulatory agencies take their roots in militaristic modes of operating, precisely because they function as part of the state's monopoly on the use of coercive force. Clearly, most regulatory agencies wield more coercive control through lawyers than lieutenants; nevertheless, the legitimate capacity to (en)force conformity and compliance provides a strong base of power for these agencies. Second, accountability internal to these agencies depends to a great extent upon professional monitoring. Individuals within these agencies, then, can create and enforce regulation and exercise considerable discretion in doing so. Of course, the large number of professionals itself provides some status for the agencies. (The corrections area offers less professional stature, but more coercive potential.) In any case, some of the general power of these agencies depends upon the benefits it provides to wider society through their regulatory work. In terms of gender power, the professional autonomy has conventionally been more common to men, as has the independence of action involved in regulation, but women are increasingly entering into these professional arrangements as well.

Distributive and redistributive policies offer more striking analytic potential. Consider, for example, the longstanding analytic conclusion that redistributive policies manipulate the allocation of wealth, property, or rights, while distributive policies foster and promote the interests of their clientele. Is not fostering and promoting the interests, say, of agriculture, a manipulation of wealth? It is remarkable that logrolling and pork barrel politics somehow can be categorized as "producing only winners," when the most direct benefits go to major producers of those goods or services. Highway construction firms derive tremendous particularistic gain from public contracts, a fact that goes unnoticed in this account of policy. All taxpayers contribute to government support of sport hunting, for example, so through this public investment we see a redistribution from nonhunting taxpayers to those who hunt. Clearly, spillover benefits are such that all citizens benefit from quality highway systems and wildlife habitat. What is interesting is that the same understandings do not exist for programs like Aid to Families with Dependent Children. Surely society understands the spillover benefits of investing wisely in the next generation of workers, taxpayers, and citizens. Society also should understand the widespread costs of crime and violence, much of which can be traced back to poverty and inadequacies of childhood. Similarly, poverty breeds innumerable social ills, yet attempts to alleviate poverty generate considerable contention.

We need to think more clearly about how we have come to understand policies as we do and to unquestioningly accept analyses that "see" transfers of wealth when poor people are involved but not when wealthy contractors or sportsmen receive benefits. We need to notice that the distributive "decision-making process is tantamount to a conspiracy to keep larger social questions from becoming issues of public policy."[35] Such is governance deployed to legitimize status quo power arrangements. How have these perceptions been shaped? Distributive policies and the agencies that accompany them "appear to produce only winners" and so are characterized by cooperation and limited conflict. In contrast, redistributive agencies lead to perceptions that distinct winners and losers result, so they are marked by high degrees of visibility and conflict. The very way we think about policies is imbued with assumptions that mask power relations.

Organizational consequences similarly carry multiple assumptions about power relations that flow from their missions, the people who work in these agencies, and the opportunities structures that follow. For example, distributive agencies' functions are said to require decentralization, with more professionals and fewer underlings, while redistributive policies demand centralized organizations and hierarchical arrangements. Of course, then, the degree of autonomy would vary directly, with top positions in distributive agencies being offering much more latitude (and opportunity for leadership) than the internally controlled redistributive organizational positions. Furthermore, the trusting patterns of personal interactions within distributive agencies make them much more akin to a "club" atmosphere than the rule-driven redistributive model. Distributive agencies would seem a more productive place to work if much less time and energy needed to be displaced onto rule compliance. If the work environment is more productive, the opportunity to shine in terms of career enhancement is greatly improved, and the chance to provide leadership to policy areas would also be facilitated. If we look to opportunities from the nature of hiring practices, we find heavy emphasis to recruit at the bottom in redistributive agencies, while distributive ones offer much better paying, higher status professional employment. To the extent that employment is itself an opportunity and a resource to transfer wealth, as the literature on representative bureaucracy suggests, then even by this measure these organizations are not created equal.

One need not look long to see gendered patterns in the clientele of distributive and redistributive agencies. Women are more likely to need the services of redistributive agencies than are men. Men are more likely to be the direct recipients of public spending on highways (as owners and employees of construction companies), fish and game projects, and other distributive policy areas. Gender power, then, is embedded into these agencies in terms of clientele. Gender power also is implicated in the understandings of what is perceived as a transfer of wealth and what is understood to generate conflict. The question we must ask is how these assumptions have for so long gone unnoticed and unchallenged. Chapter 1 of this volume would point to ideological arrangements under masculinism that render such imbalance in gender power arrangements invisible.

The Florida Experience: Individuals in Organizations

Let us examine how individuals integrate with opportunity structures inside these agencies. Upon closer inspection, we may unearth elements relevant to gender power and leadership. What are the implications for career advancement and leadership potential in terms of the nature of organizations? Does the structure of opportunity differ according to agency type? The findings from the Florida case study enable us to comment effectively on these larger questions. The Florida study replicates a study organized by Rita Mae Kelly. It is part of a "systematic, comparative empirical study of women administrators in ... state governments."[36] The data upon which the findings of the Florida study are based were generated by means of a questionnaire sent to the universe of female upper-level administrators, and a sample of 50 percent of their male counterparts in twenty-eight agencies of the state government of Florida. From a total target population of 253 executives, 108 responded within a workable time frame. When those respondents in constituent agencies are excluded, the number of subjects is reduced to 89 (women, 29; men, 60). The study sought answers to questions of representation, patterns of career advancement, and the work experiences of these upper-level administrators. While Lowi's categories "appear to be neither mutually exclusive nor collectively exhaustive,"[37] the models do offer some deeper insights into the dynamics of career success. Agency type, categorized in both functional and policy terms, appears a significant determinant of the structure of opportunity within those agencies. As a caveat, it should be noted that the following analyses are limited strictly to one segment of the Florida state government, the Senior Management Service upper-management level.

Representation: Gendered Patterns

As expected, the findings reveal that, in terms of representation, the majority (53 percent) of female Senior Management Service executives are employed in the redistributive agencies. Approximately one-third of the women are found in the regulatory agencies (31 percent), with only 17 percent in the distributive agencies. By contrast, the distribution of male subjects in each of the three agency types finds the most (40 percent) in distributive agencies, with 30 percent in the regulatory agencies and 30 percent in the redistributive agencies.

Moreover, agency type and professional occupation apparently must be entered into any leadership opportunity equation, as opportunity structures may differ, and differ by gender, across agency types. That is, one type of agency may offer more opportunity for career advancement than another, and with it comes greater opportunity to exert more leadership. For example, lawyer-dominated or regulatory agencies, such as business regulation and legal affairs, may provide more opportunity for women, while engineer-dominated or distributive agencies, such as highway safety, motor vehicle, and agriculture, are traditionally, if not notoriously, male dominated. Opportunity for advancement in such agencies may be severely limited for women. The Florida findings are illustrative on this point. The female subjects are represented equally with their male counterparts in one agency only, a regulatory agency (Business Regulation). In strict numerical terms, most female upper-level administrators are found in redistributive agencies, especially Health and Rehabilitative Services (fourteen). And while men are overrepresented in the upper-level managerial ranks across all twenty-eight state agencies, there are no women at the top of two distributive agencies (Highway Safety and Motor Vehicle, and the Game and Fish Commission). As we have said throughout this book, gender and gender power permeates all social arrangements, and the arrangements of these agencies appears not to deviate from this generality.

"Types and Fit" of Agencies and People

Can generalizations be made in terms of the characteristics of upper-level administrators in each agency type? That is, can a representative profile of the typical respondent in each of Lowi's agency categorizations be drawn from the data? The Florida findings offer a preliminary personal sketch. Indeed, Lowi's typology of agencies predicts the "goodness of fit" for women in management. The latent implications for career and/or leadership success are suggested in the process.

As shown in table 8, there are a number of similarities and differences across the agency types. Not surprisingly, most respondents come from a

TABLE 8. Characteristics of Women and Men in Management by Agency Types

	Regulatory		Distributive		Redistributive	
	Female	Male	Female	Male	Female	Male
	%	%	%	%	%	%
Characteristics	(n = 9)	(n = 18)	(n = 5)	(n = 24)	(n = 15)	(n = 18)
Social class of family while growing up						
Upper	33	17	20	13	13	11
Middle	33	44	60	46	53	61
Lower	33	39	20	38	33	28
Sex-role socialization						
Father's highest levels of education						
Less than high school	22	50	0	42	13	22
High-school graduate	33	17	40	25	33	44
Father's occupation						
Professional/technical	11	22	20	17	27	28
Manager/administrator	33	17	40	17	33	17
Craftsman/Foreman	22	22	20	25	20	28
Mother's highest level of education						
Less than high school	11	28	0	21	7	11
High-school graduate	22	50	60	38	40	56
Mother's occupation						
Professional/technical	11	11	0	13	20	17
Manager/administrator	11	11	40	8	0	6
Housewife	68	56	60	54	53	33
Education						
Undergraduate degree	44	68	100	67	73	67
Masters	44	39	80	25	53	56
Doctorate	0	22	0	17	13	33
Domestic environment						
Marital status						
Not married	44	28	20	13	53	17
Married	56	72	80	88	47	83
Living situation						
Living alone	38	6	0	13	36	6
Living with others (adult(s) and/or dependents)	63	83	100	87	64	88
Political persuasion						
Democrat	56	61	80	54	87	50
Republican	33	22	0	33	7	39

Note: Numbers may not add to 100 because of missing data (responses not given) or the fact that not all categories are included herein.

middle-class background in all three types of agencies. Most respondents have a higher-educated mother than father. The highest level of their father's formal education is less than high school for the regulatory- and distributive-agency "types" (regulatory, 41 percent [20 percent of women's fathers, 48 percent of men's fathers]; distributive, 42 percent [men only]). Most respondents in redistributive agencies have a somewhat more educated father (high-school graduate, 39 percent [33 percent of women's fathers, 44 percent of men's fathers]). Mothers, on the other hand, are most likely to be high-school graduates. Despite the educational gap between respondents' parents, a majority of their mothers are housewives, not employed outside the home. Their fathers tend to be employed in the public domain. In all three agency types, fathers of the female subjects were most likely to work as managers or administrators, while fathers of male subjects were least likely to have been employed in managerial or administrative work. To the extent that such factors shape these subjects as adult professionals, table 8 provides interesting contextual information.

Education is often important to positions of public leadership and surely is an investment worth making if one hopes to move into top positions. While the majority of respondents have an advanced education, those in redistributive agencies are more highly qualified than the typical regulatory or distributive type. Generally speaking, men as a group are better educated than these women. The one exception occurs in distributive agencies, where women are more likely to hold advanced degrees (80 percent have a Masters, although 17 percent of the men also have a Ph.D.). Only in redistributive agencies do we find any women with a Ph.D. Of course, obtaining similar educational credentials is one way to enhance the similarity of workers regardless of gender, as equivalent degrees level the playing field. Perhaps more importantly, education and training provide socialization to the profession and a shared knowledge base.

Lowi's thesis speaks to the importance of professional training, especially in distributive agencies.[38] However, distributive agencies are populated with top-level posts that demand training in traditionally male-dominated professions (such as engineering). Consequently, training and education for these positions in distributive agencies are themselves highly gendered, and educational requirements then become a barrier to women moving into leadership roles in these agencies. In comparison, the gendered nature of training required in redistributive agencies such as health and education, for example, is consistent with areas women have traditionally been attracted. Of course however, advanced degrees in the overwhelming majority of fields have traditionally gone to men regardless of gender role assumptions.

The Florida findings show that the most highly qualified female respondents work in redistributive agencies, where, probably not coincidentally, their representation is the highest. Regardless of gender, these findings support

Lowi's thesis that redistributive agencies seek "the best management at the top," including those whose status is derived from education. These findings are similar to those of the U.S. Department of Labor's 1991 private-sector study, which found advancement opportunities also vary in staff and line functions according to corporate culture. For example, a high-tech organization might lean toward individuals with advanced and scientific degrees, while a consumer products company looks to its sales and marketing divisions for future senior executives.[39]

Another way to fit into an organization is to have a lifestyle similar to those of colleagues, such as patterns in living arrangements. While the majority of respondents in all cases are married, except for women in redistributive agencies, there are some subtle differences in respondents' domestic environments across agency types. Regardless of the subjects' sex, those in distributive agencies are most likely to be married and to be living with one other adult. In fact, no women in this sample who work in distributive agencies live alone, while about one-third of women in the other two agency types do. Substantially more women in distributive agencies than in the other two agency types are married, 80 percent compared to 56 percent and 47 percent. These women appear to have the most traditional domestic arrangements. In contrast to the wide variation among women, roughly 85 percent of men live with one other adult regardless of agency type. These women have not solved the traditional dilemma between work and family roles; they have merely avoided it. Women in distributive agencies also do not have the same arrangements as their male counterparts in redistributive and regulatory agencies, so "fit" might prove more of an issue there.

To the extent that political party matters, regulatory agencies may be the most politically conservative for women, as the proportion of Democrats to Republicans is almost the same. In other places, Democrats dominate, especially among women.

Gender and Fit

The nature of organizations and these variables have consequences in terms of the integration of women into the elite ranks. The linkages between the qualitative characteristics and the general sociological theories about type and degree of integration suggest that agency type predicts individual type. Aspiring entrants must be perceived as fitting in with the incumbents. Because each agency type develops its own group relations,[40] a lack-of-fit model of bias may be inherent in questions of equity in the workplace. In terms of gender power, we must ask, with whom are women to fit? The answer of course is with the men who predominate in these agencies' top echelons.

The concepts of homomorphy and homogeneity are relevant to an understanding of this variable.[41] These concepts are implied in discussion of the "cloning effect" in organizations. Lowi defines integration, or "groupness," as a process involving increasing the degree of mutual awareness and mutual personal identification. Such expanded interaction increases realization of common values and experiences. "Expectations develop, involving the whole person, what he is like, what he is likely to react to, what will offend him, and so on."[42] As Lowi points out, sociologists call this kind of integration gemeinschaft, loosely translated as "fraternity," or "community."[43] Kaufman refers to the process of integration, of "fitting in," in terms of "osmosis";[44] that is, forest officers, for example, are absorbed into the organization by a kind of gradual social osmosis, "during which they, in turn, absorb many of the prevailing values, assumptions, and customary modes of operation."[45]

However, those not fitting the desired mold may be gradually excluded, resulting in a preconscious form of discrimination,[46] especially against women. Nor is such discrimination directed only toward women. Kaufman examines such discrimination in terms of the male employees of the Forest Service: "the men whose administrative behavior fits the desired pattern are the ones who win the rewards, while those who do not conform feel the weight of official disapproval."[47]

One obvious implication of homogeneity in upper-level decision makers is the built-in bias to see things from a single perspective. That is, the relative homogeneity in a group of administrators helps produce relative homogeneity in an outlook on any crucial policy question,[48] including issues of gender equity in the workplace. With issues of gender equity come issues of gender power.

Patterns of Advancement

How did these upper-level administrators reach their current positions? Does career mobility vary across these three agency types, making leadership potential more available in some agency types than others?

As shown in table 9, the subjects in regulatory agencies have spent less time in their current positions than in the other types. More significantly, women in regulatory agencies have been promoted from their second-most-recent position into their current position at a faster rate than women in the other agency types. These women have spent an average of 3 years in their second-most-recent position, compared to an average of 4 and 3.5 years, respectively, for their female colleagues in distributive agencies and redistributive agencies.

Salaries are a widely recognized measure of status and can be a measure of power in organizations. It is common knowledge that women on average earn

TABLE 9. Patterns of Career Advancement in Management, by Agency Type

	Years in Position											
	Regulatory				Distributive				Redistributive			
	Women (n = 9)		Men (n = 18)		Women (n = 5)		Men (n = 24)		Women (n = 15)		Men (n = 18)	
	Mean	Std. Dev.	Mean	Std. Dev.	Mean	Std. Dev.	Mean	Std. Dev.	Mean	Std. Dev.	Mean	Std. Dev.
Current position	2.80	2.82	4.91	5.34	2.80	1.92	4.83	3.87	3.73	2.99	3.65	3.46
Second position	3.11	3.44	3.86	2.36	4.00	2.45	3.64	3.08	3.36	2.41	5.31	8.51
Third position	4.44	4.16	4.05	2.74	3.25	1.71	3.19	2.16	2.79	2.26	4.69	4.44
Fourth position	2.00	1.77	3.56	2.53	1.67	0.58	3.82	2.30	3.85	2.73	5.55	4.93
Current salary	$61,111		$67,318		$70,000		$70,833		$68,400		$69,806	
Hours spent at work per week (expressed as %)												
41–50 hours	44		50		40		46		13		56	
51–60 hours	44		33		40		42		47		28	
61 hours or more	11		11		20		8		40		11	

less than men. Does that marker of gender power occur in these agencies? To what extent do current salaries of respondents differ according to agency type?

The findings indicate that respondents in distributive agencies receive the highest average salary ($70,690: women, $70,000; men, $70,833). They earn an average of $5,521 more than the regulatory-agency type, with the smallest wage gap between sexes. Respondents in redistributive agencies receive somewhat less ($69,167: women, $68,400; men, $69,805), even though on average they work longer hours than the other two types. The lowest average salaries and greatest gender wage gap are evident in the regulatory agencies ($65,169: women, $61,111; men, $67,317). Women earn less in all types of agencies, but the disparity is the least in distributive agencies. Women also work longer hours across the board, despite being paid less than their male counterparts.

The data on span of control suggest that agency type does produce organizational consequences in terms of opportunity structure.[49] The span of control appears to differ according to agency type. While Lowi's thesis is that redistributive agencies are characterized by narrow spans of control, the Florida findings of upper-level administrators, in their current positions, reveal that the regulatory agencies have the narrowest spans of control (with an average of fifteen subordinates per supervisor). The redistributive agencies have somewhat wider spans of control (with an average of twenty-one subordinates per supervisor), and the distributive agencies have the widest spans of control (with an average of twenty-four subordinates per supervisor). A closer examination of these averages in terms of gender reveals that female respondents supervise fewer people in regulatory agencies—an average of thirteen subordinates compared to seventeen for men—and in distributive agencies, with fourteen subordinates compared to twenty-six for the men. However, in redistributive agencies, women supervise a greater number, with twenty-nine, compared to seventeen for the men. The linkage between representation, agency type, and span of control is also noteworthy. That is, the majority of female respondents are employed in redistributive agencies, especially Health and Rehabilitative Services, a quintessential female-type agency. Women have the largest span of control in these agencies, but they get to be "boss" in agencies that are the most hierarchical and conflict laden.[50] These female upper-level administrators are responsible for supervising more than twice as many subordinates as their female counterparts in the other agency types. Remember that the sex composition of these agencies means that women are supervising other women, by and large.

Gender and Benefits from Advancing

In order to examine whether there are organizational differences pertaining to horizontal and vertical career mobility, as Lowi suggests, respondents were asked whether they received grade and salary changes for each of the last four positions held, and whether the position represented a position title change reflecting greater responsibility. The data suggest that benefits are not distributed equally across agency types, but rather accrue to male-dominated agencies. While approximately the same percentages of women and men experienced grade increases or decreases, received salary increases, and experienced position title changes, the percentages for grade and salary increases are higher in the distributive agencies, where patronage politics prosper, than the other two agency types. For approximately three-quarters of the respondents in distributive agencies, their current positions represent a grade increase, in contrast to regulatory agencies, with 63 percent, and redistributive agencies, with 58 percent. The data on salary increases for the current position held reflect the findings above. For 93 percent of respondents in distributive agencies, their current positions represent a salary increase. This compares to regulatory agencies, with 81 percent; and redistributive agencies, with 70 percent. There are no significant differences in position title changes for respondents across all three agency types. No clear pattern of organizational differences emerges from the analyses of the second, third, and fourth positions held. In other words, in the distributive agencies that men dominant, advancement meant both a salary and grade increase for more people than in agencies less associated with masculinity.

Three final observations regarding career mobility are significant. First, according to Lowi, redistributive agencies are characterized by upper-level administrators who have been promoted from within. The Florida findings reveal that more respondents in the distributive agencies (41 percent) than the regulatory (30 percent) or redistributive agencies (29 percent) believe that continuous employment in one state agency has been helpful to their career success. There are no significant gender differences.

Second, lateral entry into government positions is defined as entry at any level, as opposed to entry only at the beginning level. Lowi suggests that lateral entry is characteristic of regulatory agencies. The Florida findings reveal that, while the percentages are low for each agency type, slightly more respondents in the redistributive agencies (14 percent) than the regulatory (11 percent) or distributive agencies (11 percent) believe that lateral moves in state agencies have helped their careers. In terms of gender, it is revealing that while about one in four (26 percent) men in distributive agencies perceive such moves as a facilitator to career success, none of the women so indicate. And while one in three (33 percent) of the women in regulatory agencies perceive such moves as helpful, only one in six (17 percent) of the men so indicate. A gendered pattern exists, although its consequences are unclear.

Third, Lowi posits that distributive agencies are characterized by a large number of specialists in the upper managerial ranks. The Florida findings reveal that a slightly higher proportion of respondents in the distributive agencies (79 percent) than the redistributive (76 percent) or regulatory agencies (52 percent) agree that they are employed in a job concerned with the subject matter in which they specialized for their highest degree. By contrast, a greater proportion of respondents in the regulatory agencies (44 percent) than the redistributive (24 percent) or the distributive agencies (7 percent) respond negatively. Somehow the fit between educational training and a respondent's current job is best in distributive agencies.

It is interesting to speculate on the differences in agency type in the Florida personnel as compared to differences Lowi observed in the federal personnel. First, the differences appear to confirm the validity of the scheme itself. Lowi's typology allows most Florida state agencies to "be categorized with little, if any, damage to the nuances."[51] Second, the differences between federal and state outcomes, empirically speaking, could possibly be attributable to fundamental differences between state agencies and federal agencies, without regard to the policy scheme itself. Local agencies, for example, are functionally quite different from federal agencies. This issue is further explored in Newman and Kelly.[52]

Bureaucracy and Gender

Do respondents exhibit management styles unique to an agency type? Are behavioral characteristics determined, at least in part, by the nature of the organization as Lowi suggests? Duerst-Lahti and Johnson examine the theoretical structure of the Weberian bureaucracy and consider whether bureaucracy "is a masculine organization that undervalues, and possibly excludes, the feminine."[53] This raises a very fundamental question of whether women are universally discriminated against in bureaucracy, or whether bureaucracy is, as purported, neutral, in treating all persons in terms of function and role with no implications for gender. The Florida study allows for an improved formulation of this general Weberian principle.

The Florida findings suggest that organizational behavior is determined by agency type; that is, the nature of bureaucracy is shaped by the type of policies administered therein. The respondents in the regulatory agencies characterize their behavioral styles as follows, in diminishing order of importance: loyal, team oriented, straightforward and frank, independent, and assertive. Those subjects in the distributive agencies characterize their behavioral style as: loyal, straightforward and frank, team oriented, and trusting. Those respondents in the redistributive agencies characterize their behavioral styles as: loyal, team oriented, straightforward and frank, managerial, skilled in interpersonal relations, and do things "by the book."

While respondents in all three agency types characterize their behavioral styles as loyal, straightforward and frank, and team oriented, there are a number of differences. Those respondents in the regulatory agencies are more likely to exhibit behavior characterized as independent and assertive. Those respondents in the distributive agencies indicate they are more trusting. And those respondents in the redistributive agencies are more skilled in interpersonal relations, managerial, and likely to do things by the book. In terms of gender, the majority (83 percent) of female respondents work in either redistributive or regulatory agencies, agencies characterized as rule oriented.[54] Their predilection to manage by the book supports Lowi's thesis that organizational behavior ("group relations")[55] is determined by the type of policies being administered within those agencies.[56] Rule orientation may also indicate that women operate from weaker structural power bases, as people in general who have positions with weak bases are more likely to operate by the book. More to the point for gender power, the fact women have a large presence in top levels of these agencies may have in some fashion caused these agencies to develop more rules; historically, women have been seen as incapable of properly handling the autonomy granted to men in distributive agencies. Conversely, gender power perhaps has dictated that women would advance in these agencies in part because they are more rule bound and therefore have less discretion, a key structural power resource in organizations. The data cannot inform these musings, but the correspondence with gender leads one to muse nonetheless.

Opportunities and Advancement

A central organizing principle of this chapter is an examination of structures of opportunity and the differences that exist in terms of agency type. What are the barriers encountered by the respondents, and do these barriers exist equally across all three agency types? What is there about the organizational environment that might produce significant variations in work environment, particularly of relevance to women? Is there something peculiar about the work environment of a regulatory-, distributive-, or redistributive-agency type and the degree of bureaucratization, professionalization, or the values inherent· in the type of policy? The Florida findings suggest some preliminary answers.

According to the respondents, a number of attitudinal and systemic barriers to career advancement remain in the workplace. First, sex-role stereotyping manifests itself as discriminatory attitudes toward workforce diversity. Almost one in four (22 percent) of the respondents in regulatory agencies believe they have been discriminated against in either hiring or promotion (33 percent of women, 17 percent of men). In distributive agencies only 10 percent report they have been discriminated against, but within that smaller proportion a clear gender pattern exists, with 40 percent of women but only 4 percent of men. In other words, in male-bastion agencies, we see dramatic gender differences in perceived discrimination. A similar but less striking pattern occurs in redistributive agencies, with 12 percent of respondents, but a gendered distribution of 20 percent women and only 6 percent of men. So even in agencies most aligned with feminine gender roles and most populated by women at the top, women still report disproportionately more discrimination in attempts to advance into the most influential leadership posts. Not surprisingly, more support exists for a representative workforce and affirmative-action policy in redistributive agencies (66 percent of respondents so indicate) than the other agency types (regulatory, 33 percent; distributive, 47 percent).

Second, do these attitudes spill over into access to informal networks? According to the literature, access to informal, collegial networks within an organization is critical for career advancement.[57] Many more respondents in distributive agencies (76 percent) than in redistributive (48 percent) or regulatory (33 percent) indicate that they are rarely or never left out of informal discussions with colleagues where important decisions are made. This finding supports Ripley and Franklin's assertion that managers in distributive agencies (typically men) are characterized by long-established patterns of personal inter-action.[58] Reading with a gender lens, one might cynically call this the old-boys network taking care of itself. One might also see it as a reasonable outcome of agencies who grant considerable autonomy to its executives and then develop an ethos that makes that autonomy functional.

Third, to what extent does sexual harassment exist at the highest level of the bureaucratic structure of each agency type? Are respondents in one agency type more or less likely to report knowledge and/or experiences of sexual harassment in the workplace than their counterparts in the other agency types?

Equal Employment Opportunity Commission data show that Florida ranks third highest of the fifty states in the number of sexual harassment filings in 1991. After California and Texas, Florida recorded 377 filings with the EEOC.[59] While the sheer size of the state would likely elevate its ranking, findings here underscore the pervasiveness of sexual harassment in this workplace.

As is shown in table 10, women in redistributive agencies report the highest incidence of sexual harassment. While none of the men so indicate, 20 percent of the women in redistributive agencies indicate they have experienced the most blatant form of sexual harassment, unwelcome sexual advances in exchange for an employment opportunity by a superior. In regulatory agencies 11 percent of women report harassment, and, amazingly, no women in distributive agencies report having been harassed. Perhaps the fact that these women are the most traditional, with 80 percent being married and none living alone, contributes to this harassment-free setting. It invites further inquiry. Nonetheless, redistributive agencies offer the agency type with the greatest advancement potential for women, so finding the most harassment in them is particularly disturbing. A greater proportion of respondents in redistributive agencies than the other two agency types report experiencing requests for sexual favors from work col-

TABLE 10. Sexual Harassment and Agency Type

	Regulatory				Distributive				Redistributive			
	Experienced		Heard About		Experienced		Heard About		Experienced		Heard About	
Type	Women	Men	Women	Men	Women	Men	Women	Men	Women	Men	Women	Men
A	10	0	30	39	0	0	20	17	20	0	67	50
B	30	0	40	48	0	4	40	21	33	0	47	22
C	30	0	60	43	20	0	40	33	33	11	53	39
D	70	39	50	57	40	29	60	50	53	39	67	39

Note: n = 89. Figures are percentages. Type *A* refers to unwelcome sexual advances. Type *B* refers to requests for sex favors from work colleagues. Type *C* refers to other offensive physical contact of a sexual nature. Type *D* refers to offensive verbal behavior.

leagues (redistributive: 15 percent of respondents, 33 percent of women only; regulatory: 11 percent of respondents, 33 percent of women only; distributive: 3 percent of respondents, 4 percent of men only). Not surprisingly, more respondents in the redistributive agencies than the other two agency types report hearing about sexual harassment. Fifty-eight percent of respondents in the redistributive agencies have heard about the most blatant form of sexual harassment (67 percent of women, 50 percent of men), compared to 37 percent of respondents in regulatory agencies and 17 percent of respondents in distributive agencies. Taken together, the findings reveal that sexual harassment creates a significantly "hostile" working environment,[60] especially for women in redistributive agencies. Such an environment translates into a powerful barrier to the career advancement of women in the very place women have the most positional power and the most gender power. This speaks loudly to the power-rooted basis of sexual harassment.

Conclusion

Taken together, the data suggest that the work environment of each agency type is distinctive. Policy types interact with institutional dimensions to produce different opportunities for leadership, unequal distribution of benefits, and varying levels of conflict. Benefits are said to be redistributed in policies with considerable female involvement, and these policies are marked by high degrees of conflict. Policies of greatest interest to men seem to generate less conflict and, tellingly have been interpreted to distribute benefits universally, even though closer inspections shows male advantage. For example, the distributive-agency work environment is conducive to collegial informal networks and cooperation, while regulatory agencies are the most formal in communications; redistributive agencies, where the most women work and hold top posts, are the most centralized and rule bound. Discrimination against respondents in hiring and promotion are more peculiar to regulatory agencies than the other agency types. In this study, female respondents experience the most discrimination in hiring and promotion in distributive agencies, but the least proportional incidence of sexual harassment is reported therein. Redistributive agencies are most supportive of affirmative-action practices, yet have the highest proportional incidence of sexual harassment. Analysis of the work experiences of elites reveal implicit masculinity and advantages accruing to those who work in male-bastion agencies.

Career advancement is a consequence of a myriad of factors. Gender is one such factor. An examination of the difference that gender makes is a necessary prerequisite to understanding and explaining the dynamics of career success. Yet, such an approach is limiting. Broadening the focus to encompass the nature of the organizations in which individuals encounter glass ceilings and glass walls produces additional fruitful and revealing insights.

Organizations are not created equally. Organizational consequences flow from the peculiarities of mission. Such consequences encompass both structure and behavior. Each of Lowi's three models exhibit distinctive organizational features, which reflect substantial gender power differentials. The Florida findings illustrate the characteristics of the structures of opportunity in terms of representation, the fit between the individual and the agency type, patterns of career advancement, and work experiences. This begs the question, Which agency type is most conducive to the career advancement of women? The foregoing analysis is revealing, but not telling. It suggests that the theoretical structure of the Weberian bureaucracy rests, not on a unisex foundation, but a masculine one. Even the construction of the policy typology itself can be thought of in gendered terms. It reflects the masculine ideology inherent in Weberian bureaucracy. At the very least, the peculiarities of mission and agency type are the silent partners in any analysis of structures of opportunity and gender power.

Notes

1. H. George Frederickson, "Public Administration and Social Equity," *Public Administration Review* 50 (2) (1990): 228–37.
2. Gregory B. Lewis, "Men and Women toward the Top: Backgrounds, Careers, and Potential of Federal Middle Managers" (paper presented at the annual meeting of the American Society for Public Administration, Los Angeles, 1990).
3. United States Merit Systems Protection Board, *A Question of Equity: Women and the Glass Ceiling in the Federal Government* (Washington, D.C.: Government Printing Office, 1992).
4. Angela M. Bullard and Deil Spencer Wright, "Circumventing the Glass Ceiling: Women Executives in American State Governments," *Public Administration Review* 53 (3) (1993): 189–202.
5. Rita Mae Kelly, Mary Ellen Guy, Jane Bayes, Georgia Duerst-Lahti, Lois L. Duke, Mary M. Hale, Cathy Marie Johnson, Amal Kawar, and Jeanie R. Stanley, "Public Managers in the States: A Comparison of Career Advancement by Sex." *Public Administration Review* 51 (5) (1991): 402–12.
6. Meredith A. Newman, "Career Advancement: Does Gender Make a Difference?" *The American Review of Public Administration* 23 (4) (1993): 361–84. This framework was first presented in Mary M. Hale and Rita Mae Kelly, *Gender, Bureaucracy, and Democracy,* 1989.
7. For example, C. Wright Mills, *The Sociological Imagination* (New York: Oxford University Press, 1959).
8. Herbert Kaufman, *The Forest Ranger: A Study in Administrative Behavior* (Baltimore: Johns Hopkins University Press, 1960).
9. John Ferejohn, "Comment," in *Regulatory Policy and the Social Sciences,* ed. R. G. Noll (Berkeley, Calif.: University of California Press, 1985): 105–10.
10. Theodore J. Lowi, "The State in Politics: The Relation Between Policy and Administration," in Noll, *Regulatory Policy.*
11. Theodore J. Lowi, "American Business, Public Policy, Case-studies, and Political Theory," *World Politics* 4 (July 1964): 689–90.

12. Theodore J. Lowi, "Four Systems of Policy, Politics, and Choice," *Public Administration Review* 32 (4) (1972): 298–310; Deil Spencer Wright, *Understanding Intergovernmental Relations* (Pacific Grove, Calif.: Brooks/Cole Publishing Company, 1988).

13. The Weberian principle of bureaucracy is based upon rationality and efficiency. As such, Weber's ideal-typical bureaucratic organization is characterized by such qualities as: hierarchy, the direction of subordinates by superordinates, the profile of the organization being pyramidal; a clear specification of the functions and responsibilities of each position in the hierarchy; regular routines and the conduct of activities according to rules; appointment and promotion according to merit; the existence of career ladders in the organization and the expectation of a career within the organization. Dwight Waldo, *The Enterprise of Public Administration: A Summary View,* 5th ed. (Novato, Calif.: Chandler and Sharp Publishers, Inc., 1992).

14. Lowi, "The State in Politics"; Wright, *Understanding Intergovernmental Relations.*

15. Lowi, "The State in Politics."

16. Wright, *Understanding Intergovernmental Relations.*

17. Lowi, "The State in Politics."

18. Lowi, "The State in Politics"; Wright, *Understanding Intergovernmental Relations.*

19. Lowi, "The State in Politics."

20. Theodore J. Lowi, *Incomplete Conquest: Governing America,* 2d ed. (New York: Holt, Rinehart and Winston, 1981).

21. Wright, *Understanding Intergovernmental Relations.*

22. Theodore J. Lowi and Benjamin Ginsberg, *Poliscide: Big Government, Big Science, Lilliputian Politics* (New York: MacMillan, 1976; rpt. Lanham, Md.: University Press of America, 1990), 291.

23. Ibid., 292.

24. Theodore J. Lowi and Benjamin Ginsberg, *American Government: Freedom and Power* (New York: Norton, 1990), 635.

25. Lowi, "The State in Politics."

26. Lowi, *Incomplete Conquest.*

27. Lowi, "The State in Politics."

28. Randall B. Ripley and Grace A. Franklin, *Congress, the Bureaucracy, and Public Policy,* 4th ed. (Chicago: Dorsey Press, 1987).

29. Lowi, "The State in Politics"; Wright, *Understanding Intergovernmental Relations.*

30. Ripley and Franklin, *Congress.*

31. Wright, *Understanding Intergovernmental Relations.*

32. Ripley and Franklin, *Congress,* 93.

33. Ibid.

34. Ibid.

35. Lowi and Ginsberg, *Poliscide.*

36. Debra W. Stewart, "Women in Public Administration" in *Public Administration: The State of the Discipline,* ed. Naomi B. Lynn and Aaron Wildavsky (Chatham, N.J.: Chatham House Publishers, 1990), 224.

37. Ferejohn, "Comment," 107.

38. Lowi, "The State in Politics."

39. United States Department of Labor, *A Report on the Glass Ceiling Initiative* (Washington, D.C.: Government Printing Office, 1991), 16.

40. Lowi, "American Business."

41. Kaufman, *The Forest Ranger;* Ripley and Franklin, *Congress;* Mary Ellen Guy and Lois L. Duke, "Personal and Social Background as Determinants of Position," in *Women and Men of the States,* ed. Mary Ellen Guy (Armonk, N.Y.: M. E. Sharpe, 1992).

42. Theodore J. Lowi, *The Politics of Disorder* (New York: Basic Books, 1971), 37.

43. Ibid.
44. Kaufman, *The Forest Ranger,* 181.
45. Ibid., 182.
46. Ann-Marie Rizzo and Carmen Mendez, *The Integration of Women in Management: A Guide for Human Resources and Management Development Specialists* (Westport, Conn.: Greenwood Publishing, 1990).
47. Kaufman, *The Forest Ranger,* 158.
48. Ripley and Franklin, *Congress.*
49. Span of control is of course a larger concept than the number of employees that a position supervises, taking into account the range and nature of responsibilities, latitude in decision making, size of budget, and the like. Here I use span of control as Lowi and others have done and confine it to number supervised.
50. Ripley and Franklin, *Congress.*
51. Lowi, "American Business," 689.
52. Meredith A. Newman and Rita Mae Kelly, "The Gendered Bureaucracy: Agency Mission and Equity of Opportunity," in progress.
53. Georgia Duerst-Lahti and Cathy Marie Johnson, "Gender and Style in Bureaucracy," *Women and Politics* 10 (4) (1990): 67–120.
54. Lowi, "The State in Politics"; Ripley and Franklin, *Congress.*
55. Lowi, "American Business," 690.
56. Results of factor analysis tentatively suggest a linkage between behavioral characteristics and agency type. These findings are explored in the context of the agency typology in Newman and Kelly, "The Gendered Bureaucracy."
57. Rizzo and Mendez, *Integration of Women;* Rosabeth Moss Kanter, "Presentation VI," *Signs* 1 (3) (1976): 282–91.
58. Ripley and Franklin, *Congress.*
59. Marcia Lynn Whicker and R. A. Strickland, "An Analysis of EEOC Sexual Harassment Filings by State" (paper presented at the annual meeting of the American Political Science Association, Chicago, 1992).
60. S. J. Adler, "Lawyers Advise Concerns to Provide Precise Written Policy to Employees," *Wall Street Journal,* October 1991, B1.

Part 4: Gender Power as a Set of Practices: The Interpersonal Dimension

The interpersonal interactions between men and women involve gender power. The national concern for domestic violence, sexual harassment, and date and stranger rape make dramatically evident the fact that sexual differences and sexuality intrude into physical and psychological power differentials in male/female relations. We also know that women and men generally approach communication differently, often with the consequence of men dominating the conversation while women contribute supportive facilitating messages. To date little attention has been paid to whether or how these types of gender power shape efforts of women to become part of the U.S. governance and leadership structure. If men and women approach conversations differently in private, personal interactions, as Deborah Tannen detailed, does this carry over to the legislature and other political organizations? If the answer is yes, then what does this mean for female leadership? Especially when, as Tannen fails to note, men and women are not situated similarly in terms of societal power. How do alternative styles of communication or patterns of men's sexualized violence toward women, which are themselves embedded in larger power differentials, shape women's ability to gain and hold power in our governing institutions once they are elected or appointed to office?

Lyn Kathlene in "Position Power versus Gender Power: Who Holds the Floor?" directly addresses these questions. Recognizing that leadership requires verbal communication and that control of such communication can determine policy agendas and outcomes, Kathlene examines how traditions of gender power in interpersonal interactions can perpetuate male dominance of policy discussions and outcomes in legislative committees. Gender power becomes evident in that men's verbal activity becomes the greatest in circumstances where women have attained specific position power, including when women become committee chairs and bill sponsors, and in those situations where policies have particular significance for women. This explicit focus on interpersonal gender power draws attention to the intractability of the problems involved in attempts to alter gender power in leadership and governance. The more women "intrude" into the masculinist governance, the more men resist. The most troubling aspect is that legislators—female as well as male—seem not to recognize that these communication patterns occur.

Rita Mae Kelly in "Offensive Men, Defensive Women: Sexual Harassment, Leadership, and Management" shows how male displays of sexual dominance in the workplace reduce the leadership potential of high-level civil servants. Sexual harassment has been called "psychological warfare in the workplace." As with most warfare, winners of the war gain control over positions of leadership, power, and policy outcomes, while losers retreat or defer. Kelly uncovers a link between sexual harassment and the performance of leadership functions by female public administrators, with the offending behavior of men who harass putting their targets into defensive postures contrary to widely acknowledged leadership behavior.

The studies of Kathlene and Kelly combined clearly show that interpersonal gender power is able to neutralize the position power attained by being elected or appointed to a governing office. More is involved than sexism in the fabric of the institutions. Gender power pervades interpersonal conduct in such a way to undermine even those women who attain positions of public leadership. Full equality in the world of governance and leadership may be more difficult to attain than previously recognized. The focus on multiple levels of gender power here helps clarify particular sets of practices that need immediate attention.

Chapter 7

Position Power versus Gender Power: Who Holds the Floor?

Lyn Kathlene

An implicit assumption behind advocating for more women in elected office is that these officials will bring a new power and influence to their underrepresented group. However, this idealized viewpoint ignores the gender power dynamics that subordinate women's words and actions even in "well-balanced" male and female group interactions. An extensive body of research on gender in a variety of disciplines, including management, psychology, communication, linguistics, sociology, and political science, has shown that women are not equally situated with men or adequately captured through models built upon male behavior.[1] Women, whether they be 10, 20 or 60 percent of an organization, work within the larger confines of gendered institutions and socially prescribed roles.[2] As Janice Yoder demonstrates, simply increasing women's presence in the workplace to combat the negative effects of tokenism and bring about gender equality ignores the pervasive sexism in society.[3] Yoder reports that studies on tokenism have found that token men do not experience the same negative consequences as token women; thus sexism rather then group size produces inequities; and that highly masculinized occupations become more, not less, resistant to rapidly increasing numbers of women, a phenomenon Yoder labels the "intrusiveness" effect.

Yoder's assessment, alone, has serious implications for women in politics. Few social and occupational domains are more masculinized than politics. One does not need a thorough review of American history to recognize that elected offices have belonged almost solely to men (especially at the state and national levels) until just very recently—the last twenty or so years. While on one hand we may bemoan that women are making slow (but steady) increases in state legislatures (less than a 1 percent gain per year), historically understood, women's pace could be classified as rapid and "intrusive" in a highly masculinized institution.[4] If individual power and influence over policymaking occurs mainly in legislative committees and subcommittees,[5] women may face barriers not considered within existing models of legislative-committee behavior that ignore the presence and effect of gender power.

In the legislative setting, individuals (and therefore groups) obtain influence primarily through two methods: (1) appointments to powerful positions, and (2) assignments to and participation in committees. Theoretically, in a gender-neutral institution, all committee chairs have the power to set the agenda and guide committee discussions. If women have more of an interest in certain types of issues, as research on their legislative priorities and sponsorship of bills indicates,[6] then in an equitable setting, female committee chairs would have opportunities to imprint their concerns while directing hearings. Similarly, if committees are composed of some critical mass of women, then the effects of tokenism and marginalization should be eliminated, allowing women to join freely in the debate on bills. Yet Yoder's work suggests that women chairs will not receive the same respect or have the same influence over committee hearings as men; and the more feminized a committee becomes, the more overt the hostility will be directed at women by men.

Although it is possible that men always dominate verbal interactions in mixed-sex dyads, triads, and groups,[7] other research indicates that the dynamics of dominance are more complex.[8] Factors such as the positional power of speakers play an important role in gendered verbal behavior.[9] Appointed leaders (such as committee chairs) have "enhanced status" through institutional legitimization,[10] which confers upon them power and respect, as well as access to more resources.[11] In this case, we should expect that women leaders will have more power than women and men not in leadership positions; but they will not necessarily have as much institutional power as men leaders. Women in state legislatures are disproportionately assigned to lower-status social-policy committees (education, health, and welfare) and are largely absent on business-related committees and powerful budget committees.[12] While research has found that women "freely choose" these committees,[13] the choice is largely conditioned by sex socialization that shaped women and men's interests in gendered ways, which is, not surprisingly, directly reflected in the power and prestige these issues have within the legislative body. Men dominate "status" committees; their masculine presence reinforces the given that these are the power committees. Women leaders may be additionally disadvantaged by being assigned to chair lower-status committees,[14] thus perpetuating a cycle of limited opportunities for women.[15] Women leaders also may be disadvantaged to the extent that men and women have or are perceived to have gendered leadership styles in an institution that places higher value on masculinized behavior, such as formal settings with well-defined goals.[16] Finally, other people at a committee hearing may respond to the sex of the chairperson in gendered ways that could validate or challenge a leader's authority.[17]

From the perspective and behavior of women leaders, the issue of gender power becomes particularly salient. Research has found that women do not either use or perceive their positions of power like their male counterparts.[18] Eagly and Johnson's meta-analysis of experimental and organizational research on gender and leadership style found that women tended to lead more democratically, while men tended to be more autocratic.[19] Similar results were found in a legislative setting, where women chairs were more likely to use their position as a facilitator or moderator of committee discussion rather than use it to control witness testimony, direct committee discussion, and join in the substantive debates.[20] Yet it is the latter approaches that are associated with the notion of positional power. That women do not use the position in the same way brings up three important questions: (1) Will gaining access to powerful positions result in truly equal influence? And if women use their positions differently, is this due to (2) men's negative reaction to women in power or (3) women's freely chosen redefinition of power?

With regard to rank-and-file committee members, we should expect similar asymmetrical gender power arrangements. Theoretical and empirical research discussed previously strongly indicates that women and men will not be equal participants in group discussions. The indirect consequences of male-dominated participation in committee hearings may be even more profound than the actual event, as women may be passed over for leadership positions based on both stereotypic perceptions of gender differences (their inappropriateness for leadership) and actual behavioral differences due to the effects of gender power.[21]

Applying gender power to our analyses recognizes that gender is a complex and interacting construct representing struggles over the use and definition of power, methods of managing conflict and building consensus, paths toward implementing change, and resistance by supporters of the status quo. Gender power, like class struggle, is a fundamental category of political analysis, not just an independent variable representing biological sex.[22] Simply increasing the numbers of elected women in public office will not automatically change the power balance.

Documenting how and when women are effectively kept out of policy decision making and under what circumstances women are successful is important for understanding and countering how the status quo resists change despite numerical gains in elected women representatives. This chapter summarizes research documented elsewhere[23] and considers the normative implications of its findings. The focus is on the verbal dynamics of individuals participating in one important decision-making setting: the committee hearing. While the research examines the interpersonal level of co-verbal interaction between women and men, the gender power dynamics that are uncovered represent manifestations of the larger society through a lifetime of sex socialization. Moreover, a gendered organizational component is embedded in the legislative institution, which is structured in ways that enhance men's activity while simultaneously silencing women's voices. Gender power, as seen through an analysis of verbal participation of individuals in committee hearings, does not exist separate from the other social spheres but rather interacts in complex ways that reinforce existing power structures.[24]

Research Design and Methodology

All the data were collected from the 1989 Colorado State House during the regular legislative session. The Colorado legislature has long been among the states with the highest proportion of elected women and is a particularly excellent site for examining both women's impact and legislative decision making in committee hearings.[25] During 1989, Colorado ranked fifth among the fifty states in the number of women elected to state government, with 33 percent (n = 22 out of 65) seated in the house and 20 percent (n = 7 out of 35) in the senate.[26] For testing gender differences in participation rates at committee hearings, the house committees provided a variety of sex compositions. The percentage of women assigned to standing committees ranged from a low of 9 percent on the powerful State Affairs Committee to a high of 55 percent on the Education committee. Two of the ten committees of reference were chaired by females; six committees had female vice-chairs. Both committees chaired by females also had a female vice-chair. All committees were proportionally representative of the legislature's party distribution, with the committee chairs and vice chairs selected from the majority Republican party. Table 11 provides descriptive information about the committees.

Sample Selection of Hearings

Twelve committee hearings, representing 13.2 hours of committee discussion and 204 speakers acting in one of four positions (e.g., sponsor, chair, committee member, witness), were selected from the sixty-eight taped and transcribed hearings gathered.[27] All eight family/children bills taped during the 1989 session were selected for this analysis, based on the presumption that women were likely to engage in discussions about family and children issues, since other research has found that women are more likely to prioritize and sponsor these issues.[28] Four other nonfamily bills, selected on the basis of hearing and sponsor charac-teristics comparable to the family/children bills (i.e., sponsor's sex, chair's sex, the proportion of women on the committee, and the first committee assigned to the bill) provide for a comparison between family and nonfamily bills. Overall, the sample is representative of both the bills and the legislators across many important characteristics.[29] Table 12 lists the characteristics for each of the hearings analyzed.

Dependent Variables

To determine "who holds the floor" in legislative committee hearings, five dependent variables were tested: the percentage of time elapsed at the point when a speaker enters the discussion, the expected frequency of words spoken and turns taken, and the percentage of interruptions made and received.[30]

Results

Positional role at the hearing is an important determinate of speaking behavior. Chairpersons, committee members, and witnesses all differed significantly from sponsors on the five dependent measures. Chairpersons took the most turns speaking, while sponsors dominated hearings in speaking time. Sponsors and chairpersons both made and received more interruptions than committee members or witnesses.[31]

Position continued to distinguish among different speaking behaviors after controlling for sex of the speaker, indicating that men and women chairs (or sponsors, committee members, witnesses) act more like each other than like their male or female counterparts in other positional roles. However, after taking into account the effect of positional role, sex was also significant. Of particular

TABLE 11.   Committees of Reference, 1989 Colorado State House

Committee	n	% Female	Sex of Chair	Sex of Vice Chair
Education	11	55	female	female
Judiciary	11	45	male	female
Finance	11	45	male	male
Local Government	12	42	male	female
Business Affairs and Labor	13	31	female	female
Health, Environment, Welfare and Institutions	10	30	male	female
Agriculture, Livestock, and Natural Resources	12	25	male	male
Appropriations	10	20	male	male
Transportation	11	18	male	male
State Affairs	11	9	male	male

TABLE 12. Committee Descriptions and Legislative Outcomes of Selected Bills

Bill	Title	Issue Area	Assigned Committee	Sex of Sponsor	Sex of Chair	% Female[a]	Outcome[b]
1066	Disabled Children Home Care Program	Family	HEWI[c]	female	female	12	passed/law
1089	Medical Benefits for Children	Family	HEWI	female	male	36	passed/law
1193	Encourage Opportunities for Child Care	Family	HEWI	female	male	25	passed/ postponed indefinitely
1344	Concerning Custody Proceedings	Family	Judiciary	female	female	55	postponed indefinitely
1071	Domestic Abuse Restraining Orders	Family	Education	male	female	56	passed/law
1234	Enforcement of Support Obligations	Family	Judiciary	male	male	44	passed/law
1269	Child Care Expenses and Income Tax	Family	Finance	male	male	36	tabled
1339	Reporting Child Abuse	Family	HEWI	male	male	27	postponed indefinitely
1105	School Dropout Prevention Ace	Education	Education	male	female	64	passed/ postponed indefinitely
1118	Adult High School Diplomas	Education	Education	female	female	56	passed/lost
1263	Reparation Payments and Social Services	Social Services	Finance	male	male	36	passed/law
1309	Superfund Implementation	Environment	HEWI	female	male	36	postponed indefinitely

[a]The percentage female at the hearing includes all legislators (committee members, sponsor, chair). The variation shown within the same committee reflects one or more of the following conditions: (1) one or more legislators assigned to the committee did not attend the hearing; (2) the sponsor could be a man or a woman; (3) the chair of a committee could be a man or a woman since chairs and vice chairs directed hearings.

[b]Outcomes reported: outcome of bill in committee hearing in study or final outcome of bill in the 1989 legislative session.

[c]HEWI = Health, Environment, Welfare, and Institutions.

importance was the finding that female chairs differed significantly from male chairs. Supporting research findings on small-group tutorials,[32] women chairing committees spoke less, took fewer turns, and made fewer interruptions than their male counterparts, suggesting that men and women have different leadership styles. The same gendered pattern holds for female committee members and female witnesses in comparison to their male counterparts, although these differences were not statistically significant.[33] The interaction between gendered leadership styles and its effect on committee members and witnesses will be explored in the following sections.

Gendered Behavior of Committee Members

A look at which group of legislators hold the floor in committee hearings most closely mirrors the environment found in linguistic research on conversational dynamics. While clear and important differences are evident between informal groups (i.e., a group of friends, a set of couples, etc.) and the formality of a public hearing with its political and parliamentary constraints, the committee member plays the most "natural" role of the four types of participants studied in this research. Committee members are relatively free to engage in discussion at any point in time, unlike the witnesses, who must wait for their initial turn and subsequent requests for comments. Unlike the sponsor, committee members are not necessarily advocates of a particular bill, although they may be strongly aligned with a particular issue area. Rather than "campaigning" for the bill as the sponsor does, the committee members' task is to examine the proposed legislation from a multitude of perspectives—personal, professional, and politi-cal—that each brings with them. In this way, committee members have the freedom to act more like individuals in a conversation than the witnesses, who are "outsiders" or merely "guests" at the legislative table, the sponsor, whose self-interest is tightly bound to the passage of the bill, or the chair, whose primary formal responsibility is directing and coordinating the hearing within the boundaries of parliamentary procedures.

Thomas and Welch's study of legislative activity found that men and women reported similar levels of participation in committee hearings.[34] How-ever, given the research discussed earlier on mixed-sex conversational dynam-ics, we would expect gender differences between committee members, with men dominating the hearing. Unlike an informal conversation among friends, several political and institutional factors could produce differentiated patterns beyond or instead of gender. Partisan differences seem very likely. We might expect that the minority party, in this case the Democrats, to be less vocal than the majority Republican party. Or, as Hall's research indicates,[35] minority-party members may be particularly active in committee hearings in order to vocalize their objections to or imprint their concerns on the bill before it reaches the highly partisan dynamics of the House floor debates.[36] Or, party differences may not be discernable, since committees are viewed by the legislators, themselves, as one of the least partisan arenas in the legislature.[37]

Other factors could also be important. Hall found that the desire of members of Congress to make an imprint on a piece of legislation was strongly related to their participation in committee hearings.[38] Having a personal interest or expertise in the issue area of the bill could explain differences in verbal behavior. Interest in the bill should increase a legislator's activity in the committee hearing.

Finally, legislative expertise may account for greater participation. The number of terms served in the legislature can be used as a general measure of legislative expertise. We would expect that newly elected legislators are inexperienced in state legislative policymaking at a number of different levels (e.g., parliamentary procedures, detailed knowledge about failed bills in previous years, and general insider politics) and lack the clout to be included in important off-the-record dealings with legislative leaders, state bureaucrats, and lobbyists. Because the first-term legislators in this research were in the first sixty days of their two-year term, the differences in speaking behavior between the newest members and more seasoned legislators might be very pronounced. Hall found that freshman status was negatively related to participation in congressional policymaking, and the same may hold true in state legislative committee hearings.[39]

Table 13 shows that only sex is highly significant across all the measures of speaking behavior. Male committee members engaged in discussion much earlier than females. Women, on average, waited until more than two-thirds of the hearing was over before they uttered their first words, while men engaged before half the hearing had passed. Men spoke an average of fifty-seven more words, while women spoke an average of seventy-nine fewer words than an equal distribution of words spoken per committee member predicts. Similarly, men took an average of 1.0 more turns than expected and women took an average of 1.4 less turns than expected. In addition, men both made and received more interruptions than women. In other words, women were not the targets of men's more aggressive turn-taking methods; rather, men challenged men. Clearly, these patterns of differences indicate that men dominated the discussion produced by committee members.

Interest in the issue area also proved to be significant on three of the five dependent measures. Committee members who had a personal or professional interest in the bill under consideration spoke more, took more turns, and were interrupted more frequently than the other legislators. Party affiliation and legislative tenure were insignificant.

TABLE 13. Differences in Speaking Behavior of Committee Members by Sex, Party, Freshman Status, and Interest in Issue Area

	Sex Mean Scores			
Speaking Behavior	Male (n = 62)	Female (n = 44)	t	p
% hearing elapsed until first utterance	46.10	64.91	-2.65	.010
Discrepancy word score average in speaking time	56.64	-78.50	2.41	.018
Discrepancy score average in speaking turns	1.00	-1.43	2.39	.018
% interruptions made	4.59	1.05	3.84	.000
% interruptions received	4.91	2.10	2.18	.032
	Party Mean Scores			
Speaking Behavior	Republican (n = 60)	Democrat (n = 46)	t	p
% hearing elapsed until first utterance	52.76	55.09	-.34	.738
Discrepancy word score average in speaking time	-8.35	12.15	-.33	.741
Discrepancy score average in speaking turns	-.21	.25	-.41	.682
% interruptions made	3.61	2.39	1.15	.251
% interruptions received	3.40	4.04	-.46	.650
	Interest in Issue Area Mean Scores			
Speaking Behavior	No (n = 68)	Yes (n = 38)	t	p
% hearing elapsed until first utterance	56.45	49.85	.94	.352
Discrepancy word score average in speaking time	-56.17	107.41	-2.30	.026
Discrepancy score average in speaking turns	-1.08	1.91	-2.71	.008
% interruptions made	2.60	3.73	-1.05	.297
% interruptions received	2.68	5.23	-1.65	.106
	Term Mean Scores			
Speaking Behavior	Freshman (n = 41)	2d+ (n = 65)	t	p
% hearing elapsed until first utterance	50.82	55.62	-.67	.504
Discrepancy word score average in speaking time	-15.39	10.60	-.39	.698
Discrepancy score average in speaking turns	-.42	.25	-.59	.554
% interruptions made	3.56	2.75	.74	.461
% interruptions received	3.18	4.00	-.57	.569

The univariate statistical tests indicate that sex is a powerful predictor of verbal participation in committee hearings. However, it is possible that men's heightened engagement and verbal aggressiveness were related to other factors, most notably interest in the bill. To disentangle the interactions, the four independent variables for each of the five dependent variables were analyzed using ordinary least squares (OLS) multiple regression. Table 14 demonstrates that sex continues to be significant across the five measures even after accounting for committee members' interest in the bill, their party affiliation, and their freshman status. In each of the measures, it was the male committee members who dominated the committee hearings. Gender power operates such that men dominate discussion overall; in part they do so by focusing on men more—shutting out the "intrusive" women. Perhaps most insidious, women apparently do not even realize that men participate more. This pattern is so inculcated that it is nonconscious.

Gendered Dynamics of Committee Hearings

Leadership

Chairing a committee is an important position of power because the chair can control much of the hearing dynamics, including how witnesses are treated, the

TABLE 14. Multivariate Analyses of Speaking Behavior among Committee Members, $n = 106$

Independent Variables	Dependent Variables: Unstandardized Regression Coefficients				
	% Time Elapsed[a]	Words Spoken[b]	Turns Taken[b]	Interruptions Made (%)[c]	Interruptions Received (%)[c]
Female	.19[****]	-144.49[***]	-2.66[***]	-.04[****]	-.03[***]
Interest	-.05	153.23[***]	2.73[***]	.01	.02[*]
Minority party	.05	- 10.53	-.12	-.02[**]	-.01
Freshman status	.03	- 63.48	-1.34	-.01	-.02
Constant	.45	34.33	.69	.05	.05
R^2:	.09	.11	.12	.17	.10

[a]Measures the percent of the hearing that has elapsed when the speaker first talks. Smaller percentages indicate early engagement in committee discussion.
[b]Discrepancy scores computed as expected frequency minus actual frequency. Negative numbers reflect less activity; positive numbers reflect more activity than average. *Words Spoken* measures the time a speaker holds the floor; *Turns Taken* measures how often a speaker initiates and engages in discussion.
[c]Calculated by summing the number of all the types of interruptions a speaker made (or received) divided by the total number of turns in the hearing.
[*]significant at .15 level; [**]significant at .10 level; [***]significant at .05 level; [****]significant at .01 level.

order in which committee members will be recognized to speak, which committee members' ideas will be encouraged or cut off, and whether the bill will
receive a final committee vote or be tabled (usually resulting in the death of the
bill). Earlier we saw that women as chairpersons differed significantly from the
men in measures of their verbal behavior, which raises several important
questions, including (1) what is the substantive nature of this difference? and
(2) how does it affect committee members' verbal behavior? There is some basis,
derived from research of all female groups, to believe that women leaders are
more likely to guide the committee discussion through supportive and cooperative, rather than competitive, linguistic strategies,[40] and to have a more democratic style than men.[41] However, Smith-Lovin and Brody found that the
inclusion of even just one male changed the verbal dynamics of a group toward
more competitiveness.[42] Our expectations, then, are mixed. On the one hand,
women committee members may find the style of women chairs to be more
conducive to their participation, but at the same time men committee members
may become more verbally active and aggressive in response to a woman
chairing the committee and/or her gendered leadership style.

There is even more reason to believe that the leadership style of chairs will
have a strong effect on witnesses' participation. Witnesses have many constraints on their speaking behavior, most notably that they must wait for the chair
to call them forward to speak. Therefore, gender differences in speaking behavior among witnesses may not reflect gender differences between the witnesses
but rather differential treatment by the chair (who determines the order of
testimony[43] and has the power to limit testimony) and the committee members
(who may ask questions of the witnesses). Witnesses may be treated differently
depending upon their formal affiliation (e.g., lobbyist, bureaucrat, expert, or a
citizen) and other important characteristics. Speakers who come to testify at the
request of a legislator should receive more opportunity to speak than witnesses
who come forward on their own initiative. And, relatedly, witnesses who testify
in favor of the bill may be treated differently than those who are against it.
Finally, theories of gender power tell us that male and female witnesses with
different affiliations and roles may be not be equally situated with regard to how
committee members and chairpersons evaluate their importance and credibility.

Sponsorship

The sex of the sponsor may have an effect on the committee members' speaking
behavior. If women are bringing a "different voice" to policymaking,[44] then bills
that women sponsor should reflect this difference and perhaps strike a responsive
cord among the other women committee members and increase their participation at the hearing. Other research on this legislative session found that women

who sponsored traditional women's bills (e.g., family issues) took a more comprehensive and innovative approach to the problem,[45] and even in the case of an issue not traditionally understood as among women's issue, the problem of prison recidivism, men and women conceptualized and recommended solutions in starkly different terms.[46]

Findings

To begin to answer questions of the chair's control and substantive engagement in the committee discussion, the *type of turns* taken by chairs were coded into one of three categories.[47] Beyond taking the floor away from speakers, male chairs also influenced and controlled committee hearing discussions through engaging in substantive comments more than female chairs did. Women were more likely to act as a facilitator of the hearing; while men, in one out of six turns, on average, interjected personal opinions or guided the committee members and witnesses to a topic of their interest. Men used their position of power to control hearings in ways that we commonly associate with the notion of positional power and leadership.[48]

Compared to men's propensity to control committee discussion through interrupting speakers, producing a competitive verbal arena, and selecting issues to be debated, indicating an autocratic leadership style, women chairs acted as moderators guiding the hearing participants toward issue consensus. Did these gendered leadership styles differentially affect the gendered participation rates of committee members and witnesses? The answer is definitively yes in its effect on witnesses. For committee members, the dynamics are complicated by interactions between the sex of the sponsor, percent of females present at the hearing, and policy issue area.

Witnesses began speaking earlier in hearings chaired by a woman because she tended to move directly to witness testimony; whereas a man chairing the committee tended to delay witness testimony through his substantive questioning of sponsors, particularly female sponsors, during the introduction of their bill. Male witnesses, under a female chair or when the hearing was on a family bill, demonstrated heightened verbal aggressiveness through their use of interruptions, with male witnesses interrupting female chairs! Clearly, this is a breach of position power. This suggests that when women are in power and when women's traditional interests are being discussed, there is a backlash practiced by male witnesses.

Gender Overrides Position Power

Gender overrides position power, and the pattern persists in other dynamics, in what can be considered a gender credibility gap. Regardless of who chaired the committee, female witnesses opposed to a bill had significantly less opportunity to participate in the hearing than male witnesses opposed to a bill. And female citizens spoke less than male citizens, who were asked more questions by committee members, as evidenced in the greater number of turns male witnesses took.[49] While we might expect that citizens and witnesses opposed to bills would receive fewer opportunities to participate in the hearing, this is actually only the case for those who are women. Among the less "politically connected" witnesses, there appears to be a significant gender credibility gap. Even among the more politicized witnesses, there were gender differences. Male bureaucrats were asked more questions (they took more turns) but also received more interruptions. Female bureaucrats took significantly fewer turns and made and received fewer interruptions, indicating that they were asked far fewer follow-up questions by the legislators after their initial testimony. And finally, female witnesses who testified on their own accord (rather than being asked by the sponsor) spoke earlier in the hearing than their male counterparts. These women also took more turns, made more interruptions, and received more interruptions, but they did not speak significantly more words than the men.[50] The verbal patterns indicate that these women were persistent in trying to take the floor away from other speakers but were unable to hold it long enough to actually say more than the men.

The differential effect of female legislators' presence (ranging from a low of 12 percent female to a high of 64 percent female) and the sex of the chair and sponsor on committee members' participation in the hearing is complicated. Importantly, men rather than women became significantly more vocal when women comprised greater proportions of the committee, supporting Yoder's "intrusiveness" theory.[51] And, similarly, male committee members engaged earlier, and female committee members later, when the sponsor of the bill was a woman. An examination of the transcript revealed that male committee members asked questions of female sponsors immediately after their introduction and that more male committee members engaged early in questioning witnesses who testified for a female-sponsored bill, regardless of the proportion of women at the hearing. Both behaviors tended not to be present when a man sponsored a bill. In other words, females, but not males, in positions of importance have their ideas scrutinized by rank-and-file men.[52] Seemingly, men's gender power advantage enables them to diminish women's credibility, which in turn reinforces men's gender power advantage.

While the male committee members engaged significantly earlier, they were not speaking or taking more turns under the different situational characteristics of the hearing. The same cannot be said for female committee members. Women not only engaged later when there were more women at the hearing, but they also spoke fewer words. And, women, contrary to the expectation, spoke significantly less than men at hearings addressing a family issue, even after controlling for interest in the issue area (which remained significant). So, gender power advantages do not even accrue to female legislators on a "women's issue."

The statistical measures miss other very distinctive treatments that male chairs used when addressing or acknowledging female witnesses. A woman who testified was usually addressed by her first name by male chairpersons, whether she was an unknown expert or citizen or a familiar lobbyist or bureaucrat; but a witness who was a man received a title in front of his name, both at the time of introduction and at the conclusion of his remarks. Female chairpersons used titles with both men and women who were unknown to them and reserved first names for witnesses of both sexes with whom they were familiar.[53] The most egregious example of this sexist treatment occurred in a hearing on a health issue where several doctors testified. Although the woman witness clearly stated her title and name as "Dr. Elisa Jones,"[54] the male chairperson addressed her repeatedly as "Elisa" and finally thanked "Mrs. Jones" for her testimony. Needless to say, none of the male doctors were referred to as anything but "Dr. Surname."

This all too familiar unconscious downgrading of women's authority and position in society, while not affecting the participation rate of female expert witnesses, may be providing another view of the sexist culture in committee hearings that permeates the participation rates for some female witnesses and most female committee members. Women experts may be given equal opportunity to speak, but one has to wonder if women's expert testimony is seen as equally credible with men's. Such practices reinforce gender power differences, and the persuasiveness of the practices confound obvious remedies through women's increased positional power, expertise, interest, and advocacy, and even their greater numbers. These dynamics of committee hearings unmask the multiple and reinforcing dynamic of gender power arrangements.

Consideration of Nonlinguistic Features

The findings so far suggest that women legislators, despite their numerical and positional gains, may be seriously disadvantaged in committee hearings and unable to participate equally in legislative committee hearings. These findings are not actually surprising given our culture and the social construction of male power. Perhaps most disturbing are the results that substantiate Yoder's thesis of intrusiveness.[55] Contrary to some scholarly expectations and legislators' self-reported behavior,[56] the more women on a committee, the more silenced women became. It may be that women are particularly active in behind-the-scenes negotiations; but as Hall points out,[57] informal participation that alters a bill has to surface as formal participation in the form of amendments in committee or on the floor, which are governed by formal rules.

Does this leave us with no hope that women can participate equally with men in the near future? Perhaps yes, but again, research in conversational dynamics suggests that male dominance is not universal but rather thrives in certain types of settings, some of which are particularly salient to legislative policymaking. Women held their own with male colleagues in university committee meetings when the talk was informal, i.e., not led by the chairperson. But when the meeting turned to formal procedures, men dominated the discussion.[58] This implies that the parliamentary rules and procedures adversely affect women and benefit men. This apparent male advantage in formalized discussion then further compounds informal gender power imbalances during discussion. Changing the way hearings are held is a tall order and probably will not happen any time soon.

However, Swann argues that nonlinguistic features such as the seating arrangement—whether males and females are either grouped together or interspersed—may be a powerful factor in linguistic behavior.[59] According to Caldeira and Patterson,[60] spatial proximity helps create political friendships in the legislature, which can be important influences in legislative decision making. Yet, Blair and Stanley found that women had greater difficulty in establishing political friendships, especially with their male colleagues, despite being surrounded by men.[61] Given the importance of political friendships and women's tendency to find other women more friendly toward them, would women on committees speak earlier and more often if they sat next to each other? Maybe women do not have to sit next to each other to make use of their common interests. Other research has found that women were more aware of and responsive to nonverbal social and emotional cues.[62] Given women's sensitivity to nonverbal behavior, it seems possible that the arrangement of the hearing table could be important for women in ways that have little affect on men. If the table is shaped in a V or in a semicircle, rather than one long straight table, women would be able to see and make eye contact with other women committee members. Would visual contact between women increase their verbal interactions?

To answer these questions, I cluster-analyzed the previous three factors hypothesized to be important to bringing out women's voices, sex of the chair, sex of the sponsor, and percentage of females present at the hearing, and added two new variables: (1) the seating arrangement of female committee members, measured as at least one pair of females seated together at the table or no pairs of females seated together, and (2) the shape of the table, where two hearing rooms with very different table shapes were represented.

Three clusters emerged from the analysis. Four of the five clustering variables were statistically significant across the three clusters. The most powerful variables (most differentiating as measured through an analysis of variance) were (1) seating arrangement of females (F = 20.13, df = 2, p = .000); (2) shape of the table (F = 17.91, df = 2, p = .000); (3) sex of the sponsor (F = 16.02, df = 2, p = .000); (4) sex of the chair (F = 9.26, df = 2, p = .000). The five speaking-behavior variables were then compared by sex within each of the clusters. Table 15 shows the characteristics of each cluster.

TABLE 15. Characteristics of and Gendered Verbal Behavior in Hearings

	Cluster 1	Cluster 2	Cluster 3
Hearing characteristics (used in cluster analysis)			
Females paired?	Yes	Yes	No
Table shape	V-shaped or straight	V-shaped	Straight
Sponsor	Female	Male	Male or female
Chair	Female	Male or female	Male
Average % of females	40% (range: 12–56%)	48% (range: 36–64%)	33% (range: 25–44%)
Verbal behavior (not clustered)			
Committee Members			
First utterance	males early	no difference	no difference
Words spoken	no difference	no difference	males more
Turns taken	no difference	no difference	males more
Interruptions made	males more	males more	males more
Interruptions received	no difference	no difference	males more
Witnesses			
First utterance	females early	no difference	males early
Words spoken	no difference	no difference	males more
Turns taken	no difference	no difference	no difference
Interruptions made	no difference	no difference	males more
Interruptions received	no difference	no difference	males more
Hearing characteristics (not clustered)			
Number of bills	4	4	4
Number of family bills	3 (75%)	2 (50%)	3 (75%)
Average time (minutes)	82.2	54.8	65.1
Range of time (minutes)	38–138	26–87	42–80
% female witnesses	43%	30%	52%
Number with fiscal impact	3	2	2
Number passed	3 (75%)	3 (75%)	2 (50%)

When women committee members sit together (as in clusters one and two), women committee members and women witnesses have verbal behaviors similar to their male counterparts. When the chair and sponsor is also a woman (cluster one), the overall percentage of women at the hearing can range from a small minority (12 percent) to a majority (56 percent) without negatively affecting women's "voice," although male committee members do initiate their first turn substantially earlier than female committee members. This early turn appears to be in response to the early initiation of female witnesses in cluster one. When women hold both positions of power (as chair and as sponsor) and bring women to the witness table early, male committee members engage quickly. While women's voices are strong in both these clusters, men committee members are significantly more likely to make interruptions than the women.

Quite the opposite pattern appears in cluster three. When none of the women committee members sit next to each other at the hearing, men as committee members and witnesses dominate the hearing. The gender imbalance in verbal behavior is striking, and one gets the sense that the hearings themselves are male-dominated competitive arenas, where men as committee members and witnesses both make and receive more interruptions than the women. This reflects patterns uncovered earlier: hearings chaired by males had the highest percentage of speaker turnovers through interruptions. Importantly, having women sit together appears to have a moderating affect on these dynamics associated with male-chaired hearings (see cluster two).

The differences in verbal behavior among the cluster types is not related to issue area or the fiscal impact of the bill. Family bills are found in each cluster, as are bills that require state monies. Six of the eight bills heard in clusters one and two, where gender differences were the least, were passed out of the committee. A somewhat smaller ratio of bills, two of the four, heard in the male-dominated cluster three were passed. But what about the table shape? When women dominate the hearing and are seated together (cluster one), either table will do. But when women make up less of a presence yet continue to sit together (cluster two), the V-shaped table appears most conducive to bringing out women's voices. The straight table where no women sit together and the hearing is dominated by men (cluster three) does not enhance women's verbal interactions. An examination of figure 6 provides the visual context to interpret these results.

As hypothesized, when women sit next to each other and/or can see each other (as is the case in the V-shaped table), women will be more active participants in committee hearings. With the absence of both these nonlinguistic features, women's voices are muted. The features of clustering would have the effect of minimizing isolation and providing a "reality check" for the women

Hearing table 1: V-shaped

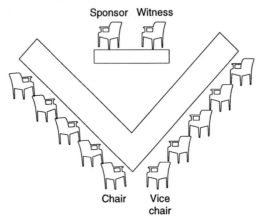

Hearing table 2: Straight*

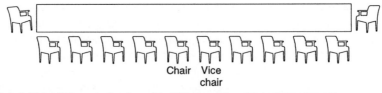

*Labeled "straight" because the wings of the table were not used to seat more than one committee member.

Fig. 6. Table shapes and seating arrangement of legislators

that indicates similar reaction to events in the hearing. This support may be sufficient to have women enter men's "intrusive reaction" competition.

Recommendations

The cluster analysis indicates that there are specific circumstances that produce a more favorable environment for women's active participation in committee hearings: (1) First and foremost, women committee members should sit next to at least one other woman. (2) A woman sponsor concerned about having a gender-balanced treatment of her bill should attempt to have a woman chair the hearing. In Colorado, 50 percent of the vice chairs were women, and vice chairs frequently directed the hearing. The alternative, having a woman-sponsored bill heard in a committee chaired by a man, received the most unbalanced gender treatment. (3) If the shape of the table does not automatically provide a clear view of other committee members, then women should seat themselves so they can make eye contact with as many other women as possible. If the table has a long straight middle section with short "wings" on either side, women should not sit solely in the middle section where they cannot see another woman (other than those seated next to her). This advice, summarized in table 16 below, might be particularly useful for women in legislative positions.

Discussion

Two major issues regarding women and governance are raised by this research. First, gender power in the legislature disadvantages women in all four positions of policymaking activity to the extent that men assert more control over the access to and content of the committee hearing debate. However, the control is not absolute, and there are simple and effective ways for women to counterbalance gender power. In these terms, the research provides both an examination of gender dynamics and proactive prescriptions for change.

Second, the normative implications of gender power in our political institutions are nothing less than seriously disturbing. To the extent that a democracy entails some semblance of representativeness of individuals and groups, the systematic imbalance of power between men and women across every position of the committee hearing defies the numerical and social gains women have made. Sex discrimination and patriarchal control have only become more subtle and insidious, rather than reformed or eliminated, and the worst part may be that female legislators remain unaware of their differential participation. Under masculinest ideology, the "givenness" of these gender power assumptions run deep, out of conscious awareness.

Gender power not only creates problems for women's opportunities but for governance as well. First, power concentrated among certain groups of elected officials at every level of the institution is systemic discrimination that is neither just for the individuals working within the organization nor enabling of the

TABLE 16. Overcoming Gender Power in State Legislative Hearings: Three Simple Strategies for Legislative Women

1. Women should sit together, at least in pairs.

2. A woman should have her bill heard in a committee chaired by a woman.

3. Women should seat themselves so they have eye contact with other women.

institution to produce fair policies. Second, the masculine leadership style—verbally aggressive and substantively autocratic—is itself contrary to the tenets of democratic policymaking, yet it largely goes unnoticed. If this is business as usual, we have come to accept a distorted, or at least a partial, notion of what governance can be. Even Webster's definition of governance as a noun meaning "control [and] authority" demonstrates this monolithic, masculinized view of political institutions.[63] But this institutionalized view of governance reflects an approach to leadership more common to men. Women who chaired committees created a policymaking arena that allowed for more participation by witnesses and more opportunity for committee members and witnesses to debate the issue—minimizing the "control and authority" typically imposed by a chair's personal or political agenda.

This brings us back to a set of questions posited earlier. Is women's alternative leadership style created out of (1) men's negative reaction to women in power, or (2) women's freely chosen redefinition of power?[64] Research done by Smith-Lovin and Brody can help disentangle these issues.[65] They found that men, but not women, differed in their interruption rates and the type of interruption made (i.e., positive or negative) based on the sex composition of the group. In all-male groups, men used more supportive or positive interruptions with each other; but in mixed-sex groups, men's style changed: they were more than twice as likely to interrupt a woman, and when they interrupted a man, the odds that the interruption would be supportive declined steeply in relation to the proportion of women in the group. In contrast to the men, women's interruption behavior did not differ regardless of the sex composition of the group. The authors conclude that "men are acting as if sex is a status characteristic ... [but] women are behaving as though sex were not a status characteristic for them."[66] Their research implies that men's verbal behavior in committee hearings chaired by a woman was, indeed, a reaction to her sex. In addition, Smith-Lovin and Brody's work also found that women's verbal behavior was consistent across various settings, suggesting that women's leadership style was not in response to men's increased aggressiveness but rather women's preferred way of conducting hearings. Such suggests that when women enter a scene, their presence prompts men to protect masculinist gender power arrangements through heightened aggression.

What is the basis for these gendered leadership styles? Are women socialized to be subordinate and dependent, and therefore they act cautiously, tending not to use their institutional power to command and control? Or are women socialized to be "nice and caring of others" and feel compelled to hear everyone's opinion and politely wait until a person stops speaking? Or have women learned caution from life experience of men who "attack" verbally in respond to their mere presence? The connotations of these questions are themselves illustrative.

Women's qualities, thus far argued to represent a more empowering and demo-cratic approach to policymaking, suddenly sound like a weakness when juxta-posed against the masculine "norm" of dominance and independence. But consider the following questions, which we should be asking in addition to or instead of pondering why women are "different": Are men socialized to be dominant, and therefore they act without self-restraint, which becomes espe-cially pronounced when they acquire positions of power in institutions? Or are men socialized to be "independent thinkers," producing a false sense of certainty about what is best and what is important, creating individuals who undervalue, override, or ignore the opinions and concerns of others unlike themselves? These latter two questions ask why are men different than women, while giving implicit positive value to the so-called feminine qualities rather than vice-versa. Surely, if we are to ask questions of gender difference, we must take care to ask questions about both feminine and masculine behavioral constructs.

Is the answer to these questions to be found, given the totality of sex socialization and the complexity of human behavior? Probably not; at least not as long as sex socialization exists. Do we need to know the answer? Again, probably not, because ultimately the issue is not which leadership style is best but rather what circumstances or points in the process are best served by a particular style. The problem has been (and continues to be) that one leadership style has been institutionalized and rewarded. So while leadership styles that lean more toward consensus building may be less efficient and not as conducive to moving an issue through the legislative process in the short term, they provide participants with opportunities to learn about different views and arguably then lead to improved long-term solutions to public problems. Clearly forums open to multiple perspectives and free from domination benefit the early stages of policymaking. When more people and more perspectives are incorporated into the policy formulation process, the better our public policies will reflect the affected communities.[67]

First, committee hearings in state legislatures (i.e., those like the ones examined in this research) are usually the first open public airing and discussion of a proposed policy. While much work has already been done behind the scenes in drafting the bill, unless the legislator was able or willing to bring together all who could have an interest in the bill, the committee hearing is the first and sometimes last chance for interested parties (which includes both witnesses and committee members) to participate in the policymaking process interactively. To "control" the dialogue at this point in the process is to increase the probability that policies will be poorly designed, insensitive to the needs and realities of its target population and the public at-large.[68]

Governance as control may have an important place later in the process, after the public debate has been aired. But as this research demonstrates, men tend to control the policy debate early in the process. This has special significance for all public policy, but I would argue it is especially disconcerting for policy issues in which women have a special stake, for example, women's rights, women's health concerns, and domestic violence. If male chairpersons have a propensity to interrupt speakers and choose the points to be discussed, women's issues will probably not receive a fair or informed hearing. If rank-and-file men are propelled to "take up" and "take away" the floor from rank-and-file women when a female sponsors a bill or the issue heavily affects women, then women's imprint on the policy process will be undermined. The more the status quo is challenged—by the presence of women as participants in the policymaking process and by the inclusion of women's issues on the policy agenda—the more stridently its defenders resist. Such a reaction calls into question the quality of women's representation and the legitimacy of our democracy. No evidence suggests that gender power dynamics will change on their own with the increase of women in legislative positions or even necessarily come with the passage of time, as there were no generational differences in gendered behavior.[69]

Ultimately, to understand these gender power differentials, we need to examine how the content of a bill changes as it passes through the process and look closely at who is influencing the changes. Does male verbal aggression directed at women-sponsored bills or women's issues result in a transformation of women's bills so that their bills become disproportionately influenced by male voices? Or do women as chairs or committee members have ways, other than verbal participation in committees, to imprint their concerns on legislation as it moves through the process? For example, are ideas raised by women in committee hearings reflected in amendments sponsored by men? Are women influential in derailing potential changes to their bills? Do stereotypic female communication tactics[70] result in more substantive impact than women's actual verbosity would predict? These other behaviors may be occurring, as women were as successful as men in getting their bills through the legislative process even in the context of men's more vocal participation in committees.[71]

While the gender power dynamics uncovered in this research demonstrate a severe imbalance in participation in committee hearings, there is room for optimism. Women's alternative leadership styles suggest a future where governing may be defined as both the process of building a public consensus and the authority to direct society toward common goals. But we need not wait for the future. Given the right committee hearing configuration, women as elected officials and women as witnesses can increase their impact on the content of today's public policies.

Summary

Examining the speaking behaviors of legislators during committee hearings provides us with yet another view of the power of gender in our culture. Bringing more women into politics will not translate directly into a proportionate amount of female power and influence. In fact, a powerful backlash may occur when women exceed a certain critical mass in a highly masculinized institution such as legislative politics.[72] This competitive arena is simply an enhancement of the status quo where men, as committee members and witnesses, interrupt speakers to deliver a monologue (rather than participate in a dialogue) and male chairpersons use their position of power to control the hearing by manipulating the substantive debate through interjecting personal opinions and interrupting participants. Governance, as we have come to know it, is the reflection of this masculinized version of power and control. Governance, as we have come to know it, is a product of masculinist ideology.

Yet, over time the presence of more women legislators will lead to more women sponsoring bills and chairing committees. When women chaired committees, the dynamics of the hearing changed for witnesses and female sponsors in complex ways, some of which may provide for more democratic policymaking, particularly when the negative effects of increased verbal aggressiveness by men can be countered. So, while women in legislatures face these double binds, their efforts remain important to good governance.

Notes

The research was funded, in part, by the Revson Foundation through its grant to the Center for the American Woman and Politics (CAWP), a unit of the Eagleton Institute of Politics at Rutgers University, and, in part, by the Purdue Research Foundation. The author is solely responsible for all analyses and interpretations. An earlier version of this paper was presented at the annual meeting of the Western Political Science Association, March 1993, Pasadena, Calif.

1. Rosabeth Moss Kanter, *Men and Women of the Corporation* (New York: Basic Books, 1977); Carol Gilligan, *In a Different Voice: Psychological Theory and Women's Development* (Cambridge, Mass.: Harvard University Press, 1982); Lyn Kathlene, "Uncovering the Political Impacts of Gender: An Exploratory Study," *Western Political Quarterly* 42 (1989): 397–421; Belle Rose Ragins and Eric Sundstrom, "Gender and Power in Organizations: A Longitudinal Perspective," *Psychological Bulletin* 105 (1989): 51–88; Mary Ellen Guy, ed., *Women and Men of the States* (Armonk, N.Y.: M. E. Sharpe, 1992).

2. Lynn Zimmer, "Tokenism and Women in the Workplace: The Limits of Gender-Neutral Theory," *Social Problems* 35 (1988): 64–77; Mary Ellen Guy and Georgia Duerst-Lahti, "Agency Culture and Its Effect on Managers," in Guy, *Women and Men.*

3. Janice D. Yoder, "Rethinking Tokenism: Looking beyond Numbers," *Gender and Society* 5 (1991): 178–92.

4. Center for the American Woman and Politics (CAWP), *Women in State Legislatures 1993,* fact sheet (New Brunswick, N.J.: National Information Bank on Women in Public Office, Eagleton Institute of Politics, Rutgers University, 1993).

5. Wayne L. Francis and James W. Riddlesperger, "U.S. State Legislative Committees: Structure, Procedural Efficiency, and Party Control," *Legislative Studies Quarterly* 7 (1982): 453–71; Richard L. Hall, "Participation and Purpose in Committee Decision Making," *American Political Science Review* 81 (1987): 105–27.

6. Sue Thomas and Susan Welch, "The Impact of Gender on Activities and Priorities of State Legislators," *Western Political Quarterly* 44 (1991): 445–56; Michelle A. Saint-Germain, "Does Their Difference Make a Difference? The Impact of Women on Public Policy in the Arizona Legislature," *Social Science Quarterly* 70 (1989): 956–68.

7. Jessie Bernard, *The Sex Game* (New York: Atheneum, 1972); Marjorie Swacker, "The Sex of the Speaker as a Sociolinguistic Variable," in *Language and Sex: Difference and Dominance,* ed. Barrie Thorne and Nancy Henley (Rowley, Mass.: Newbury House, 1975); Don H. Zimmerman and Candace West, "Sex Roles, Interruptions, and Silences in Conversation," in Thorne and Henley, *Language and Sex;* Frank N. Willis and Sharon J. Williams, "Simultaneous Talking in Conversation and Sex of Speakers," *Perceptual and Motor Skills* 43 (1976): 1067–70; Pamela M. Fishman, "Interaction: The Work Women Do," *Social Problems* 25 (1978): 397–406; Joan Swann, "Talk Control: An Illustration from the Classroom of Problems in Analyzing Male Dominance of Conversation," in *Women in Their Speech Communities,* ed. Jennifer Coates and Deborah Cameron (London: Longman, 1988); Nicola Woods, "Talking Shop: Sex and Status as Determinants of Floor Apportionment in a Work Setting," in Coates and Cameron, *Women in Speech Communities;* D. Craig and M. K. Pitts, "The Dynamics of Dominance in Tutorial Discussions," *Linguistics* 28 (1990): 125–38.

8. Mary E. Correa, Edward B. Klein, Walter N. Stone, Joseph H. Astrachan, Ellen E. Kossek, and Meera Komarraju, "Reaction to Women in Authority: The Impact of Gender on Learning in Group Relations Conferences," *Journal of Applied Behavioral Science* 24 (1988): 219–33; Stephen O. Murray, Lucille H. Covelli, and Mary Talbot, "Women and Men Speaking at the Same Time," *Journal of Pragmatics* 12 (1988): 103–11.

9. Peter Kollock, Philip Blumstein, and Pepper Schwartz, "Sex and Power in Interaction: Conversational Privileges and Duties," *American Sociological Review* 50 (1985): 34–46.

10. Correa et al., "Reaction to Women."

11. Ragins and Sundstrom, "Gender and Power."

12. After controlling for a variety of demographic and political factors, Thomas and Welch, "Impact of Gender," found men and women differed only in their assignments to business-related committees (men more) and health and welfare committees (women more). However, for purposes of understanding how gender power is distributed in the legislature through who sits on what committees, the proportion of men and women assigned to committees regardless of control factors is the important measure.

13. Susan Carroll and Ella Taylor, "Gender Differences in the Committee Assignments of State Legislators: Preferences or Discrimination?" (paper presented at the Midwest Political Science Association, Chicago, April 13–16, 1989).

14. Thomas and Welch, "Impact of Gender."

15. Ragins and Sundstrom, "Gender and Power."

16. Correa et al., "Reaction to Women."

17. Dore Butler and Florence L. Geis, "Nonverbal Affect Responses to Male and Female Leaders: Implications for Leadership Evaluations," *Journal of Personality and Social Psychology* 58 (1990): 48–59.

18. Georgia Duerst-Lahti and Cathy Marie Johnson, "Gender and Style in Bureaucracy," *Women and Politics* 10 (1990): 67–120; Diane D. Blair and Jeanie R. Stanley, "Personal Relationships and Legislative Power: Male and Female Perceptions," *Legislative Studies Quarterly* 16 (1991): 495–507; Debra L. Dodson and Susan J. Carroll, *Reshaping the Agenda: Women in State*

Legislatures (Rutgers, N.J.: Center for the American Woman and Politics, Eagleton Institute of Politics, Rutgers University, 1991).

19. Alice H. Eagly and Blair T. Johnson, "Gender and Leadership Style: A Meta-analysis," *Psychological Bulletin* 108 (1990): 233–56.

20. Lyn Kathlene, "A New Approach to Understanding the Impact of Gender on the Legislative Process," in *Feminist Research Methods: Exemplary Readings in the Social Sciences,* ed. Joyce McCarl Nielsen (Boulder, Colo.: Westview Press, 1990). Research on women in management supports these findings in the legislative setting. See Judy Rosener, "Ways Women Lead," *Harvard Business Review* (Nov.–Dec. 1990): 119–25.

21. Ragins and Sundstrom, "Gender and Power."

22. Gertrude A. Steuernagel, "Reflections on Women and Political Participation," *Women and Politics* 7 (1987): 3–13; Helene Silverberg, "What Happened to the Feminist Revolution in Political Science? A Review Essay," *Western Political Quarterly* 43 (1990): 887–903.

23. Lyn Kathlene, "Who Holds the Floor? Overcoming Gender Differences in Legislative Committee Hearings" (paper presented at the annual meeting of the Western Political Science Association, Pasadena, Calif., March 18–20, 1993); Lyn Kathlene, "Power and Influence in State Legislative Policy Making: The Interaction of Gender and Power in Committee Hearing Debates," *American Political Science Review* (September 1994), forthcoming.

24. Ragins and Sundstrom, "Gender and Power."

25. Kathlene, "Power and Influence."

26. CAWP, *Women in State Legislatures.*

27. The larger sample of 68 bills were selected from all 360 bills introduced in the 1989 session of the Colorado State House based on a number of criteria: (1) sex of the sponsor; (2) terms in the legislature of the sponsor; (3) issue area of the bill; (4) state fiscal impact; and (5) public visibility. The sample of 68 bills was representative of the 360 bills introduced in the 1989 session in terms of the above criteria and legislative-outcome factors, including House committee hearing outcomes, amendment action, House and Senate floor action, and governor action.

28. Saint-Germain, "Does Their Difference"; Thomas and Welch, "Impact of Gender"; Sue Thomas, *How Women Legislate* (New York: Oxford University Press, 1994).

29. Kathlene, "Power and Influence."

30. Percentage time elapsed was calculated by dividing the number of words spoken at the hearing prior to a speaker's first utterance by the total number of words spoken at the hearing. Words spoken and Turns taken are discrepancy score measures computed as expected frequency (the sum of the speaking behavior divided by the number of people present at the hearing) minus actual frequency. Negative numbers reflect less activity—positive numbers, more activity—than average. The discrepancy score standardizes for differences in the length of the hearing time to make inter-hearing speaking behavior comparable. Percentage interruptions made and Percentage interruptions received were coded according to the scheme in Craig and Pitts, "Dynamics of Dominance," which identified five types of interruptions. See Kathlene, "Power and Influence," for a diagram of how interruptions were coded.

31. Kathlene, "Power and Influence."

32. Craig and Pitts, "Dynamics of Dominance."

33. Kathlene, "Power and Influence."

34. Thomas and Welch, "Impact of Gender."

35. Hall, "Participation and Purpose."

36. Wayne L. Francis, *The Legislative Committee Game: A Comparative Analysis of Fifty States* (Columbus: Ohio State University Press, 1989).

37. Francis and Riddlesperger, "U.S. State Legislative Committees."

38. Hall, "Participation and Purpose."

39. Ibid.

40. Jennifer Coates, "Gossip Revisited: Language in All-Female Groups," in Coates and Cameron, *Women in Speech Communities*.

41. Eagly and Johnson, "Gender and Leadership Style."

42. Lynn Smith-Lovin and Charles Brody, "Interruptions in Group Discussions: The Effects of Gender and Group Composition," *American Sociological Review* 54 (1989): 424–35.

43. It was common for the chair to ask the sponsor if they had a preference for the order of the witnesses. Sometimes the sponsor was interested in ordering all of the witnesses, but usually the sponsor had a preference only for who spoke first. Therefore, any gender differences found in the amount of hearing time elapsed before speaking could be an indicator of gendered sponsor treatment of the witnesses as much as, if not more than, differential treatment by the chair.

44. Saint-Germain, "Does Their Difference"; Kathlene, "Uncovering"; Kathlene, "Gendered Approaches to Policy Formation in the Colorado Legislature" (paper presented at the annual meeting of the Midwest Political Science Association, Chicago, April 18–20, 1991); Debra L. Dodson, ed., *Gender and Policymaking: Studies of Women in Office* (Rutgers, N.J.: Center for the American Woman and Politics, Eagleton Institute of Politics, Rutgers University, 1991); Beth Reingold, "Concepts of Representation among Female and Male State Legislators," *Legislative Studies Quarterly* 17 (1992): 509–37.

45. Lyn Kathlene, Susan E. Clarke, and Barbara A. Fox, "Ways Women Politicians are Making a Difference," in Dodson, *Gender and Policymaking*.

46. Kathlene, "Gendered Approaches."

47. The three categories were (1) *parliamentary turns* (which were procedural turns, such as when the chair would call a witness or recognize a committee member who wanted to speak); (2) *clarification turns* (which requested an affirmation from a previous speaker about the content or meaning of their statement); and (3) *question/opinion turns* (which interjected a new idea into the discussion).

48. Kathlene, "Power and Influence."

49. Ibid.

50. Ibid.

51. Yoder, "Rethinking Tokenism."

52. Kathlene, "Power and Influence."

53. It is not hard to distinguish between familiar and unfamiliar witnesses. When a chairperson knows the witness, he or she usually makes a remark indicating their familiarity, such as "Nice to see you again," or "It's been a long time since you've come to this committee." A witness who is unknown elicits slower and more careful (if not mistaken) enunciation of their name, along with the chairperson offering precise directions to the witness to "state your name and whom you represent for the tape."

54. Dr. Elisa Jones is a fictitious name.

55. Yoder, "Rethinking Tokenism."

56. Thomas and Welch, "Impact of Gender."

57. Hall, "Participation and Purpose."

58. Carole Edelsky, "Who's Got the Floor?" *Language in Society* 10 (1981): 383–421.

59. Swann, "Talk Control."

60. Gregory A. Caldeira and Samuel C. Patterson, "Political Friendship in the Legislature," *Journal of Politics* 49 (1987): 953–75.

61. Diane D. Blair and Jeanie R. Stanley, "Personal Relationships and Legislative Power: Male and Female Perceptions," *Legislative Studies Quarterly* 16 (1991): 495–507.

62. Ross W. Buck, Virginia J. Savin, Robert E. Miller, and William F. Caul, "Communication of Affect through Facial Expressions in Humans," *Journal of Personality and Social Psychology* 23 (1972): 362–71; Barbara Westbrook Eakins and R. Gene Eakins, *Sex Differences in Human Communication* (Boston: Houghton Mifflin, 1978); Mary Glenn Wiley and Arlene Eskilson,

"Speech Style, Gender Stereotypes, and Corporate Success: What If Women Talk More Like Men?" *Sex Roles* 12 (1985): 993–1007.

63. *Webster's Dictionary of the English Language* (New York: Lexicon Publications, 1989).
64. I do not mean to imply that these styles are strictly tied to sex; rather, I respond to the empirical pattern found here.
65. Smith-Lovin and Brody, "Interruptions in Group Discussions."
66. Ibid.
67. Lyn Kathlene and John A. Martin, "Enhancing Citizen Participation: Panel Designs, Perspectives, and Planning," *Journal of Policy Analysis and Management* 10 (1991): 46–63.
68. This discussion assumes an idealized hearing where all people representing the variety of perspectives attend. This, of course, is a problematic assumption, and the solution to low levels of citizen participation is another topic in and of itself. Nevertheless, if the forum for citizen participation is discriminatory (e.g., women get less opportunities to join in the discussion) and biased (i.e., the perspective of the chair carries more force because of the power and control a chairperson can wield), then citizens' physical access to public hearings still will not result in citizen input.
69. Kathlene, "Who Holds the Floor?"
70. Georgia Duerst-Lahti, "But Women Play the Game Too: Communication Control and Influence in Administrative Decision Making," *Administration and Society* 22 (1990): 182–205.
71. Kathlene, "Gendered Approaches," and "Power and Influence."
72. Yoder, "Rethinking Tokenism."

Chapter 8

Offensive Men, Defensive Women: Sexual Harassment, Leadership, and Management

Rita Mae Kelly

Throughout the 1990s sexual harassment has been a hot topic in America. Prior to the 1970s this age-old practice was typically considered a personal matter. Courts rarely dealt with it, and when they did, they approached unwanted sexual attention as a individual personal-injury issue, not as a matter of sex discrimination against women as a group. In the last quarter of the twentieth century, however, dramatic changes in thinking about gender power and its sources and links with sexual harassment have led to a different, less tolerant view of such types of behavior.

The women's movement pushed strongly for the recognition that male/female interactions were, for the most part, not biologically decreed, but rather were socially constructed behaviors, approved and condoned to perpetuate a power structure that subordinated women. Catherine A. MacKinnon argued persuasively that sexuality involves practices enforcing existing gender statuses.[1] In her view, unwanted sexuality in the workplace constitutes a group injury of sex discrimination. Moreover, sexually based behaviors, such as sexual harassment, rape, and pornography, are major causal factors contributing to the cumulative oppression of women and their lower status and pay in the workplace.

In 1976, in *Williams v. Saxbe* a U.S. court ruled that sexual harassment in the workplace was a violation of the Title VII of the Civil Rights Act of 1964, thereby setting a precedent that sexual harassment constituted sex discrimination.[2] In 1980 the Equal Employment Opportunity Commission (EEOC) defined sexual harassment: It is a discriminatory action, sexual in nature, that negatively impacts equality in the work environment. Interpretations of Title VII have since clarified that sexual harassment violates a constitutional right to equality in the workplace and in educational access. Throughout the 1980s the range and scope of the occurrence of sexual harassment has been extensively documented.

Although some men report being victims of such harassment, the vast majority, typically 90 percent plus, of the victims of such harassment are women.

A 1992 study by the American Association of University Women, *Hostile Hallways: The AAUW Survey on Sexual Harassment in America's Schools,* reported that four of every five students experienced sexual harassment and that the majority were girls.[3] The incidence is at least one of every five women in the workforce,[4] and about two of every five women employed in the federal government.[5] At the state level, Kelly and Stambaugh reported in 1992 that in Arizona and Wisconsin only one-third of the women sampled at both the middle and upper levels of the state civil service experienced no harassment; one-third experienced verbal harassment, and another one-third experienced more severe forms of harassment.[6] A follow-up study including data from Alabama, Florida, Texas, Utah, and Wisconsin revealed the following about the type and extent of sexual harassment experienced by female civil servants around the nation.[7]

1. *Women in substantially higher proportions than men have experienced all forms of sexual harassment.* Specifically, whereas from 6 percent to 16 percent of high-level female public administrators have experienced unwanted sexual advances, almost none of their male counterparts have. Up to 24 percent of the females experienced requests for sexual favors, while fewer than 7 percent of males in any of the states did. Whereas up to 36 percent of the women experienced offensive physical contact, 3 percent or fewer of the men did. In addition, whereas a low of 33 percent and a high of 57 percent of the women experienced offensive verbal behavior, in no state bureaucracy did more than 36 percent of the men experience it.

2. *Similarly, women reported hearing about these types of sexual harassment at higher levels than men.* Specifically, the proportion of women hearing about unwelcome sexual advances and offensive physical contact ranged from three of every ten in Texas to two of every three in Arizona; for men the range went from one and one-half of every ten to four of every ten.

Studies documenting the high incidence of sexual harassment have increased in the 1990s simultaneously as the demand for "breaking the glass ceiling" has intensified. The question this chapter addresses is, How is sexual harassment linked to the glass ceiling? More specifically, the question explored is, What impact does sexual harassment have on the leadership and management potential of women in state bureaucracies?

Pereia, a lawyer for the Securities and Exchange Commission in the 1980s, describes sexual harassment as "psychological warfare with an old-boy network."[8] The implication is that harassment is a form of oppression grounded in gendered sexual power differentials. These differentials work to prevent women from achieving economic and political power by means of sexual intimidation and the threat of physical domination. Male gender power in the private, personal arena is used to maintain control over women's destiny in the public, leadership-management arena.

Using data from Alabama, Arizona, Florida, Texas, and Wisconsin, I explore the impact sexual harassment has on women's ability to perform specific management or leadership tasks and to be an effective employee, poised to move to higher-level positions. The analysis across the five states allows an assessment of whether sexual harassment is a consistently powerful negative weapon reinforcing the glass ceiling, a situation where offensive men are able to intimidate and dominate women placed on the defensive because of unwanted sexual attention. The analysis also facilitates examining gender power as a set of interpersonal practices that demonstrate that the personal is indeed political.

Research Design

The Questionnaire

The data used in this study were collected as part of a multiple-state study completed between 1986 and 1992.[9] The instrument was designed to obtain comparative data from male and female middle- and upper-level public administrators on several topics: career patterns, perceptions of career success and satisfaction, employment behavior, self-perceived competencies and functions performed on the current job, perceptions of structural barriers and discrimination patterns. It included items pertaining to sexual harassment as part of the latter queries. The questionnaire was pretested with public servants at a federal training center in Colorado and with a randomly selected group as well as a focus group of public administrators in Arizona.

Sampling

Various sample designs were used (see appendix). In Texas, Wisconsin, and Arizona, the state in which the study was first conducted, systematic probability samples were used. In Alabama, all upper-level managers were surveyed. All studies sought to distinguish upper-level from middle-level managers. Criteria used to do this included salary levels, duties performed, and grade schedules. Due to the different personnel systems in each state, the precise definition of the upper-echelon managers varied slightly from state to state.

Statistical Analyses
To explore how sexual harassment impacts a woman manager's ability to lead, make decisions, and in general perform her job effectively, a sexual-harassment index (hereafter called SHI) was created. This additive index was scored as follows: those respondents who had not experienced any form of either verbal or other harassment were given a zero; those who had experienced verbal

harassment in the form of only jokes and/or snide remarks were give a one; those who had experienced offensive physical conduct of a sexual nature, requests for sexual favors from work colleagues, or unwelcome sexual advances in exchange for an employment opportunity by a supervisor were given a two. This index is an ordinal scale of the seriousness of the sexual harassment experienced.

The argument that sexual harassment is a serious form of sexual discrimination derives from the assumption that harassment has a critical impact on a woman's ability to perform a job and to be an effective employee. All respondents in each of the five states were asked to rate twenty-two job tasks on a scale from one to five (with five being the highest) in terms of how important the tasks were for their performance evaluation and how important they were for the respondent's effectiveness on the job. To examine the impact sexual harassment has on job performance and effectiveness, analyses were completed correlating the SHI scores with twenty-two different types of job functions and competencies.[10]

Sexual harassment is also thought to affect how individuals perceive their chances of success for themselves and others. Hence, analyses of various perceptions of the factors contributing to the respondent's success and her perception of the factors contributing to the success of male and female colleagues were also conducted.

Results and Discussion

Background Characteristics and Harassment

Not all women experience or hear about sexual harassment. Table 17 presents the distribution by severity of harassment experienced by upper-level women and men in Alabama, Arizona, Florida, Texas, and Wisconsin (no data on males were obtained for Florida). Data on middle-level managers are also presented for Arizona and Wisconsin, the only two states for which such extended analyses were completed.

All states except Texas and Arizona show that about two-thirds of women experienced some type of sexual harassment. Texas reveals less sexual harassment, while Arizona shows more. Other than in Texas, a substantial majority of women experienced verbal or more severe forms of harassment. Texas exhibited a different distribution, with the majority (60.3 percent) of women reporting no sexual harassment, 18.1 percent experiencing only verbal harassment, and 21.6 percent reporting more severe forms of harassment. In Arizona and in Florida a higher percentage of women experienced the more severe forms of sexual harassment than the percentage of those who did not experience any harassment. In Arizona close to three-fourths of the upper-level women experienced some

TABLE 17. Harassment Experienced by State Administrators

State	Type of Harassment	Female Management Level 18–22	n	Management Level 23–30	n	Male Management Level 18–22	n	Management Level 23–30	n
Arizona	None	35.8	19	26.2	11	60.2	71	61.2	12
(Female N = 95)	Verbal	28.3	15	33.3	14	33.9	40	29.6	61
(Male N = 324)	Other	35.8	29	40.5	17	5.9	7	9.2	19
Wisconsin	None	40.7	44	32.7	17	65.5	150	61.2	126
(Female N = 161)	Verbal	36.1	39	44.2	23	27.5	63	29.6	61
(Male N = 229)	Other	23.1	25	23.1	12	7.0	16	9.2	19
Alabama	None	—	—	37.3	31	—	—	63.2	146
(Female N = 83)	Verbal	—	—	32.5	27	—	—	34.6	80
(Male N = 231)	Other	—	—	30.1	25	—	—	2.2	5
Florida	None	—	—	34.2	13	—	—	—	—
(Female N = 38)	Verbal	—	—	28.9	11	—	—	—	—
	Other	—	—	36.8	14	—	—	—	—
Texas	None	—	—	60.3	78	—	—	82.2	—
(Female N = 116)	Verbal	—	—	18.1	21	—	—	14.7	—
(Male N = 129)	Other	—	—	21.6	25	—	—	3.1	—

form of sexual harassment in their careers. Having risen in the administrative ranks provided no apparent protection against harassment. Indeed, the pattern of the Arizona and Wisconsin data in table 17 suggest that upper-level women might actually experience more harassment than middle-level women. These statistics suggest that Pereia might well be correct in considering sexual harassment part of psychological warfare in the workplace. This supposition gains greater credibility when background data are analyzed.

An examination of the relationship of the SHI to various background characteristics (age, race, religion, parental social class, income, party affiliation, years of service, and marital status) revealed that the person who is most likely to be severely harassed is not the youngest but rather the modal female administrator: a white woman between the ages of thirty-six and fifty whose parental family came from the middle class who is not currently married and does not live with another adult. Some notable differences existed within states.

For example, in Alabama, unlike other states, being over the age of fifty-one was not a protective factor for more severe forms of harassment. Also in Alabama, 60 percent of minority women experienced the most severe forms of sexual harassment, unlike the four other states, where percentages for minority women who were severely harassed were relatively low.

Some protection against sexual harassment seems to derive from one's family's socioeconomic standing. Except for Florida, women from upper-middle- and upper-class backgrounds were least likely to suffer any harassment in all states except Florida. While other states show women from the upper-middle class being much less likely to be harassed at all, Florida's results show only 12.5 percent of upper-middle-class women reporting never being sexually harassed. In Texas and Alabama the lower-middle- and lower-class women tended to be more victimized than the other classes. Although being married did not at all preclude the possibility of being harassed, not being married clearly raised the probability of experiencing more severe sexual harassment. Apparently, marriage still connotes that a woman "belongs to" someone else and, therefore, adds some additional protection from harassment by the men with whom women work. The data from all states suggest that if a woman lives alone or with dependents, she also has a higher chance of being harassed.

Impact of Harassment on Job Performance and Effectiveness

If sexual harassment is indeed a means for keeping women from being successful as leaders and reducing their numbers in leadership ranks, then a connection should exist between experiencing higher levels of harassment and job performance. Tables 18 and 19 summarize the main findings for each state regarding how sexual harassment is related to respondents' perceptions of the importance of particular tasks for the evaluation of their job performance and its impact on their effectiveness. Table 18 presents only significant negative correlations, indicating the lower the sexual-harassment index, the higher the rating of the importance of the item.

The data reveal that those women who experienced the least sexual harassment were more likely to link the more leadership-related items to their job performance. Such items include communication abilities; taking the initiative and showing creativity; leadership; interpersonal relations; personnel management; affirmative action, budgetary resource management; keeping up with policies, priorities, and trends; selling and defending work unit activities; coordinating and integrating work unit activities; identifying policy and program alternatives; managing programs; monitoring program compliance; and research and development.

TABLE 18. Importance of Job Functions and Competencies for Upper-Level Female Administrators: The Lower the SHI the Higher the Rating of Importance of Item

	Alabama	Arizona	Florida	Texas	Wisconsin
Job Performance					
Communication abilities			-.14*	-.08*	
Taking the initiative/creativity				-.15***	
Leadership	-.17***			-.12***	
Interpersonal relations/sensitivity		-.19**			
Personnel management	-.12*			-.09*	
Affirmative action/EEO	-.20***				-.20**
Budgetary resource management	-.15**				-.16*
Keeping up policies/priorities/trends			-.25***		
Selling/defending work unit activities				-.13**	
Coordinating and integrating work unit	-.10*				
Identifying policy and program alternatives				-.19****	
Managing programs				-.19****	
Monitoring program compliance	-.17***			-.11**	-.18*
Research and development	-.18***			-.16***	-.17*
Job Effectiveness					
Organizational/conflict management		-.24***			
Results/goal achievement					-.19*
Taking initiative/creativity			-.16*		
Leadership	-.18***				
Interpersonal relations/sensitivity		-.16*			
Personnel management		-.17*			-.16*
Affirmative action/EEO	-.35****	-.13*			-.20**
Budgetary resource management	-.16**				-.16*
Keeping up with policies/priorities/trends			-.23***		
Selling work unit activities				-.12**	
Managing programs				-.11***	
Monitoring program compliance	-.16**			-.13***	-.18*
Research and development				-.16*	-.17*

*p < .15   **p < .10   ***p < .05   ****p < .01.

TABLE 19. Importance of Job Functions and Competencies for Upper-Level Female Administrators: The Higher the SHI the Higher the Rating of Importance of Item

	Alabama	Arizona	Florida	Texas	Wisconsin
Job Performance					
Specialized expertise		.25***			
Sensitivity to the environment		.23**			
Job effectiveness					
Organizational/conflict management			.22**	.09*	
Specialized expertise		.25***			
Adaptability/flexibility	.10*			.10**	
Balancing long and short-term considerations	.11*	.18**		.16***	
Collecting/analyzing information/judgments	.08*			.07**	
Sensitivity to the environment					.17*
Goal achievement	.10*				
Keeping up policies/priorities/trends				.08***	
Identifying policy and program alternatives		.17**			

$^*p < .15$ $^{**}p < .10$ $^{***}p < .05$ $^{****}p < .01$

These same women scoring lower on the SHI also believed that the following tasks were important for their job effectiveness: organization and conflict management; focusing on results and goal achievement; taking the initiative and showing creativity; leadership; interpersonal relations and sensitivity; personnel management; affirmative action; budgetary resource management; keeping up with policies, priorities, and trends; selling work unit activities; managing programs; monitoring program compliance; and research and development.

Table 19 presents items that were *positively* correlated with the SHI, indicating those respondents who scored higher on the SHI also gave higher ratings of importance to the following items for job performance: specialized expertise; and sensitivity to the environment. Those items positively correlated with the SHI for job effectiveness included organization and conflict management; specialized expertise; adaptability and flexibility; balancing short- and long-term considerations; collecting and analyzing information; sensitivity to the environment; goal achievement; keeping up with policies, priorities, and trends; and identifying policy and program alternatives.

Although differences in those items that are statistically significant exist in the data between the five states, patterns of how sexual harassment reinforces the glass ceiling are made more visible by these analyses. First, the items focusing most directly on leadership and actual management of tasks and people were consistently negatively related with sexual harassment, even if not always at a statistically significant level. This pattern was true for the respondents whether the respondent is addressing the importance of the task for their performance evaluation or for their personal effectiveness doing the task. Conversely, those women who scored highest on the SHI tended to see items related to their interpersonal behavior and specific expertise as being more important for their jobs and effectiveness than the other women respondents did. For example, those suffering from more harassment were also more concerned with specialized expertise, sensitivity to the environment, being adaptable, balancing short- and long-term goals, getting information, and keeping up and coordinating activities. Although these tasks are important, they are not as related to direct line jobs of supervision and leadership, such as in the first grouping, where little or no sexual harassment is most directly linked with stressing the importance of taking the initiative, being a leader, and managing programs and people.

One might think that one should argue these negative correlations simply reflect a power differential that is typical of sexual harassment, that is, the women experiencing more sexual harassment have less power and therefore these women are more vulnerable. However, these women either constitute the universe or are from random samples of the highest levels of public administrators in each of the five states. No reason exists to assume that the respondents scoring highest on the SHI have less position power than their counterparts in the sample. Indeed, table 17 illustrates that in Arizona and Florida, where both higher- and lower-level administrator percentages are provided, the higher-level women received a greater amount of sexual harassment. Therefore, sexual harassment itself is likely producing these differences in responses. Sexual harassment appears to reinforce the glass ceiling by diverting attention away from leadership and management toward interpersonal relations and more specific job tasks.[11]

This finding is not totally unexpected. As a power weapon, sexual harassment would be expected to deter scoring high on such job functions and competencies. Its supposed intent and impact is to reduce women's desire and ability to compete and perform in traditional male roles. Positive correlations in table 19 between a job function/competencies and sexual harassment would suggest that function/competency has become either a substitute for other behaviors or a means of defense. Most of the items in table 19 (other than organizational/conflict management) are relatively power neutral and do not suggest assertiveness or even competitiveness. The contrast between the patterns in the tables 18 and 19 leads me to conclude that sexual harassment does succeed in producing hesitation, defensiveness, and less competitiveness in women.

Inconsistencies across the states in positive and negative correlations are few, indicating that sexual harassment is indeed one of the key barriers contributing to the creation of the glass ceiling in public organizations. Because the trends across the five samples are significantly greater than the few inconsistencies, this provides evidence for an even stronger linkage between sexual harassment and the glass ceiling.

Impact of Harassment on
Perception of Reasons for Career Success

If sexual harassment is indeed a type of psychological warfare in the workplace, then the women experiencing its worst forms ought to react differently to how they view reasons for career success than women not experiencing such harassment. To examine this possibility several additional items were examined.

First, women in each of the five states were asked if they felt they had lost advancement opportunities because of their gender. In examining how these responses were related to sexual harassment, significant positive correlations were obtained for three states—Florida,[12] Texas,[13] and Wisconsin.[14] Women who suffered more sexual harassment in these states strongly felt they had lost advancement opportunities due to gender discrimination.

Second, in exploring some of the reasons why this pattern across states might exist, the SHI was run against responses on how often, if at all, the respondent felt she was left out of discussions and how much time the respondent spent on the job. In terms of being left out of discussions, none of the relationships was very strong. The tendency, nonetheless, was for the women with the higher SHI scores to be most likely to be left out in three of the states.[15] In terms of time spent on work activities, different results were found for Alabama and Texas. In Alabama, women who were less sexually harassed spent more time at work,[16] while in Texas the opposite relationship was found.[17]

Because sexual harassment tends to increase the saliency of gender issues to women, the SHI was correlated with support for four gender-related issues (pay equity, child care, job sharing, and flextime) to see if any connection empirically exists for these high level female administrators. Women experiencing more severe sexual harassment gave more support to pay equity in Florida,[18] job sharing in Texas,[19] and flexible time work schedules in both Alabama[20] and Arizona.[21] A significant negative correlation was found only for child care.[22] Apparently those women who suffer the greatest amount of harassment are more likely to desire comparable pay adjustments (possibly feeling that traditional equal competition is impossible). They also tend to want to work either less than full-time (which usually does not lead to advancement) or to work hours of their choosing, perhaps to avoid the possibility of harassment. Women who experience a lesser degree of harassment may desire child care to enable them to work more hours, or to be less constrained in opportunities for advancement by familial duties. These findings indicate that sexual harassment impacts how women managers look at other gender work issues.

Third, the attributions respondents give for their own and their colleagues' success were explored. A previous study compared the male and female upper-level Arizonan administrators' attributions of how gender is linked to success.[23] This study found that hard work and ability were central reasons given for career success for oneself and for one's male and female colleagues, constituting an "Alger factor" (after the Horatio Alger myth). The study also found that professional contacts were viewed as substantially more important for each woman's success than either nonprofessional (political or personal contacts) or luck. Nonetheless, women were more likely than men to see a positive connection between luck, hard work, and ability. The authors suggest that this male-female difference stems from differential feelings of entitlement to having career success.

Given that harassment derives in part from a gender power differential and gives males an unfair advantage in the workplace, it is likely that women experiencing more severe harassment will view the factors contributing to their own success and that of male and female colleagues differently than women experiencing less. Indeed, this is so.

Only those women who were less sexually harassed felt ability[24] and hard work[25] were significant factors contributing to male success. Women with higher SHI scores were more likely to attribute male success to whom men know,[26] political connections,[27] professional contacts,[28] or luck.[29] Overall results indicate a strong tendency for women with higher SHI scores to view the male pathway to success negatively, attributing success to external factors.

Women with higher SHI scores tended to attribute the success of their female colleagues also to whom they know,[30] political connections,[31] professional contacts,[32] and luck,[33] in a fashion similar to how their male colleagues were viewed. Wisconsin respondents were the only outliers with this pattern. The reason why is not clear.

In Alabama[34] and Arizona[35] ability and hard work were seen by the more harassed women as critical to career success of female colleagues, but not for their own success. The patterns suggest that the more harassed women tend to attribute success to external factors rather than to a person's ability or hard work. Only less harassed women thought ability[36] and hard work[37] were significant factors in their own success. The more harassed the women were the higher they rated whom they know,[38] political connections,[39] professional contacts,[40] and luck[41] as factors facilitating their own success. These responses indicate sexual harassment may have a negative overall effect on the psychological well-being of women in their careers. Thus sexual harassment on female administrators appears to impact not only perceptions of job-related performance and effectiveness, but also personal feelings of self-worth and esteem.

The data from these five states confirm that sexual harassment impacts how women think about how they had attained their current positions and how their male and female colleagues attained theirs. It is obvious that the more harassed the respondent was the more negatively she viewed how men achieved career success. When rating themselves, more harassed women seemed to lose self-esteem, attributing their own success to connections, contacts, and luck at higher rates than their less harassed peers.

To determine if sexual harassment is related to individual overall perceptions of her own career success and satisfaction, the harassment index was correlated with the items asking how successful and how satisfied each respondent felt. Significant results for success were found only in Alabama.[42] However, in the other four states trends were in the same direction, indicating women who are less harassed are more likely to be satisfied with their careers and to be feel they are more successful.

Conclusion

These data from the five states of Alabama, Arizona, Florida, Texas, and Wisconsin indicate that substantial percentages of both mid- and high-level female administrators in state government experience sexual harassment and that these experiences impact on their job performance and behavior. Such harassment appears to affect work style, self-perception, and a women's ability to perform particular job functions, especially those functions linked most directly to line leadership and management rather than staff and interpersonal responsibilities. Such harassment remains a contributor to the "glass ceiling effect," which both keeps women out of upper-levels of management and from seeking entrance to those levels. Having offensive men pushing unwanted sexual attention on women makes women defensive; defensiveness runs counter to an ability to lead and manage well at the upper levels of the bureaucracy.

If states are serious about ending discrimination then efforts to end this particular form of gender "psychological warfare" also must be serious. Without such attention to this problem that debilitates the leadership of women, men in public decisionmaking positions—those who govern—are at least complicit in the harassment that undermines women's ability to lead and skews gender power to their advantage.

Appendix

State Sample Designs

In Alabama, all persons in positions paying $60,000 and above in spring 1989 were selected except for physicians and other high-paid professionals who clearly were not managers. Individuals in the lower-paying levels III, IV, and V were selected if the job being performed was managerial regardless of salary. These criteria resulted in a universe of 806. Only 796 surveys reached their destination; 317 were returned (40 percent). The final sample consisted of 229 male respondents out of a population of 618 (37 percent), 83 females out of a population of 151 (55 percent), and five of twenty-seven (19 percent) questionnaires from individuals who did not indicate their sex.

The Arizona study drew two samples: one (that used for this chapter) was drawn from all 478 employees who held upper-level positions in January 1987. Of these 87 percent ($n = 414$) were males, and 13 percent ($n = 64$) were females. All the 53 women who could be reached and who were still in their positions at the time of the survey in spring of 1987 were sampled. Of these, 79 percent ($n = 42$) responded. Of the 414 men, a systematic probability sample of 305 was drawn; 208 responded, for a response rate of 68.2 percent. These Arizona administrators were in the state personnel grade schedules of 23 to 30. They include those generally considered management, who have more responsibilities and authority and make more autonomous decisions, and supervise more employees than other personnel. The second sample was a systematic probability sample of 171 of 4,447 individuals in grades 18 through 22. As with the upper-level administrators, a sample size was sought that would allow predicting the number of years an employee had served in Arizona state government with an error of no more than one year at the 0.05 probability level. Arizona state employees in these ranks are considered "career track" personnel who make highly technical contributions (i.e., are first- and second-line supervisors).

In Florida, a list of the entire population of state employees in the Senior Management Service was provided by the Division of Personnel Management Services of the Florida Department of Administration. This listing included those employed in twenty-eight of the thirty-two state agencies. Those agencies excluded from this list are: (1) Health Containment Care Cost Board; (2) Florida School for the Deaf and Blind; (3) Correctional Educational School Authority; and (4) Lottery. The entire universe of women ($N = 87$) and a systematic probability sample of fifty percent of the men ($n = 166$) was drawn to obtain a study population ($n = 253$). The sample that provides the data for the following analysis includes 38 women and 70 men.

The Texas state personnel system is highly decentralized, with over two hundred relatively independent state agencies. Fewer than 25 percent of all state employees are included in a state merit employment system. Most upper-level managers appear to be in grades 19 to 21. For the Texas survey, a random study of the 400 state employees in these grades was selected. Of these, 130 men and 117 women responded, for an overall response rate of 62 percent.

The Wisconsin universe consisted of 640 professional and executive employees in the state's pay ranges that were numbered 13 and higher. The response rate was 61 percent, yielding a sample of 389. For the purposes of this chapter, only those falling in pay ranges 16 to 24 and in the Executive Salary Group (ESG denotes political appointees) were included, as they are the upper-level elite corps of the state's civil service. Women were oversampled to yield sufficient cases for analysis. All men and women in the ESG were surveyed, resulting in a sample of 16 women and 36 men; and 125 men and 125 women in ranges 16 to 24 were surveyed, with a resulting response of 84 men and 95 women. The final sample used for this study consisted of 100 women and 131 men.

Notes

1. Catherine A. MacKinnon, *Sexual Harassment of Working Women* (New Haven, Conn.: Yale University Press, 1979).
2. *William v. Saxbe*, 413 F. Supp. 654, 657 (D.D.C. 1976).
3. Anne L. Bryant, "Hostile Hallways: The AAUW Survey on Sexual Harassment in America's Schools" (Annapolis Junction, Md.: American Association of University Women, 1992).
4. Barbara A. Gutek, *Sex and the Workplace* (San Francisco: Jossey-Bass, 1985).
5. U.S. Merit Systems Protection Board, *Sexual Harassment in the Federal Workplace: Is It a Problem?* (Washington, D.C.: Government Printing Office, 1987). See also the 1988 update published under the same title.
6. Rita Mae Kelly and Phoebe Morgan Stambaugh, "Sexual Harassment in the States" in *Women and Men of the States,* ed. Mary Ellen Guy (Armonk, N.Y.: M. E. Sharpe, 1992).
7. Rita Mae Kelly, "Sexual Harassment in State Agencies (A Comparison of Five States: Implications for Leadership and Management)" (paper presented at the annual meeting of the Western Political Science Association, March 18–20, 1993, Pasadena, Calif.).
8. J. L. Pereia, "Women Allege Sexist Atmosphere in Offices Constitutes Harassment," *Wall Street Journal,* February 10, 1988, sect. 2:23.
9. The questionnaire used in these studies was developed by Mary M. Hale, Rita Mae Kelly, and Dail Neugarten, with assistance from Jane Bayes, Dorothy Riddle, Nancy Felipe Russo, Beverly Springer, and Jeanie Stanley. It is printed in Mary M. Hale and Rita Mae Kelly, *Gender, Bureaucracy, and Democracy,* (Westport, Conn.: Greenwood Press, 1989), appendix.
10. Tau C correlations were used because of the ordinal nature of the data. Chi-square analyses were performed to determine if selected background characteristics are related to higher SHI scores. Since this study is exploring how sexual harassment relates to the glass ceiling, probability levels of p .15 are reported. Patterns of relationships and commonality of patterns across states are more important at this juncture than specific levels of statistical significance.
11. It must be noted here that the data across the five states are not consistent in terms of the number of statistically significant relationships found. Some of these differences are undoubtedly due

to the number of cases in each state: in table 18 Texas ($n = 116$) has thirteen items significant at the less than .15 level; Alabama ($n = 83$) has eleven; Wisconsin ($n = 52$) has ten; Arizona ($n = 42$) has five; and Florida ($n = 38$) has four.

12. Tau C = .29, $p < .05$.
13. Tau C = .33, $p < .01$.
14. Tau C = .17, $p < .15$.
15. Ariz.: Tau C = -.17, $p < .15$); Fla.: Tau C = -.05, $p < .20$; Tex.: Tau C = -.05, $p < .30$.
16. Tau C = -.18, $p < .05$.
17. Tau C = .12, $p < .05$.
18. Tau C = .24, $p < .05$.
19. Tau C = .09, $p < .15$.
20. Tau C = .17, $p < .05$.
21. Tau C = .23, $p < .05$.
22. Ala.: Tau C = -.16, $p < .05$.
23. Nancy Felipe Russo, Rita Mae Kelly, and Melinda Deacon, "Gender and Success-Related Attributions: Beyond Individualistic Conceptions of Achievement," *Sex Roles* 25 (5–6) (1991): 331–51.
24. Wisc.: Tau C = -.25, $p < .05$.
25. Ariz.: Tau C = -.21, $p < .05$; Tex.: Tau C = -.10, $p < .15$; Wisc.: Tau C = -.27, $p < .05$.
26. Ala.: Tau C = .28, $p < .01$); Tex.: Tau C = .12, $p < .15$.
27. Ala.: Tau C = .21, $p < .05$; Tex.: Tau C = .14, $p < .05$.
28. Ala.: Tau C = .31, $p < .01$.
29. Tau C = .31, $p < .01$.
30. Ala.: Tau C = .17, $p < .05$.
31. Ala.: Tau C = .13, $p < .15$.
32. Ala.: Tau C = .31, $p < .01$; Ariz.: Tau C = .20, $p < .10$.
33. Ala.: Tau C = .24, $p < .05$.
34. Tau C = .17, $p < .05$.
35. Tau C = .21, $p < .05$ for ability; Tau C = .23, $p < .05$ for hard work.
36. Fla.: Tau C = -.11, $p < .10$.
37. Fla.: Tau C = -.12, $p < .15$; Wisc.: Tau C = -.20, $p < .10$.
38. Ala.: Tau C = .15, $p < .10$; Fla.: Tau C = .24, $p < .10$.
39. Fla.: Tau C = .16, $p < .15$.
40. Ala.: Tau C = .18, $p < .05$; Ariz.: Tau C = .37, $p < .01$.
41. Ala.: Tau C = .18, $p < .05$; Fla.: Tau C = .22, $p < .10$.
42. Tau C = -.17, $p < .05$.

Part 5: Gender Power and Social Symbolic Meaning: Norms of Gender and Gender in Norms and Concepts

Masculinism as an ideology or worldview permeates governance and leadership. Because masculinism has been so pervasive, its ideas have become the uncritically accepted givens, the norms, in our thinking and beliefs about governance. Alternative worldviews offered by various versions of feminism have seemed strange or radical because they deviate from this masculinist norm. These norms are buried so deeply in our belief systems that few even grant ideological status to power arrangements developed under masculinity that advantage the masculine, while efforts to shift these power arrangement through feminism are understood as highly charged ideologically. Making this masculinist ideology visible is a cause of concern; for, its invisibility and apparent universality make masculinism even more powerful. Unchallenged, it allows men to ignore or diminish women and their concerns and leaves women in the implacable position of either being known as the radical "other" or trying to improve their lot inside power arrangements established to support masculinity. At a minimum, women become irrelevant because they and their vantage points do not readily fit within the existing conceptual frame. More often, women, and what they represent, become known as dangerous because their actions, even their presence in a power capacity, threatens existing power arrangements. Therefore when women enter governance and leadership in a powerful way, they become symbolically charged, larger than the individuals involved. The meaning of reactions to women's entry cannot be fully understood without considering symbolic dimensions.

The two chapters by Georgia Duerst-Lahti and Dayna Verstegen and Mary Ellen Guy contribute to challenging the social symbolic meaning given to women's political efforts and roles. In "Making Something of Absence: The Year of the Woman and Women's Political Representation," Duerst-Lahti and Verstegen explore how "the year" emerged, the way it was constructed in print media, and its unfolding in terms of political representation. Throughout, the tricky problem of women's representation, and why we so readily dismiss the importance of descriptive representation, is highlighted. Evidence of the effects of gender power arrangements pervades "the year."

Evidence of gender power arrangements also pervade "Hillary, Health Care, and Gender Power" as Guy shows dominance/deference parallels among health care professionals, men and women, husbands and wives, leaders and followers. Hillary becomes the symbolic locus of all these gender power arrangements as she conducts herself beyond the bounds of masculinist expectations through her work on health care reform. By not initially masking her personal competence and establishing herself as a fully professional advisor capable of power duties, she contradicts the role of "lady" so symbolically laden in the "First Lady." By supplementing her personal power with position power as official head of a presidential task force and by inviting nurses—women— centrally into health care reform plans, she upsets masculinist power expectations in a major leadership and governance arena. In the process she lays gender power on the table for all to see.

The Year of the Woman and Hillary capture symbolic dimensions of gender power. No understanding of gender power in leadership and governance is complete if the potency of symbolic meaning is ignored.

Chapter 9

Making Something of Absence: The "Year of the Woman" and Women's Political Representation

Georgia Duerst-Lahti and Dayna Verstegen

The "year of the woman" during the 1992 election cycle surely achieved prominence as a political phenomenon known to all of the attentive public. It became a media catchphrase for just about anything related to women and politics, gaining sufficient prominence to become Newsweek's "story of the year."[1] The year of the woman (the year) might be regarded as a political spectacle. Like any political spectacle, it was "constituted by news reporting [that] continuously constructs and reconstructs social problems, crises, enemies and leaders and so creates a succession of threats and reassurances.... [It] also play[ed] a central role in winning support and opposition for political causes and policies."[2] In this case, women became the leaders in demand, change in incumbents became the crises (based upon many other crises), the Senate Judiciary Committee became the enemy, and women's absence from the halls of national elective power became the social problem that superseded all social problems.

Political spectacles are manufactured. To a great extent, the fact that "the year" had only a marginal effect on the actual voting patterns matters far less than the construction of it portrayed by the press. The year came into the public eye through news media coverage and then was used by organized feminism to perpetuate that coverage as a tactic to help women win public-leadership posts.[3] Of course, numerous others also had a hand in the phenomenon of the year. Had gender power relations not so effectively excluded women from governance in the past, such a spectacle would neither have been possible nor seen as necessary by women's groups. Women would have been better represented among the governing ranks.

But what does "better represented" mean for women? It is a topic that has received very little attention throughout the hoopla and extensive coverage the year inspired. For example, in all the articles written about the year in the *New York Times* and the *Washington Post,* fifty-eight articles total, we could find only seven mentions about the lack of representation for women, and even then the term *representation* was rarely used. Instead, it was cast as the lack of women in office. Yet women's representation seems central to the dynamics of the year. It is also a topic that should be of critical interest to those who care about women's political interests. That women's political interests and the topic of representation can so readily be divorced suggests a closer look is in order.

In this chapter, we explore ideas surrounding women's representation through analysis of the year of the woman. We seldom think about gender and political representation in their complicated meaning. In fact, most empirical considerations of representation substitute numerical counts for representation or focus narrowly on behavior styles. These approaches direct attention away from analyses of the consequences of gender power which so clearly favors men. Therefore, we begin by reviewing the concept of representation in order to remind readers of its full complexity. We also revisit the tricky problem of women's representation and how we have come to think about gender parity in representation as untenable. Special attention is focused upon the need to be aware of the absence of representation for women and the consequences of that absence. Because 1992 as "the year of the woman" in politics occurred in a historical context, we cover elements of the context that led the hearings to act as a catalyst for this political spectacle. Finally, we return to the concepts of representation and examine the media construction of the year as it reveals gender power's influence. To conduct this analysis, we identified every article published in the *New York Times* and *Washington Post,* thirty and twenty-eight articles respectively, that included discussion of the year and/or of women candidates for leadership posts as U.S. senators. All fifty-eight articles ran between September 1991 and December 1992.[4] Such analysis allows us to illustrate how these nationally distributed, opinion-shaping papers constructed the year. It also provides a means to examine women's representation.

As this book details in part 1, women have been largely absent from images of political leaders as well as from the set of practices involved with leadership and governance. These articles, then, inevitably had to deal with the complexity of inventing a way for women to be understood both as women and as (potential) political leaders, something imbued with masculine gender.[5] Because image and symbols have much to do with attributes of leadership and governance, the way these newspapers covered these candidates and races arguably shaped a much larger understanding of gender and leadership. Important to us here is the relationship between the phenomenon of the year and its implicit companion, women's political representation. This analysis should reveal dynamics involved in gender power as it operates in crucial gatekeeping functions for offices with considerable political power. How did the year make something of absence?

On Representation

No contemporary political theorist has written more eloquently on political representation than Hanna Fenichel Pitkin. It is fitting to discuss absence and representation together, according to Pitkin, because "representation, taken generally, means the making present *in some sense* of something which is nevertheless *not* present literally or in fact."[6] It is equally fitting to discuss women, absence, and representation together because women have long been represented "in some sense" as extensions of their fathers or husbands, or by men under viriarchy—rule by adult men—more generally.[7] Clearly, when we look at the proportions of women holding public-leadership posts over time, women have in fact not been literally present beyond occasional tokens. So U.S. women have largely only known representation as absence made present in some nonliteral sense.

Representation: A Review

To understand the representational potency of the Hill-Thomas hearings, held by the Senate Judiciary Committee, and the emergence of "the year of the woman," we might fruitfully begin with a review of Pitkin's conceptual analysis of representation. She considers four dimensions of representation: formal, descriptive, symbolic, and substantive and makes an important distinction between "standing for" and "acting for" as modes of representation.

Formal representation, as conceived first in these terms by Hobbes,[8] consists of formal arrangements that actually precede and initiate representation through *"authorization,* the giving of authority to act," and of formal arrangements that follow and terminate representation, that is, *"accountability,* the holding to account of the representative for his actions."[9] A prime mechanism

TABLE 20. Representation Concepts

Concept	Definition/Characteristic
Formal	Mechanism that grants *authority* to act on another's behalf and/or to hold *accountable* for actions as a representative. Elections: a process to make representation possible.
Descriptive	When being like another is important for representation, often because of access to information relevant to decision making. Standing for.
Symbolic	Occurs if one feels represented. Affective and emotive more than cognitive. Related to, but seldom in the form of, that which is symbolized. Subject to manipulation. Standing for.
Substantive	Pursuing the interests and policy preferences of constituents. Acting for.

Source: Hannah F. Pitkin, *Concepts of Representation* (Berkeley and Los Angeles: University of California Press, 1967).

for both authorization and accountability is the electoral process. Elections, then, are mechanisms to grant authority for another to act on one's behalf and to terminate that authority if a representative's actions do not meet one's desires. Elections enable representation but do not themselves constitute representation. Nonetheless, elections play a key role in representation.

Descriptive representation is concerned with representatives' characteristics, what they *are* or are *like,* "on being something rather than doing something."[10] For proponents of descriptive representation, what a legislature does is less important than how it is composed. Portraits, mirrors and maps can be used to illustrate. A map is judged by its accuracy. While not the actual territory it represents, if accurate, a map has the same structure as the territory. The territory is then accurately represented *by* the map. Crucial here is representative*ness.* Is the legislative body sufficiently like those represented to be seen as "truly representative?"

Appearances, in the case of "representative," become inextricably linked to legitimacy. The image of a mirror is useful. Because representation involves "standing for" someone who is absent, descriptive representation of a person involves "being sufficiently like them," of what they are or are like, to be seen as representing them. An accurate reflection of what they are or are like, a mirror, helps enormously in being seen as sufficiently like them to legitimately be accepted as their representative. Appearances, then, remain important to being seen as representing (but the function of being sufficiently like them in appearances trespasses into symbolic representation, which will be discussed shortly). More important is a context that makes descriptive representation relevant: "contexts where the purpose of representation is to supply information about something not actually present ... [to] draw accurate conclusions about the represented, gather information about the represented, because it is in relevant ways like the represented."[11] Standing for, through shared characteristics that legitimate other actions, is a kind of activity then, even if it is not itself acting for.

Finally, descriptive representation ties to the legitimacy of the whole body politic by providing assurances through an accurate correspondence to the nation. If descriptive representation corresponds, then legislatures can justify their actions, not only in terms of accurate information, but as "what the nation would have done" if it had in fact been present. As a mirror of the nation, theoretically at least, all are present through re-presentation.

Symbolic representation is another kind of standing-for representation.[12] Symbols make something present when it is not, although rarely do symbols represent in the form or make recognizable aspects of what it represents. A flag, for example represents a nation even though it does not have the form or characteristics of the country. Symbols are never wholly arbitrary, however. The

U.S. flag has a number of stars equal to the number of states, certain flag colors are more prevalent in certain regions of the world, and so on. Humans beings too can be thought of as symbols—police officers, judges, the queen of England, the president of the United States.

In contrast to descriptive representation, symbolic representation emphasizes the power of symbols to evoke feelings or attitudes. Symbolizing is "an exact reference to something indefinite,"[13] yet one can never fully capture in words what a symbol symbolizes, evokes, implies. Nonetheless, the symbol is the only possible embodiment of what is symbolized. Again in contrast to descriptive representation, symbolic representation is *not* a source of information about what it represents but rather a recipient or object of feeling, expressions of feelings, or actions intended for what it represents. If we ask what *makes* symbols out of anything, "the answer is clearly the beliefs, attitudes, assumptions of people."[14] A symbol has meaning beyond itself, not because of its actual resemblance, or any real connection, but just because someone believes it does.

Symbolic representation "is a condition, primarily a frame of mind."[15] As a form of representation it is existential, present or absent in people's beliefs, not necessarily dependent upon results. Symbolic representation rests upon emotional, affective, psychological responses more than rationally justifiable criteria. It exists when the audience receiving the symbolic message of representation believes it does. Those under representative authority must agree to the representative(s) as being believed in or accepted as the symbol of representation. Symbolic representation is based upon a system of shared values, functioning as a two-way correspondence, agreement between the ruler and the ruled.

The activity involved in the standing-for representation of symbolism most often has little to do with acting for in terms of substance. Murray Edelman has spoken forcefully on "symbolic politics" through "words that succeed and policies that fail."[16] Rather, the activity attempts to foster belief, loyalty, and satisfaction among the people with the leader. Pitkin points to fascism as the extreme case. But even in cases not so extreme, spin doctors have a place (and name) in U.S. politics. Leaders become symbol makers. Most significantly, representation functions as a power relation, that of leaders' power over followers. The danger is that consent can be created by leaders who skillfully create a belief in representation, a feeling that individuals are represented. But followers also must consent to follow, and symbols have the potential, at least, to work against leaders who fail symbolically.

Substantive representation is most directly and clearly an acting-for mode of representation. The substance of representation is activity, deliberate action. "In this sense a man represents what (or whom) he looks after or concerns himself with, the interests that he furthers.... [It says] something about who gets his way, or what forces can be thought of as acting by or through the government."[17] Using a colorful analogy, representation of a rural Wisconsin district could be done by a green Martian if the Martian looks after dairy interests and other concerns of rural Wisconsin. The substance of the issues, policies, and legislation the representative pursues determines whether or not representation occurs. If the representative acts for the interests of the represented, then representation has occurred. This possibility has served to justify white males as representing every other type of citizen.

To act for another that action must be deliberate, if the representative will be held accountable. The representative's role can be expressed in a number of ways: to act "on behalf" of others, "in their place" or "stead," "in their interests," "in accord with their desires," pursuing their "welfare," and so on.[18] The representative might assume various roles in representing, and much contemporary writing on representation has focused on this representational behavior rather than on its theoretical meaning. The three most common roles to serve as the basis of action are trustee (one who substitutes his or her own best judgment for the often ill-informed, unknown, or conflicting opinion of the represented), delegate (one who attempts to discern the exact position of the represented and acts accordingly), and politico (one who weighs a variety of political concerns). Any or a combination of any of these roles might serve as the basis of acting for another.

Pitkin steadfastly holds that all aspects of representation must be considered. Nonetheless, formal, descriptive, and symbolic representation receive less attention than substantive representation. Some attention is directed toward the best electoral arrangements, especially in emerging democracies, but most aspects of authorization and accountability— formal representation—have simply been assumed. Elections are formal opportunities to "vote the bums out" if representatives don't follow the wishes of citizenry; they present the opportunity to "vote change in" if citizens are dissatisfied with their representative. Descriptive representation collides with notions of majority rule, one person, one vote, majority rule; and the reality of multiple aspects of identity and pluralistic interests and characteristics. No one representative can have all characteristics, and few, if any, districts are entirely homogeneous. Descriptive representation proves impossible when we vote for only one person. Finally, although we may fear spin doctors and demagogues, the U.S. public seems to accept some role for symbolic representation from its political leadership without much comment. However, rarely do we consider the converse, the possibility that followers may create politically potent symbols that require leaders to respond (although interest groups regularly attempt to create symbols for their purposes).

For Pitkin, and for many who think about political representation, substantive representation is vitally important. "This substantive concept is the 'something' that was missing from the authorization (formal) view.... In descriptive and symbolic representation, we saw hints of what that something might be, but we saw also that those views could not be directly applied in the realm of actions.... The activity of representing as acting for others must be defined in terms of what the representative does and how he does it."[19] And while the writing of Edmond Burke about the wisdom of trustee representation surely launched this mode of reasoning, most recent studies have explored the style deployed in substantive representation and have given scant attention to other concepts of representation.[20] So if the substance of women's interests can reasonably be said to be deliberately pursued, then women can be said to be represented.

The Tricky Problem of Women's Representation

Generally speaking, public discussion about women and representation seldom moves beyond the notion of counting the number of women and calculating their proportion of all officials in a category of office. Such is a form of descriptive representation that fails to justify why description matters. Usually, the argument runs that elective officials ought to look like the U.S. and women are 53 percent of the population; anything less is underrepresentation. Unfortunately, the discussion too often ends there, probably because in practice, descriptive representation is fraught with problems. The most mutable problem has been that more men than women seem to want to be politicians. That can change and in fact appears to be changing. Less resolvable is that *many* characteristics have political salience—race, sexual orientation, age, (dis)ability, ethnicity, gender, and so on—yet only a few seats exist in most elective bodies. No district is perfectly homogeneous, so no single representative meets the descriptive needs of a district. With the executive, we find a single seat, and again no one person can embody all the salient political characteristics.[21] Any attempt to have perfect descriptive representation challenges the capacity to represent all those characteristics within a given elected body.

　　Perhaps most to the point for any constituent or for a serious consideration of women and representation is the fact that no one representative can be both male and female, so no one person's body can share the characteristic of sex with half of the citizenry. Either a representative is male or female.[22] Similar problems exist for age. Race presents a raft of related problems with its own complications.[23] As a result, and most importantly, we long have apparently believed that representing according to the substance of policy—substantive representation—is far more important than other dimensions of representation.[24] So, men (mostly white men) have predominated the national posts. Seldom has the lack of gender parity been identified as a real problem. Given the futility of perfect demographic matching for descriptive representation, better to focus on policy. Thus, we face a tricky problem, both for its invisibility and for its practical resolution. While the practical aspects may be irresolvable, at the level of an individual representative, changes in gender power can readily illuminate the problems of gender disparity in representation.

Still, women's representation is tricky for gender power reasons as well. Inside feminist circles the paucity of women in office has consistently been called into question. Nonetheless, because many men in office have "voted right" for feminist policies (substantive representation), and also because they hold positions of power too great to ignore, even organized feminism often endorses men for office. In Pennsylvania for example, the state-level National Organization for Women (NOW) endorsed Senator Arlen Specter in 1992. In many states the National Women's Political Caucus (NWPC)—an organization dedicated to getting more women into elective and appointive office—still endorses men. It is quite rational to endorse male candidates who possess incumbent influence and a friendly voting record. This becomes especially true given the nagging problem of demographic characteristics and an individual representative, especially in single-member districts.[25]

Enter the year of the woman in politics when absence became something—something visible and important— for women's representation.

Absence as Something for Women's Representation

The absence of women as political leaders can be found in many venues. Most obviously, few female bodies populate political bodies of governance. Thus, women simply are absent from leadership posts disproportionate to their presence in the population and as voters. As a result, then, women's concerns receive less committed attention in the congressional legislative realm, as Karin Tamerius shows elsewhere in this volume. Studies conducted under the auspices of the Center for the American Woman and Politics similarly reveal the importance of women in state legislatures.[26] Likewise, our image of political leaders remains tied to men if we have few opportunities to witness women in leadership capacities. When we don't see women as leaders, we continue to think of leaders as men. As importantly, women are not present to raise questions or to pose alternative perspectives, perhaps especially on issues not commonly associated with women but that also affect them, such as tax policy or foreign-development issues.

Women are not present to add a range of female experiences to gender-"neutral" policies, they are absent from posts to sponsor special-concerns legislation effectively, and we seldom see them in leader positions and so continue to lack models who challenge our assumptions about gender and leadership. All of this combines into greatly diminished influence potential and tenuous access to important avenues of social power. And these in turn combine through multiple and reinforcing mechanisms to make the current power arrangements more difficult. In circular fashion, the absence of women as political leaders contributes to the continued absence of women as political leaders.

At a national level, we faced a virtual absence of women as public leaders in the United States in 1991.[27] The White House seemed beyond reach, although women could count on a few national cabinet posts under any president. Importantly also, more women had been elected as governors. But women were 5 percent of the U.S. Congress before the 1992 elections. With those elections, women doubled their presence in Congress, in by far the biggest single expansion of the number of women in Congress, especially, in the Senate.

These advances clearly culminated the process of making 1992 the "year of the woman" in politics, yet they do not explain how the phenomenon of the year came to be originally, nor why this "story" stayed in the news so long. Women stepped forward to run in record numbers and were supported by record numbers of women. Women stepped forward at least partly because, as political analysts have amply noted, many factors converged to offer opportunities for any nonincumbent. The opportunities helped, to be sure, but something more was necessary, and that something has received almost no explicit coverage.

The key ingredient, we contend, was an *awareness of the consequences of the absence of women in public leadership posts.* To make 1992 the year of the woman in politics, the U.S. public needed a widespread awareness that, despite advances made over the years, women still had not achieved many seats in the whole of political leadership. Women were not well represented in this regard, and this fact needed to come to the fore in the minds of many. Mainstream U.S. society had to be(come) aware that women were largely absent from leadership and governance. Once it was aware, a second ingredient was necessary; the missing link—that absence has consequences—needed to be added for absence to become something with political meaning.

As our analysis should make evident, translating the fact of small numbers of female political leaders into an awareness that women were absent from governing and leading is not at all straightforward. It is tricky business because women have neither been present in large numbers in U.S. elective office, nor, as earlier chapters in this volume detail, has there been a cultural expectation that women are, or even could be, leaders.[28] Traditional patterns of gender power lead us to *not* question this absence.

A conscious awareness of women as absent, then, demanded a shift in the ways large numbers of Americans thought about women, leadership, and governance, especially, we will argue, a shift that involves conceptions of women's representation. To break with past understandings and to shift gendered cultural expectations about leaders generally and leaders who govern more specifically, the citizenry needed incentives to see current political leadership arrangements as salient for women. For the shortage of women in governance posts to "be seen"—to come into public awareness—the very normality of the masculine/male assumption had to be called into question. Something had to be made of women's absence.

Laying the Groundwork for the Year: Women Advance

"The year" did not spring fully forth on New Year's Day of 1992. Patterns of American politics had been changing for some time, and events surrounding the year must be viewed within the wider focus.[29] It is worth remembering that women constitute 53 percent of U.S. voters and have voted such that Democrats benefit from women's votes. In addition, pollsters can trace a gender gap on issues such as violence, peace, and children's welfare back to the 1930s.[30] On the positive side for women and governance, a critical mass of women had been making their way into positions of political leadership since the rebirth of feminism during the 1960s. Women filled about one-fifth of state legislative seats, for example. The pipeline—lower offices, political appointees, board members and commissioners—now had a female presence that gave these women qualifications to be seen as viable political candidates for higher office. Because the number of women holding public office had risen dramatically since 1970, these women now had the credentials to move into public office.

As importantly, by 1991 women, especially feminist women, now populated many of the authoritative arenas adjacent to political office and central to leadership as opinion influencers.[31] Journalism became a "female" occupation in 1985,[32] and despite persistent discrimination, women could be heard and seen covering and reporting news on radio and television. Nina Totenberg, Helen Thomas, and Leslie Stahl serve as prominent examples.

Women such as Kathleen Frankovic and Celinda Lake attained prominence as pollsters and were in a position to influence our understanding of the year. For example, consider the potency of the following December 1991 coverage for influencing opinion and launching the year.

> "The 1990s are a uniquely good time for women candidates," noted Democratic strategist and pollster Celinda Lake. "In an era when voters are strongly anti-incumbent in their mood, women run as the ultimate outsiders, turning what was once a disadvantage at the polls to a strong advantage."[33]

The phrase "ultimate outsider" stayed with women for the entire campaign, and other elements seen as shortcomings for women candidates in the past were recast positively.

The Center for the American Woman and Politics (CAWP) of Rutgers University also contributed. Gathering statistics on women in politics since 1971, CAWP fortuitously was in a position to provide facts to help persuade voters of the merits of women in offices. CAWP contributed one element important to "the year," even though it remain largely outside the awareness of the mass public. In November 1991, it released several scholarly studies documenting the heretofore illusive "impact of women in public office."[34] For the first time in a comprehensive fashion, scholars were able to document "gender in policymaking," including the far-reaching ways that women were "reshaping the agenda." Although impossible to predict when the studies began in 1988, the release could not have been better timed to fuel women's campaign speeches and the more general work of feminist groups who had been pushing for more female elected officials at least since the demise of the Equal Rights Amendment. Organized feminism made use of their findings.

Organized feminism also had evolved into a constellation of sophisticated interest groups savvy in the ways of political influence. Surely the failed battle for the ERA had taught them the techniques of interest groups politics. Feminist organizations such as the NWPC, which celebrated its twentieth anniversary in 1991, and NOW, which turned twenty-five in 1992, had matured over the decades into permanent fixtures beside more long-standing women's organizations like the American Association of University Women and the National Federation of Business and Professional Women. In addition, independent political action committees that contribute exclusively to female candidates also had developed. The Women's Campaign Fund, which emerged in the late 1970s, gave money to women of either party. Democratic candidates could now appeal to EMILY's List since the mid-1980s and Republicans to the newly formed WISH List (Women in the Senate and House). Women had penetrated the structures that made developing a viable campaign possible.

The Larger Political Context

Without belaboring these commonly known points, 1992 also offered unique opportunities, especially for women. Due to reapportionment and a special retirement incentive, more seats than usual were open in Congress, a condition that helps nonincumbents generally. Because so few women were incumbents, this advantage accrued to them. Congress also faced a series of ethical scandals that made voters leery of incumbents. As "ultimate outsiders," women tended to benefit by being free from the taint of politicians, but women also have been seen at least since suffrage as more moral and ethical in politics. In addition, the cold war had ended and the focus turned toward the domestic agenda. Women have stereotypically been seen as better able to handle issue like health, education, and welfare, key components of the domestic agenda. For a change, gender stereotypes and the political agenda coalesced in a way that advantaged women. Finally, change served as a ready theme for the 1992 elections. Because so few women held national office, electing them would automatically mean change; female candidates could ride the change theme easily. The 1992 election was an election of opportunity for women. These electoral conditions directly shaped rising awareness of the absence of women as public leaders and provided particular advantages for women.

Backlash: Conditions and Context

The rhetoric employed by the far Right since the early 1980s established one crucial condition to set the possibility of seeing a lack or absence as something. Conservatives mobilized public support for their particular depredations of social programs by moving "in two interrelated directions: against social welfare and the poor, and against feminism and women."[35] These depredations, of course, especially affect and depreciate women. Women who did not fit the traditional helpmate and mother roles had been the target of conservative public proclamations for more than a decade. Conservatives succeeded, to some extent at least, in socially constructing feminists in a negative way.[36] For example, in 1986, a Gallop poll conducted for *Newsweek* found a majority of women described themselves as feminists and only 4 percent described themselves as "antifeminists." At this same time the media began to discuss the "postfeminist generation." By 1989, the number of women calling themselves feminists had dropped to one in three, according to a Yankelovich poll for *Time*/CNN.[37] An October 1991 poll by *Newsweek* found 34 percent of women self-identified as feminists.[38] The onslaught had an effect.[39]

Importantly, many of the women who were active in the 1970s faded from the activist scene. In comparing 1984 to 1988, Michelle Brophy-Baermann finds that the New Right's onslaught on women corresponds to a six-percentage-point decline in warmth feelings among "modernist" women (self-identified feminists or equal-rights-oriented women) toward women as a group, and to a whopping twenty-seven-percentage-point decline in such women's feelings of warmth toward feminism. In other words, a major portion of the least traditional women surveyed had become disenchanted with feminism under the onslaught during the Reagan years. Even many feminists no longer felt warmly about feminism.[40] Interestingly, traditionalist and other categories showed a warming toward women as a group during this same time period. So while the women's movement's vanguard had cooled, less "modern" women had actually begun to warm toward women as a group, with the traditionalists showing the biggest change through a nine-percentage-point decline in the "cool" column. In any case, talking about women in feminist ways had become harder during the 1980s. The context was one of backlash against feminism and women that had taken on the terms of a "cultural war" often announced by Reagan pinch hitter William Bennett.

This cultural war with feminism at its center is readily acknowledged by both Republicans and Democrats and was fully evident at the 1992 national conventions, although its roots go back at least to 1984, according to Jo Freeman.[41] The notion of cultural wars emerged partly from debates about abortion that crystallized in extreme language in the 1988 Republican platform, language that spurred the rise of Republicans for Choice and the National Republican Coalition for Choice. But the cultural war, especially with its focus on feminism, is larger than abortion. The context of this war was expressed by Pat Buchanan in first Iowa and also before the Republican delegates at the 1992 convention. "It is a cultural war, as critical to the kind of nation we will one day be—as was the Cold War itself ... [R]adical feminism [is] the agenda Clinton & Clinton would impose on America—abortion on demand, a litmus test for the Supreme Court, homosexual rights, discrimination against religious schools, women in combat.... It is not the kind of change we can tolerate."[42] For Democrats, the war seems peaceably internalized. The Democratic National Committee has a long history of working with established women's groups, even when they disagree. Its director of political programs, formally political director for NWPC, claimed that "the Democratic Party is a feminist organization. We don't have to lobby and march outside any more. We march together. It's not Us. v. Them. The Party stands for the same thing that the movement stands for."[43]

In 1991, conditions then could be described as those of "absence or lack" of discussion about women's concerns *as women*'s concerns under Reagan. Arguably, the silencing of feminist voices over the 1980s left emotions tinder dry and primed for a spark. Ironically, while feminism chilled, "prowoman" feelings warmed, even among the characteristically quiet traditional women. Conditions were set to have an incident like the Hill-Thomas hearings set something into motion, a response of "feminine (though not necessarily feminist) resentment."[44]

The Hill-Thomas Catalyst and the Rise of "the Year"

Susan Faludi documented the "undeclared war against American women" waged since the late 1970s in messages delivered throughout popular culture. The war was waged by declaring that the women's movement had succeeded in making women equal and then, paradoxically, reporting how feminism had made women miserable. Coincidentally, and perhaps fortuitously, Faludi's book was released in October 1991, the same time as the Hill-Thomas hearings. One gains a sense of just how catalytic these hearing were for making "the year" by looking to Faludi's closing remarks on backlash. Expressing gloom, she questions various forecasts made at the start of the 1990s that declared them as "the Decade of Women." Then, on her last page, she turns to Ruth Mandel, director of the Center for the American Woman and Politics:

> when the media set out to report this [year of the woman] story, they had the usual trouble rounding up evidence. "I get press calls every election season," Ruth Mandel ... wearily told a reporter. "But the answer is no, this isn't the year (for women)—it wasn't the year in 1986 or 1988, and it won't be in 1990 or 1992."
> One might hope, or dream, that Mandel's gloomy prediction is proved wrong.[45]

And of course, it was wrong. Ruth Mandel, surely among the most astute students of women in political leadership, alludes directly to the symbolic potency of Hill-Thomas hearings as reason to change her position on the possibility of a year of the woman. In her remarks for the plenary at the CAWP Forum for Women State Legislatures, delivered November 15, 1991, just one month after the hearings, Mandel said,

> I'm positively, absolutely delighted to tell you ... we were right! Women in politics *do* make a difference!
> What you're going to hear at this session makes us even more certain that a political world dominated by suits and ties is not just incomplete—it's unacceptable. Last month gave us a searing image of men with power presiding, investigating and grappling with an issue which almost exclusively affects women, men who admitted they know little about the subject about which women feel so strongly. Now we have data to reinforce and give solid backing to what people across the country came to understand so well during those days of intense emotion in October 1991—that a society governed by men alone cannot be a society well governed. This feeling conforms to an opinion expressed more and more frequently in recent years ... the opinion that the educational, business, and political leadership of a diverse community or nation should reflect the community's variety, at least to a greater extent than we have witnessed historically.[46]

While the context at the time of the Hill-Thomas hearings incorporated the countervailing forces of advances for women with simultaneous backlash against women's advances, clearly Ruth Mandel describes those hearings in catalytic terms.

While the hearings had little overall affect on involvement by the mass public in the 1992 election, the gender content of the election directly affected the relevance of the Hill-Thomas hearings. Those who leaned toward Anita Hill also reported much greater interest in the campaign, especially where women were running for office.[47] More importantly for the creation of news coverage surrounding the election, and hence the interpretation given to gender in this election, political and cultural elites followed the hearings closely. They then commented upon the gendered impacts of the hearings and were covered by journalists who also followed the hearings closely. The result was an exaggerated account of the importance of the hearings to the electorate. Nonetheless, the hearings created a foil for organized feminism to make something of women's absence in political leadership.

In fifty-eight articles in the *Washington Post* and *The New York Times,* we find the Clarence Thomas confirmation hearing mentioned thirty-two times, most often by NWPC president Harriett Woods.[48] The effects were notable as they rippled outward in the political system. Using an event like the Hill-Thomas hearings as a reference point for the poor treatment of women, NWPC updated press fact sheets regularly and did continual press releases about the power of women in this country and the need for more women in office. The hearings also galvanized feminist organizations, dramatically increasing their membership and donations. This network of women and money was in turn given to women candidates. With money for their campaigns, women candidates could buy media time and materials that increased their name recognition. All of these women supporting a record number of women candidates made a very good story to cover, so organized feminism had repeated opportunities to claim the catalytic effect of the hearings, thereby helping to create a reaction. The importance of the Hill-Thomas hearings carried to the end in the year's construction, as this November 4, 1992 news story confirms.

> They took their inspiration from Anita F. Hill, saw their opportunity in an electorate hungry for change and cast themselves as outsiders in a year when outsiders could be fashionable. And it worked. Yesterday, a record number of women won seats in congress, making the "Year of the Woman" a reality.[49]

The hearings served as a catalyst and a framing idea for news stories. We have had an absence of women in politics since we ratified the Constitution, but something sparked intense emotion for 1992; that something became evident as Anita Hill faced the senators. It involves women's representation and the quality of governance.

Women's Representation and the Construction of the Year

To gain a sense of how ideas important for women's representation may have unfolded in press coverage, we searched the fifty-eight articles for related ideas. Table 21 presents the number of mentions of each of the following ideas and the number of articles including each idea. Such analysis provides some guideposts for the construction of the year through press coverage in two highly influential newspapers. We also can better see the picture painted by the print press of women candidates for the U.S. Senate, and aspects of gender power relevant to this picture.

In terms of sheer mentions, the idea of women supporting women candidates outstrips all others by an extraordinary margin of thirty-one mentions. By far the most remarkable occurrence was the widespread and strong support of women by women. Second, with forty mentions, was the construction of male incumbents as negative. Interestingly, in terms of articles, these ideas were covered with equal frequency, twenty-five times, or in 43 percent of the articles. While aspersions were cast at male incumbents, the idea repeated, and repeated again, was women's support of women. Thus, nearly half of the year developed around the ideas of male incumbents as negative, but women supporting women candidates figured most importantly.

Other ideas received nearly as much coverage in articles as "negative men." Women's stereotypical policy associations appeared in 41 percent of the articles. But interestingly, coupled with gender stereotypes was a similar level of attention to women's previous political experience. Also close behind in amount of coverage was the cry for women to be leaders, with mention in 36 percent of articles. Other themes persisted: Women were outsiders and therefore by their very presence served as vehicles for change. And women were portrayed as important to (domestic) policymaking—three related ideas that appeared in about 30 percent of articles.

These ideas affirmed a desire for more women to hold public-leadership posts and to do so for positive change and policy reasons. The year clearly built itself upon the idea that change was needed and change included women contributing to public leadership because they had important insights into some policy areas. The focus remained on the something women wanted, rather than dwelling on the absence.

Interestingly for an investigation that pursues the theme of making something of absence, the lack of women in office or the lack of women's repre-

TABLE 21. Ideas of Representation during the "Year"

Idea	Paper	Number of Mentions	Number of Articles	% Articles
Women supporting women candidates	Post[a]	39	14	43
	NYT[b]	32	11	
	Total	71	25	
Male incumbent as negative	Post	18	11	43
	NYT	22	14	
	Total	40	25	
Stereotypic/innate female functions/characteristics	Post	8	7	41
	NYT	28	17	
	Total	36	24	
Women's previous political experience	Post	10	9	39
	NYT	24	14	
	Total	34	23	
Cry for women to be leaders	Post	14	10	36
	NYT	18	11	
	Total	32	21	
Women as outsiders	Post	14	8	31
	NYT	17	10	
	Total	31	18	
Women as advocates/agents/vehicles for change	Post	18	11	31
	NYT	11	7	
	Total	29	18	
Women as important to policymaking	Post	15	12	29
	NYT	7	5	
	Total	22	17	
Value of incumbent status	Post	3	3	12
	NYT	6	4	
	Total	9	7	
Women or feminist organization noting lack of representation	Post	3	3	12
	NYT	4	4	
	Total	7	7	

Note: $N = 58$ (*Washington Post* = 28, *New York Times* = 30).
[a]*Washington Post.*
[b]*New York Times.*

sentation was mentioned only seven times in as many articles. Few of those mentions were as directly related to representation. The following excerpt was among the few that directly addressed representation itself, and this discussion appears to be in response to a direct question:

> "Women's perspective and experience is definitely missing," said Pennsylvania Senate candidate Lynn Yeakel, who is running neck-and-neck with Republican Senator Arlen Specter. "And so, yes, our values are not well represented because we're not well represented—and those values are now the nation's values, which is why I think this is all coming together in this year."[50]

Ironically, although probably coincidentally, the value of incumbent status was covered in seven articles as well. The year was explicitly constructed far more on positive ideas than upon a sense of absence or lack. Nonetheless, lack or absence remains implicit throughout.

Representation as the Year Unfolds

Representation is not static. It dynamically adjusts to circumstances, forming and transforming in response to new information and changing situations. Arguably, the need for any elected official to perpetually put forward the image of representing constituents is the central reason spin doctors or handlers have become a fixture in U.S. politics. Their presence is larger than elections. Ace handler David Gergen's recall to the White House as press secretary serves as an example. Much of politics today surely has enormous symbolic aspects worthy of attempts to control or manipulate. The public seems to respond, at least in the short term, to symbolic politics. The year was fraught with symbolic politics.

To consider what the year had to do with women's representation we analyzed the evolution of events, "spins," and responses over time. Using key markers of the campaign season, we look at the unfolding of the year in terms of Pitkin's four concepts of representation. Table 22 presents the findings. To gain a full appreciation of the dynamics involved in representation during the year, both the interaction across categories and the evolution of each concept are important.

Pitkin predicates her entire discussion of representation upon two questions: "when can something be considered present although in fact it is not? ... And, upon whose view does the existence of representation depend?"[51] The simple answers to these questions in terms of the year are that something can be said to be present for purposes of representation when those represented feel like it is, and especially in terms of the year of the woman and the Hill-Thomas hearings, the existence of representation depended upon the view of women opinion influencers (and men who cared about how women viewed their own representation).

TABLE 22. The "Year" and Women's Representation Dynamics

Evolution of "Year"	Formal	Descriptive	Symbolic	Substantive
Thomas/Hill hearing	Cry for accountability	Lack of women as Senate Judiciary Committee becomes salient	Senate Judiciary Committee as elite white men who "didn't get it"	Sexual harassment as evidence of gender difference in policy
Early announcement	Desire for accountability propels women candidates	Specific male targets; need for women seen	Begin move to generalize men; anti-incumbent; first hint of "year of woman"	Treatment of women/Anita Hill; question all policy important for women
Early primary wins	Braun, Yeakel emerge; accountability confirmed	Affirm women; generalized male	Phenomena with momentum; women as not incumbent	Emerge domestic agenda and feminine stereotypes
Democratic convention	Begin to authorize woman as outsider	Parade of women; women as positive	Woman as change; outsider; positive phenomenon	Rise of domestic agenda; pro-choice
Republican convention	Court traditional women; authorized tradition; some backfire	Gender as irrelevant; internal conflict about proper woman	Women as politically same as men; questionable phenomenon	Antifeminist policy; antiabortion; proexperience
Late primaries	Quest to authorize women	Women as positive but some tarnish in NY; power of incumbents emerges	Phenomenon as phenomena; change; outsider	Domestic agenda; abortion contention; hints of inexperience
Home stretch— general election	Quest to authorize; must authorize in specific candidates	Power of incumbents as important to representation	Time to prove phenomena or actual; open seats	Domestic agenda; incumbent records positive

Representation Concepts Interact

To illustrate the interaction across concepts of representation, let us refer to the Hill-Thomas hearings marker in the campaign season. Citizens, especially women, saw (white) men handling the substance of policy about sexual harassment.[52] Many interpreted their initial assessment of the problem as insufficient; senators were perceived to see sexual harassment as too unimportant to warrant further concern. For women who cared about sexual harassment, the senators provided evidence of poor representation. Rarely do members of Congress cross chambers. Nontheless, congresswomen from the House stormed the Senate in angered action, bringing female leadership to this issue. The need for members of the House to go to the Senate highlighted the absence of male senators' leadership and presentation on this issue important to women.

As events unfolded, alternative views on sexual harassment along gender lines became very evident. Such a divergence left the impression and fostered a feeling that these men had not represented women well on this issue. Impressions and feelings are, of course, fuel for symbolic representation. Given the considerable distance between women and men in understandings of this issue, the relevance of demographic characteristics in offering information and perspective on policy became apparent. Throughout the hearing, the conduct of the senators themselves began to call into question the universality of "appropriate" conduct of political leaders. Several, especially Republican, senators were seen as unnecessarily insulting to Hill, ungentlemanly at best, ridiculing and harassing at worst. Democratic senators' conduct was generally perceived as closer to condescending than harassing but still did not put them in a positive light. In either case, the senators "didn't get it."

Because men—exclusively elite white men to be more exact—represented women on a policy clearly divided by gendered perspectives, descriptive representation came to have meaning for many female opinion-influencers. Women no longer felt represented, and descriptive representation took on symbolic proportion precisely because these male political leaders were perceived to have failed women in terms of substance. And if these male senators failed with this policy so important to women, questions were raised about other such policies. But perhaps more importantly for symbolic representation, the male senators dramatically failed women affectively through their conduct and attitudes they displayed. Women reacted at an emotional level to perceived unjust treatment of the symbol of all women who had ever been sexually harassed, Anita Hill. In the process, specific men on the committee—and as the campaign season unfolded, all male incumbents—became symbols of what was wrong with governance for women.

Descriptive representation then became symbolic representation when substantive representation failed. The campaign and election became the medium through which to hold these officials accountable, to exercise formal representation. Hence, through representation becoming something very important to/for women, an absence in governance and leadership was very much at the heart of the year, even though few spoke about representation directly.

The Year Unfolds

Similar interaction among concepts of representation probably occurs in any politically relevant event, especially those that take on proportions of a political spectacle. A similar analysis could be conducted for any of the markers developed in table 22. Here, however, we will consider the evolution of each representation concept over the unfolding of the campaign season. As we move beyond the Hill-Thomas hearings, into the early announcements, to spring primaries, the Democratic and Republican conventions, the late primaries, and finally the home stretch and general elections, how do ideas related to representation evolve?

Formal representation clearly began with a demand to hold specific senators accountable for their actions during the hearings. To do so, (often unlikely) women stepped forward as candidates. The significance of holding specific senators accountable was confirmed through the primary victories of Braun and Yeakel. By May, references to the Hill-Thomas hearings faded away, to be replaced by rhetoric on outsiders and change. With the spotlighting of women at the Democratic convention, an effort to shift from the negative of accountability to the positive of authorizing occurred. In contrast, the Republican convention attempted to court and authorize tradition and traditional women, but experienced some backfire for this effort. By September, the focus moved almost exclusively to explanations of why women should be authorized—why voters should support women candidates—but much was still cast in broad "symbolic woman" terms. In the end however, voters authorize one specific person to represent them, and the effort shifted accordingly.

Descriptive representation is more tricky, as indicated above. Nevertheless, its unfolding occurs in a clear pattern. After the lack of women on the Senate Judiciary Committee became meaningful, specific men—Senators Specter and Dixon—were the immediate and prominent targets, although the phenomenon was also more widespread. Quickly, the notion that women had much to offer politics became central, and the negative interpretation of a generalized male incumbent emerged. The Democratic convention served to reinforce this notion. The Republican convention, in contrast, attempted to make gender irrelevant to politics and governance, spotlighting wives and ignoring elected Republican women. Their strategy led to significant internal conflict that was played out on page 1 of leading publications.[53] The New York primary between Ferarro and Holtzman called into question the distinctiveness of women's politics, probably to the detriment of the year's message. In the end, the importance of power to representing constituents, especially the power available to key incumbents, inevitably weighed back into descriptive-representation ideas.

Symbolic representation offers a plethora of ideas for the year. The year arguably was most of all symbolic representation. With the hearing, the Judiciary Committee became the symbol of all (elite white) men who abused their power and ignored concerns of women. Anita Hill became the symbol of all women who suffer under governance of such political leaders. The failings of the Judiciary Committee became the failings of all incumbents/insiders, and women were defined as outsiders (regardless of incumbency). As the Clinton campaign escalated the "change" theme, the outsider theme merged with change, and female candidates became symbols of both. Republicans tried to challenge the notion that women were politically different from men, all the while touting the complementarity of wives in traditional marriages. However, Republicans probably succeeded in beginning a move to question whether the year was something meaningful or a mere phenomenon created by certain kinds of women. In the end, the question became whether the year was merely a phenomenon without substance or an idea that would actually produce concrete results.

Substantive representation began with the sexual harassment but quickly expanded into gender stereotypes. With the treatment of Anita Hill and her charges generally, gender differences in our comprehension of "important" policy concerns became apparent. The move from sexual harassment to other policy areas was swift, in part because domestic policy more generally gained prominence given other political events. Domestic policy readily corresponds with feminine stereotypes, and that fact was not lost on Ann Richards and other leaders at the Democratic convention.[54] As described earlier, the Republican convention painted the need to reject feminist policy initiatives and instead to recognize the value of experience for substantive policy success. The domestic agenda remained central, and abortion occupied an uncomfortably prominent role. In the end, voters and even feminist interests had to acknowledge the importance of incumbent records in judging who would be supported with the vote.

Conclusion

Time will reveal how important this political spectacle proved for U.S. politics. Writing only a few years past its unfolding, we can imagine that the year might have marked a turning point, where women's involvement in national elective office became seen as normal. In this case, a fundamental shift in gender power would have begun with the year. Alternatively, the year might merely go down as a passing fad, a flash in the pan, important in the short term but with little lasting effect. A close analysis of elements of its unfolding should help us understand the consequences involved in any case.

Two points are clear. First, the very idea of women supporting women as candidates for positions of public leadership was by far the most noteworthy aspect of the entire year phenomenon. The fact that this simple idea was so remarkable speaks to the power of masculinism to make women supporting women at a mass level unthinkable in the first place. Second, seldom was women's representation, or the lack thereof, the explicit theme of the year of the woman in politics. Something—indeed many things—was made of women's absence in leadership and governance. But the quality of women's representation, as representation, rarely received attention. Perhaps the most important legacy of the year would be if the political spectacle of the year of the woman in politics made the link between descriptive and substantive representation a permanent part of our ideas about political representation, leadership, and governance. Such a linkage would indeed mark a fundamental shift in gender power.

Notes

1. See the final issue of the year for a cluster of articles on the year of the woman in politics, *Newsweek,* December 27, 1994.
2. Murray Edelman, *Constructing the Political Spectacle* (Chicago: University of Chicago Press, 1988).
3. For an account of the uses made by organized feminism see Georgia Duerst-Lahti, "Year of the Woman, Decade of Women: Wisconsin Legislative Elections" (paper presented at the Midwest Political Science Association, 1993).
4. Dayna Verstegen conducted the original search using nineteen different combinations of words and phrases such as "women and elections," "female candidates," "Clarence Thomas," and "the year of the woman" to identify 106 articles total. We discarded articles having to do with candidates for an office other than U.S. Senate that have no mention of the year, or just with the Hill-Thomas hearings but with no mention of women candidates. All of the articles included explicitly deal with the year or with women running for Senate posts.
5. See Kim Fridkin Kahn and Edie N. Goldenberg, "Women Candidates in the News: An Examination of Gender Differences in U.S. Senate Campaign Coverage," *Public Opinion Quarterly* 55 (1991): 180–99. Kahn has published extensively in this area.
6. Hanna Fenichel Pitkin, *The Concept of Representation* (Berkeley and Los Angeles: University of California Press, 1967), 8–9.
7. See Jeff Hearn, *Men in the Public Eye* (London: Routledge, 1992) for an extended discussion of viriarchy.
8. Pitkin, *The Concept of Representation,* 250, credits Hobbes with the etymological shift from "representer" to representative. She also believes he identified the term with "legal agency" or "acting for"; this constitutes a fundamental shift from the mystic or symbolic "standing for" that began with the notion that Parliament represented the whole realm.

9. Pitkin, *The Concept of Representation,* 9.

10. This paragraph is drawn from Pitkin, *The Concept of Representation.* See 61, 70, 71, 75, 80, and 84 especially.

11. Ibid., 81.

12. Ibid., 92–105.

13. Ibid., 97.

14. Ibid., 100.

15. Ibid.

16. Murray Edelman, *The Symbolic Uses of Politics* (Urbana: University of Illinois Press, 1964), and *Political Language: Words That Succeed and Policies That Fail* (New York: Academic Press, 1977).

17. Pitkin, *The Concept of Representation,* 116.

18. This is a partial list of the terms Pitkin includes as "adverbial expressions" purporting to summarize the representative's role, ibid., 119.

19. Ibid., 142–43.

20. See Roger H. Davidson and Walter J. Oleszek, *Congress and Its Members,* 2d. ed. (Washington, D.C.: Congressional Quarterly Press, 1985), esp. 122–24 and the sources used there as an example of contemporary writing.

21. Although usually more positions are attached to the executive in related appointed positions, so the executive is not really singular. It can be "made to look like America," as President Clinton said he would do.

22. As elaborated in chapter 1 the equation is not necessarily this simple. However, gender demands that representatives present themselves as either men or women.

23. Race as a salient political characteristic is more complex in many regards than sex. Governor of Virginia Douglas Wilder, for example, had only one-quarter African heritage and yet self-identified and was identified as African-American. Furthermore, race is highly charged politically, as the Hill-Thomas hearings clearly revealed. See, for example, Jane Mansbridge and Katherine Tate, "Race Trumps Gender: The Thomas Nomination in the Black Community," *Political Science and Politics* 25 (3) (1992): 488–92.

24. This point begs the very important question of how we arrived at believing demographic representation was as difficult as it is or that substantive representation somehow was so fully distinct from the demographic characteristics of representatives or the represented.

25. See Wilma Rule and Joseph F. Zimmerman, *United States Electoral Systems: Their Impact on Women and Minorities* (Westport, Conn.: Greenwood Publishing, 1992) for extensive coverage of electoral arrangements and outcomes.

26. Debra L. Dodson, ed., *Gender and Policymaking: Studies of Women in Office* (Camden, N.J.: Center for the American Woman and Politics, Rutgers University, 1991).

27. We can far too easily name the handful of prominent women, Pat Schroeder, Ann Richards, Olympia Snowe, Nancy Kassebaum, and Sandra Day O'Connor. The handy list of recognized women leaders is very short even as the pipeline continues to fill. See Tolleson-Rinehart and Stanley, *Claytie and the Lady,* for an important look at gender and governance. Ann Richards's election in 1990 may have actually started the year.

28. For a good historical accounting see Robert Darcy, Susan Welch, and Janet Clarke, *Women, Elections, and Representation* (New York: Longman, 1987).

29. Marian Lief Palley, "Elections 1992 and the Thomas Appointment," *Political Science and Politics* 26 (1) (1993): 28–31.

30. See Michale X. Delli Carpini and Ester R. Fuchs, "The Year of the Woman: Candidates, Voters, and the 1992 Elections," *Political Science Quarterly* 108 (1) (1993): 29–36, for a listing of citations documenting these differences.

31. Feminism, or gender consciousness, is an important medium for creating and transmitting gendered points of views. See Sue Tolleson Rinehart, *Gender Consciousness and Politics* (New York: Routledge, 1992).
32. That is, journalism enrollments are about 60 percent females, although women were not yet in positions to define the news in meaningful ways. See Maurine Beasely, "Newspapers: Is There a New Majority Defining the News?" in *Women in Mass Communication: Challenging Gender Values,* ed. Pamela J. Creedon, (Newbury Park, Calif.: Sage, 1989), who draws upon a University of Maryland study entitled *The New Majority: A Look at What the Preponderance of Women in Journalism Education Means to the Schools and to the Professions.*
33. "When Politics Lose, Women Win," *Washington Post,* December 29, 1991, C3.
34. Dodson, *Gender and Policymaking.*
35. Taken from Christine Stansell, "White Feminists and Black Realities: The Politics of Authenticity," in *Race-ing, Justice, En-gendering Power,* ed. Toni Morrison (New York: Pantheon, Books, 1992), 262, who quotes Rosalind Pollack Petchesky, "Antiabortion, Antifeminism, and the Rise of the New Right," *Feminist Studies* 7 (summer 1981): 222.
36. Anne Schneider and Helen Ingram, "Social Construction of Target Populations: Implications for Politics and Policy," *American Political Science Review* 87 (2) (1993): 334–47.
37. Data taken from Susan Faludi, *Backlash: The Undeclared War against American Women* (New York: Crown Publishers, 1991), 465, n. xix.
38. *Newsweek,* October 21, 1991 as reported by Kathleen Frankovic and Joyce Gelb, "Public Opinion and the Thomas Nomination," *Political Science and Politics* 25 (3) (1992): 481–84. Another article in the same issue of *PS* by Mansbridge and Tate, "Race Trumps Gender," indicates the 1986 Gallop poll probably elicited a higher level of feminist identification due to methodological flaws.
39. See also Naomi Wolf, *Fire with Fire: The New Female Power and How It Will Change the Twenty-first Century* (New York: Random House, 1993), for an account of negative connotations for the term *feminist.*
40. Michelle D. Brophy-Baermann, "The 'Intra-Gender' Gap: The New Right's Impact on the Women's Movement in the 1980s" (paper prepared for the Midwest Political Science Association, 1991). Survey data are drawn from the 1984 and 1988 National Election Studies. She divided the female respondents into categories of traditionalists, modernists, and others. All three categories indicate a cooling toward feminism, with a sixteen-percentage-point decline overall.
41. Information in this paragraph is drawn entirely from Jo Freeman, "Feminism versus Family Values: Women at the 1992 Democratic and Republic Conventions," *Political Science and Politics* 26 (1993): 21–28.
42. Ibid., 27.
43. Ibid., 23.
44. Marian Lief Palley and Howard A. Palley, "The Thomas Appointment: Defeats and Victories for Women," *Political Science and Politics* 25 (3) (1992): 473–77, esp. 476.
45. Faludi, *Backlash,* 464–65.
46. Ruth B. Mandel, prepared remarks for Plenary Session on "Reshaping the Agenda: The Impact of Women in Public Office," CAWP Forum for Women State Legislators, Friday, November 15, 1991, 2–3.
47. Virginia Sapiro and Pamela Johnson Conover, "Gender in the 1992 Electorate" (paper prepared for the annual meeting of the American Political Science Association, Washington, D.C., 1993), 5.
48. NWPC was the most quoted women's organization during this time frame, as one might expect given the group's focus on getting more women into public office.
49. "'Year of the Woman' Becomes Reality as Record Number Win Seats," *Washington Post,* November 4, 1992, A30.

50. "Flexing Their Electoral Muscle," *Washington Post,* June 5, 1992, C3.
51. Pitkin, *The Concept of Representation,* 9.
52. This accounting does not assess the important and confounding factor of race. See Morrison, *Race-ing, Justice, En-gendering Power,* for an enlightening analysis of race in gender in the hearing.
53. "Family Values and Women: Is GOP a House Divided?" *New York Times,* August 21, 1992, A1; and "GOP Women Complain about Roles in Shadows," *Washington Post,* August 19, 1992, A1.
54. The linking of feminine stereotypes with domestic policy involves many more complicated processes related to assumptions about women's capacity to govern at all, of course. Women have advanced first in administrative agencies associated with feminine stereotypes, however—so the pattern is consistent. See Mary Guy and Georgia Duerst-Lahti, "Agency Culture and Its Effect on Managers," in *Women and Men of the States,* ed. Mary Ellen Guy (Armonk, N.Y.: M. E. Sharpe, 1992).

Chapter 10

Hillary, Health Care, and Gender Power

Mary Ellen Guy

Government institutions, as well as the media and the general public, treat the First Lady much as they would a puppet. She is carried to center stage to perform a scripted role, then tossed in the trunk to await the next performance. As is so often the case, the exception proves the rule. This cultural and political choreography has never been so obvious as it is with Hillary Rodham Clinton, for she does not quite fit back into the trunk.

The ongoing tug of war between the scriptwriter and the living puppet has placed the issue of gender power and leadership squarely on center stage. The stagehands seem not to be able to close the curtain and clear the stage. Contrary to their intent, the show goes on. And the story line is brought to life through the parable of the Clinton administration's attempt at health reform. Hillary's critics are responding in large part to the fact that her performance places gender power on the table leaving no choice but to acknowledge it.

Gender shapes power capacity. Although not to the same degree as in Abigail Adams's day, women are still expected to speak through the voices of their husbands, brothers, sons, or fathers to be heard. The First Lady is no exception. The traditional interpretation of the role reinforces the customary gender power differential: men have considerable and broad power, women have limited and highly circumscribed power. But Hillary's execution of the role turns the traditional notion of gender power on its head. By her appointment as chair of the White House Task Force on National Health Care Reform, Hillary Rodham Clinton became a lightning rod for that power differential. With the controversy that surrounds the interpretation of "proper behavior" for a *lady*—especially a First Lady, with all of her symbolic potency—and with the prospects of a changing health care system coupled with partisan politics, sparks were inevitable. This confluence of gender, power, and leadership occurs in three dimensions: institutional (gender relations, medical establishment); individual (Hillary Rodham Clinton), and symbolic (gender, power, and leadership).

Institutional refers to that which has been customary in the health policy arena. Physicians, most of whom are men, have controlled policy debates, while nurses, most of whom are women, have been encouraged to sit on the sidelines as spectators. *Individual* refers to Hillary Rodham Clinton and the fact that her presence as head of the health reform task force placed her in a position of power and leadership usually accessible only to men. *Symbolic* refers to the norms and counternorms that are triggered by Hillary's performance and expectations of her role as first lady.

Gender power has been a central, although silent, construct in the policy-making arena. The political culture is constructed in such a way that women are expected to be helpmates rather than drivers, and when women do drive, they are expected to drive a pink car. Despite notable gains made by women in the Clinton administration, women generally are to play the supportive role, while the limelight is supposed to shine on (their) men. I use the relationship between health reform and gender power to demonstrate this fact. I argue that Hillary Rodham Clinton's performance of her role as First Lady reveals the contradiction between the "wifely" role of the First Lady and the power of her position as chair of the health reform task force.

Discussion first turns to health reform to provide the background for this explication.

Reforming Health Policy

A problem like health care does not get to government until the private sector has determined that a profit cannot be made from some aspect of it and until it is too big for the nonprofit sector to handle. Attempts have been made throughout the century to reform America's health system in such a way that access to care would be ensured regardless of one's income. One of the early attempts was the Committee on the Cost of Medical Care in 1932. This committee reported persistent gaps in access to health care for various rural and urban regions and income groups.[1] Later, President Truman proposed a national health insurance that was successfully opposed by the American Medical Association.[2] A national commission appointed by President Eisenhower concluded that "access to the means for attainment and preservation of health is a basic human right," although no legislation was passed to correct the problem until Lyndon Johnson's administration.[3] The passage of Medicare and Medicaid satisfied some of the need for reform. These programs instituted a major expansion of federal responsibility for health care services. But rising costs and problems of access gave rise to repeated calls for additional system reform during the Nixon, Carter, Reagan, and Bush administrations.[4]

In recent years, exploding health care costs resulted in state governments joining the call for system reform. In 1980, Medicaid expenditures comprised 9 percent of state budgets. In 1985 these expenses comprised 10 percent of state budgets. But by 1990 they had climbed to 14 percent of state budgets, and, if costs had continued to climb at the same rate, projections showed that by 1995 Medicaid costs would consume 25 percent of state budgets.[5] Pushed to the point of desperation, by 1993 a number of states, including Florida, Minnesota, Vermont, Washington, and Oregon had already taken the initiative and designed their own versions of health reform. Other states, including Iowa, Kentucky, Maryland, New York, and Maine had either adopted piecemeal reforms or were on the verge of adopting statewide reforms.[6]

When compared with citizens in comparable nations, Americans report less satisfaction with their health care system.[7] In a Harris poll that compared ten nations, the U.S. public was the least satisfied with its health care.[8] Nations with national health systems, including Great Britain, Germany, the Netherlands, Sweden, and Canada, report higher satisfaction.[9] (In fact, Germany has had a national health insurance program since 1883, and Great Britain since 1911).[10]

For all these reasons, public dissatisfaction, budget-busting health care costs, and humanitarian need, the 1992 presidential campaign witnessed all candidates, George Bush, Ross Perot, and Bill Clinton, advocating health reform. For several years, polls had shown less controversy among the public in regard to changing the system than in leaving it unchanged.[11] Furthermore, a substantial majority of Americans already favored a national health insurance plan financed through taxation.[12] However, the consensus that change was needed was broad but thin. As an example of the difficulty of health reform, this joke made the rounds in the winter of 1993:

> A physician died and went to heaven. Upon being met by God, the doctor said, "Tell me, God, will there ever be health reform?" God replied, "Yes, doctor, but not in my lifetime."

Humor captures cultural contradictions and frustrations, and this example shows the extenuation of health reform efforts.

Policy development was controversial because of the enormous financial stakes involved for the pharmaceutical, insurance, medical products, and hospital industries, as well as for physicians, nurses, and other health professionals. Yet, the basics of the reform had been generally agreed upon by the major stakeholders before President Clinton's inauguration. The Enthoven plan, which provided the foundation for the health reform proposed by the White House Task Force on National Health Care Reform, was a revision of the plan first proposed in 1980.[13] The plan had been discussed, bandied about, and modified for so long that the major hospital associations, physicians' groups, and insurance companies were familiar with it and were adapting their practices to it before the task force ever completed its deliberations in the spring of 1993. Called "managed competition," the plan represented a compromise resulting in a health maintenance organization approach that retains some degree of consumer choice.

Although unacceptable to the American Medical Association (AMA) in the past, managed competition represented the inevitability of reform and, by 1993, it became the lesser of evils. Physicians had tried to block managed care for decades, with mixed success.[14] For example, in 1943, the U.S. Supreme Court upheld a conviction of the American Medical Association and the Medical Society of the District of Columbia for conspiring to block Group Health Association, a prepaid medical plan, from operating. As health maintenance organizations have cropped up in community after community, however, organized medicine has grown accustomed to them, and physicians have adapted their practices accordingly.

Thus, the process of health reform was well on its way to closure before President Clinton was inaugurated. When he named his wife to head the health reform task force, those who stood to be most affected by the reform already knew what shape it would take. President Clinton's calls for health care reform came on the heels of a groundswell of public support for it—a groundswell that had been developing for the greater part of this century. So why all the fuss about Hillary Rodham Clinton as head of the task force? To understand this, we must include gender in the equation. Much like a silent partner in the policy process, gender is always present, along with a presumption of the proper role for men and the proper role for women. The following discussion outlines the gendered norms of the health care establishment.

Health Care and Institutionalized Sexism

Professional hegemony and gender hegemony converge in health care, for it is an industry governed by men but delivered by women. While females comprise the vast majority of health care workers, they are employed in relatively low paying occupations. For example, 95 percent of nurses are women, and nurses earn only 20 percent of physicians' average earnings. Health care pricing mechanisms are built around physicians, even though a patient will have more contact time with a nurse than with a physician[15] and will be more dependent on a nurse than on a physician for the provision of services. While educational differences account for some of the earnings spread, it cannot fully account for the differential value accorded to nurses and doctors.

Accustomed to an industry where women stay in the background while policy decisions are made, the AMA found itself confronted not only by a day in which input from nursing was sought and listened to, but worse: A woman, who did not hold an M.D. degree, was heading the policy development process that would affect the way physicians conducted their business and charged their fees. To rub salt in the wound, both the secretary of the U.S. Department of Health and Human Services and the U.S. surgeon general were women. In a system in which the power differential between women and men is more often accepted without question than challenged, everything was topsy-turvy.

To accentuate the change, Hillary's task force reached into the states and brought state nursing directors and key nursing initiatives to the table. The inclusiveness of the task force changed the face of the health care debates. The fee-for-service providers (physicians and hospitals) were having less of an influence than that to which they had grown accustomed. The AMA, which has 290,000 members and is a powerful lobbying force in Congress, was further aggravated when representatives from nursing associations and deans of nursing schools were invited to a meeting of the health reform task force on April 20, 1993.[16] At that time, the task force was considering how to increase the utilization of advanced practice nurses, such as nurse practitioners, nurse-midwives, and nurse anesthetists, who are underutilized in the current system. The slogan that appeared in the spring of 1993, "In the future your family doctor may be a nurse," threatened both the professional power and personal finances of physicians.

Gender power relations in medicine are an exaggeration of power relations embedded in the political culture. Patients spend more time with nurses but pay physicians. Health care treatment teams are comprised of physicians; nurses; various therapists; pharmacists; laboratory technologists; and a stable of technicians but all providers other than physicians are categorized as "ancillary" professionals. Most reimbursement schedules are predicated on whether the physician orders the services of the ancillary professional. If a physician does not prescribe the service, reimbursement is usually not allowed. Imagine any other industry as lucrative as health care where one discipline has had such occupational and financial control over the income of all other professionals. Dr. James Todd, executive vice president of the AMA, said that his organization does not approve of anyone treating patients independent of a physician's advice.[17] The fact that much of what any physician sees in daily practice is routine and programmable, easily diagnosed, and easily treated, makes it obvious that the AMA's insistence on the professional hegemony of physicians is based less on concerns about quality of care than on self-interest.[18]

The Politics of Medical Practice

A brief scan of the 1993 issues of the *New England Journal of Medicine* shows several articles on managed competition, but little attention to revising practice norms. Apparently, the medical establishment assumes that physicians will continue to decide how practice is conducted. In fact, after Hillary addressed the

Association of American Medical Colleges and explained the new priority on training primary-care physicians, medical students complained that they resented "the government's dictating the direction" of their careers.[19] The nursing literature, on the other hand, shows the voice of those on the outside who want inside. Reading the journals of the American Nursing Association compared to those of the American Medical Association is instructive. While articles in the former focus on wanting changes in the system and a devolution to community care, articles in the latter focus on managed competition—the business aspects of the enterprise. And while nursing journals have advertisements, they cannot compare to the multicolored, expensive advertisements of the pharmaceutical companies that are scattered throughout the physicians' journals, obviously intending to influence the readers' use of their products. Scanning the journals, one sees that the enterprise that physicians write about is quite different from the enterprise that nurses write about.

The historical tension between physicians and nurse-midwives provides another window on the institutional sexism of medical practice. The twentieth century witnessed a tug of war, with physicians struggling (successfully) to wrest the normal delivery of babies from the hands of nurse-midwives. Midwives have been a threat to physicians' incomes for years. In fact, in 1900 midwives delivered about half of the babies born in the United States.[20] There is substantial evidence that nurse practitioners and nurse-midwives achieve higher scores than physicians on resolving pathological conditions, achieving patient satisfaction and functional status, and securing patient compliance. Their patients experience fewer hospitalizations than those of physicians and the cost per patient visit for nurse practitioners is two-thirds of that for physicians.[21]

Barbara Redman, executive director of the American Nurses Association, describes the nursing agenda as being proactive in favor of taking health care to the people in the communities where they live. She argues that the consumers of health systems are the people, not the providers, and that the public should have convenient access to care. She also argues that empowerment is an important piece of healing; that basic, primary care must be offered in balance with acute, high-tech care; and that nurses are cost-effective providers.[22] In sum, she argues that today's health care system provides medical care, but not health care.

The institutional sexism of the medical profession is made obvious by the lengths to which the AMA has gone to deny nurses a voice in health policy debates. In medicine, more so than in any other moneymaking enterprise, differentials in gender power have led to institutional sexism, which then reinforces gender power differentials through differential political and economic power.

A Woman Overseeing a "Man's" Enterprise

Given the cultural construction of that which is viewed as feminine and that which is viewed as masculine, Hillary's role as wife contradicts her role as head of the White House Task Force on National Health Care Reform. The public is accustomed to "appropriate" masculine and feminine behavior, and that which breaches the bounds of appropriateness induces a sexual static that everyone finds uncomfortable, especially the syndicated columnists that bear down on Hillary Rodham Clinton when she steps from appropriately *wifely* and *motherly* duties to power duties.

The White House Task Force on National Health Care Reform involved more than five hundred people working in deep secrecy. In her position as head of the task force, Hillary Rodham Clinton is credited by her advocates as having smashed the stereotype of a First Lady as primarily a hostess and helpmate whose public advocacy is a sideline.[23] By March 24, a mere two months following the Clinton inauguration, she had made ten trips to Capitol Hill for policy discussions with senators and representatives.[24] But her iconoclastic leadership was not without its detractors, both from those in the medical profession and from those in the media and general public.

The topic of gender power, written in lay language, means that men have it and women do not. Barbara Kellerman argues that leadership is all about dominance and deference.[25] Men dominate, women defer. And the presidency is all about dominance and the amount of deference that the public give to the office, a pattern consistent with masculinized understandings of leadership delineated throughout this volume. Thus, when the president's wife enters the picture, everyone becomes confused. Is she an extension of the president, the president's proxy, if you will, and therefore able to rightfully claim dominance and to expect deference given to the presidency? But in the gender role of woman and wife, should she not defer to men and her husband? In this case as proxy, she has indirect power at best—pseudopower more accurately. Far more tolerable is a First Lady who is a proxy with pseudopower than someone with real power. Pseudopower is the thin veneer that everyone accords the wife of an important man. Real power, on the other hand, is quite different. It refers to the power any First Lady garners from the confluence of her proximity to the president plus Hillary's expertise based on her own skills plus her legendary ability to get things done. In Hillary's case, these elements of personal power converge with her legitimate and formal position as official head of a presidential task force and power derived from the position. Pseudopower is to be expected, and there are protocols according the wife of the president commensurate deference. Real power for the First Lady, on the other hand, challenges funda- mental images of husband/head of household/public representative and wife/helpmate/private caretaker, the old breadwinner/homemaker dichotomy of 1950s conventions.

The cultural discomfort that accompanies this twist to the mythical American household is reflected in the mass media. Hillary Rodham Clinton became the recipient of criticism by those who resist change in gender power. Of the many diatribes against her, a particularly vitriolic one was written by Paul Gigot for the *Wall Street Journal*. In this he lambasted not only her, but anyone who might agree with her. He claimed that she benefits from coverage by feminist reporters because they

> have a stake in her success as a woman with power. So they stress her role as a cultural icon while ignoring the quality of her policy advice. And of course anyone who criticizes Hillary is accused of wanting to enslave women in the kitchen. Such coverage is not better than what used to run in old newspaper "women's pages." If Hillary has power, Americans deserve to know how she uses it.[26]

Of course, Gigot remains blissfully uncritical of his gender power stake in her failure as a symbolic woman with power. He also seems simply to assume his structural power (space to voice his opinion in a major newspaper) to shape public opinion. Data on gender distribution in journalism suggest few women, let alone feminists, have such access to this resource.

Criticism also bore down on Hillary from those who feared their economic toes were being stepped on. Take, for example, the lawsuit *Association of American Physicians and Surgeons, Inc., et al. v. Hillary Rodham Clinton, et al.* Ostensibly the suit was about separation of powers and whether the task force had to comply with the Federal Advisory Committee Act and give a fifteen-day advance notice of formal sessions.[27] The 1972 law requires that any committee established to give advice to the president or Congress that includes members who are not government employees must abide by open meetings laws. Since the Federal Advisory Committee Act applies only to intragovernment groups, the litigation hinged on whether the First Lady is, or is not, a government employee. The Justice Department, representing the White House, contended that the 1972 law did not apply because Hillary Rodham Clinton, as First Lady, was the functional equivalent of a federal employee. Because the First Lady is neither a federal officer nor a full-time federal employee, the plaintiffs contended that the task force's meetings had to be open to the public under the 1972 law. Obviously, the highly gendered assumption that two people contribute to one career, but that only one spouse, the husband, can be understood as the employee, is implicated, as is its consequences for gender power.

The significance of this case is that, after two hundred years, the executive branch and the judicial branch are just now deciding how to classify what category of government official the First Lady is. If the First Lady's formal and proper role is on a pedestal, then to step off of it and use her professional skills is to topple the house of cards that deny the fact that First Ladies function in political ways or that they occupy a distinct portion of the institution of the presidency. One step threatens the system that has been designed to let men govern and women follow. And no one should be surprised that the challenge was registered by physicians, not nurses.

As the health care industry braced for reforms, they began to speak of the "Hillary Factor." "Hillary" was shorthand for changes in the system that would challenge the industry to be more cost efficient and provide access to health care for all Americans, not just the privileged.[28] They feared that reform measures would impose price controls and disallow excessive earnings that had been the rule in the past, thus ending windfall profits. Such changes were credited to the Hillary Factor, and, hence, she was seen to have power. But Hillary was only leading the parade that was already up and moving when President Clinton was elected. The fact that the president's wife was leading the charge complicated the momentum for change because her visibility explicitly added gender power to the equation.

In sum, the health reform movement was already rumbling around before President Clinton assumed office. And challenges to the traditional medical model have been voiced for years. But when Hillary Rodham Clinton was named chair of the health reform task force, the appointment brought to a head a convergence of conflicts between women and men, doctors and nurses, and government and the health care industry. To complicate matters, attention turned to the tensions inherent in the role of First Lady, for with that role comes its own tangled web of expectations and norms. All of this makes gender power and its differential advantages hard to hide.

The Role of First Lady

First ladies usually are credited with a policy agenda, but one that has two essential features: first, it reflects a stereotypical "woman's" issue, and, second, it is relatively noncontroversial. For example, Barbara Bush (1989–93) adopted illiteracy and AIDS; Nancy Reagan (1981–89) addressed drug abuse; Rosalynn Carter (1977–81) focused on mental health; Betty Ford (1974–77) targeted women's rights; Patricia Nixon (1969–74) addressed volunteerism; Lady Bird Johnson (1963–69) emphasized landscape beautification; Jacqueline Kennedy (1961–63) adopted the arts and historical restoration; Eleanor Roosevelt (1933–45) addressed poverty and human rights; Nellie Taft (1909–13) advanced women's right to vote; Lucy Hayes (1877–81) addressed better prisons and asylums; and Abigail Adams (1797–1801) pushed for women's rights.[29]

None of these initiatives has been as controversial as health reform, for at least two reasons. First, the more debatable of the reasons, health reform confronts organized opposition that has been effective at halting reform movements for the past century. Thus, whatever change effort is promulgated in the 1990s will incur similar levels of opposition by the American Medical Association and other economic forces. Johnson ran into economic forces because her beautification efforts curtailed advertising; however, roadside advertising is but one small part of larger systems, unlike medicine and health care reform. Taft's and Adams's initiatives were controversial, but they were only marginally economic and were not in an era of modern presidencies, when television highlights such activities. Second, when former First Ladies adopted issues, any controversy was mitigated by the "ladyhood" of the president's wife. Only Eleanor Roosevelt begins to compare in the challenge she brought to the "lady" factor. Hillary, on the other hand, does not shy from claiming authority based on her personal expertise and credentials, rather than by virtue of her position as the president's helpmate.

Given the fact that many presidents' wives have possessed personal expertise, how can we explain the seeming necessity that each has felt to package herself as a lady rather than as a powerful government agent? Why has the role of First Lady remained with its power so curtailed? While the complete answer is complex and confounded by gender, the straightforward answer is simple: Power comes when one prevails in a controversy. Ladies, as myth would have it, shirk controversy.

"Ladyness" is a reflection of gender power and the invisibility that marriage brings to women. For those who doubt this assessment, note that criticism is levied at presidents' wives who step to the podium without having been properly escorted there on the arms of a man. Edith Wilson (1915–21), for example, was criticized for managing President Wilson's office, albeit behind the scenes, after he suffered a debilitating stroke. Eleanor Roosevelt, despite the gender appropriateness of her policy interests, was reviled by her detractors for being too prominent and speaking too openly. This was in spite of the fact that she was sensitive to her critics and worried that her activism would incur charges of a "petticoat government."[30] And even Abigail Adams was criticized for speaking through her husband for greater rights of citizenship for women. For example, Kellerman quotes John Adams's political opponents as asking questions about Abigail Adams, "this unelected woman's influence over her husband."[31] And Rosalynn Carter was faulted for being "too equal." During the 1980 presidential campaign, revelations of her involvement in substantive decision making were responsible for her being "rescripted" as the dutiful wife. Similar stories were now appearing about Hillary Clinton. As long as the practice of reining in president's wives is condoned, the charade that wives are mere decorations will continue.

A further confirmation of the passivity that is expected of presidents' wives is the fact that it is not unusual for entire books to be written analyzing a president's performance with barely a mention of his wife.[32] Barbara Kellerman's *All the President's Kin* shows how the president's wife is just one of several family members who play various ancillary roles, ranging from decorations, extensions, and humanizers who take it upon themselves to play to the public, to helpmeets, moral supports, and alter egos who "stand by their Man."[33] The kin include siblings, parents, children, and wives, and there is little differentiation between the kinship connection and the role.

Hillary and Power

It is the appearance, the symbolics, of a woman having power that so disturbs traditionalists. Hillary Rodham Clinton's mere existence is making political waves,[34] in spite of the fact that 37 percent of married women do not assume their husband's name, 42 percent of law students are women, and 59 percent of married couples have two wage-earner households (and in 21 percent of these couples the wife earns more than her husband). Presidents have always used unelected male advisors, but a woman has to be seen as distinctly "unfeminine" to be accepted as a proper advisor or she must be the man's wife. And even then, she is supposed to advise cautiously and passively, not directly and proactively. The particularly threatening aspect of wives compared to blood kin rests in the fact that the relationship is voluntary and intimate. Both of these factors lead to a feared potential to influence the one man who is seen as the leader of the nation.

But we didn't elect her! is the complaint lodged against presidents' wives. "We" did not elect Richard Nixon's pal, Bebe Rebozo, or Franklin Roosevelt's pal Harry Hopkins, either. The public is much less likely to accept a First Lady as an adviser than they are to accept a male buddy of the president. The "We didn't elect her!" argument is specious at best. Marriage seems to be an unwritten prerequisite for the job, since unmarried men, apparently, are not viable presidential candidates. Even though a wife is required, she is expected to serve as a decoration, where her inaugural gown and hairdos will be described in detail, but any exertion of power is to be sub rosa. An activist wife, someone who would be seen as a positive force and hailed as a community leader in other circumstances, brings criticism both to herself and to her husband. Such is the wrath that Hillary Rodham Clinton has incurred.

As first lady, Hillary must walk a fine line between power and familiarity with the president, an awkwardness that continues to disarm the political and editorial establishment. In the spring of 1993, only a few months after President Clinton's inauguration, popular television journalist Ted Koppel devoted two entire sessions of his network news program *Nightline* to whether Hillary Rodham Clinton had too much power. Pollitt quotes former president Ronald Reagan's advisor, Michael Deaver: "This is not some kind of a woman behind the scenes who's pulling the strings. This woman's out front pulling the strings."[35] Perhaps Michael Deaver longs for the days when first lady Nancy Reagan was known for manipulating President Reagan's schedule of activities from behind the scenes. The inference is that it is not the behavior of the First Lady that is objectionable. Rather, it is her *visibility* that is troublesome. Perhaps the visibility of a president's wife makes it impossible to ignore the fact that the president is merely mortal. Perhaps such reality unwraps the aura of superhumanness that the public want to accord the president. Perhaps such reality is all about visibility. When a woman's power is exerted from behind the scenes, the charade of man in charge, woman as helpmate is perpetuated. However, when a woman's power is visible, it threatens the myth of omnipotent male superiority.

As the first First Lady with an overt power agenda, Hillary has fascinated journalists with her involvement in policy matters. In the pattern of thesis-antithesis, by May 1993, a backlash against the media's criticism of Hillary Clinton was beginning to develop. But not before nationally syndicated columnist Lewis Grizzard bemoaned the fact that the First Lady insisted on being more than a decoration in the White House. His distaste or fear for a powerful First Lady results in his magnification of her actions and a diminution of President Clinton's actions. Take, for example, this excerpt from a column he wrote:

> Personally, I think Co-President Clinton wants her maiden name used so that when history remembers her, she can have a set of famous initials.... What we have to accept here is that HRC is one powerful lady who, before it's all over, probably will affect our lives more than her husband will.[36]

Hillary Clinton's use of power is better received by the general public than by those who are the usual opinion shapers. Based on the trends in polling data since the Clinton administration began, Hillary has developed a positive image among the public that surpasses the opinions written in the national press.[37] Editorial writers have shown themselves to be one of the last strongholds of male privilege. In May 1993, *Time* magazine reported a poll showing that 63 percent of those responding answered yes to the question: "Is Hillary Clinton's prominent role in national policy appropriate?"[38] The most powerful woman to emerge from 1993, supposedly the "year of the woman" in electoral politics, was a wife, Hillary Rodham Clinton. This woman, who as a high schooler was voted "most likely to make her husband president," is the enigma of those who have been satisfied with the First Lady as icon rather than doer.[39]

As the health reform debates died down, she remained a target, as the March 21, 1994 *Time* magazine cover makes clear. "Hard Times for Hillary" declares the cover caption, "How much is she to blame?"—for the problems with Whitewater real estate deal that marred the presidency. Despite careful efforts to cultivate Hillary's image, softening it and making her more feminine, she still was described in extraordinary terms.

> Hillary functions in the White House rather like the queen on a chessboard. Her power comes from her unrestricted movement; but the risk of capture is great, and a player without a queen is at a fatal disadvantage. Clinton's presidency would be severely disabled by a direct hit to his wife. So, as the Whitewater story has wound tighter around her, opponents, supporters and observers of the Clinton Administration alike have been faced with the simultaneously giddy and unnerving prospect of seeing the capture of such a powerful figure.[40]

Hillary insists that the extraordinary attention focussed on her "was a Republican plot to discredit her," and while several polls conducted in March 1994 showed that the public agreed with that assessment, trust in the president had diminished to 35 percent, down from 40 percent in January. "Caesar's wife" remained the target of right-wing conservatives, perhaps as a predictable assault on an strong, outspoken feminist, perhaps because they recognized the threat to gender power arrangements if Hillary were to succeed in transforming expectations for power within marriages and for women as professionals generally.

The chasm between traditional behavior for the First Lady and Hillary's behavior marks a watershed in the publicness with which dual-career couples are experiencing the power differential in their own marriages. Accommodation to prescribed gender roles continues to have a lasting effect on women's and men's views about Hillary and her relationship to President Clinton. Attitudes toward gender roles evolve, but if the evolution were to be charted, the progress would be a jagged rather than a straight line. Women are more likely than men to favor empowered roles for women who are active in politics. For example, support for Hillary cuts across partisan lines.[41] Senator Nancy Kassebaum (R-Kans.) has shown admiration for her activist stance, as has Heather Foley, wife and unpaid aide to former Speaker of the House Thomas Foley. Conversely, women and men who favor "traditional" gender roles tend to converge in their levels of disapproval of Hillary's performance.[42]

The president's wife is expected to be, in Camilla Stivers's words, on "tap but not on top," to be seen rather than heard, and to be loyal rather than assertive.[43] This results in the "proper" place for the wife: a compliant deferent to her husband. And when a woman in a visible position and visible marriage challenges that which is customary, the traditional gender power relationship is magnified. For example, a typical office joke passed around shortly after it was announced that Hillary would head the health reform task force went like this:

> Three people died and showed up at the Pearly Gate. God asked them who they were. The first cleared his throat and answered that his name was George Bush, the late president of the United States. God said, "Well, that was a very important position, so please come sit in this chair to my left." God then looked at the second person, who answered that his name was Bill Clinton and explained that he was president of the United States. God replied that Clinton was also an important person and that he should take a seat on his right. The third person then spoke up. She looked straight at God and said, "My name is Hillary Clinton and I believe someone is in my place."

Humor is used to relieve tension and to communicate those fears and circumstances that defy the ordinary. This joke, as did several at the time, captures the discomfort that the teller has with a woman's power and the exaggeration of it by those who fear it.

Conclusion

The post of First Lady carries social symbolic meaning that transcends the woman who holds the position. Despite many strong wives of former presidents, no modern First Lady has challenged the symbolics of the office as much as Hillary Rodham Clinton. By taking the visible lead in the Clinton administration's health reform effort, she challenged the power relationship between the president's wife, the public, and powerful constituencies. In presidential marriages, as in all nuptials, wives generally have influence with their spouses. It is ironic that her influence has done less to upset the reality of such relations than it has to upset the *perception* of that reality. In the process of reforming health care, she also illuminated gender power relations within the health care industry.

As First Lady, Hillary Clinton is regarded not as a political advisor but as a wife, first and foremost. For example, within a month and a half after President Clinton's inauguration, political observers for the *Wall Street Journal* were warning that "Mrs. Clinton has taken on the most intractable problem the country faces—health care."[44] And with the load, Democratic strategist Alan Baron warned that "people working for the president will be afraid to challenge her."[45] And Democratic strategist Greg Schneider was warning that "It's hard to get rid of your wife if she's not performing in her job."[46] Republican theoretician Kevin Phillips speculated that if she were to fail in the health reform process, there would be legal and political questions raised about the process. And, if she were to succeed, "I think it raises the question of whether we don't have a new type of relationship that I hate to call quasi-monarchical, but how else do you get a chief of state and an unelected consort except in a quasi-monarchical situation?"[47] The message to these comments from both Democrats and Republicans is that the First Lady is to be "the lady consort" and not enter the "manly" arena of politics. Their message is that Hillary is a woman with a power agenda, and they do not like it one bit.

The controversy surrounding health reform and Hillary's performance as First Lady is in part due to the fact that she put gender power on the table. People had no choice but to acknowledge it. The power dimension between physicians and nurses is challenged in these debates as well. Nursing as a profession is struggling to loosen its tradition of being a rule-driven nondiscretionary enterprise and is just learning to exert its political muscle. Hillary and her policy performance consciously and explicitly challenge the dominance and deference pattern evident in masculinity/femininity, husbands/wives, doctors/nurses, leaders/followers.

In sum, Hillary Rodham Clinton walks a balance beam over a cultural divide. A poll taken three months after the inauguration showed that the public admired the role that she was playing. To the question, "Do the Clintons set a good example as role models for the country," 74 percent responded that they were a good or very good example. The majority of respondents (55 percent) said that Hillary Rodham Clinton had the right amount or too little power.[48] She is expected to be the compassionate First Lady while her head and heart are dedicated to engineering a more just nation. But after being trounced in the media for being smart, well educated, and competent, a major media blitz appeared, and each article featured Hillary Rodham Clinton as the compassionate wife and mother. Apparently attempting to rid herself of the chilly image of social engineer (read *dynamic power broker* if describing a man), personal interviews and homey photographs appeared in *Family Circle, People, Time,* and *Parade,* the weekly magazine inserted in Sunday newspapers across the nation. The articles depicted her as a woman trying to balance work and home, able to work round the clock on health care yet manage to make scrambled eggs for a sick Chelsea.[49] For example, "Hillary still has something in common with women everywhere: a day that contains only twenty-four hours, and responsibilities that extend way beyond what happens in the office. Family duties fall primarily to her—from attending soccer games and helping Chelsea with her homework to shopping and organizing birthday parties."[50]

Summary

By taking the lead in the Clinton administration's health reform effort, Hillary Rodham Clinton transformed the gender power of the post in spite of White House public relations efforts to depict her as a stereotypical wife and mother at every opportunity. For example, the *New York Times* published a story entitled "A Warm and Fuzzy White House Christmas" in December 1993, complete with a photograph of Hillary in front of the first family's Christmas tree. The article describes her red suit and rhinestone pin and details the Christmas cookies that Hillary has baked.[51] *Parade* published "A Holiday Message from Our Family to Yours" that included a homey photograph of President Clinton and his wife.[52]

In the process of reforming health care, she also challenged gender power relations within the politics of the health care establishment by including nurses in the health policy debates and by refusing to accept carte blanche the proposals of the American Medical Association. At the close of the first year of the Clinton presidency, a front-page article in the *Wall Street Journal* reported that "the most powerful woman in American national politics is arguably Mr. Clinton's unelected wife, Hillary, and only after a campaign by her husband that deliberately soft-pedaled her influence and interests."[53]

This transformation in progress illustrates the power and politics of gender. It points out one more difficulty in a woman being elected president—what will we do with her husband? Until our politics achieves the awareness of our gendered concept of governance, as described by Wendy Brown in *Manhood and Politics* and Anne Phillips in *Engendering Democracy*,[54] this question will loom large over any woman attempting a presidential campaign.

This chapter has used Hillary Rodham Clinton's interpretation of the role of First Lady to illustrate the knotty problems surrounding power, politics, and meaning, of gender. Any evaluation of Hillary's performance as chair of the task force must take into consideration the gendered underpinnings of the process and the assumptions that surround them. The knot harbors a number of threads and loops all entangled: gender, medical establishment, economic power, partisan politics. Gender often is wrapped in the garb of some other topic. To look at gender power directly challenges the social order. To look at gender as a piece of something less personal makes it less threatening and less challenging. But the challenge cannot be denied.

As more women graduate from professional schools, as they gain an economic toehold in the workplace, as they contribute their wages to household income, gender power shifts and women expect to be accorded the same respect and influence as that which men possess. The Hillary Factor in national health reform challenged the political norm that in the United States, power duties belong to men while family duties belong to women. As time passes, and the public grows more accustomed to the Hillary Factor, it is possible that she is on her way to creating a new paradigm for First Ladies, and with it, a new paradigm for gender power in governance and leadership.

Notes

1. Jennie Jacobs Kronenfeld, *Controversial Issues in Health Care Policy* (Newbury Park, Calif.: Sage Publ., Inc., 1993).
2. Alice Sardell, *The U.S. Experiment in Social Medicine* (Pittsburgh, Pa.: University of Pittsburgh Press, 1988).
3. Kronenfeld, *Controversial Issues,* 135.
4. Ibid.
5. Penelope Lemov, "States and Medicaid: Ahead of the Feds," *Governing,* (July 1993): 27–28.
6. Ibid.
7. Kronenfeld, *Controversial Issues.*
8. Morris L. Barer and Robert G. Evans, "Perspective: Interpreting Canada: Models, Mind Set, Myths," *Health Affairs* 11 (Spring 1992): 44–61.
9. Kronenfeld, *Controversial Issues.*
10. Sardell, *The U.S. Experiment.*
11. Robert J. Blendon and Jennifer N. Edwards "Conclusion and Forecast for the System," in *System in Crisis: The Case for Health Care Reform,* ed. Robert J. Blendon and Jennifer N. Edwards (New York: Faulkner and Gray, 1991), 269–78.
12. Ibid.
13. Kronenfeld, *Controversial Issues,* 135.
14. Barnett, Alicia A. "Antitrust Exemption: Are Health Providers Crying Wolf?" *Journal of American Health Policy* 3 (3) (May–June 1993): 38–41.
15. Chris Hafner-Eaton, "Will the Phoenix Rise, and Where Should She Go?" *American Behavioral Scientist,* 36 (6) (1993): 841–56.
16. "Initially, Hillary Likes HRC," *Birmingham News,* March 18, 1993, B1.
17. Timothy McNulty, "Proposed Role of Nurses Concerns Doctors," *Birmingham News,* June 21, 1993, E1, E4.
18. Ibid.
19. Stephen Burd, "Mrs. Clinton Wins Few Converts among Medical-College Officials," *Chronicle of Higher Education,* November 17, 1993, A34–A35.
20. Sardell, *The U.S. Experiment.*
21. *Journal of American Health Policy* 3 (3) (May–June 1993): 44.
22. Ibid.
23. Julia Malone, "Cutting Her Own Swath: Mrs. Clinton Taken Seriously in D.C.," *Birmingham Post-Herald,* March 24, 1993, E1.
24. Ibid.
25. Barbara Kellerman, *Leadership: Multidisciplinary Perspectives* (Englewood Cliffs, N.J.: Prentice-Hall, 1984).
26. Paul A. Gigot, "It's Time We Knew More about Hillary's 'Meaning'," *Wall Street Journal,* May 28, 1993, A10.
27. Robert L. Bartley, "Executive Power: A First Lesson for Bill & Hillary," *Wall Street Journal,* March 25, 1993, A14.
28. George Anders and Ron Winslow, "Health-Care Industry Is Now Restructuring; With It Comes Pain," *Wall Street Journal,* June 16, 1993, A1, A6.
29. Malone, "Cutting Her Own Swath."

30. Barbara Kellerman, *All the President's Kin* (New York: New York University Press, 1984).
31. Ibid.
32. See, for example, James David Barber, *The Presidential Character* (Englewood Cliffs, N.J.: Prentice-Hall, 1977); Joseph A. Califano Jr., *A Presidential Nation* (New York: W. W. Norton, 1975); Fred I. Greenstein, ed., *The Reagan Presidency: An Early Assessment* (Baltimore, Md.: Johns Hopkins University Press, 1983); Louis W. Koenig, *The Chief Executive* (San Diego: Harcourt Brace Jovanovich, 1986); James I. Lengle and Byron E. Shafer, *Presidential Politics* (New York: St. Martin's Press, 1983); Paul C. Light, *The President's Agenda* (Baltimore, Md.: Johns Hopkins University Press, 1983); Richard E. Neustadt, *Presidential Power: The Politics of Leadership with Reflections on Johnson and Nixon* (New York: John Wiley and Sons, 1976); John L. Palmer and Isabel V. Sawhill, *The Reagan Record* (Washington, D.C.: The Urban Institute, 1984); Stephen J. Wayne, *The Road to the White House* (New York: St. Martin's Press, 1992); or Marcia Lynn Whicker and Raymond A. Moore, *When Presidents Are Great* (Englewood Cliffs, N.J.: Prentice Hall, 1988) among a myriad of others.
33. Kellerman, *All the President's Kin.*
34. Katha Pollitt, "Not Just Another Hillary Magazine Cover Story," *The Nation,* May 17, 1993, 657–60.
35. Ibid.
36. "Initially, Hillary Likes HRC," *Birmingham News,* March 18, 1993, B1.
37. Barbara C. Burrell, "How's She Doing? Hillary Clinton, the People, and the Polls" (paper presented at the annual meeting of the Southern Political Science Association Savannah, Ga., November 4–6, 1993).
38. Margaret Carlson, "At the Center of Power," *Time,* May 10, 1993, 29–36.
39. "Hillary High School Yearbook," *Fun and Stuff,* March 1993, 6.
40. Nancy Gibbs, "The Trials of Hillary," *Time,* March 21, 1994, 33.
41. David Rogers, "Hillary Rodham Clinton Is Walking a Fine Line in Corridors of Power Long Dominated by Men," *Wall Street Journal,* March 26, 1993, A12.
42. Linda L. M. Bennett and Stephen E. Bennett, "Changing Views about Gender Equality in Politics: Gradual Change and Lingering Doubts," in *Women in Politics: Outsiders or Insiders?* ed. Lois L. Duke (Englewood Cliffs, N.J.: Prentice Hall, 1993), 46–56.
43. Camilla Stivers, *Gender Images in Public Administration* (Newbury Park, Calif.: Sage Publications, 1993).
44. James M. Perry, "Pundits Praise Clinton's Start, But See Dangers in Three H's: Hillary, Health Care and Hubris," *Wall Street Journal,* March 8, 1993, A14.
45. Ibid.
46. Ibid.
47. Ibid.
48. Kenneth T. Walsh, "America's First (Working) Couple," *U.S. News and World Report,* May 10, 1993, 32–34.
49. Robin Toner, "Hillary Clinton Is Back!" *New York Times,* May 7, 1993, A11.
50. Margaret Carlson, "At the Center of Power," *Time,* May 10, 1993, 30.
51. Marian Burros, "A Warm and Fuzzy White House Christmas," *New York Times,* December 7, 1993, B1.
52. "A Holiday Message From Our Family to Yours," *Parade Magazine,* December 19, 1993, 4–5.
53. John Harwood and Geraldine Brooks, "Other Nations Elect Women to Lead Them, So Why Doesn't U.S.?" *Wall Street Journal,* December 14, 1993, A1, A9.
54. Wendy Brown, *Manhood and Politics: A Feminist Reading in Political Theory* (Totowa, N.J.: Rowman and Littlefield, 1988); Anne Phillips, *Engendering Democracy* (University Park: Pennsylvania State University Press, 1991).

Part 6: Summary, Conclusions, and Recommendations

The following chapter summarizes our findings, presents our conclusions, and makes recommendations for enhancing gender awareness.

Chapter 11

Toward Gender Awareness and Gender Balance in Leadership and Governance

Rita Mae Kelly and Georgia Duerst-Lahti

Those who have dabbled with the topic of gender know the pitfalls and perils. Feminists well versed in gender theory might object because we have wandered too far into postmodern and deconstructionist terrain, or conversely because we have not traversed this terrain well enough. Some might also charge that we have focused too much on men to the neglect of women. Many men likely will object because talking about men's gender is itself objectionable. Some think the entire field of gender studies superfluous or irrelevant. Others may fear having men become implicated in ideas of women. Still others, perhaps especially those who believe men have gender, may not concur with our analysis—viewing it as a gynocentric view of men and masculinity. If (only) women have the "proper" understanding of women, then (only) men have a proper understanding of men. In years of experience dealing with gender, we have also learned that for many, to raise the discussion at all is to be "antimale." In this volume we have consciously included men in the conversation about gender in an effort to help correct the partial understandings of the past. We hope men, as well as women, will better understand the process of engenderment, and that all readers, regardless of their sex or sexual identity, will recognize the need to distinguish the engenderment process from how we think about that process, or how we value the results of particular engenderment processes. We want to move into new terrain and to do so in a way that gets us passed the ruts of the past.

Throughout this book, we have covered old ground and introduced new applications. In this conclusion we first highlight the scholarly and normative implications of this book; and then we review the empirical findings presented by the various studies. In the process we explore possible avenues for improving gender awareness and gender imbalance.

Scholarly and Normative Implications

Some readers might question the ramifications of incorporating a gendered conceptual framework and gender power into the study of politics. By clarifying our conclusions in terms of the scholarly and normative implications we see, we hope that at least some of these basic questions will be answered, and that other scholars will be prompted to advance this exploration further.

One central implication of this volume is that a consistent scholarly focus on one sex, either male or female, only in the study of politics, power, leadership, and governance, can lead to distorted understandings of current social reality and future potentialities. This does not mean that studies of the behavior and actions of men as a group and women as a group should never be done or that they are without value. However, the knowledge such studies produce is necessarily partial and, if generalized widely or projected as truth for all social actors, can cause harm, and most certainly will produce greater power imbalances. We believe much harm both to individuals and to our knowledge base about politics, power, leadership, and governance has occurred as a result of the existing masculine bias in our past and current scholarship. In the study of human action and behavior, societies and social relations, gender unawareness and gender imbalance can only lead to bad scholarship and faulty knowledge.

A second major implication of this volume is that we must expand our conceptual framework for studying human behavior. Notions about sex and gender are embedded within broader understandings and logics of reality and of how societies and human beings act and develop. To see a different reality, we must examine alternative ontologies and epistemologies. The study of gender and gender power involves much more than simply relabeling the older terms of sex and sex roles. It involves developing an alternative systematic way of thinking about the universe. As noted in chapter 2, we believe such a framework involves utilizing a relational worldview rather than a classical, dualistic, and positivistic worldview.

Third, we must move beyond the simple notion of using sex as a variable representing the dichotomy of male/female, and using sex difference as a conceptual framework for studying leadership and governance or for explaining what happens to, or is possible for, individual men and women. We must move to using gender and its broader social construction as our conceptual framework. We must recognize the existence and impact of gender power. This theoretical change will facilitate recognizing that masculinism is as much of an ideology as feminism. Further, this change in view will make including men, masculinity, and manliness into our studies as well as women, femininity, and womanliness more appropriate and feasible. This change in our conceptual framework makes visible the fact that all facets of human interaction are gendered, and that ignoring gender and gender power in the political system persistently produces biased results and partial truths.

A fourth implication of our emphasis on gender and gender power is that the gender bias in existing political ideologies needs to be not only recognized and explored but also systematically considered in all of our explorations and actions. One reason students of politics have been slow to use gender analysis is because political ideologies have a power function. In essence they are plans for the best way to structure power so as to benefit a particular group or set of values. Keeping the underlying gender-biased assumptions of any ideology invisible promotes maintaining the gender status quo. The very invisibility of gender in ideology creates circumstances in which gender power can continually and consistently favor men. However, once masculinism becomes visible as *the* dominant gender ideology, then its ideological consequences for structuring the distribution of power and privilege will also become visible. In addition, conscious decisions can be made about the virtue or vices of maintaining such power and privilege.

We are *not* arguing that masculinity and masculinism are themselves inherently bad or that femininity and feminism are inherently good. Both starting points have strengths and weaknesses, both have advantages and disadvantages. We are arguing that the dominance and resulting mode of action of one gender ideology is bad. Gender unawareness (or plain ignorance) is also bad.

Since men have long controlled social and political institutions, they also have shaped the conventions of those institutions. That these conventions suited the founding fathers as men and masculine beings should not be surprising. As John Adam's letter to his wife Abigail confirms, he at least was cognizant of masculinism's influence.[1] Masculinism has continued to operate and has defined leadership and governance. As a result, women and feminism have been and remain particularly disadvantaged in these crucial domains of public life. One of the obvious disadvantages is that women have been forced to understand—even master—masculinism and its values if they are to move successfully into positions of public leadership. The converse for men is not true.

Women have been forced to adopt masculine traits and behaviors and to assume masculinist ways and values in order to succeed as leaders or governors. This way of being and doing to be successful, however, is neither a universal fact nor a historical imperative. It is a product of the historical moment, which persists largely because of the blindness to masculinity and the effects of gender. This does not deny that negative effects have also occasionally occurred through willful androcentrism; it does assert that gender unawareness and ignorance of the consequences of gender imbalance are themselves part of the problem. These phenomena enable men to promote masculinism at the expense of women, even though they do not conspire to do so. The lack of gender awareness facilitates the appearance of normality when men advantage men and disadvantage women.

In this volume we promote the idea of gender awareness, especially on the part of men and about men, masculinity, and masculinism. We also suggest a need for greater gender balance and propose a concept even beyond that—the transgendered. Projecting even beyond this notion of the transgendered to a nongendered state of being (as many science fiction writers have done) clearly is possible. Unfortunately, we contend with the empirical realities of today and must begin with the first step, that is, making all people, but especially men, gender aware. We cannot move beyond our current state of imbalance by denying gender's force.

Although creating gender awareness is itself a step forward, awareness alone is insufficient. Much like the yin and yang of Eastern thinking, imbalance itself does cause problems. At this moment in history we need to promote gender balance. Social institutions will be improved by a better balance between masculinist and feminist influence. Because we all live gendered lives, and society still needs to contend with existing levels of gender unawareness and gender power imbalance, we believe it is more likely that women will understand and give leadership to women's political interests better than men will. From this perspective, the systematic underrepresentation of women in leadership is bad. Conversely men are likely to understand and represent men's political interests better than women will. In either case, there can be no doubt that men's systematic overrepresentation in public leadership has consequences. However, in no way do we see this process as essentialistic; rather, it is the product of a world that ties sex and sex roles to structural-functionalist ways of thinking and curtails human agency in the process.

Although we promote at least equality of numbers (if not proportional representation, meaning a majority) of women in societal institutions and within governance and leadership positions, and although we advocate developing greater gender balance in terms of masculine/feminine influences, our goal is not only gender awareness or gender balance of this type. Such awareness and balance, while an improvement over the current male bias of societies, cannot be viewed as the long-term solution. Our goal must be to move toward a social and political system in which leadership and governance actions and behaviors are at least transgendered. By this we mean moving toward a world in which traits and behaviors exhibited by leaders, and actors at all levels and positions, can be seen as suitable for the socially situated context in which they occur regardless of the biological sex or sexual orientation of the person who happens to be the leader or actor at that moment and place. Ultimately, our goal might well be an ungendered society. Nonetheless, we recognize that gender still shapes our interpretation and acknowledge that gender labeling still occurs irrespective of biological bodies. We have not yet reached a time when even transgendered possibilities are widely available.

At this moment in time, as we seek to promote gender awareness and gender balance, we need to recognize that leadership must be reconceptualized to better incorporate notions from women and feminism. The first step in this process is to understand how leadership within the political arena currently is conceived and practiced within a framework of men and masculinism. This has been a major task of this book. The empirical findings reported in this volume can leave little doubt about the existence of current gender imbalance and unawareness.

The Importance of Gender and Gender Power: Empirical Findings

Progress in a discipline requires appraising core assumptions about theories, methods, and research problems, that is, our research paradigms, programs, and traditions. This volume has contributed to this appraisal by articulating the benefits of exploring masculinism within the gender frame of reference and by examining the intersection of methodology, social norms, and cognitive aims. Feminism begins with the problem of understanding the role and position of women. Gender studies consciously begin to incorporate masculinism into social analyses. By linking gender, governance, and leadership, we help make gender power visible and available for study in political systems and behavior. We think that gender power analysis has the potential to redirect much thinking in the discipline of political science as well as in related social sciences. The fundamental premise about masculinity as an ideology rests at the heart of gender power analysis. We assert that that premise has transformative prospectives.

In this work we have sought to achieve the following basic purposes: (1) to articulate gender and gender power as concepts central to the analysis of governance and leadership and to show that gender and gender power are grounded in masculinism as well as in feminism; (2) to sharpen our analytical understanding of the difference between analyzing sex or sex-role variations and analyzing gender power; (3) to demonstrate how institutional sexism (historical as well as contemporary) leads to differential gender-based political power within our governing structures, even by women who hold the same elected or appointed positions as their male counterparts; and (4) to illustrate how gender and gender power undergird symbolic meanings of daily political life and public-policy discourse, as well as constrain what individual men and women are expected or permitted to do. To accomplish these objectives we systematically introduced gender power as an empirical tool of analysis for the discipline of political science.

We built on the knowledge that masculinism functions as an ideology, a metaideology, one that is largely invisible and ignored, but an ideology nonetheless. We assert not only that men as well as women have gender, but also that feminism is at some levels the normative equivalent of masculinism. Gender power arrangements historically have rested on a masculinist ideological base, with its assumptions about human nature, appropriate power arrangements, and the plan of action that follows from these assumptions. Though feminist political philosophers have critiqued theorists and the discipline for their masculinist biases and bases, the translation of these critiques to empirical research has not yet fully occurred. This volume has launched this progressive stage in a comprehensive way.

In order to study gender power as it shapes public leadership and governance, we first needed to make the case that gender was important to these analyses. We also needed to clarify the concept of gender because its conceptual richness has developed rapidly since the mid-1980s and because the term has been used in many ways, some inappropriately. Throughout this book, we have examined gender and the theorizing around it in four broad ways consistent with the evolution of the scholarship on gender. We looked at gender as a variable applied to individuals; as a property of persons, roles, and organizations; as a set of practices; and as a normative stance permeating concepts and reality with symbolic meanings.

One problem with the use of gender has been the tendency to associate the term exclusively with women and females; another has been the tendency to associate its ideological base only with feminism. A primary conclusion of this work is that all social scientists, but particularly political scientists, must recognize that men have gender too. As we explore facets of any ideology—the assumptions made about humans, the power arrangements deemed appropriate, and the plan of action that follows—we simultaneously must assess its gendered metaideological overlay. We also must assess the way gender power plays out empirically in contemporary leadership and governance. The authors in this book have established a solid foundation for documenting masculinism in action.

Analyzing Sex Differences versus Analyzing Gender Power

A major problem with the understandings and uses of gender has been the confounding and conflating of sex, sex differences, and gender. In other words, too often researchers have used the term *gender* as fully synonymous with *sex*. Often this misuse is found in survey research or other quantitative studies in which all that is known about a respondent or subject is which box a male or female checked on a survey. Rather than examining the more complicated and profound interplay of societal practices, power resources, and beliefs involved in the social construction of sex-gender, these studies document sex differences or similarities but inaccurately label them as gender. As a result, such research may be called gender research when really it focuses on the more limited study of sex differences.

This approach feeds into another problem that diminishes understandings of gender and gender power. Liberalism and positivism within the empirical study of political science have joined to produce a paradigm highlighting sex differences when the issue of women or gender has been raised. This emphasis has been made possible by the unstated assumptions of masculinism, a metaideology that subsumes most of what we have thought of as political ideology. Masculinism provides the givens that become universal norms for political theory, behavior, and empirical analysis. The universality of masculinism makes feminism seem radical and different. It also has made invisible the masculinist assumptions undergirding sex difference methodologies. This invisibility enhances the gender power of masculinism and makes systematic analyses of the gender of men difficult to introduce into the study of politics. This, in turn, means that the consequences of masculinism cannot be examined clearly as well. Instead of concentrating on gender and the power arrangements accompanying gender, we become distracted by sex differences, or more accurately, how women are different from the norm men set. In this volume, we have consistently moved beyond sex difference into analyses of gender power.

Gender as a conceptual and empirical tool of analysis requires moving away from the positivist and narrow postpositivist assumptions about the individual as a unit of analysis. For example, Karin Tamerius demonstrates a need to change assumptions regarding the utility of sex as a dichotomous variable in political analyses such as roll call voting. The meaning of findings derived from such studies clearly needs reexamination because the studies miss the mark of crucial insights about politics. Innumerable studies of congressional voting examine sex differences only to find minimal differences in voting. Though these studies may be factually correct, they are extremely limited, and in some ways invalid, erroneously leading to conclusions that the sex of a member of Congress makes no difference. Instead, a focus here on gender shows that lack of sex differences in roll call votes does not signify identical views of female and male legislators, or the same level of general commitment to or leadership on a women's policy agenda. Also at the individual level, Cheryl King shows us that in studying decision styles, no significant sex differences exist despite the growing literature on women's management styles, which include decision-making styles. She takes us into sex-role identity, an individual-level aspect of identity that reveals social constructions of gender. Here she finds that more women than men identify with masculine decision styles.

Moving to gender analysis enables us to see that gender is not necessarily tied to a sexed body. More importantly, it shows the pervasiveness of "compulsory masculinity," particularly for women, in executive life. It reveals a double standard of leadership, one for women and one for men. It reveals that women often must overcompensate to demonstrate that they are assimilated to compulsory masculinity. Considering public leadership and governance in terms of gender and gender power is necessary because so many of the assumptions made about appropriateness and what is "given" reinforce male-biased gender power. Arrangements are such that men and masculinity continue to be advantaged even when women move into public-leadership posts.

To address these concerns adequately and validly, a broader understanding of the gendered nature of legislative organizations and of how masculinism is embedded into decision-making styles and structures is needed. Moreover, we need to explore other givens in our understandings and practices of leadership and governance to ascertain whether masculinism permeates them as well.

This focus on gender and gender power clarifies the need to change the goal of inquiry when studying participants in the political process, especially women in politics. The goals should not be to ascertain how women differ from men and to build a large body of literature about sex differences, thereby reifying essentialistic notions of maleness and femaleness. Nor should the goal be to make differences among human beings disappear within sameness. This disappearance often occurs when we use the grand mean in statistics to summarize findings, a statistical approach that encourages us to assimilate difference into an invisible, universal, masculinist norm. This does not mean that statistics and means ought not be used, but does suggest that we need to use them with a clearer understanding of the assumptions undergirding our analyses. Gender is complicated; it should not be confused or conflated with the dichotomous notion of sex.

Karin Tamerius illustrates this important distinction in her analysis of how women systematically do represent the interests of women more than men do. Women in legislatures who identify themselves as women, rather than just neutral legislators, do see women as a group with distinctive interests and needs. Such female legislators make a crucial difference in legislative bodies, sponsoring more bills, leading the fight for passage into law, and working actively to promote a broad women's policy agenda. Tamerius shows that descriptive representation is linked to substantive representation and the substance of policy. In terms of agenda formation, policy initiatives, and advocacy, it is clear that, regardless of party affiliation, without female legislators most women's issues would not have come before the United States as they have. Sex differences in roll call voting clearly hide these dramatic variations in male/female legislative behavior. The application of the notion of gender power to legislative governance and leadership helps make visible the actual difference having women in legislatures makes.

Institutional Sexism, Gender Power, and Political Power

The study of gender power of and within organizational structures, especially governmental structures, is only beginning. To this point most studies have focused on institutional sexism and sex differences. Although these studies are important, they all too often give the impression of the unchanging constancy of the existing structural forms and processes operating within them. Gendered organizational analyses and the gendered approach that include masculinism and feminism as sources of concepts and hypotheses enrich this discussion and analysis. The gendered conceptual framework makes visible the interdependency of masculinism, gender power, and the status quo. By identifying the specific ways and mechanisms by which gender power operates and is maintained, we can articulate how change can take place. What appeared to be universal and stable becomes contextual and part of a continuous process of change.

Noelle Norton, in her study of the U.S. Congress, shows how rarely we see women hold critical institutional positions of power. In her analysis of reproductive policies she illustrates how the historical exclusion of women and institutional patterns of gender power perpetuate the difficulties women have in accumulating power and the resources needed to shape policy in areas, such as reproduction, that are vital for women. She, like Tamerius, demonstrates how unlikely men are to undertake policies most women would support in key policy areas. Norton also highlights the importance of exploring gender power as it intersects with institutional power throughout the entire policy process within legislatures, rather than just focusing on sex differences or similarities in roll call voting.

Meredith Newman demonstrates the surprising grip gender has on our thinking and the extent to which male gender power is capable of masking masculinist assumptions and advantages. Political scientists and students of policy have long accepted the basic contours of the policy typology developed by Theodore Lowi and expanded on by others. In many regards, Newman confirms the central theses of the Lowi typology as well: Distributive agencies are comparatively pleasant work environments, with minimal conflict, considerable autonomy, professional modes of accountability, and informal but apparently effective decision processes that involve those who need to be politically included; they have a satisfied clientele and a stable structure. Redistributive agencies have narrower spans of control, top management with the highest educational status, internal conflict, and centralized decision making. Regulatory policies vary in the way Lowi predicts. What the authors using these central theses failed to notice is that men disproportionally populate the workforce of these advantageous distributive agencies, while women have made the greatest inroads into the more difficult work environment of redistributive agencies.

What Lowi and the many others who have extended his ideas also failed to notice is the gendered assumptions at the root of his assertions. Clear gender patterns exist in the clientele of agencies, especially in the distributive and redistributive policy areas. Distributive policy areas cover those that have stereotypically carried masculine gender role connections, such as transportation, agriculture, fish and wildlife, and the like. The education required for agencies that deal with these policies, like engineering, have been some of the toughest screening devices or barriers for women to overcome. Agencies associated with these fields have some of the lowest participation rates of women, especially in top-level line positions. Redistributive policy areas correspond with policy areas traditionally of special concern to women, such as welfare, affirmative action, and other social programs. These are among the most popular areas for women in terms of obtaining advanced educational programs, agencies in which they seek employment and the arenas in which women have advanced the most and the quickest.

But Lowi tells us that distributive policies generate little controversy, even stymie advancing new issues onto the public agenda, and that they benefit everyone. In contrast, redistributive policies are said to generate a great deal of controversy because they do not benefit everyone; rather, a few gain at the expense of others. A gender power lens requires reexamining these statements. On the surface Lowi's conclusions appear to reflect the gender power dynamics of the polity more than they reflect an accurate picture of reality.

Many of the "givens" in our understandings and practice of leadership and governance have been given to us by some men for most men. We need to recognize gender's effect upon operating assumptions. In order to understand them fully, analysis of gender and gender power must be incorporated into our work. If not, assumptions of universality, such as in Lowi's distributive policies, will go unchallenged and we will misinterpret root causes involved in the conflict surrounding redistributive policies.

Gender as a Set of Practices

Interpersonal interactions and relationships between men and women are typically imbued with gender power issues. Social psychologists have demonstrated that men often use verbal interactions as well as physical intimidation to dominate women. Male sense of entitlement of more verbal and physical space has been an historical cultural norm. In this volume Kathlene and Kelly demonstrate how these generalized customs of interaction have permeated political arenas. The patriarchal sociosexual structure, with its related practices, habits, and traditions, carries over into the political arena, even among women and men who ostensibly hold equal position power.

Practices of male dominance in conversation permeate the halls of legislatures and bureaucratic committee meetings. This sociosexual form of control is subtle, not something even the most astute nonfeminist political analysts would have expected. Yet, the data presented by Lyn Kathlene are most persuasive. Informal sociosexual practices can stymie or alter formal elected and appointed position power. Clearly, new ways need to be developed both to recognize and to overcome these means of domination.

Unwanted sexual attention in the workplace and in public political arenas is now widely recognized as harassment and harmful, both legally and socially. The extent to which sexual harassment constitutes psychological warfare, however, and is an additional tool of political domination, even of highly placed women with considerable position power, is only now being empirically explored. Kelly's study reveals a patterned linkage between sexual harassment and leadership behaviors among women who by position should be exercising considerable leadership and power in our governing structures. Offensive men do seem to compel women to behave defensively at even upper levels of administration, thereby reducing their potential as leaders.

The works in this volume clearly point to a need for more explicit studies of these sociosexual practices. Verbal domination and sexual harassment, although major and common examples of how these sets of gender power practices intrude into political life, are not the only phenomena requiring attention. These studies should encourage others to examine a broader range of these practices.

Gender and Symbolic Meaning

The contemporary approach of the social construction of reality couples with recent insights gleaned from deconstruction to provide a way to understand the meanings assigned to gender, and hence to better interpret the gender power emanating from social symbolic meanings. Analysis at the social symbolic level enables us to see the way patterns found among individuals transform into normative assumptions with political power even when their gendered elements remain obscure to the uncritical eye.

Throughout this work we have highlighted the importance of recognizing masculinism as a metaideology. The way in which masculinism is embedded in our understanding of universal norms for rights, governing and leadership behavior, and even in the concepts of governance and leadership themselves has been emphasized. This volume points to the need for more systematic empirical studies of how masculinism permeates our concepts and methodologies as well as our theories and hypotheses. Until masculinism is better understood, feminism will seem novel and, to some, beyond the pale of most political analyses. By making visible the invisible, new light on almost everything is initiated.

Duerst-Lahti and Verstegen's emphasis on the "year of the woman" points to how the visual absence of women on the Judiciary Committee in the Hill-Thomas hearings made visible the lack of women in the U.S. Senate, raising the consciousness of U.S. women nationwide to their lack of substantive as well as descriptive representation. The hearings made visible not only the gender power of sexual harassment but also how women's absence in leadership and governance is related to the gender power of the masculinist-based political system. This sudden national awareness of accumulated gender power itself assumed symbolic importance, enabling the beginnings of a stronger political base for women in Congress. And, much like Newman's analysis of policy typologies, this study calls into question why the value of descriptive representation so thoroughly was dismissed. Such dismissal, of course, contributes to beliefs that the predominance of men in public leadership has no consequences of importance. We conclude that strategies for revealing other aspects of masculinism and its dominance within the political system could do much to promote greater gender balance, at least to increase the numbers of women in higher-level political positions.

The degree to which Hillary Rodham Clinton has become the symbolic center of these multiple gender power issues is almost startling, though not unexpected by feminists focusing on power and leadership. The parallels of the contradictory forms of gender power held by and surrounding the First Lady and of the health care industry produce a fascinating puzzle. Guy's analysis demonstrates well the importance and need for further exploration of the power of symbolic meaning. It also shows how overwhelming the accumulation of gender power at the individual, institutional, interpersonal, and symbolic levels can be. Even a person of extraordinary training, ability, experience, and expertise with a power base grounded in interpersonal relations (wife of the president) cannot easily withstand the masculine gender power of society's health and political institutions and the symbolic gender biases within them.

Conclusion

Gender and gender power are critical concepts with related analytical tools that need to be incorporated into political and policy studies. Arguably, studies that ignore their implications simply represent faulty scholarship. The conceptual frame of gender power facilitates giving serious consideration to the way masculinism operates as a metaideology whose presence underpins other ideological positions. Considering public leadership and governance in terms of gender and gender power is necessary because so many of the masculinist ideological "givens" both visibly and invisibly support and reinforce the polity. Arrangements are such that men and masculinity continue to be advantaged even when women move into public leadership posts. To move the United States to a more democratic place, gender and gender power can no longer be ignored.

Notes

1. Letter from John Adams to Abigail Adams, April 14, 1781, in Abigail Adams's "Remember the Ladies," in *The Feminist Papers,* ed. Alice Rossi (New York: Columbia University Press, 1973).

Bibliography

"Abortion Agreement Ends Funding Deadlock." *Congressional Quarterly Almanac.* 95th Cong., 1st sess., 1977. 295–313.

' "Abortion Dispute Derails First HHS Bill." *Congressional Quarterly Almanac.* 102nd Cong., 1st sess., 1991. 501–12.

"Abortion Funding Ban Added to Labor-HHS Budget." *Congressional Quarterly Weekly.* 103rd Cong., 1st sess., June 26, 1993. 1657–58.

"Abortion Funding Rebuff Shows House Divided." *Congressional Quarterly Weekly.* 103rd Cong., 1st sess, July 3, 1993. 1735–39.

Acker, Joan. "Hierarchies, Jobs, Bodies: A Theory of Gendered Organizations." *Gender and Society* 4 (1990): 146.

Alexander, Deborah, and Kristi Andersen. "Gender as a Factor in the Attribution of Leadership Traits." *Political Research Quarterly* 46 (1990): 527–45.

Aries, Nancy. "Fragmentation and Reproductive Freedom: Federally Subsidized Family Planning Services, 1960–1980." *American Journal of Public Health* 77 (1987): 1465–71.

"As Reform Nears, RNs Aim to Claim Primary Care Role." *American Journal of Nursing* 93 (May 1993): 91, 94.

Bach, Stanley. "Representatives and Committees on the Floor: Amendments to Appropriations Bills in the House of Representatives, 1963–1982." *Congress and the President* 13 (1986): 41–53.

Bach, Stanley, and Steven S. Smith. *Managing Uncertainty in the House of Representatives: Adaptation and Innovation in Special Rules.* Washington, D.C.: Brookings Institution, 1988.

Bachrach, Samuel B., and Edward J. Lawler. *Power and Politics in Organizations.* San Francisco: Jossey-Bass, 1981.

Barber, James David. *The Presidential Character.* Englewood Cliffs, N.J.: Prentice-Hall, 1977.

Barer, Morris L., and Robert G. Evans. "Perspective: Interpreting Canada: Models, Mind Set, Myths." *Health Affairs* 11 (spring 1992): 44–61.

Barnett, Alicia A. "Antitrust Exemption: Are Health Providers Crying Wolf?" *Journal of American Health Policy* 3 (3) (May–June, 1993): 38–41.

Beasely, Maurine. "Newspapers: Is There a New Majority Defining the News?" In *Women in Mass Communication: Challenging Gender Values,* edited by Pamela J. Creedon, 180–94. Newbury Park, Calif.: Sage Publications, 1989.

Belenky, Mary Field, Blythe McVicker Clinchy, Nancy Rule Goldberger, and Jill Mattuck Tarule. *Women's Ways of Knowing: The Development of Self, Voice, and Mind.* New York: Basic Books, 1986.

Bem, Sandra L. *The Bem Sex-Role Inventory.* Palo Alto, Calif.: Consulting Psychologists Press, 1981.

Bennett, Linda L. M., and Stephen E. Bennett. "Changing Views about Gender Equality in Politics: Gradual Change and Lingering Doubts." In *Women in Politics: Outsiders or Insiders?*, edited by Lois L. Duke, 46–56. Englewood Cliffs, N.J.: Prentice-Hall, 1993.

Berkman, Michael B., and Robert E. O'Connor. "Do Women Legislators Matter? Female Legislators and State Abortion Policy." *American Politics Quarterly* 21 (1993): 102–24.

Bernard, Jessie. *The Sex Game.* New York: Atheneum, 1972.

Blair, Diane D., and Jeanie R. Stanley. "Personal Relationships and Legislative Power: Male and Female Perceptions." *Legislative Studies Quarterly* 16 (1991): 495–507.

Blendon, Robert J., and Karen Donelan. "The Public and the Future of U.S. Health Care System Reform." In *System in Crisis: The Case for Health Care Reform,* edited by Robert J. Blendon and Jennifer N. Edwards, 173–94. New York: Faulkner and Gray, 1991.

Blendon, Robert J., and Jennifer N. Edwards. "Conclusion and Forecast for the System." In *System in Crisis: The Case for Health Care Reform,* edited by Robert J. Blendon and Jennifer N. Edwards, 269–78. New York: Faulkner and Gray, 1991.

Block, Sharon. "Congressional Action on Abortion: 1984–1991." In *Abortion, Medicine, and the Law,* 4th ed., edited by J. Douglas Butler and David F. Walbert, 648–66. New York: Facts on File, 1992.

Bologh, Rosalyn Wallach. *Love or Greatness: Max Weber and Masculine Thinking: A Feminist Inquiry.* London: Unwin Hyman, 1990.

Brod, Harry. *The Making of Masculinities.* Boston: Allen and Unwin, 1987.

Brophy-Baermann, Michelle D. "The 'Intra-Gender' Gap: The New Right's Impact on the Women's Movement in the 1980s." Paper prepared for the Midwest Political Science Association, 1991.

Brown, Wendy. "Reproductive Freedom and the Right to Privacy." In *Families, Politics, and Public Policy: A Feminist Dialogue on Women and the State,* edited by Irene Diamond, 322–38. New York: Longman, 1983.

———. *Manhood and Politics: A Feminist Reading in Political Theory.* Totowa, N.J.: Rowman and Littlefield, 1988.

Bryant, Anne L. *Hostile Hallways: The AAUW Survey on Sexual Harassment in America's Schools.* Annapolis Junction, Md.: American Association of University Women, 1992.

Buck, Ross W., Virginia J. Savin, Robert E. Miller, and William F. Caul. "Communication of Affect through Facial Expressions in Humans." *Journal of Personality and Social Psychology* 23 (1972): 362–71.

Bullard, Angela M., and Deil Spencer Wright. "Circumventing the Glass Ceiling: Women Executives in American State Governments," *Public Administration Review* 53 (3) (1993): 189–202.

Burd, Stephen. "Mrs. Clinton Wins Few Converts among Medical-College Officials." *Chronicle of Higher Education,* November 17, 1993, A34–A35.

Burrell, Barbara C. "How's She Doing? Hillary Clinton, the People, and the Polls." Paper presented at the annual meeting of the Southern Political Science Association, Savannah, Ga., November 4–6, 1993.

Butler, Dore, and Florence L. Geis. "Nonverbal Affect Responses to Male and Female Leaders: Implications for Leadership Evaluations." *Journal of Personality and Social Psychology* 58 (1990): 48–59.

Butler, Judith. *Gender Trouble: Feminism and the Subversion of Identity.* New York: Routledge, 1990.

———. *Bodies That Matter: On the Discursive Limits of "Sex."* New York: Routledge, 1993.

Caldeira, Gregory A., and Samuel C. Patterson. "Political Friendship in the Legislature." *Journal of Politics* 49 (1987): 953–75.

Califano, Joseph A., Jr. *A Presidential Nation.* New York: Norton, 1975.

Carlson, Margaret. "At the Center of Power." *Time,* May 10, 1993, 29–36.

Carroll, Susan J. *Women as Candidates in American Politics.* Bloomington: Indiana University Press, 1985.

Carroll, Susan J., and Ella Taylor. "Gender Differences in the Committee Assignments of State Legislators: Preferences or Discrimination?" Paper presented at the Midwest Political Science Association, Chicago, April 13–16, 1989.

Cartwright, Dorwin, ed. *Studies in Social Power.* Ann Arbor: University of Michigan Press, 1959.

Center for the American Woman and Politics. *Women in State Legislatures 1989.* New Brunswick, N.J.: National Information Bank on Women in Public Office, Eagleton Institute of Politics, Rutgers University, 1989.

——. *Women in Elective Office 1990.* New Brunswick, N.J.: Center for the American Woman and Politics, Eagleton Institute of Politics, Rutgers University, 1991.

——. *Fact Sheet: Women in Elective Office 1993.* New Brunswick, N.J.: Eagleton Institute of Politics, Rutgers University, 1993.

——. *Women in State Legislatures 1993.* New Brunswick, N.J.: National Information Bank on Women in Public Office, Eagleton Institute of Politics, Rutgers University, 1993.

Chafetz, Janet Saltzman. *Gender Equity.* Newbury Park, Calif.: Sage Publications, 1990.

Chodorow, Nancy. "Family Structure and Feminine Personality," In *Women, Culture, and Society,* edited by Michelle Zimbalist Rosaldo and Louise Lamphere, 43–66. Stanford, Calif.: Stanford University Press, 1974.

Clatterbaugh, Kenneth. *Contemporary Perspectives on Masculinity: Men, Women, and Politics in Modern Society.* Boulder, Colo.: Westview Press, 1990.

Cleveland, Harlan. *The Knowledge Executive: Leadership in an Information Society.* New York: Dalton Books, 1985.

Coates, Jennifer. "Gossip Revisited: Language in All-Female Groups." In *Women in Their Speech Communities,* edited by Jennifer Coates and Deborah Cameron, 94–122. London: Longman, 1988.

Collie, Melissa P., and Joseph Cooper. "Multiple Referral and the New Committee System in the House of Representatives." In *Congress Reconsidered,* 4th ed., edited by Lawrence C. Dodd and Bruce I. Oppenheimer, 245–72. Washington, D.C.: Congressional Quarterly Press, 1989.

Correa, Mary E., Edward B. Klein, Walter N. Stone, Joseph H. Astrachan, Ellen E. Kossek, and Meera Komarraju. "Reaction to Women in Authority: The Impact of Gender on Learning in Group Relations Conferences." *Journal of Applied Behavioral Science* 24 (1988): 219–33.

Craig, Barbara Hinkson, and David M. O'Brien. *Abortion and American Politics.* Chatham, N.J.: Chatham House, 1993.

Craig, D., and M. K. Pitts. "The Dynamics of Dominance in Tutorial Discussions." *Linguistics* 28 (1990): 125–38.

Dahl, Robert A. "The Concept of Power." *Behavioral Science* 2 (1957): 201–15.

——. *Who Governs? Democracy and Power in an American City.* New Haven, Conn.: Yale University Press, 1989.

Darcy, Robert, Susan Welch, and Janet Clark. *Women, Elections, and Representation.* New York: Longman, 1987.

Davidson, Roger. "Subcommittee Government: New Channels for Policymaking." In *The New Congress,* edited by Thomas E Mann and Norman J. Ornstein, 99–133. Washington, D.C.: American Enterprise Institute, 1981.

——. "Emergence of the Postreform Congress." In *The Postreform Congress,* edited by Roger Davidson, 3–24. New York: St. Martin's Press, 1992.

Davidson, Roger H., and Walter J. Oleszek. *Congress and Its Members.* Washington, D.C.: Congressional Quarterly Press, 1985.

Davis, Angela Y. *Women, Race, and Class.* New York: Random House, 1981.

Davis, Susan, ed. *Women under Attack: Victories, Backlash, and the Fight for Reproductive Freedom.* Boston: South End Press, 1988.

Delli Carpini, Michale X., and Ester R. Fuchs. "The Year of the Woman: Candidates, Voters, and the 1992 Elections." *Political Science Quarterly* 108 (1) (1993): 29–36.

Derr, C. Brooklyn, and André Laurent. "The Internal and External Career: A Theoretical Cross-Cultural Perspective." In *Handbook of Career Theory,* edited by Michael B. Arthur, Douglas T. Hall, and Barbara S. Lawrence, 454–74. New York: Cambridge University Press, 1989.

Desjardins, Carolyn. "Gender Issues in Community College Leadership." *American Association of Women in Community and Junior Colleges Journal* 25 (1989): 125–37.

Diamond, Irene. *Sex Roles in the State House.* New Haven, Conn.: Yale University Press, 1977.

DiStefano, Christine. "Masculinity as Ideology in Political Theory: Hobbsian Man Reconsidered." *Women's Studies International Forum* 6 (1983): 633–44.

———. *Configurations of Masculinity: A Feminist Perspective on Modern Political Theory.* Ithaca, N.Y.: Cornell University Press, 1991.

Dodd, Lawrence C., and Bruce I. Oppenheimer. "Consolidating Power in the House: The Rise of a New Oligarchy." In *Congress Reconsidered,* 5th ed., edited by Lawrence C. Dodd and Bruce I. Oppenheimer, 39–64. Washington, D.C.: Congressional Quarterly Press, 1992.

Dodson, Debra L., ed. *Gender and Policymaking: Studies of Women in Office.* Rutgers, N.J.: Center for the American Woman and Politics, Eagleton Institute of Politics, Rutgers University, 1991.

Dodson, Debra L., and Susan J. Carroll. *Reshaping the Agenda: Women in State Legislatures.* Rutgers, N.J.: Center for the American Woman and Politics, Eagleton Institute of Politics, Rutgers University, 1991.

Donnell, Susan M., and Jay Hall, "Men and Women as Managers: A Significant Case of No Significant Differences." *Organizational Dynamics* 8 (4) (1980): 60–77.

Doyle, James. *The Male Experience.* Dubuque, Ia.: William C. Brown, 1984.

Duerst-Lahti, Georgia. *Gender Power Relations in Public Bureaucracies.* Ph.D. diss., University of Wisconsin, 1987.

———. "But Women Play the Game Too: Communication Control and Influence in Administrative Decision Making." *Administration and Society* 22 (1990): 182–205.

———. "Year of the Woman, Decade of Women: Wisconsin Legislative Elections." Paper presented at the Midwest Political Science Association, 1993.

Duerst-Lahti, Georgia, and Cathy Marie Johnson. "Gender and Style in Bureaucracy." *Women and Politics* 10 (4) (1990): 67–120.

———. "Management Styles, Stereotypes, and Advantages." In *Women and Men of the States,* edited by Mary Ellen Guy, 125–56. Armonk, N.Y.: M. E. Sharpe, 1992.

Duke, Lois L., ed. *Women in Politics.* Englewood Cliffs, N.J.: Prentice-Hall, 1993.

Durst, Samantha L., and Ryan W. Rusek. "Different Genders, Different Votes? An Examination of Voting Behavior in the U.S. House of Representatives." Paper presented at the annual meeting of the American Political Science Association, Washington, D.C., September 2–5, 1993.

Dyson, James W., and John W. Soule. "Congressional Committee Behavior on Roll Call Votes: The U.S. House of Representatives, 1955–64." *Midwest Journal of Political Science* 14 (1970): 626–47.

Eagly, Alice H., and Blair T. Johnson. "Gender and Leadership Style: A Meta-Analysis." *Psychological Bulletin* 108 (1990): 233–56.

Eakins, Barbara Westbrook, and R. Gene Eakins. *Sex Differences in Human Communication.* Boston: Houghton Mifflin, 1978.

Edelman, Murray. *The Symbolic Uses of Politics.* Urbana: University of Illinois Press, 1964.

———. *Political Language: Words That Succeed and Policies That Fail.* New York: Academic Press, 1977.

———. *Constructing the Political Spectacle.* Chicago: University of Chicago Press, 1988.

Edelsky, Carole. "Who's Got the Floor?" *Language in Society* 10 (1981): 383–421.

Eisenstein, Zillah. *The Radical Future of Liberal Feminism.* New York: Longman, 1981.

———. "The State, the Patriarchal Family, and Working Mothers." In *Families, Politics and Public Policy: A Feminist Dialogue on Women and the State,* edited by Irene Diamond, 41–58. New York: Longman, 1983.

Etzioni, Amatai. *A Comparative Analysis of Complex Organizations.* New York: Macmillan, 1975.

Fagenson, Ellen. "Perceived Masculine and Feminine Attributes Examined as a Function of Individual's Sex and Level in the Organizational Power Hierarchy: A Test of Four Theoretical Perspectives." *Journal of Applied Psychology* 25 (2) (1990): 204–11.

Faludi, Susan. *Backlash: The Undeclared War against American Women.* New York: Crown Publishers, 1991.

Family Planning Services and Population Research Act of 1970 (Title X of the Public Health Service Act), PL 91–572; Pregnancy Sex Discrimination Prohibition, PL 95–555, 92 STAT. 2076.

Farrell, Warren. *Why Men Are the Way They Are.* New York: McGraw-Hill, 1987.

Fenno, Richard F., Jr. *Power of the Purse.* Boston: Little Brown, 1966.

———. *Congressmen in Committees.* Boston: Little Brown, 1973.

Ferejohn, John. "Comment." In *Regulatory Policy and the Social Sciences,* edited by Roger G. Noll, 105–110. Berkeley and Los Angeles: University of California Press, 1985.

Ferguson, Kathy. *The Feminist Case against Bureaucracy.* Philadelphia: Temple University Press, 1984.

Fierman, Jaclyn. "Why Women Still Don't Hit the Top." *Fortune,* July 30, 1990, 40–62.

Fisher, Anne B. "When Will Women Get to the Top?" *Fortune,* September 21, 1992, 44–56.

Fishman, Pamela M. "Interaction: The Work Women Do." *Social Problems* 25 (1978): 397–406.

Flammang, Janet A. "Female Officials in the Feminist Capital: The Case of Santa Clara County." *Western Political Quarterly* 38 (1985): 94–118.

Flax, Jane. "Postmodernism and Gender Relations in Feminist Theory." *Signs* 12 (summer 1987): 621–43.

Francis, Wayne L. *The Legislative Committee Game: A Comparative Analysis of Fifty States.* Columbus: Ohio State University Press, 1989.

Francis, Wayne L., and James W. Riddlesperger. "U.S. State Legislative Committees: Structure, Procedural Efficiency, and Party Control." *Legislative Studies Quarterly* 7 (1982): 453–71.

Frankovic, Kathleen, and Joyce Gelb. "Public Opinion and the Thomas Nomination." *Political Science and Politics* 25 (3) (September 1992): 481–84.

Frederickson, H. George. "Public Administration and Social Equity." *Public Administration Review* 50 (2) (1990): 228–37.

Freeman, Jo. "Feminism vs. Family Values Women at the 1992 Democratic and Republic Conventions." *Political Science and Politics* 26 (March 1993): 21–28.

French, J. R. P., and B. H. Raven. "The Bases of Social Power." In *Studies in Social Power,* edited by Dorwin Cartwright. Ann Arbor: University of Michigan Press, 1959.

Fried, Marlene, ed. *From Abortion to Reproductive Freedom: Transforming a Movement.* Boston: South End Press, 1990.

Gehlen, Frieda L. "Women Members of Congress: A Distinctive Role." In *A Portrait of Marginality,* edited by Marianne Githens and Jewell Prestage, 304–19. New York: McKay, 1977.

Gelb, Joyce, and Marian Lief Palley. *Women and Public Policies.* Princeton, N.J.: Princeton University Press, 1987.

Gertzog, Irwin N. *Congressional Women: Their Recruitment, Treatment, and Behavior.* New York: Praeger, 1984.

Gibbs, Nancy. "The Trials of Hillary." *Time,* March 21, 1994, 27–37.

Gigot, Paul A. "It's Time We Knew More About Hillary's 'Meaning.'" *Wall Street Journal,* May 28, 1993, A10.

Gilder, George. *Sexual Suicide.* New York: Bantam Books, 1973.

Gilligan, Carol. *In a Different Voice: Psychological Theory and Women's Development.* Cambridge, Mass.: Harvard University Press, 1982.

Gilligan, Thomas, and Keith Krehbiel. "Organization of Informative Committees by a Traditional Legislature." *American Journal of Political Science* 34 (1990): 531–64.

Gilson, Edith, and Susan Kane. *Unnecessary Choices: The Hidden Life of the Executive Woman.* New York: Paragon Press, 1989.

Glendon, Mary Ann. *Abortion and Divorce in Western Law: American Failures, European Challenges.* Cambridge, Mass.: Harvard University Press, 1987.

Goldberg, Herb. *The Hazards of Being Male: Surviving the Myth of Masculine Privilege.* New York: Signet, 1976.

———. *The New Male.* New York: Signet, 1979.

Goldberg, Steven. *The Inevitability of Patriarchy.* New York: William Morrow, 1974.

Greenstein, Fred I., ed. *The Reagan Presidency: An Early Assessment.* Baltimore, Md.: Johns Hopkins University Press, 1983.

Gregware, Peter, and Rita Mae Kelly. "Relativity and Quantum Logics: A Relational View of Policy Inquiry." In *Policy, Theory, and Policy Evaluation: Concepts, Knowledge, Causes, and Norms,* edited by Stuart S. Nagel, 29–42. Westport, Conn.: Greenwood Press, 1990.

Gutek, Barbara A. *Sex and the Workplace.* San Francisco: Jossey-Bass, 1985.

Guy, Mary Ellen, ed. *Women and Men of the States.* Armonk, N.Y.: M. E. Sharpe, 1992.

Guy, Mary Ellen, and Georgia Duerst-Lahti. "Agency Culture and Its Effect on Managers." In *Women and Men of the States,* edited by Mary Ellen Guy, 157–88. Armonk, N.Y.: M. E. Sharpe, 1992.

Guy, Mary Ellen, and Lois L. Duke. "Personal and Social Background as Determinants of Position." In *Women and Men of the States,* edited by Mary Ellen Guy, 43–60. Armonk, N.Y.: M. E. Sharpe, 1992.

Haeberle, Steven H. "The Institutionalization of the Subcommittee in the United States House of Representatives." *Journal of Politics* 40 (1978): 1054–65.

Hafner-Eaton, Chris. "Will the Phoenix Rise, and Where Should She Go?" *American Behavioral Scientist* 36 (6) (1993): 841–56.

Hagemann-White, Carol. "Gendered Modes of Behavior—a Sociological Strategy for Empirical Research." Paper presented at the Third International Interdisciplinary Congress on Women, July 1987, Dublin, Ireland.

Hale, Mary M., and Rita Mae Kelly. *Gender, Bureaucracy, and Democracy.* Westport, Conn.: Greenwood Press, 1989.

Hall, Elaine. "Waitering/Waitressing: Engendering the World of Table Servers." *Gender and Society* 7 (3) (September 1993): 329–46.

Hall, Richard L. "Participation and Purpose in Committee Decision Making." *American Political Science Review* 81 (1987): 105–27.

Hall, Richard L., and C. Lawrence Evans, "The Power of Subcommittees," *Journal of Politics* 52 (1990): 335–54.

Hardin, Clifford M., Kenneth A. Shepsle, and Barry R. Weingast, "Government by Subcommittee." *Wall Street Journal,* June 24, 1983, 22.

Harding, Sandra. *The Science Question in Feminism.* Ithaca, N.Y.: Cornell University Press, 1986.

Harwood, John, and Geraldine Brooks. "Other Nations Elect Women to Lead Them, so Why Doesn't U.S.?" *Wall Street Journal,* December 14, 1993, A1, A9.

Hawkesworth, Mary. "Confounding Gender." Paper presented at the annual meeting of the Western Political Science Association, Albuquerque, N.M., March 10, 1994.

Hearn, Jeff. *Men in the Public Eye: The Construction and Deconstruction of Public Men and Public Patriarchies.* New York: Routledge, 1992.

Hearn, Jeff, Deborah L. Sheppard, Peta Tancred-Sheriff, and Gibson Burrell. *The Sexuality of Organization.* London: Sage, 1989.

Helgesen, Sally. *The Female Advantage: Women's Ways in Leadership.* New York: Doubleday Currency, 1990.

Henshaw, Stanley K. "Induced Abortion: A World Review 1990." In *Abortion, Medicine, and the Law,* 4th ed., edited by J. Douglas Butler and David F. Walbert, 426. New York: Facts on File, 1992.

Hill, David. "Women State Legislators and Party Voting on the E.R.A." *Social Science Quarterly* 64 (1982): 318–26.

"Hillary High School Yearbook." *Fun and Stuff,* March 1993, 6.

Hinckley, Barbara. "Policy Content, Committee Membership and Behavior." *American Journal of Political Science* 19 (1975): 543–57.

Hochschild, Arlie. *The Second Shift.* New York: Avon Books, 1989.

Hoffman, Frances L. "Sexual Harassment in Academia: Feminist Theory and Institutional Practice." *Harvard Educational Review* 56 (2) (1986): 105–21.

Hofstede, Geert. *Culture's Consequences: International Differences in Work-Related Values.* Newbury Park, Calif.: Sage Publications, 1984.

"A Holiday Message from Our Family to Yours." *Parade Magazine,* December 19, 1993, 4–5.

Hoover, Kenneth. *Ideology and Political Life.* 2d ed. Belmont, Calif.: Wadsworth Publishing, 1994.

Jaggar, Alison M. *Feminist Politics and Human Nature.* Totowa, N.J.: Rowman and Allanheld, 1983.

Jamieson, Kathleen Hall. *Beyond the Double Bind: Women and Leadership.* New York: Oxford University Press, 1995.

Johnson, Pamela. "Women and Power: Towards a Theory of Effectiveness." *Journal of Social Issues* 32 (1976): 99–110.

Jonasdottir, Anna. *Power, Love, and Political Interests.* Sweden, 1990. Reprinted as *Why Women Are Oppressed.* Philadelphia: Temple University Press, 1994.

Jones, Bryan D., ed. *Leadership and Politics: New Perspectives in Political Science.* Lawrence: University Press of Kansas, 1989.

Jones, Kathleen B. *Compassionate Authority: Democracy and the Representation of Women.* New York: Routledge, 1993.

Jones, Kathleen B., and Anna G. Jonasdottir, eds. *The Political Interests of Gender: Developing Theory and Research with a Feminist Face.* London: Sage, 1988.

Journal of American Health Policy. May–June 1993, 42–45.

Jung, Carl. *Psychological Type.* New York: Pantheon Books, 1923.

Kahn, Kim Fridkin, and Edie N. Goldenberg. "Women Candidates in the News: An Examination of Gender Differences in U.S. Senate Campaign Coverage." *Public Opinion Quarterly* 55 (1991): 180–99.

Kahn, Mark. "Fortune Is a Man." Paper presented at the Western Political Science Association, Pasadena, Calif., March 1993.

Kanter, Rosabeth Moss. "Presentation VI." *Signs* 1 (3) (1976): 282–91.

———. *Men and Women of the Corporation.* New York: Basic Books, 1977.

———. "Some Effects of Proportions on Group Life: Skewed Sex Ratios and Responses to Token Women." *American Journal of Sociology* 82 (1977): 965–90.

Kathlene, Lyn. "Uncovering the Political Impacts of Gender: An Exploratory Study." *Western Political Quarterly* 42 (1989): 397–421.

———. "A New Approach to Understanding the Impact of Gender on the Legislative Process." In *Feminist Research Methods: Exemplary Readings in the Social Sciences,* edited by Joyce McCarl Nielsen, 238–53. Boulder, Colo.: Westview Press, 1990.

————. "Gendered Approaches to Policy Formation in the Colorado Legislature." Paper presented at the annual meeting of the Midwest Political Science Association, Chicago, April 18–20, 1991.

————. "Who Holds the Floor? Overcoming Gender Differences in Legislative Committee Hearings." Paper presented at the annual meeting of the Western Political Science Association. Pasadena, Calif., March 18–20, 1993.

————. "Power and Influence in State Legislative Policy Making: The Interaction of Gender and Power in Committee Hearing Debates." *American Political Science Review.* Forthcoming.

Kathlene, Lyn, and John A. Martin. "Enhancing Citizen Participation: Panel Designs, Perspectives, and Planning." *Journal of Policy Analysis and Management* 10 (1991): 46–63.

Kathlene, Lyn, Susan E. Clarke, and Barbara A. Fox. "Ways Women Politicians Are Making a Difference." In *Gender and Policymaking: Studies of Women in Office,* edited by Debra L. Dodson. Rutgers, N.J.: Center for the American Woman and Politics, Eagleton Institute of Politics, Rutgers University, 1991.

Kaufman, Herbert. *The Forest Ranger: A Study in Administrative Behavior.* Baltimore: Johns Hopkins University Press, 1960.

Keller, Evelyn Fox. *Reflections on Gender and Science.* New Haven, Conn.: Yale University Press, 1985.

Kellerman, Barbara. *All the President's Kin.* New York: New York University Press, 1984.

————. *Leadership: Multidisciplinary Perspectives.* Englewood Cliffs, N.J.: Prentice-Hall, 1984.

————, ed. *Political Leadership: A Source Book.* Pittsburgh: University of Pittsburgh Press, 1986.

Kellough, J. Edward. "The 1978 Civil Service Reform Act and Federal Equal Opportunity Act." *American Review of Public Administration* 19 (1989): 313–24.

————. "Integration in the Public Workplace: Determinants of Minority and Female Employment in Federal Agencies." *Public Administration Review* 50 (5) (1990): 557–66.

Kelly, Rita Mae. *The Gendered Economy: Work, Careers, and Success.* Newbury Park, Calif.: Sage Publications, 1991.

————. "Sexual Harassment in State Agencies (A Comparison of Five States: Implications for Leadership and Management)." Paper presented at the annual meeting of the Western Political Science Association, Pasadena, Calif., March 18–20, 1993.

Kelly, Rita Mae, and Jane Bayes, eds. *Comparable Worth, Pay Equity, and Public Policy.* Westport, Conn.: Greenwood Press, 1988.

Kelly, Rita Mae, and Mary Boutilier. *The Making of Political Women.* Chicago: Nelson-Hall, 1978.

Kelly, Rita Mae, and Phoebe Morgan Stambaugh. "Sexual Harassment in the States." In *Men and Women in the States,* edited by Mary Ellen Guy, 109–24. Armonk, N.Y.: M. E. Sharpe, 1992.

Kelly, Rita Mae, Mary Ellen Guy, Jane Bayes, Georgia Duerst-Lahti, Lois L. Duke, Mary M. Hale, Cathy Marie Johnson, Amal Kawar, and Jeanie R. Stanley. "Public Managers and the States: A Comparison of Career Advancement by Sex." *Public Administration Review* 51 (5) (1991): 402–12.

Kelly, Rita Mae, Mary M. Hale, and Jane Burgess. "Gender and Managerial/Leadership Styles: A Comparison of Arizona Public Administrators." *Women and Politics* 11 (2): 119–39.

Kimmel, Michael S., ed. *Changing Men: New Directions in Research on Men and Masculinity.* Newbury Park, Calif.: Sage Publications, 1987.

King, Cheryl Simrell. "Gender and Management: Men and Women and Decision-Making in Public Organizations." Ph.D. diss., University of Colorado at Denver, 1992.

————. "Gender and Administrative Leadership in Colorado." Paper presented at the Western Political Science Association, Pasadena, Calif., 1993.

Kingdon, John W. *Congressmen's Voting Decisions,* 3d ed. Ann Arbor: University of Michigan Press, 1989.

Kleinberg, Seymour. "The New Masculinity of Gay Men, and Beyond." In *Beyond Patriarchy,* edited by Michael Kaufman, 120–38. Toronto: Oxford University Press, 1987.

Koenig, Louis W. *The Chief Executive.* San Diego, Calif.: Harcourt Brace Jovanovich, 1986.

Kohlberg, Lawrence. *The Philosophy of Moral Development.* San Francisco, Calif.: Harper and Row, 1981.

Kollock, Peter, Philip Blumstein, and Pepper Schwartz. "Sex and Power in Interaction: Conversational Privileges and Duties." *American Sociological Review* 50 (1985): 34–46.

Kommers, Donald P. "Abortion in Six Countries: A Comparative Legal Analysis." In *Abortion, Medicine, and the Law,* 4th ed., edited by J. Douglas Butler and David F. Walbert., 303–32. New York: Facts on File, 1992.

Korda, Michael. *Male Chauvinism: How It Works.* New York: Random House, 1973.

Krehbiel, Keith. "Why Are Congressional Committees Powerful?" *American Political Science Review* 81 (1987): 929–35.

———. *Information and Legislative Organization.* Ann Arbor: University of Michigan Press, 1991.

Kronenfeld, Jennie Jacobs. *Controversial Issues in Health Care Policy.* Newbury Park, Calif.: Sage Publications, 1993.

"Labor-HEW Funds: Abortion Compromise." *Congressional Quarterly Almanac.* 95th Cong., 2nd sess., 1978. 105–15.

Lauretis, Teresa de. *Technologies of Gender.* Bloomington: Indiana University Press, 1987.

Leader, Sheila Gilbert. "The Policy Impact of Elected Women Officials." In *The Impact of the Electoral Process,* edited by Louis Maisel and Joseph Cooper, 265–84. Beverly Hills, Calif.: Sage Publications, 1977.

Lemov, Penelope. "States and Medicaid: Ahead of the Feds." *Governing* 6 (July 1993): 27–28.

Lengle, James I., and Byron E. Shafer. *Presidential Politics.* New York: St. Martin's Press, 1983.

Le Veness, Frank P., and Jane P. Sweeney, eds. *Women Leaders in Contemporary U.S. Politics.* Boulder, Colo.: L. Rienner, 1987.

Lever, Janet. "Sex Differences in the Games Children Play." *Social Problems* 23 (1976): 478–87.

Lewis, Gregory B. "Changing Patterns of Sexual Discrimination in Federal Employment." *Review of Public Personnel Administration* 7 (1987): 1–13.

———. "Progress toward Racial and Sexual Equality in the Federal Civil Service." *Public Administration Review* 48 (3) (1988): 700–707.

———. "Men and Women toward the Top: Backgrounds, Careers, and Potential of Federal Middle Managers." Paper presented at the annual meeting of the American Society for Public Administration, Los Angeles, Calif., 1990.

Light, Paul C. *The President's Agenda.* Baltimore: Johns Hopkins University Press, 1983.

Lipman-Blumen, Jean. *Gender Roles and Power.* Englewood Cliffs, N.J.: Prentice-Hall, 1984.

Loden, Marilyn. *Feminine Leadership, or How to Succeed in Business without Being One of the Boys.* New York: Times Books, 1985.

Lorber, Judith. "Believing Is Seeing: Biology as Ideology," *Gender and Society* 1 (1987): 125–51.

Lowi, Theodore J. "American Business, Public Policy, Case-Studies, and Political Theory." *World Politics* 4 (July 1964): 677–715.

———. *The Politics of Disorder.* New York: Basic Books, 1971.

———. "Four Systems of Policy, Politics, and Choice." *Public Administration Review* 32 (4) (1972): 298–310.

———. *Incomplete Conquest: Governing America.* 2d ed. New York: Holt, Rinehart, and Winston, 1981.

———. "The State in Politics: The Relation Between Policy and Administration." In *Regulatory Policy and the Social Sciences,* edited by Roger G. Noll, 167–205. Berkeley and Los Angeles: University of California Press, 1985.

Lowi, Theodore J., and Benjamin Ginsberg. *American Government: Freedom and Power*. New York: Norton, 1990.

———. *Poliscide: Big Government, Big Science, Lilliputian Politics*. Lanham, Md.: University Press of America, 1990.

Lyons, Nona Plessner. "Two Perspectives on Self, Relationships, and Morality." *Harvard Educational Review* 53 (1983): 125–45.

Maccoby, Eleanor Emmons, and Carol Nagy Jacklin. *The Psychology of Sex Differences*. Stanford, Calif.: Stanford University Press, 1974.

MacKinnon, Catherine A. *Sexual Harassment of Working Women*. New Haven, Conn.: Yale University Press, 1979.

———. *Towards a Feminist Theory of the State*. Cambridge, Mass.: Harvard University Press, 1987.

Mandel, Ruth B. Prepared remarks for plenary session on "Reshaping the Agenda: The Impact of Women In Public Office." CAWP Forum for Women State Legislators, November 15, 1991.

Mansbridge, Jane, and Katherine Tate. "Race Trumps Gender: The Thomas Nomination in the Black Community." *Political Science and Politics* 25 (3) (Sept. 1992): 488–92.

McClelland, David C. *Power: The Inner Experience*. New York: Irvington, 1975.

McClelland, David C., and David H. Burnham. "Power Is the Great Motivator." *Harvard Business Review* 54 (2) (1976): 100–110.

McGlen, Nancy E., and Meredith Reid Sarkees. *Women in Foreign Policy: The Insiders*. New York: Routledge, 1993.

Mechanic, David. "Sources of Power of Lower Participants in Complex Organizations." *Administrative Science Quarterly* 7 (1962): 349–64.

Meehan, Elizabeth, and Selma Sevenhuijsen, eds. *Equality Politics and Gender*. London: Sage, 1991.

Mezey, Susan Gluck. "Does Sex Make a Difference? A Case Study of Women in Politics." *Western Political Quarterly* 31 (1978): 492–501.

Mills, Albert J., and Peta Tancred, *Gendering Organizational Analysis*. Newbury Park, Calif.: Sage Publications, 1992.

Mills, C. Wright. *The Sociological Imagination*. New York: Oxford University Press, 1959.

Milwid, Beth. *Working with Men: Professional Women Talk about Power, Sexuality, and Ethics*. Hillsboro, Ore.: Beyond Words Press, 1987.

Mintzberg, Henry. *The Nature of Managerial Work*. New York: Harper and Row, 1973.

Morrison, Anne M., and Mary Ann Von Glinow. "Women and Minorities in Management." *American Psychologist* 45 (2) (1990): 200–208.

Morrison, Ann M., Randall P. White, and Ellen Van Velsor. *Breaking the Glass Ceiling: Can Women Reach the Top of America's Largest Corporations?* Reading, Mass.: Addison-Wesley, 1987.

———. "Executive Women: Substance Plus Style." *Psychology Today*, August 1987, 18–26.

Morrison, Toni, ed. *Race-ing, Justice, En-gendering, Power*. New York: Pantheon, 1992.

Mughan, Anthony, and Samuel C. Patterson, eds. *Political Leadership in Democratic Societies*. Chicago: Nelson-Hall Publishers, 1992.

Mumby, Dennis K., and Linda L. Putnam. "The Politics of Emotion: A Feminist Reading of Bounded Rationality." *Academy of Management Review* 17 (3) (1992): 465–86.

Murray, Stephen O., Lucille H. Covelli, and Mary Talbot. "Women and Men Speaking at the Same Time." *Journal of Pragmatics* 12 (1988): 103–11.

Neustadt, Richard E. *Presidential Power: The Politics of Leadership with Reflections on Johnson and Nixon*. New York: John Wiley and Sons, 1976.

Newman, Meredith A. "Career Advancement: Does Gender Make a Difference?" *American Review of Public Administration* 23 (4) (1993): 361–84.

Newman, Meredith A., and Rita Mae Kelly. *The Gendered Bureaucracy: Agency Mission and Equity of Opportunity*. Forthcoming.

Newson, John, Elizabeth Newson, Diane Richardson, and Joyce Scaife. "Perspectives in Sex Role and Stereotyping." In *The Sex Role System: Psychological and Sociological Perspectives,* edited by Jane Chetwynd and Oonagh Hartnett, 28–49. London: Routledge and Kegan Paul, 1978.

Nicholson, Linda. "Interpreting *Gender.*" *Signs: Journal of Women in Culture and Society* 20 (1994): 79–105.

Noll, Roger G., ed. *Regulatory Policy and the Social Sciences.* Berkeley and Los Angeles: University of California Press, 1985.

Norton, Noelle H. "Committee Position Makes a Difference: Institutional Structure and Women Policy Makers." Paper presented at the annual meeting of the Western Political Science Association, Pasadena, March 1993.

———. "Women Lawmakers, Reproductive Policy and Congressional Anomie, 1969–1992." Paper presented at the annual meeting of the American Political Science Association, Washington, D.C., September 1993.

———. "Congressional Committee Power: The Reproductive Policy Inner-Circle, 1969–1992." Ph.D. diss., University of California at Santa Barbara, 1994.

Otis, Gerald D., and Naomi L. Quenk. "Care and Justice Consideration in 'Real Life' Moral Problems." *Journal of Psychological Type* 18 (1989): 3–10.

Palley, Marian Lief. "Elections 1992 and the Thomas Appointment." *Political Science and Politics* 26 (1) (March 1993): 28–31.

Palley, Marian Lief, and Howard A. Palley. "The Thomas Appointment: Defeats and Victories for Women." *Political Science and Politics* 25 (3): 473–77.

Palmer, John L., and Sawhill, Isabel V. *The Reagan Record.* Washington, D.C.: Urban Institute, 1984.

Pateman, Carol. *The Sexual Contract.* Stanford, Calif.: Stanford University Press, 1988.

Perry, William Graves. *Forms of Intellectual and Ethical Development in the College Years.* New York: Holt, Rinehart and Winston, 1970.

Petchesky, Rosalind. *Abortion and Woman's Choice: The State, Sexuality, and Reproductive Freedom.* New York: Longman, 1984.

———. "Antiabortion, Antifeminism, and the Rise of the New Right." *Feminist Studies* 7 (summer 1981): 206–46.

Phillips, Anne. *Engendering Democracy.* University Park: Pennsylvania State University Press, 1991.

Pitkin, Hanna F. *The Concept of Representation.* Berkeley and Los Angeles: University of California Press, 1967.

———. *Fortune Is a Woman.* Berkeley and Los Angeles: University of California Press, 1984.

Pleck, Joseph. *The Myth of Masculinity.* Cambridge, Mass.: MIT Press, 1981.

Pleck, Joseph, and Jack Sawyer. *Men and Masculinity: Gender and Politics in the Thought of Niccolo Machiavelli.* Englewood Cliffs, N.J.: Prentice-Hall, 1974.

Pollitt, Katha. "Are Women Morally Superior to Men?" *Nation,* December 28, 1992, 799–807.

———. "Not Just Another Hillary Magazine Cover Story." *Nation,* May 17, 1993, 657–60.

"Population Control: Increased Federal Concern." *Congressional Quarterly Almanac.* 91st Cong., 1st sess., 1970. 570–74.

Powell, Gary N. *Women and Men in Management.* Newbury Park, Calif.: Sage Publications, 1988.

Powell, Gary N., and D. A. Butterfield. "The Good Manager: Masculine or Androgynous?" *Academy of Management Journal* 22 (1979): 395–403.

"Pregnancy Disability, Rights." *Congressional Quarterly Almanac.* 95th Cong., 2nd sess., 1978. 597–99.

Price, David E. "Policy Making in Congressional Committees: The Impact of Environmental Factors." *American Political Science Review* 72 (1978): 548–74.

Pringle, Rosemary *Secretaries Talk: Sexuality, Power, Work.* London: Verso, 1989.

Ragins, Belle Rose, and Eric Sundstrom. "Gender and Power in Organizations: A Longitudinal Perspective." *Psychological Bulletin* 105 (1) (1989): 51–88.

Reingold, Beth. "Concepts of Representation among Female and Male State Legislators." *Legislative Studies Quarterly* 17 (1992): 509–37.

Reskin, Barbara F., and Heidi Hartmann, eds. *Women's Work, Men's Work: Sex Segregation on the Job.* Washington, D.C.: National Academy Press, 1986.

Rinehart, Sue Tolleson. *Gender Consciousness and Politics.* New York: Routledge, 1992.

Ripley, Randall B., and Grace A. Franklin. *Congress, the Bureaucracy, and Public Policy.* 4th ed. Chicago: Dorsey Press, 1987.

Rizzo, Ann-Marie, and Carmen Mendez. *The Integration of Women in Management: A Guide for Human Resources and Management Development Specialists.* Westport, Conn.: Greenwood Publishing, 1990.

Rodman, Hyman, Betty Sarvis, and Joy Bonar. *The Abortion Question.* New York: Columbia University Press, 1987.

Rosenbach, William E., and Robert L. Taylor, eds. *Contemporary Issues in Leadership.* 2d ed. Boulder, Colo.: Westview Press, 1989.

Rosener, Judy B. "Ways Women Lead." *Harvard Business Review* 68 (6) (Nov.–Dec. 1990): 119–25.

Rossi, Alice, ed. "Remember the Ladies." In Abigail Adams's *The Feminist Papers: From Adams to DeBeauvoir.* New York: Columbia University Press, 1973.

Rowe, Alan J., and Richard O. Mason. *Managing with Style: A Guide to Understanding, Assessing, and Improving Decision-making.* San Francisco: Jossey-Bass, 1987.

Rubin, Eva. *Abortion, Politics, and the Court.* Westport, Conn.: Greenwood Press, 1982.

Rule, Wilma, and Joseph F. Zimmerman. *United States Electoral Systems: Their Impact on Women and Minorities.* Westport, Conn.: Greenwood Publishing, 1992.

Russo, Nancy Felipe, Rita Mae Kelly, and Melinda Deacon. "Gender and Success-Related Attributions: Beyond Individualistic Conceptions of Achievement." *Sex Roles* 25 (5–6) (1991): 331–51.

Saint-Germain, Michelle A. "Does Their Difference Make a Difference? The Impact of Women on Public Policy in the Arizona Legislature." *Social Science Quarterly* 70 (1989): 956–68.

Sapiro, Virginia. "Women's Studies and Political Conflict." In *The Prism of Sex*, edited by Julia A. Sherman and Evelyn Torton Beck, 253–65. Madison: University of Wisconsin Press, 1979.

———. "The Political Uses of Symbolic Women: An Essay in Honor of Murray Edelman." *Political Communication* 10 (1993): 137–49.

Sapiro, Virginia, and Pamela Johnson Conover. "Gender in the 1992 Electorate." Paper prepared for the annual meeting of the American Political Science Association, Washington, D.C., 1993.

Sardell, Alice. *The U.S. Experiment in Social Medicine.* Pittsburgh: University of Pittsburgh Press, 1988.

Schneider, Anne, and Helen Ingram. "Social Construction of Target Populations: Implications for Politics and Policy." *American Political Science Review* 87 (2) (March 1993): 334–47.

Schwartz, Felice N. "Management Women and the New Facts of Life." *Harvard Business Review* 67 (1) (1989): 65–76.

Shapiro, Judith. *Body Guards.* New York: Routledge, 1991.

Shapiro, Thomas. *Birth Control Politics: Women, Sterilization, and Reproductive Choice.* Philadelphia: Temple University Press, 1985.

Sherif, Carolyn Wood. "Needed Concepts in the Study of Gender Identity." *Psychology of Women Quarterly* 6 (1982): 375–98.

Sherman, Julia. "Social Values, Femininity, and the Development of Female Competence." *Journal of Social Issues* 32 (3) (1976): 181–95.

Silverberg, Helene. "What Happened to the Feminist Revolution in Political Science? A Review Essay." *Western Political Quarterly* 43 (1990): 887–903.

Smith, Steven S. *Call to Order: Floor Politics in the House and Senate.* Washington, D.C.: Brookings Institution, 1989.

Smith, Steven S., and Christopher J. Deering. *Committees in Congress.* 2d ed. Washington, D.C.: Congressional Quarterly Press, 1990.

Smith-Lovin, Lynn, and Charles Brody. "Interruptions in Group Discussions: The Effects of Gender and Group Composition." *American Sociological Review* 54 (1989): 424–35.

Snodgrass, Jon, ed. *A Book of Readings for Men against Sexism.* Albion, Calif.: Times Change Press, 1977.

Stansell, Christine. "White Feminists and Black Realities: The Politics of Authenticity." In *Race-ing, Justice, En-gendering, Power,* edited by Toni Morrison, 251–68. New York: Pantheon Books, 1992.

Stetson, Dorothy McBride. "The Abortion Politics Triad in Russia, France, and the United States." Paper presented at the annual meeting of the American Political Science Association, Chicago, September 1992.

Steuernagel, Gertrude A. "Reflections on Women and Political Participation." *Women and Politics* 7 (1987): 3–13.

Stewart, Debra W. "Women in Public Administration." In *Public Administration: The State of the Discipline,* edited by Naomi B. Lynn and Aaron Wildavsky, 203–27. Chatham, N.J.: Chatham House Publishers, 1990.

Stiehm, Judith, ed. *Women's Views of the Political World of Men.* Dobbs Ferry, N.Y.: Transactional Publishers, 1984.

Stivers, Camilla. *Gender Images in Public Administration: Legitimacy and the Administrative State.* Newbury Park, Calif.: Sage Publications, 1993.

Swacker, Marjorie. "The Sex of the Speaker as a Sociolinguistic Variable." In *Language and Sex: Difference and Dominance,* edited by Barrie Thorne and Nancy Henley, 76–83. Rowley, Mass.: Newbury House, 1975.

Swann, Joan. "Talk Control: An Illustration from the Classroom of Problems in Analyzing Male Dominance of Conversation." In *Women in Their Speech Communities,* edited by Jennifer Coates and Deborah Cameron, 123–40. London: Longman, 1988.

Tamerius, Karin L. "Does Sex Matter? Women Representing Women's Interests in Congress." Paper presented at the annual meeting of the Midwest Political Science Association, Chicago, April 1993.

Tannen, Deborah. *You Just Don't Understand: Women and Men in Conversation.* New York: Morrow, 1990.

Tavris, Carol. *The Mismeasure of Women.* New York: Simon and Schuster, 1992.

Thomas, Sue. "Voting Patterns in the California Assembly: The Role of Gender." *Women and Politics* 9 (1989): 43–53.

———. "The Impact of Women on State Legislative Policies." *Journal of Politics* 53 (1991): 958–76.

———. *How Women Legislate.* New York: Oxford University Press, 1994.

Thomas, Sue, and Susan Welch. "The Impact of Gender on Activities and Priorities of State Legislators." *Western Political Quarterly* 44 (1991): 445–56.

Tolleson-Rinehart, Sue, and Jeanie R. Stanley. *Claytie and the Lady: Ann Richards, Gender, and Politics in Texas.* Austin: University of Texas Press, 1994.

Tong, Rosemary. *Feminist Thought: A Comprehensive Introduction.* Boulder, Colo.: Westview, 1989.

Tribe, Lawrence H. *Abortion, the Clash of Absolutes.* New York: Norton, 1990.

U.S. Department of Labor. *A Report on the Glass Ceiling Initiative.* Washington, D.C.: Government Printing Office, 1991.

U.S. Merit Systems Protection Board. *Sexual Harassment in the Federal Workplace: Is It a Problem?* Washington, D.C.: Government Printing Office, 1987.

————. *A Question of Equity: Women and the Glass Ceiling in the Federal Government.* Washington, D.C.: Government Printing Office, 1992.

Van Nostrand, Catherine. *Gender-Responsible Leadership: Detecting Bias, Implementing Interventions.* Newbury Park, Calif.: Sage Publications, 1993.

"Veto of Labor-HEW Funds Bill Overridden." *Congressional Committee Almanac.* 94th Cong., 2nd sess, 1976. 790–804.

Waldo, Dwight. *The Enterprise of Public Administration: A Summary View.* 5th ed. Novato, Calif.: Chandler and Sharp Publishers, 1992.

Walsh, Kenneth T. "America's First (Working) Couple." *U.S. News and World Report,* May 10, 1993, 32–34.

Wayne, Stephen J. *The Road to the White House.* New York: St. Martin's Press, 1992.

Weber, Max. *From Max Weber: Essays in Sociology.* Ed. and trans. Hans Gerth and C. Wright Mills. New York: Oxford University Press, 1946.

Weingast, Barry. "Floor Behavior in the U.S. Congress: Committee Power under the Open Rule." *American Political Science Review* 83 (1989): 795–815.

————. "Fighting Fire with Fire: Amending Activity and Institutional Change in the Postreform Congress." In *The Postreform Congress,* edited by Roger Davidson, 142–68. New York: St. Martin's Press, 1992.

Weingast, Barry, and W. Marshall. "The Industrial Organization of Congress." *Journal of Political Economy* 96 (1988): 132–63.

Welch, Susan. "Are Women More Liberal Than Men in the U.S. Congress?" *Legislative Studies Quarterly* 10 (1985): 125–34.

West, Candace, and Don Zimmerman. "Doing Gender." *Gender and Society* 1 (1987): 125–51.

Whicker, Marcia Lynn, and Raymond A. Moore. *When Presidents Are Great.* Englewood Cliffs, N.J.: Prentice-Hall, 1988.

Whicker, Marcia Lynn, and R. A. Strickland. "An Analysis of EEOC Sexual Harassment Filings by State." Paper presented at the annual meeting of the American Political Science Association, Chicago, 1992.

Whyte, William F. *Man and Organization: Three Problems in Human Relations in Industry.* Homewood, Ill.: R. D. Irwin, 1959.

Wiley, Mary Glenn, and Arlene Eskilson. "Speech Style, Gender Stereotypes, and Corporate Success: What If Women Talk More Like Men?" *Sex Roles* 12 (1985): 993–1007.

Williams, Christine. *Gender Differences at Work: Women and Men in Nontraditional Occupations.* Berkeley and Los Angeles: University of California Press, 1989.

Willis, Frank N., and Sharon J. Williams. "Simultaneous Talking in Conversation and Sex of Speakers." *Perceptual and Motor Skills* 43 (1976): 1067–70.

Wilson, Woodrow. *Congressional Government: A Study in American Politics.* Cleveland: Meridan, 1885.

Witz, Anne, and Michael Savage. "Theoretical Introduction: The Gender of Organizations." In *Gender and Bureaucracy,* edited by Michael Savage and Anne Witz, 3–62. Oxford: Blackwell Publishers, 1992.

Wolf, Naomi. *Fire with Fire: The New Female Power and How It Will Change the Twenty-first Century.* New York: Random House, 1993.

Woods, Nicola. "Talking Shop: Sex and Status as Determinants of Floor Apportionment in a Work Setting." In *Women in Their Speech Communities,* edited by Jennifer Coates and Deborah Cameron, 141–57. New York: Longman, 1988.

Wright, Deil Spencer. *Understanding Intergovernmental Relations.* Pacific Grove, Calif.: Brooks/Cole Publishing Company, 1988.

Yoder, Janet. "Rethinking Tokenism: Looking Beyond Numbers." *Gender and Society* 5 (2) (1991): 178–93.

Yukl, Gary A. *Leadership in Organizations.* Englewood Cliffs, N.J.: Prentice-Hall, 1981.

———. "Managerial Leadership: A Review of Theory and Research." *Journal of Management* 15 (2) (1989): 251–59.

Zimmer, Lynn. "Tokenism and Women in the Workplace: The Limits of Gender-Neutral Theory." *Social Problems* 35 (1988): 64–77.

Zimmerman, Don H., and Candace West. "Sex Roles, Interruptions, and Silences in Conversation." In *Language and Sex: Difference and Dominance,* edited by Barrie Thorne and Nancy Henley, 105–29. Rowley, Mass.: Newbury House, 1975.

Contributors

Georgia Duerst-Lahti is Associate Dean of Beloit College and Associate Professor of Government and Women's Studies. She researches topics related to gender in organizations, organization theory, state politics, and political symbolism. Her work has appeared in numerous journals including *Political Science Quarterly, Administration and Society,* and *Women and Politics.* She also co-authored three chapters of *Women and Men of the States,* edited by Mary E. Guy.

Rita Mae Kelly is Director and Chair of the School of Justice Studies and Professor of Justice Studies, Political Science, and Women's Studies at Arizona State University. She has written widely in the field of women and politics, including *The Gendered Economy: Work, Careers, and Success* (1991); *Gender, Bureaucracy, and Democracy* (with Mary M. Hale, 1989); *Women in the Arizona Political Process* (1988); and *The Making of Political Women* (with Mary Boutilier, 1978). Dr. Kelly is the recipient of the Aaron Wildavsky Award from the Policy Studies Organization for the best book on policy studies published in 1992; the Distinguished Research Award of the American Society for Public Administration, Section on Women in Public Administration (1991); a Fulbright Fellowship Award to Brazil (1991), the Outstanding Mentor in the Discipline Award given by the Women's Caucus of Political Science (1991); the Policy Studies Organization's Appreciation Award (1990); the American Society for Public Administration's Achievement Award (New Jersey, 1981).

Mary Ellen Guy is Chair of the Department of Political Science and Public Affairs at the University of Alabama at Birmingham. Her research interests focus on issues related to gender and management. Her work has appeared in numerous books and journals, including *Public Administration Review, Review of Public Personnel Administration,* and *Public Productivity and Management Review.* Her most recent book is *Women and Men of the States: Public Administrators at the State Level.* Dr. Guy's work on women in the workforce won a

1992 Lilly Award for Outstanding Research in Public Administration by the American Society for Public Administration. It also won the 1992 Distinguished Research Award for the best research on women in public administration, awarded by the Section of Women in Public Administration.

Lyn Kathlene is Assistant Professor of Political Science at Purdue University. She has published articles in the *Western Political Quarterly, Journal of Policy Analysis and Management, Policy Sciences,* and *Knowledge in Society,* and contributed chapters to various edited volumes. She is currently working on a book manuscript entitled *Gender, Public Policy, and the Legislative Environment.* Her research interests include women as political elites; violence against women, in particular rape and sexual attacks on campus; feminist methodology; and citizen participation.

Cheryl Simrell King is currently a Member of the Faculty in the Graduate Program in Public Administration at The Evergreen State College in Olympia, Washington. In the Fall of 1993, she will be moving to the University of Akron in Akron, Ohio as an Assistant Professor in the Department of Public Administration and Urban Studies. Dr. King received her Ph.D. in Public Administration from the University of Colorado at Denver and her M.A. in Psychology from the same institution. Prior to joining academe, Dr. King worked in the private sector as a management researcher where she was involved in over fifty research projects that yielded industry publications and presentations. She is the author of a chapter on Strategic Planning and Program Evaluation for a book on grassroots administration, the co-author of a series of articles on gender and competitive/cooperative success strategies published in the *Journal of Social Psychology,* and the author of numerous conference papers on gender style and management in public organizations and on sex and sexuality in the workplace.

Meredith Ann Newman received her Ph.D. in policy studies from Deakin University, Australia. She is Assistant Professor, Department of Political Science, Washington State University. She teaches public administration in the Master of Public Affairs program. Her research interests include comparative public policy, organizational theory and behavior, gender and politics, intergovernmental affairs, and public management. Her articles appear in a number of scholarly journals including *Public Administration Review, The American Review of Public Administration,* and *Public Administration Quarterly.* Newman is an Executive Board Member of SWPA and Region IX Representative on the National Council of ASPA.

Noelle Norton is an Assistant Professor of Political Science at the University of San Diego. She received her Ph.D from the University of California at Santa Barbara. Her dissertation is entitled "Congressional Committee Power: The Reproductive Policy Inner-Circle in the 88th to 102nd Congresses." Her publications can be found in the *Journal of the History of the Behavioral Sciences.*

Karin L. Tamerius is a National Science Foundation Graduate Research Fellow in the Department of Political Science at the University of Michigan. She conducted the interview for her study while interning with the Congressional Caucus for Women's Issues and undertook the quantitative portion of her analysis while at the University of California, Berkeley. Her current research interests have to do with the sources and participatory consequences of politicized group consciousness among women and racial minorities in American politics.

Dayna Verstegen is a doctoral candidate at the University of Wisconsin–Madison in the department of Journalism and Mass Communication. Formerly a producer for Wisconsin Public Television, she is currently the Executive Director of WYOU Community Television in Madison. Ms. Verstegen is a policy and legislative specialist and author of numerous works on women in politics.

Index